WITHDRAWN

Craven Place

To Enfield

To Edmonton

Tindal's Burying Ground

To Walthamstow

Swan and Hoop

D1029883

4 Pancras Lane

Guy's Hospital

LONDON

MOOR FIELDS

THE TOWER

Scale of half a Mile
The Divisions on the Scale round the Plan are Miles and Furlongs from the Meridian and Parallel of St Pauls Church.

George Keats of Kentucky

GEORGE KEATS
OF KENTUCKY

A Life

LAWRENCE M. CRUTCHER

FOREWORD BY JOHN E. KLEBER

Scholarly publisher for the Commonwealth,
serving Bellarmine University, Berea College, Centre College of Kentucky, Eastern
Kentucky University, The Filson Historical Society, Georgetown College, Kentucky
Historical Society, Kentucky State University, Morehead State University, Murray
State University, Northern Kentucky University, Transylvania University, University
of Kentucky, University of Louisville, and Western Kentucky University.
All rights reserved.

Editorial and Sales Offices: The University Press of Kentucky
663 South Limestone Street, Lexington, Kentucky 40508-4008
www.kentuckypress.com

16 15 14 13 12   5 4 3 2 1

Library of Congress Cataloging-in-Publication Data

Crutcher, Lawrence M.
  George Keats of Kentucky : a life / Lawrence M. Crutcher ; foreword by John E.
Kleber.
     p. cm. – (Topics in Kentucky history)
  Includes bibliographical references and index.
  ISBN 978-0-8131-3688-2 (hardcover : acid-free paper) —
  ISBN 978-0-8131-3689-9 (pdf) — ISBN 978-0-8131-4098-8 (epub)
  1. Keats, George, 1797-1841. 2. Louisville (Ky.)—Biography. 3. Bluegrass Region
(Ky.)—Biography. 4. Pioneers—Kentucky—Louisville—Biography. 5. Businessmen
—Kentucky—Louisville—Biography. 6. English—Kentucky—Louisville—Biography.
7. Keats, John, 1795-1821—Family. 8. Brothers—Biography. 9. London (England)
—Biography. I. Title.
  F459.L853K43 2012
  976.9'03092—dc23
  [B]   2012025759

Manufactured in the United States of America.

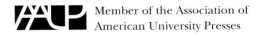
Member of the Association of
American University Presses

CONTENTS

Illustrations follow page 176

FOREWORD

Less than four months after the death of George Keats from a gastrointestinal ailment on Christmas Eve 1841, his fellow countryman, Charles Dickens, paid a brief visit to Louisville. The city was, he wrote, "regular and cheerful; the streets laid out at right angles, and planted with young trees. . . . There did not appear to be much business stirring; and some unfinished buildings and improvements seemed to intimate that the city had been over-built in the ardor of 'going ahead' and was suffering under the reaction consequent upon such feverish forcing of its powers." The previous fall, Abraham Lincoln most likely saw the same conditions while visiting his friend Joshua Speed's plantation. If business was lethargic and the city overbuilt, one might say the responsibility was partially due to Keats and his business friends, who "forced its powers" only to suffer economic reversals in the Panic of 1837. Dickens witnessed a nation and a city slowly returning to economic health.

George Keats and his young wife, Georgiana, settled in the small Ohio River town in 1819. They had emigrated from England in July 1818 seeking economic advancement. George left behind a family of siblings that included his sister, Frances Mary, and two brothers, Thomas and the poet John. By the time he died, he had made and lost a fortune, served on numerous prestigious boards, supported the town's intellectual life, and, by moving in the upper echelons of society, seen his children marry well.

The Keats siblings were the children of Thomas Keats and his wife, Frances Jennings. Thomas died after a fall from his horse in April 1804. Within a year his widow had married William Rawlings. It was an unhappy union. In time the children were placed in the care of two guardians, one of whom, Richard Abbey, assumed major responsibility for their welfare. Among other things, he managed their trusts, a deed that resulted in unfortunate misunderstandings. In addition, he saw to their education and apprenticeships. All the boys were educated at John Clarke's School in Enfield, where much of their character was formed.

"All happy families resemble one another; every unhappy family is unhappy in its own way," wrote Tolstoy. The Keats family was shattered by early death, alcoholism, and consumption. As John was aware, "I have fears that I may cease to be/Before my pen has glean'd my teeming brain." Their unique unhappiness, however, lay in the tragic constellation of economic woes, personal misunderstandings, and the jealousies of friends. For George, these matters were exacerbated by the vast distance between England and the American frontier.

If it were not for John Keats, it is doubtful this book would have been written. Important as George's contributions were to his city, it is his brother's name that places him apart from and above other early entrepreneurs, thus adding a dimension that justifies a major biographical study. Modern criticism has placed John Keats beside Shakespeare. As one critic wrote, "The faultless force and the profound subtlety of his deep cunning instinct for the absolute natural beauty can hardly be questioned or overlooked; and that is doubtless the one main distinctive gift or power which denotes him to rank beside Coleridge and Shelley." To be ranked so highly in the pantheon of poets requires true genius. Biographers have explained John's genius, but they have not explored in great detail the influence of his younger brother George. Their closeness was evident when John wrote to George and Georgiana on 14 October 1818, "I would sooner fail than not be among the greatest. I think I shall be among the English Poets after my death." That John achieved such greatness is what drew Lawrence Crutcher's attention to George. In doing so, he could not ignore the latter's ties to his adopted city and what he accomplished there in two decades.

In the *Sketch Book* Washington Irving warned us not to judge the English character on London alone but to go forth into the country "and cope with the people in all their conditions, and all their habits and humor." Although London was central to the lives of all the Keats boys, their character was imprinted by rural values when they went to the countryside for their education and to commune with nature.

George was born in London on 28 February 1797 into a middling family. Orphaned at the age of thirteen, he eventually went to work in his guardian's countinghouse. Unlike his literary brother, he gravitated to the realm of finance. When an inheritance proved insufficient to give him independence in business, he began to think of opportunities in America. Four weeks after their marriage, the Keatses left England, arriving in Philadelphia on 26 August 1818. They quickly set off by stage and boat for the frontier, confident that the West held the promise of fortune. Their destination was the prairie of Illinois and a model English community.

Very quickly the Keatses realized that the Utopian experiment was both unsustainable and undesirable, so they removed to the river town of

Henderson, Kentucky, in late October. It was there that they first met and lived with John James Audubon and his wife, Lucy. Their personal association was anything but close, even after both families relocated to Louisville. The men's financial dealings involving steamboats were the cause of the strained relationship. One significant contribution of this book is Crutcher's explanation of those dealings, based on lawsuits found in archives, and his vindication of Audubon's actions, despite John Keats's harsh criticisms.

At the time George settled in Louisville in early 1819, steamboats were a marvelous new invention that offered prime opportunities for investment and profit. Louisville's growth was inextricably tied to this new innovation, beginning with the arrival of the first steamboat on western waters on 28 October 1811. Its frightening cacophony was music to the ears of the town's entrepreneurs and heralded Louisville's ascendancy as the commonwealth's premier city. George's arrival eight years later was nothing if not timely, and his fortune grew along with the town's population. Historian George Yater tells us that Keats invested part of his fortune in a lumber mill, built a flour mill, and speculated in real estate. His profits enabled him to build a grand house on Walnut (now Muhammad Ali Boulevard), between Third and Fourth Streets. Dubbed the "Englishman's palace," it was a meeting place for city leaders, including James Guthrie. It took a while for George to be accepted, but by the time Louisville was given city status in 1828, he was a man to be reckoned with.

Although those interested in personal correspondence will find the Keats brothers' relationship enlightening, it is mainly historians who will thank Crutcher for plowing new ground. George's two decades in Louisville are seen from an Englishman's perspective, which is very different from the descriptions of America by early British travel writers such as Morris Birkbeck (*Notes on a Journey in America* [1818]). Washington Irving accused such writers of being intent "to diffuse error rather than knowledge, and so successful have they been that . . . there is no people concerning whom the great mass of the British public have less pure information or entertain more pure prejudices." In viewing George's life in Kentucky, a British citizen might be forgiven for thinking the streets were paved with gold. He and Georgiana became part of Louisville's upper echelon, something that would have been impossible in England, given their circumstances. In addition to serving on a number of prestigious business boards (Bank of Kentucky), he participated in an intellectual salon (Philosophical Society); this resulted in leadership positions in the Louisville Lyceum, the Kentucky Historical Society, the Harlan Museum, and the Louisville College, precursor to the University of Louisville. He advocated for free public education. He worked to make something more of Louisville's culture than the raw mercantile atmosphere he had encountered upon arrival. He became a Kentuckian and Crèvecoeur's "new man." By doing so, he contributed to Milton's America—"a noble and puissant nation rousing herself like a strong man after sleep, and shaking her invincible locks."

In the early nineteenth century the United States was a puissant nation, half free and half slave. To George, part of the appeal of Illinois had been its status as a new free state. The family's circle in England had been abolitionists. Finding himself in Kentucky—a slave state—George agonized over the use of enslaved labor. At first he compromised by leasing black mill hands, a common practice in Louisville. Eventually he owned three household slaves. Most of George's circle disapproved of the peculiar institution, but not enough to eschew owning slaves. Had he lived, he probably would have joined the Union cause while continuing to own slaves himself, as many Louisvillians did.

From the time he built the "Englishman's palace," George had a need for household slaves because the family lived extravagantly. He would discover that America provided opportunity but did not guarantee security. The land held economic promise and peril, and George experienced both. The truth is that George was never as good a businessman as his brother was a poet. When he alone guaranteed Tom Bakewell's note for a large steamboat in 1841, only to see the note called by the Portland Dry Dock Company, he was wiped out. Had he lived, he may have recouped. Instead, the bank acquired and sold his house.

In this book, economic pitfalls and insecurities abound. It sometimes reads like a Dickens novel. One is reminded of the economic machinations of *Bleak House,* along with other references to Chancery Court, creditors, contested wills, and errant loans. The entire Keats family experienced all these things, and the issue of money fills many pages. In doing so, Crutcher sorts out more plainly than ever before the John-George financial tangle and the Keats-Jennings family inheritance. As a consequence, he clears George of any monetary malfeasance.

This financial information constitutes only a small part of the new material found here. A digression about a horse stolen from father Thomas in London is newly unearthed from Old Bailey transcripts. Georgiana Keats's family situation is deciphered with the discovery of cousins who were already living in Montreal. Louisville's Harlan Museum is described for the first time. Political articles written by George and appearing in the

Louisville Journal, a Whig publication, are newly discovered. The appendix includes two previously unpublished slave agreements—one a sale and the other a lease. Throughout, topics touched on peripherally or as footnotes to John's story are reconstituted here as George centered. As such, the reader gains a valuable new perspective on the poet, the entire Keats family, their friends, and life in early-nineteenth-century Louisville.

The dimensions of this book, however, reach beyond Louisville's city limits or Kentucky's boundaries. They go back to England and the origins and early developments of the Keats and related families. For both George and Georgiana, England was always their home, and they returned to visit. While separated, John and George carried on an illuminating correspondence. In 1823, two years after John's death, George paid off his brother's debts, showing that George never abandoned him. Efforts to depict the brothers' relationship as anything other than close must be attributed to the jealousies or misunderstandings of others, and perhaps their physical separation. The geographic distance between them caused John to fall under the influence of his friend Charles Brown and Fanny Brawne, whom he loved.

Brown's name raises the specter of John's legacy and who would shape it. Brown, who disliked George, tried to do so. Distance and a lack of material handicapped George and prevented him from contributing greatly to that legacy. Shortly before his death, George released an injunction on his brother's poetry, enabling a biography of John to be written. But for the most part, George could only ruminate about how his brother's legacy was being handled. He did not live to see Richard Monckton Milnes's *Life, Letters, and Literary Remains of John Keats* (1848), the first of many examples of the poet's legacy as determined by others.

From editing both state and city encyclopedias, I know what a great contribution Lawrence Crutcher's book makes to Louisville and Kentucky history. The relatively few words that Yater wrote on George Keats are expanded here into a complete, well-deserved, and definitive biography. Here George rightly steps out of the shadow of his illustrious brother and sidesteps the criticisms of Charles Brown. He had his faults and weaknesses, but in the end, I would agree with James Freeman Clarke's 1843 sketch of him in the transcendental publication the *Dial,* where he called George one of the finest men he ever knew. Clarke and his assistant Samuel Osgood stayed their defense of Keats for the next thirty years in correspondence with Milnes. A century and a half later, Crutcher takes up the cause, giving us a portrait of a good man who loved his family and promoted his city. In his will George insisted that his creditors be paid first, leaving us this example of his character and so much more in the lives and institutions he touched and the progeny he sired. Like their notable poet ancestor, many Keatses have bequeathed to Louisville their own proud legacies, and Crutcher wrote of them in an earlier book. In 1821 John wrote an epitaph for himself: "Here lies one whose name was writ in water." How wrong he was. And thanks to Crutcher's efforts, the same can now be said of George.

John E. Kleber
Louisville, Kentucky

PREFACE

George Keats deserves better. John Keats's multiple biographers, themselves poets and scholars, have seconded George to younger brother status or, worse, the "business" brother. George's sudden death at age forty-four, as he approached his prime as a civic and cultural leader, caused Louisville to forget him. As Hyder Edward Rollins notes, "George Keats [has] a definite place in English literary history."[1] John Keats has been the subject of at least a dozen biographies, but the details of George's life have scarcely been published. Now it is his turn.

Their sister Fanny Keats, who married a Spanish liberal and outlived her brothers by decades, was the subject of a generous biography by Marie Adami, so I deal with her sparingly. Likewise, I deal fleetingly with younger brother Tom Keats, who died at age nineteen in 1818 after a prolonged struggle with consumption, leaving behind virtually no accomplishments other than his companionship and dependency. This book complements Adami's to provide a comprehensive view of George, his good works, and his complex family relationships.

George was a principal figure in John Keats's life, arguably the most important among a shifting and contentious group of influences on the poet during his early creative years. Dismissed by many writers and unfairly excoriated by William Haslam and Charles Brown, George lived a multidimensional life both as a youth in London and as a civic and cultural leader in America.

Biographers who write behind the facts and delve into the characters of their subjects are dependent on the availability of source materials. The paucity of these materials has been a problem in George's case. A clutch of marvelous letters from John to George reveals much about John; George's few surviving letters do not reciprocate. His notes to Fanny are stilted by their difficult sibling relationship. Contemporary accounts of George are few. No member of the family wrote his story, even though a grandson, John Gilmer Speed, completed a three-volume set on John. Speed arguably had the necessary materials to write a biography of George, but did not. Speed's niece, Emma Keats Speed Sampson, was a prolific and skillful writer, but she stuck to girls' fiction. Compounding the problem, many letters, including several from George to John, were destroyed. Unfortunately, a disproportionate number of the surviving letters that mention George relate to the contretemps between Charles Brown and Charles Wentworth Dilke over George's and John's finances. Most Keats biographers have felt obliged to report that Brown accused George of taking more than his proper share of an inheritance, only to conclude that it probably was not true. But by prolonging the issue (perhaps because only those particular letters were saved), they have cast an undeserved pall over George's reputation.

Other original source materials are scarce. Unitarian Church leader James Freeman Clarke penned a favorable "Memorial Sketch" of George in 1843, shortly after his death,[2] as did Clarke's successor, Samuel Osgood. A few of George's surviving letters in Harvard's Houghton Library were edited and collected in a small volume in 1955 by Rollins, titled *More Letters and Poems of the Keats Circle.*

Naomi Joy Kirk, a high school English teacher in New Albany, Indiana, presented a master's thesis entitled "The Life of George Keats" to Columbia University in 1933. Kirk patched together a narrative derived from various books and original materials available at the time. She also contacted three Keats family members, including Emma Sampson, for brief oral history anecdotes. She expanded her thesis into a manuscript titled "Shared Porridge," which she attempted to publish into the early 1940s, with no success. Maurice Buxton Forman included a brief synopsis of it in *The Poetical Works and Other Writings of John Keats* (Hampstead edition).[3] In 1953 Dr. Ernesto Paradinas y Brockmann, a descendant of Fanny, sold a cache of letters, including twenty from George, to Arthur A. Houghton Jr., who in turn donated them to the Harvard Keats Collection. These letters present another window into George's character.

George is my great-great-great-grandfather, and I became interested in updating Kirk's research in order to publish it, but ultimately I decided to put it aside and start over. I recognized the challenge in developing George's character—quite different from John's—which has generally been lost in the shadows of the many excellent John Keats biographies.

George's early story has been gleaned mostly from contemporaries who contributed to biographies of John, as well as from the poet's numerous letters. Several Keats biographers have included George only tangentially. Amy Lowell's monumental two-volume *John Keats* assembled troves of previously unpublished material in 1925. She was followed by Aileen Ward (1963), Walter Jackson Bate (1963), and Robert Gittings (1968), either poets themselves or Romantic literature scholars.

Preface

This biography of George, written by neither a poet nor an academic, attempts a fair and balanced picture of the man, his times, and the issues he faced. I relied on and am grateful to many people and institutions for enabling this research. Hyder Rollins assembled, edited, and published all the key letters in *Letters of John Keats* (1958) and *The Keats Circle* (1965), including those from George to Fanny. Robert Gittings, with Oxford and Cambridge credentials, a twenty-five-year career as a BBC writer and producer, and status as a minor poet, wrote several Keats books that set a high standard for fact-based research. And I would not have undertaken this project were it not for my discovery of the Naomi Joy Kirk materials in Louisville.

Keats scholar Nicholas Roe at St. Andrews University and historian John E. Kleber at the University of Louisville helped make this a better book. Stanford University professor Denise Gigante, author of *The Keats Brothers: The Life of John and George*, gave advice, as did Louisville historian Samuel W. Thomas. Curator James J. Holmberg and associate curator Robin Lynn Wallace at the Filson Historical Society, where so many Louisville documents and images are housed, were always helpful. Shirley Harmon, a prodigious researcher affiliated with Filson, provided invaluable Kentucky research. Ken Page, the interpretation officer at Keats House Hampstead, may know the whereabouts of Keats materials better than any living person, and he was unfailingly forthcoming in sharing data. No one guided this project to publication more forcefully than Grant F. Scott of Muhlenberg College, although I cannot claim that he agrees with all the book's central themes. Finally, I must acknowledge how the Internet has revolutionized the access to source information that previous authors might have spent years rooting out.

The many other authors, scholars, and content owners whose previous works have enabled this effort are recognized throughout the notes and bibliography, with my full appreciation.

My previous work *The Keats Family* (2009), describing upwards of 600 Keats descendants (and antecedents), almost defied modern standards of fact checking and proofreading, not to mention readable prose. I am grateful to the above-named for helping me avoid such pitfalls in this effort.

THE PIVOTAL YEAR

1827–1828

Perched on a gentle bluff overlooking the falls of the Ohio River, the George Keats and Company's Steam Planeing, Grooving, and Tongueing Mill was turning out 4,000 board feet of lumber daily at a nice profit.[1] Its proprietor, who lived with his young family adjacent to the mill on Brook Street, had good reason to be pleased. It was November 1827, and Louisville's trustees, as part of a petition to the state legislature to incorporate as a city, had just asked the thirty-year-old Englishman to join the Ohio Bridge Commission, along with James Guthrie (a future U.S. treasury secretary) and other civic leaders.[2] With this action, George Keats was accepted into Louisville's leadership community, even though just three years earlier he had written to his sister, Fanny, in London, "Our circumstances will not allow us to associate with what is called the first or in other words the richest people here."[3] Given that recent years had been a struggle on many fronts, headlined by the premature loss of his brother John Keats in 1821, this was a pivotal moment, presaging a highly productive decade for George.

It was also a pivotal time for Louisville as it emerged from its rugged frontier origins and transformed into a vibrant mercantile entrepôt. Left of George's view of the falls was a vast construction project, the Louisville and Portland Canal, running about two miles from Louisville past Shippingport and south to Portland.[4] The falls, the only natural barrier on the east-southwest river system between Pittsburgh and New Orleans, were crucial to Louisville's early development. The north-south bridge project would later prove to be nearly as important. Just fifty years earlier, George Rogers Clark had placed about sixty settlers on Corn Island at the falls, as protection against Indian raids.[5] By 1827, Louisville's population had burgeoned to almost 10,000.[6]

The falls, with about a twenty-six-foot drop over two miles that required the portage of goods and people,[7] were responsible for Louisville's pioneer settlement. Later, the steamboat ushered in its mercantile boom period. These shallow-draft, paddle-wheeled vessels fascinated George Keats from

1

the moment he arrived at the headwaters of the Ohio River in Pittsburgh in 1818.[8] Steamboats would later prove to be his undoing on two occasions. The export trade from west of the Allegheny Mountains followed gravity downriver to New Orleans. At the same time, settlers in Illinois and Missouri who required farm implements and other items from the East depended on Ohio and Mississippi River haulage. Warehouses sprang up along the waterfront above and below the falls to handle the transshipment of all these necessities around the water break (before the construction of the canal).

The petition to incorporate Louisville as a city was approved by the legislature two months after it was filed.[9] The 1830s would be a golden era for Louisville and for George. The city's construction required wood, and lots of it. The city would also require hotels, and George's family had operated a London hostelry and inn.

The children of Keats and his wife, Georgiana Augusta, included Georgiana Emily, Emma Frances, Isabel, and John Henry. John Henry, the middle surviving child, was born in November 1827. Their second child, Rosalind, had died. Clarence George, Ella, and Alice Ann would arrive later during the 1830s. The parents called each other George and their eldest Georgey; thankfully, Clarence George was called Clarence.

One cannot reconstruct what was on George's mind that November day in 1827, but we do know the issues he had been dealing with during the year. In 1825 George had given his former guardian in London, Richard Abbey, the power of attorney to pay all the remaining debts of his late brother John. Although the debts had been covered, George had not received confirmation due to a mix-up with the power of attorney and the vagaries of the postal service. Meanwhile, Charles Brown, a friend of the poet, insisted that George repay Brown's loans to John, with interest. Brown had criticized George for taking £700 to America in 1820, leaving John with only £60 to £70, or about £20 less than his debts totaled (although each had upward of £1,500 in a Chancery trust, unbeknownst to them at the time). Brown's disparagement of George would continue past both their deaths in 1842 and 1841, respectively.

From the time his sister, Fanny, turned twenty-one in 1824, George had been involved long-distance in a five-way scrum to settle the estates of his brothers Tom and John, who had died in 1818 and 1821, respectively, as well as winding up Chancery trust inheritances dating to his grandfather's death in 1805. With a flurry of letters to John's friend and London solicitor James Rice between 1826 and 1828, George and Fanny finally settled matters, in her favor.[10] Meanwhile, George's mentor Richard Abbey had severely disillusioned him by borrowing funds from Fanny's trust. The Keats brothers' friend and solicitor John Hamilton Reynolds had also mishandled trust affairs, overbilled the survivors, and halfheartedly planned a biography of John Keats that never came to fruition. It was a full slate of family issues.

Litigation over George's disastrous 1818 steamboat investment with John James Audubon had continued past 1825. Although George was not a party to the lawsuits, his partner and friend Tom Bakewell, whose loans he would later endorse, was. The Audubon experience was a painful memory, albeit an important lesson learned for George on the frontier.[11]

Would George return to London? Initially he had hoped to make a quick fortune and return to England for a life of ease. But with Tom and John dead, the old circle of friends quarreling and dispersing, and his mother-in-law Ann Griffin Wylie aging, the allure of returning had faded. Instead, Georgiana and her children Georgey and infant John Henry would go for a visit in 1828.

As he surveyed his bustling family and pleasant abode, George must have thought back to his own childhood in London. He had been orphaned at age seven when his father died in an accident and his mother gave the children over to the care of their grandmother. Many of the opportunities his parents had dreamed of, such as schooling at Harrow, went unrealized. George had been withdrawn from John Clarke's school in Enfield at age fourteen. He was now working hard to provide better security for his own children.

What was his business plan? George's friend Bakewell had laid out a reasonable model for Audubon in Henderson and for himself in Louisville. It centered on a steam-powered grist- and sawmill, which led to real estate speculation and investing in steamboats. Although the mix of businesses did not prove successful for Audubon, whose real interests lay elsewhere, could George make them work in Louisville?

George's political compass was tilting rightward. He had not been overly immersed in the liberal sentiments of his brother and their friend Leigh Hunt. In Louisville he was developing a Whiggish, anti-Jacksonian political consciousness tied to concerns about the popular vote. Economics were the driving force.

Also, what could George do to improve the raw culture in Louisville? The town was a mix, peopled mainly by settlers from Virginia, Pennsylvania, and New England, as well as by immigrants like himself from England,

France, and, more recently, Germany. About a quarter of the residents were slaves.[12] Yet in 1827, the city was short on the basics of culture. As in other frontier cities, business came first, then churches, then schools, and finally culture. The schools were very weak, and there was no free public library, although the city had a theater. Could George distinguish himself by playing a role in this sector, despite his own limited education? Fellow Louisvillians knew that he was the poet's brother; perhaps they expected him to take a leading intellectual role because of it.

Finally, there was the overarching question that would remain unanswered past death. Had George failed his brother by leaving John when he needed him most? What could he do from Louisville by way of making amends to ensure that John's life, letters, and poetry would receive their proper literary recognition?

When the Keatses arrived in Kentucky, the climate was cooler than in the following decades and centuries.[13] As they tucked their children in, preparing for a cold winter, they would have had good reason to pause in front of the fire and reflect on their journey from London and where their lives might be headed.

The year 1827, when George finally achieved recognition and financial independence, provides a good bridge to look back at his earlier struggles and his relationship to John Keats, as well as to look forward to his many accomplishments in Louisville.

ABANDONED

1804–1814

George might never have come to Louisville, or even considered immigration at all, but for the death of his father, followed by the children's abandonment by their mother. The breakup of the family triggered a continuum of bad events, destroying dreams of upwardly mobile lives in London and leading to George's eventual exit. The insecurities in John's life likely propelled him into the cosmos of Romantic poets.

George was born 28 February 1797, perhaps above the Swan and Hoop, the family's hostelry located at 24 The Pavement, opposite Moorgate. In August 1803 George and John were enrolled at Clarke's School in Enfield; younger brother Tom enrolled later. It was while returning home on 15 April 1804 after visiting the boys at school that their father, Thomas Keats, had a fatal riding accident.[1] He stopped to have dinner at Southgate[2] and later passed by the family's home on Craven Street, off City Road, evidently on his way to the Swan and Hoop to stable the horse. The horse apparently shied, throwing him out of the saddle; he fell into the Bunhill Fields main gate and then to the pavement. At one o'clock in the morning, watchman John Watkins noticed the horse clattering back to the stable and found Keats lying unconscious by the gate, across from the Methodist chapel. Watkins carried him to a surgeon in a side street, but nothing could be done; Thomas had suffered a fractured skull in the fall. Later they took him back to the Swan and Hoop, where he died at eight o'clock that morning.[3] Richard Abbey, who had developed a distaste for both Thomas and his wife, Frances, later said that Keats was inebriated when the accident happened.[4] There has been no further explanation of it.

Frances Keats acted precipitously. Ten weeks later, on 27 June 1804, she married William Rawlings at the same St. George's Church where she and Thomas had married. Then the story gets murky, with historians assuming that Rawlings left a bank clerkship at Smith, Payne and Company to assume Keats's leasehold at the Swan and Hoop.[5] No one knows Frances's motives for the marriage. She may have believed that Rawlings could

5

step right into Thomas's role, running the stable and providing for the children. Perhaps her father encouraged it; John Jennings, whom Abbey described as a tyrant and a gourmand, was seriously ill with gout and did not resume management of the hostelry or the inn next door after his son-in-law's death. Frances's mother, Alice, disapproved of her hasty remarriage. The Keats children came under the care of their grandparents.

Rawlings had no assets and only a modest salary. He immediately became proprietor of the inn. Frances was faced with a year's wait for her £2,000 inheritance from Thomas, and because the lease for the entire business was due to expire on 25 March 1806, she signed a short lease in her own name for the stables only. Then she disappeared, perhaps on a wedding trip with Rawlings. When a poor-rates collector visited later in the summer, he was greeted by an Elizabeth Keats, possibly Thomas's sister.

On 8 March 1805 John Jennings died, having overly enjoyed the fruits of his labors, according to Abbey. Two months after his death, on 25 May, Rawlings, who was unsuited for managing the hostelry, abandoned the lease rather than face a rent increase by the city. The Swan and Hoop, which had been his and Frances's primary source of income, was then occupied by a new tenant, Joshua Vevers.[6] Rawlings's relationship with Frances soon collapsed; he sank into the shadows and likely died. Frances may have left Rawlings and given up the lease, but accounts of her actions also went dark. Abbey said that she had taken up "as the Wife of a Jew at Enfield, named Abraham," and had started to drink brandy heavily. He called Frances "more remarkably the Slave of other Appetites."[7] Some Keats biographers have inferred from this remark that Frances suffered from nymphomania, but Abbey may have been referring to an overindulgence in food or drink. Abbey also noted that John Jennings's "Temper appears to have influenced that of his Daughter.—He was excessively fond of the pleasures of the Table." Given the family's pub lifestyle, it was probably unavoidable that Frances succumbed to "The Growth of this degrading Propensity to liquor."[8]

John Jennings left an estate that exceeded £13,600 (equivalent to as much as 100 times that amount in contemporary currency).[9] The terms of Jennings's will were sufficiently convoluted as to trigger two intrafamily lawsuits.[10] Family tensions escalated by the summer of 1805, when Frances and Rawlings sued her brother, her mother, and an executor for interpreting Jennings's will to their own advantage. In May 1806 the Chancery Court ruled against Frances in that case; however, it did award her a £50 annuity from her father's estate. Her brother Midgley, the executor, did not remit any of those funds for two years; meanwhile, Frances, likely destitute, was living in Enfield, and her children were with their grandmother, Alice Jennings, in Edmonton. Midgley died after finally settling up with Frances in 1808, but his widow, Margaret,[11] wanted to undo the estate plan and capture Midgley's capital, which reverted to Alice, in favor of her own children. The Chancery awarded half each to Margaret and Alice. The latter then made provisions for the Jennings grandchildren, while her residual estate eventually went to the Keats children. Another lawsuit remained unresolved until 1823, with the unintended consequence of depriving John Keats (who died in 1821) of funds that were rightfully his.

Frances returned to her mother in the winter of 1809 penniless, riddled with consumption and rheumatism, and alcohol dependent. She had never fully recovered her strength after Tom's birth, and having two more children (Edward and Fanny) had further weakened her. Grief over Thomas's death and disappointment at subsequent events only compounded her woes. John, always his mother's favorite, nursed her frantically when he was home on school break, cooking for her and sitting up all night to read her novels. Frances died in the second week of March and was buried 20 March 1810 beside Thomas in the Jennings vault at St. Stephen's. John, aged fourteen, returned to Clarke's School but was so broken up over his mother's death that he hid from his classmates for several days in a nook under the master's desk, passionately inconsolable.[12] Presumably it was George who lured him out.

Alice Jennings made arrangements during May–July 1810 for two friends, Richard Abbey and John Nowland Sandell, to serve as guardians for the children from that time forward.[13] By then, she may have been quite frail. Abbey withdrew John and George from Clarke's School in September 1811 and offered George employment at his tea brokerage at 4 Pancras Lane, where Cheapside and the Poultry merge, as well as living quarters in the dormitory above.

Alice Jennings died at age seventy-eight and was buried 9 December 1814, having endured a succession of sorrows. Within ten years, her son-in-law and husband had died, followed by her grandson (Edward Keats), her son, and then her daughter. John Keats wrote of her:

There was a naughty boy [referring to himself] . . .
In spite of the might
Of the maid
Nor afraid
Of his Granny-good—[14]

The Keats siblings were now alone in the world. Orphaned and abandoned to a well-intentioned but uncreative guardian's care, what were they to do, and how?

Within six years, John transformed himself from a surgeon's apprentice to the foremost among Romantic poets. George first assisted his brother's poetic endeavors, then abruptly re-created himself as an entrepreneur and civic leader on the American frontier. John wrote to George's mother-in-law, Ann Griffin Wylie,[15] "My brother George has ever been more than a brother to me, he has been my greatest friend."[16] The consequences of this brotherhood frame the core of George's story.

FAMILY ORIGINS

1773–1804

The Keats brothers' feelings of disenfranchisement were not simply related to their abandonment. The clouded and undistinguished origins of their family also contributed to their outsider status. The ancestral history of the Keats family was typically sparse in a thinly documented Georgian England. Neither John nor George ever discussed their family, except obliquely. Biographers have speculated that the Keats children had something to hide, such as their father's possible illegitimacy, as his baptismal record has never been found.

More than seven different theories of the family's origin, including the spelling of the name, add to the confusion.[1] The Keats name was fairly commonplace in the counties ranging from London west to Cornwall. Thomas Keats, George's father, is believed to have been born in 1773 or 1774, somewhere west of London.[2] The first theory, held by Fanny Keats Llanos's Spanish descendants, relates to a family headed by Thomas Keast, who lived in Land's End, Cornwall, in 1775–1776, close to the presumed date of birth of Thomas Keats.[3]

A second theory, propounded by Keats biographer Walter Jackson Bate, involves a concentration of families named Keat and Keate living near St. Teath and Madron, Cornwall. Included among this group were a John Keat and a Shilson Keate, whose ages suggest they might have fathered Thomas Keats.[4]

Robert Gittings, another biographer, has suggested a third theory. Farther north in Reading, a successful apothecary, Dr. William Keate(s), was the father of Dr. Thomas Keate at St. George's Hospital and the uncle of Dr. Robert Keate, another noted surgeon. Two individuals named Thomas Keats were born there during a suitable time frame. One of the two was the son of a baker from nearby Stratfield Mortimer. Because he was baptized in 1773 and also had a sister named Elizabeth, baptized two years later, the symmetry of dates is appealing.[5]

At the same time, a man named Thomas Keats was running a small boat called the *Lark* out of Plymouth, Devonshire. Because Charles Brown and Charles W. Dilke both recalled that Thomas Keats was a "Devonshire man," this hypothesis gained currency, even in the absence of any confirming birth records. When John Keats and Joseph Severn stopped by Lulworth Cove on their way to Rome in 1820, Severn wrote that John "was in a part [of Devonshire] that he already knew."[6]

Amy Lowell recorded a fourth suggestion, based on a letter from Thomas Hardy's second wife. Mrs. Hardy noted that there was a "family named Keats living two or three miles from here (Dorchester, in East Dorset, the county next to Devonshire). . . . They kept horses, being what is called 'hauliers,' and did also a little farming. They were in feature singularly like the poet, and were quick-tempered as he is said to have been, one of them being nicknamed 'light-a-fire' on that account. All this is very vague, and may mean nothing, the only arresting point in it considering that they were of the same name, being the facial likeness, which my husband said was very strong."[7]

Hopeful modern-day Keatses suggest a fifth possibility. Corfe Castle, Dorsetshire, located just a few miles from Broadmayne and Lulworth, housed a Keat or Keats family that included two Thomases, but their birth dates make them unlikely candidates.[8]

A sixth theory, not inconsistent with the Land's End and Devonshire hypotheses, relates to the presence of thirteen shipmasters named Keats, Keates, or Keast licensed between 1744 and 1778. John Keats had asked that his gravestone inscription read "HERE LIES ONE WHOSE NAME WAS WRIT IN WATER." With no concurrent records, the theory speculates that the Keatses were a maritime family.[9]

Finally, a strong alternative hypothesis is that Thomas Keats was from London. Thomas Mower Keats was a hat manufacturer at 14 Poultry, just around the corner from Richard Abbey, the children's guardian. His top hats, whose felt was a by-product of rabbits, were in the cheaper category. Thomas's younger brother Joseph Keats was a partner in Hammond, Stocker at 74 Cheapside and 12 Pancras Lane. During 1816 the Keats boys lived at 76 Cheapside, next door to Joseph, who always claimed a relationship to them. Abbey suggested several times that John go into the hatmaking trade, although John's letters make no mention of any other Keats. Thomas's son Frederick Keats was elected sheriff of London for 1856–1857. Other London Keatses were booksellers, one of whom claimed to be a second cousin, and a linen draper.[10]

The only certain conclusion from these disparate versions is that one could live unrecorded in eighteenth-century England. In many respects, the only meaningful contribution by the Keats forebears was their last name. It was actually the Jennings family that provided the financial wherewithal and, in John's case, the nervous energy that spawned creative genius. Grandmother Alice Jennings was responsible for most of the years that might be described as a normal family existence.

The Jennings family left a somewhat clearer trail. Keats's grandfather John Jennings appears to have been the child of John and Mary Jennings, who had connections in Madron, Cornwall, coincident with one of the Keats family hypotheses.[11] However, no documents have been found to prove either family's Cornish origins. John Jennings married Alice Haworth Whalley on 25 February 1774, three weeks after moving into the Swan and Hoop. They wed in St. Stephen's Church on Coleman Street, an ordinary Anglican church, belying their dissident theological tendencies.[12] Alice was thirty-eight, having come down from her hometown of Colne, Lancashire, a few years earlier. Destined to become the family's anchor, Alice was born 1 November 1736 in Doughty Pasture in the Aire Valley, just west of the Yorkshire border. What brought her south to London was not recorded—perhaps service in a family or a previous marriage.

Frances Jennings was born on 19 January 1775 and was baptized 29 June 1775 at St. Stephen's, where her father was warden. She was followed by Midgley John,[13] baptized in 1777; Edward, baptized in 1782; and three other brothers. Her father's investments were prospering. John and Alice had moved to 24 The Pavement, Moorfields, next to the livery. Frances's brothers went to John Clarke's boarding school in Enfield at age six, but she likely remained home to attend a dame school.[14]

The immediate Keats family is first recorded in London in 1794, by which time Thomas Keats can reasonably be assumed to have been employed as a hostler at the Swan and Hoop.[15] That was also the year of his marriage to Frances Jennings. His employer and soon-to-be father-in-law may have hired Keats, possibly a fellow Cornishman or west countryman, earlier than 1794, as his business expanded.

The Swan and Hoop, despite its pub-like name, began as a hostelry for saddled horses and light carriages. The business was similar to a modern-day car rental agency (with a bar attached). It was sensibly located next to the Moorgate Coffee House and across from St. Bethlem Hospital (or Bedlam), which today is slightly east of central London.[16] Moorfields and neighboring Finsbury Circus were London's playground, with theaters, archery contests, bear baiting, and military drills.

Jennings leased the Swan and Hoop in 1774 for ten years. He also joined or bought into the Freedom of the City, a guild that permitted one to own property even if one was not born to it. A number of livery operators participated in this group. In 1784 Jennings renewed the lease for another twenty-one years, to 1805, and also rented the inn next door. The following year he expanded his domain by acquiring 23 The Pavement, which he rented out. The combined building frontage was 117 feet wide, sited between Moorfields and Finsbury Pavement, just outside the London Wall. The original plan, dated 1753, shows two coach houses, a spacious yard, stabling for fifty horses, and room for several carriages. Jennings spent £670 on upgrades to the original buildings in 1774.[17]

Thomas Keats was a short, thickset man with brown hair and dark hazel eyes; he was an accomplished horse handler. He married Frances on 9 October 1794 in St. George's Church, Hanover Square, London. She was nineteen, and he was not much older. The Jennings family did not belong to St. George's, and no family members signed the witness book, suggesting that it was a hasty affair.[18]

John Jennings retired in 1802 and moved with Alice to Ponders End, Enfield, about ten miles from Moorfields, renting a place from a Mrs. Fuller. By this time, his investments included a coaching line, mortgages, government funds, and East India stock. He subleased the Swan and Hoop to Thomas Keats, now a tradesman, for £44 a year. In 1803 Keats was admitted into the Innkeepers' Company and also became a Freeman of the City.

Few descriptions of Frances survive. John never wrote about his mother. George simply said, "She resembled John very much in the Face was extremely fond of him and humoured him in every whim, of which he had not a few, she was a most excellent and affectionate parent and as I thought a woman of uncommon talents."[19] It was Frances's posthumous misfortune to have her character fulsomely recorded in Abbey's 1827 interview with John Taylor:

> At an early Age she told my Informant, Mr Abby, that she must & would have a Husband; and her passions were so ardent, he said, that it was dangerous to be alone with her.—She was a handsome, [but not a tall] little woman—Her Features were [of a Superior] good & regular, with the Exception of her Mouth which was unusually wide. A little Circumstance was mentioned to me as indicative of her Character—She used to go to a Grocer in Bishopsgate Street, opposite the Church, probably out of some Liking for

the Owner of the Shop,—But the Man remarked to Mr Abby that Miss Jennings always came in dirty Weather, & when she went away, she held up her Clothes very high in crossing the Street, & to be sure, says the Grocer, she has uncommonly handsome Legs.[20]

At the time of the Taylor-Abbey interview, Fanny Keats Llanos (represented by Charles W. Dilke) and her husband, Valentin Llanos, were aggressively pushing Abbey to release the remaining funds held in her trust. By 1830, Abbey was forced to mortgage his Walthamstow property for £2,500 and his chattels for £300 to the Llanoses to cover the payments and other business indebtedness. Llanos claimed credit for forcing the sale of the house. Abbey may well have felt chagrined at the time of the 1827 interview by his entire experience with the Keats family. Keats loyalists have criticized Abbey's point of view as overly harsh, but it remains the principal description of the families.

Charles Cowden Clarke, the schoolmaster's son and a later confidant of John Keats, described Thomas as "a man so remarkably fine in common sense, and native respectability, that I perfectly remember the warm terms in which his demeanour used to be canvassed by my parents after he had been to visit his boys."[21] In other words, the Clarkes liked him.

John Keats was born within a year of his parents' marriage, on 31 October 1795.[22] No one knows whether John, named for his grandfather Jennings, was born in the living quarters adjacent to the Swan and Hoop or in a different neighborhood. He was baptized at St. Botolph-without-Bishopsgate, some distance away from St. Stephen's, the Jennings family church.

George followed on 28 February 1797, then Thomas (Tom) on 18 November 1799; Edward was born on 28 April 1801 but died within the year. Frances Mary (Fanny) was born 3 June 1803.[23] All except Fanny, who lived until 1889, died young, at least two from tuberculosis. But the early family years were apparently happy. The Keatses lived for a time at the Swan and Hoop, although after the arrival of George and Tom, they moved to a larger space in a terraced house on Craven Street off City Road, about three-quarters of a mile north of the livery.[24]

John was christened when he was two months old. The family evidently grew increasingly lax in their religious observance, christening George at four and a half years, along with Tom and Edward, at St. Leonard's Shoreditch on 24 September 1801. Edward was buried on 9 December 1801 in Bunhill Fields, City Road, where some other Jennings relatives had been interred.[25] Bunhill was also called Tindal's Burial Ground or the

Dissenters Burial Ground, populated with such nonconformists as Daniel Defoe, John Bunyan, and Isaac Watt. It appears that the Keatses' religious views were eclectic or simply casual.

A final example of the gritty life of the Thomas Keats family was recently discovered in an Old Bailey court transcript involving the theft of a horse from the Swan and Hoop by Robert Mathews. It is the only known "voice" of Thomas Keats. The proceedings of 16 February 1803 state in part:

> Proceeding t18030216–31. Robert Mathews was indicted for feloniously stealing, on the 8th of February, a mare, value £11, the property of Thomas Keates.
>
> Thomas Keates sworn—I live at the Swan and Hoop Livery stables, Moorgate. I let a mare to the prisoner, who came to me on the 8th of February, between ten and eleven o'clock, he called himself Captain Thompson.
>
> Q. Had you ever seen him before? A. Yes, he came into the yard, I asked his address, he gave it to me, Captain Thomas, 16, in the Minories; he said, he wanted a mare, to go and see a friend some where about Somers Town; I asked him how long he wanted the mare; he said, about one hour, that he should not be more than an hour gone; he asked me what I should charge him for the ride; I said five shillings; I let him the mare, and he was to pay five shillings, on his return in one hour; that was the agreement between us. Not returning that hour nor that evening, I began to be a little alarmed about my horse. I thought it was likely I should not see it any more; the next day I went to where he gave me his address, 16, in the Minories, and enquired for such a person, and no such person was known. The next morning I went about to all the other stables, thinking he might have put it up somewhere else by mistake; that he might, perhaps be intoxicated with liquor; after making this enquiry, I could not hear anything about the mare. On the 10th of February, I went to the office in Worship-Street, and had some bills printed. On the 12th, an officer from Westminster, of the name of Bly, came to me in the morning, and gave me information that my mare was at the Red Lion, Cockspur-Street, where I saw the mare; and from thence I went to Westminster, where I saw the prisoner, at a little house where the officer took me to, in a little room. I swore to the mare, and the prisoner was committed.
>
> Q. Are you sure the mare you saw at the Red Lion was your

mare? A. Yes, she was a bay mare, fifteen hands and three inches high, some white in her face, some saddle marks, with two black spavins;[26] I have had her about five months; I am perfectly satisfied it was my mare.

Cross examined. Q. On the 8th of February, a Captain Thompson came to your yard to have a horse? A. Yes.

Q. You had never seen Captain Thompson before? A. Never.

Q. And you let Captain Thompson this mare for an hour? A. I did.

Q. You agreed with him for five shillings? A. Yes.

Q. Did he give you anything at the time? A. No.

Q. Do you let horses to any stranger? A. Yes, if they give me a good address. I would let you one.

James Goadby, an ostler at the Red Lion, then testified that the prisoner had approached him at four o'clock on 8 February and offered to sell him the horse. Goadby, suspecting a problem, sought out Constable James Bly. Goadby then asked the prisoner to complete a written receipt for the sale, after which Bly asked him for proof of ownership. The proceeding continued:

James Bly sworn.—I am a constable; I took up the prisoner on the 11th, at the sign of the Hope public-house, Charing-cross, upon the information of James Goadby, who thought he had got horses improperly; I got him to write a receipt, and then took him to the Office; when he had got part of the way, he resisted, and with difficulty we got him into a coach; I asked him how he got the horses; he said, honestly, they were his own; I said, if he would bring some respectable housekeeper, in the neighborhood, I would not take him before the Magistrate.

Prisoner's defence. I hired the mare, to go to Nottingham-place, about some money. I did not find the person, I came to London, and being intoxicated, I put the mare in a stable, and as I was in want of money, I thought I would sell the mare, and I might go on a voyage, and then I should be able to pay the prosecutor for the mare; I sold her for six pounds. As to my saying I was a cheese-monger, and drove her in a cart, I said no such thing.

The prisoner called two witnesses, who gave him a good character.

Jury, to Goadby. Q. Was the prisoner intoxicated when he sold the mare?—A. No, he conducted himself so I that I could not suppose he stole it.

GUILTY, Death, aged 30.[27]

The stage was set: a kindly grandmother from Lancashire, a prosperous grandfather, and upwardly mobile parents enjoying a good living in Cockney London. Thomas and Frances Keats, after living for a few years over the hostelry, were comfortable in their house on Craven Street, City Road. Yet the Keats family, as George wrote, aspired for more: "She [his mother] would have sent us to harrow school as I often heard her say, if she could have afforded."[28] There, they would have been educated in the classics, made upper-class friends, gone on to university, and ultimately taken up professions. At the time, Harrow, founded in 1243, had an analogous reputation to Eton as Cambridge University has to Oxford University, although Londoners considered it a county school. Tuition was about £50 a year.

CLARKE'S SCHOOLBOYS

1803–1810

Family life above the Swan and Hoop and then in Craven Street seemed mostly happy and normal until the death of Thomas Keats in 1804, when the themes of abandonment and financial concern rose to the fore. George wrote:

> From the time we were Boys at school where we loved, jangled, and fought alternately untill we separated in 1818 I in great measure releived him [John] by continual sympathy, explanation, and inexhaustible spirits, and good humour, from many a bitter fit of hypochondriasm, he avoided teazing any one with his miseries but Tom and myself and often asked our forgiveness; venting, and discussing them gave him relief— . . . no one in England understood his character perfectly but poor Tom and he had not the power to divert his frequent melancholy, and eventually encreased his desease most fearfully by the horrors of his own lingering death.[1]

George communicates an enormous amount of the family story in these contorted sentences. John, who was difficult to handle from birth, required a great deal of attention.

The children attended a local dame school, similar to a day-care center, in their early years. John reportedly was the most creative at dreaming up games and little plays, unless he fell into "one of his moods," as described by Craven Street next-door neighbor Mrs. Frances Grafty.[2] George was even-tempered. Like their father, George and Fanny had dark hair and dark hazel eyes; the other children resembled their mother. Unlike his father, George grew tall, to five feet eleven inches; John topped out at five foot one, similar to his father's height.

After Thomas Keats died and Frances went missing, the situation changed. The brothers had to amuse themselves, but primarily Tom and George had to amuse John, whose "melancholy" was likely what modern psychologists would call postabandonment depression. George acknowledged that Tom was better at humoring John, but as Tom's illness worsened, his closeness to John worked in reverse, dragging down John's spirits and his health.

On 16 April 1804, when George was just seven, the happy and tight-knit family began to unravel. As recounted earlier, word arrived that day that Thomas Keats had been killed in a riding accident. John and George were too young to appreciate the consequences, being sheltered at Clarke's School, but the next year brought to an end any semblance of traditional family life. They lost their father, lost their interest in his estate, experienced their mother's remarriage and separation, lost their home, lost their grandfather Jennings, and witnessed the beginning of their mother's instability and decline (she would be dead, at age thirty-five, within five years). Alice Jennings stepped forward to become the "discreet parent" of the Keats children at age sixty-nine. Fanny Keats Llanos wrote that she and her siblings never lived with Rawlings, nor with their mother after her separation from him.[3] They moved in with their grandmother immediately. George and John returned to Alice's home on school breaks. In the early summer of 1806 she reorganized her life as a widow around the grandchildren, moving from Ponders End to Church Street in Edmonton, two miles away and closer to Clarke's School. The family continued to unravel when Frances died in March 1810.

Alice Jennings executed a deed, or indenture, in July 1810, four months after Frances's death, that presaged another dramatic chapter in the Keatses' lives. She signed over the majority of her funds and custody of the grandchildren to the control of two guardians: Richard Abbey and John Nowland Sandell. Alice picked different personalities as guardians for the Keats children. Sandell, a generous, kindly individual, was a Russian fur merchant doing business in the Broad Street buildings near Finsbury Pavement as John Schroeder and Company. Sandell played no known financial role in the arrangement and reduced his role as guardian within a year, perhaps after a disagreement with Abbey. Abbey agreed to shelter the younger children, although Fanny Keats visited Sandell as late as January 1816, the year he died.[4]

Richard Abbey was a conservative entrepreneur who had built a successful tea and coffee importing house. He was a Yorkshireman, the eldest son of farmers from Healaugh in the Vale of York, forty miles northeast of Alice's birthplace in Colne. Baptized in 1765, he had inherited sufficient funds to buy into his importing business upon arriving in London in 1786.

His wife, Eleanor Jones, whom he had married for love, was illiterate at the time.[5]

An earlier event prompted Alice to select Abbey as guardian of her grandchildren. Alice had befriended a young girl from Colne who had married, moved to Edmonton, had children, and then been murdered by her husband in a fit of rage. A neighbor asked Alice to shelter the children until the victim's family from Colne could complete custody arrangements. Alice took in the three-month-old boy and asked the Abbeys, who were childless, to look after the two-year-old girl. When the children's grandmother arrived, she took the boy but asked the Abbeys to keep the girl until she could find a home. When the time came, the Abbeys sought to keep their ward, to which the grandmother assented. The girl was in Abbey's home on the day of his interview with John Taylor in 1827, at which time she was probably at least nineteen or twenty.[6] Alice Jennings recalled the Abbeys' compassion, and the Abbeys likely saw Fanny Keats as welcome companionship for their lonely ward. Richard Abbey also may have envisioned room-and-board reimbursements as well as trustee fees.

Grandmother Jennings, having provided the Keats children with the semblance of a normal household for ten years, died on 17 December 1814. John Keats was then nineteen, George seventeen, and Tom fifteen, all of them away; Fanny was eleven and living at home. The family structure was destroyed, and Abbey, already charged with the children's financial destinies, found himself playing a larger role, housing Fanny.[7]

Robert Browning later asked, rhetorically, "What porridge had John Keats?"[8] Browning meant that it is necessary to know certain facts about a poet's creative process, and sometimes these facts can be as inconsequential as what the poet had for breakfast. Although the porridge metaphor is far-fetched, to answer Browning's question from the perspective of family and early childhood, John's porridge included a few happy early years, shattered by death, abandonment, depression, and disease. The porridge also included a wonderful grandmother, a difficult guardian, and, as the story unfolds, vital school influences and crucial friends.

Although Frances Keats had wanted the boys to go to Harrow, which offered Greek, Latin, and lots of games, along with a vicious system of bullying and discipline, the family's decision to school them at John Clarke's in Enfield turned out to be extremely fortuitous. In 1848 Keats biographer Richard Monckton Milnes attributed the decision not to enroll the Keats boys at Harrow to "financial" considerations, as did Frances Keats.[9] But that is probably not the whole story, given that Thomas Keats was flourishing at the time of his death in 1804. Keats had accumulated assets of nearly £2,000—not an inconsiderable sum for a thirty-year-old.[10] Clarke's School likely appealed to the family because of its progressive characteristics. Thomas Keats enrolled George and John simultaneously, at ages six and seven, in Clarke's School in the summer of 1803. Of the school's seventy to eighty students, the Keats boys were the youngest. They were also carrying on a family tradition, their uncle Midgley Jennings being a graduate.[11]

John Clarke was a political liberal from Northampton, where he served as a solicitor and deputy sheriff. In about 1782 he was called on to substitute for a hangman but refused the duty. He then resigned his posts and joined his father-in-law John Collett Ryland, a prominent Baptist preacher, in operating a school. Ryland's theology was dissenting but not doctrinaire. Ryland was also known to support the American cause, describing himself as an ardent friend of liberty. After reverses at the school, hastened by Ryland's charitable nature, they moved it to Enfield in 1786, with Clarke in charge.[12]

Enfield was a pleasant community ten miles north of London. The school's principal building, at the edge of the village, was a former Georgian mansion built in about 1680 after a design by Sir Christopher Wren.[13] Charles Cowden Clarke, son of the school's headmaster, later described the campus. His firsthand, period-specific prose provides a portrait of the boys' life better than any modern summary:

Enfield . . . is the very *beau-ideal* of an English village. Green, picturesque, brightened by the winding New River, it is one of the most beautiful of miniature towns. . . .

[The schoolhouse] had, by tradition, been originally built by a retired West India merchant [in] "1717."

The structure was of rich red brick, moulded into designs decorating the front with garlands of flowers and pomegranates, together with heads of cherubim, over two niches in the centre of the building. . . .

The house, airy, roomy, and substantial, with a good allowance of appertaining land, was especially fitted for a school. "The eight-bedded room," "the six-bedded room," as they were called, give some idea of the dimensions of the apartments. The school-room, which occupied the site where formerly had been the coach house and stabling, was forty feet long. In the spacious playground between the school-room and the house flourished a goodly baking-pear tree; it was made a point of honour with "the boys" that if they forbore from touching the fruit until fit for gathering, they should have it in due time for supper regales, properly baked or stewed.

From the playground stretched a garden, one hundred yards in length, where in one corner were some small plots set aside for certain boys fond of having a little garden of their own . . . and farther on was a sweep of greensward, beyond the centre of which was a pond, sometimes dignified as "The Lake." . . . Round this pond sloped strawberry-beds, the privilege of watering which was awarded to "assiduous boys" on summer evenings, with the due understanding that they would have their just share of the juicy red berries when fully ripe. . . . From the meadow beyond, whence the song of the nightingales in May would reach us in the stillness of night, there stood a rustic arbor, where John Keats and I used to sit and read Spenser's "Faery Queene" together when he had left school. . . . Beyond this a gate led into a small field, or paddock, of two acres,—the pasture-ground of two cows that supplied the establishment with fresh and abundant milk.

It was a domain of almost boundless extent and magnificence to the imagination of a schoolboy.

Several men of ability . . . issued from that Enfield schoolhouse; and three men of eminence—John Keats, the young poet; Edward Holmes, the enthusiastic and accomplished musician; and Edward Cowper, the scientific engineer and inventor, were wholly educated there.[14]

John Clarke's liberal politics led him to subscribe to Leigh Hunt's *Examiner.* He was an educational liberal as well.[15] Compared with the horrors of Charles Dickens's fictional Yorkshire School in *Nicholas Nickleby*—with its abusive tutors, student bullying, and narrow curriculum—or even the rigidly classical education offered at Eton or Westminster, Clarke's School allowed its students exceptional freedom. The boys could pick which games to play, or they might choose to simply wander down to the New River to read a book or catch fish. They were encouraged to read widely, anything in the library. The place was made to order for the Keats boys, particularly for the hypersensitive John, whose free spirit might have been smothered at a more traditional school.[16]

The academic routine was fairly relaxed by English boarding-school standards. John and George were taught reading, writing, and arithmetic, followed by Latin and later French. They studied at the same level, despite the sixteen-month age difference. There was insufficient demand for the classics, so Greek was not offered. There were courses in astronomy, physics, geology, and botany. The depth of instruction was probably not great, but the boys were offered a breadth of subjects.

Clarke's philosophy of learning was to stress individuality and independence, concepts that were far ahead of their time, in comparison to the old Anglican grammar schools. The school offered modern subjects such as mathematics and geography and utilized teaching methods that valued doubt and questioning. Students recalled that Clarke liked to teach by using examples. He demonstrated centrifugal force by twirling a mop head; he explained migration by taking the students outside in the fall to watch the swallows heading south; he constructed a solar system by arranging students in a circle. Anatomy was taught with a real human skeleton. Clarke and his wife loved music, which blended into the curriculum. The themes of humanity and tolerance were pervasive.

The school's precept was to develop the good in boys rather than to expunge the evil. Boys who were willing to water the strawberries on hot summer evenings gained an extra share of the bounty. Each boy kept his own academic tally, the "ledger of the recording angel." The grades were O for *optime*, B for *bene*, and X for negligence or misconduct. At the end of each half year, accounts were totaled and rewards handed out for academic excellence and gentlemanly behavior. Special prizes were awarded for Latin and French translations done beyond the assignment. It was a practical curriculum, designed for the sons of tradesmen who largely populated the school.[17]

The school's daily regimen was not overly Spartan. Hands and ears were inspected before an early breakfast, after which the students repaired to recitation rooms in the former coach house. The uniform included a starched shirt with frilled collar; long, high-waisted trousers; a short jacket with pearl buttons; and a tasseled cap. At eleven o'clock the students returned to the main building for dinner, which was followed by a half afternoon of continued lessons. Clarke's School had spacious grounds for semirequired, supervised play in the afternoon, but the students could choose among several recreational activities.

The school had common gardens and orchards. There was one particular morello (sour) cherry tree that all the boys were eager to climb, especially during fruit-picking season. Pymmes Brook ran through the property and into a pond. Charles Cowden Clarke described it as a rural paradise.[18]

John Keats, on his deathbed, commented to Joseph Severn that his greatest pleasure had come from watching the flowers grow.[19] Charles Brown (1786–1842) wrote in his putative biography of Keats, "From his earliest boyhood he had an acute sense of beauty, whether in a flower, a tree, the sky, or the animal world."[20] This sense of beauty was framed by Enfield, not by smoky London.

After classes, George generally habituated the cricket pitches, whereas John was more likely to be found wandering through the meadows or lying in the grass by the brook, alone. The older boys did not bully the Keats brothers, and any tensions were likely caused by the red-haired John's fiery temper. John's black moods, evident from childhood, led him into quarrels; imagined insults would precipitate fights from which George would extricate him. Although it might have been better to leave John to fend for himself, George usually intervened, a practice that continued past their school days. George's amiable demeanor and ease at making friends calmed the brothers' relationships with the other boys, who called George "Keats" and John "Little Keats." But sometimes John would even turn on George. As Charles Cowden Clarke wrote, "George, being considerably the taller and stronger, used frequently to hold him down by main force, laughing when John was in 'one of his moods,' and was endeavoring to beat him. It was all, however, a wisp-of-straw conflagration; for he had an intensely tender affection for his brothers."[21] George recalled, "My school fellows will bear witness that John's temper was the cause of all, still we were more attached than Brothers ever are."[22] And as Edward Holmes (1797–1859) later wrote about John, "His *penchant* was for fighting. He would fight any one—morning, noon or night; . . . to keep up the family reputation for courage." The younger but taller brother, who acted more socially mature, had a "passive manner."[23]

These diverse accounts of John—Holmes's description of him as an outgoing fighter, Brown's musing on his childhood contemplation of beauty, George's remark that he often had to be cheered out of his melancholia—are all perfectly consistent in a boy reacting to a numbing series of family losses.

At Clarke's, the boys made a number of friends who would play interesting roles later. Charles Briggs immigrated to America, arriving in Louisville before George. Edward Holmes later wrote the first *Life of Mozart*, from a musician's perspective. Richard Hengist Horne (1802–1884) wrote with Elizabeth Barrett (later Browning; 1806–1861) *A New Spirit of the Age*. Edward Cowper (1790–1852), though older than the boys, went on to invent a four-cylinder press that enabled printing on both sides of the sheet at the same time, presaging high-speed newspaper presses.[24]

After Frances's death, John's academic performance greatly improved, and he twice won the top academic prize before being withdrawn from the school at age fifteen by guardian Richard Abbey. Abbey concluded, perhaps wrongly, that continuing the boys' education at Clarke's School would dissipate the core principal of their inheritance. Under English law, if the beneficiary challenged the loss of principal, the guardian might be forced to make it up out of his own pocket, and Abbey was too conservative to take such a risk. He also disapproved of Clarke's School, which was too liberal for his tastes. John Keats once told Charles Cowden Clarke, smiling, that "one of his guardians [presumably Abbey], being informed of what books I had lent him to read, declared that if he had fifty children he would not send one of them to that school."[25] Abbey did not endorse a higher education for the boys because he evidently believed that their inherited funds were insufficient to propel them to a higher social status. Perhaps he thought that the money should be available to the boys so that they could buy into a trade, as he had done.

Under today's law, Abbey might have gained a dispensation from the court to invade the excess principal to pay for the boys' education. Perhaps that was not possible at the time, and Abbey concluded that it would be better to deliver the remaining funds safely to the children at age twenty-one than to invest in additional schooling. Whatever his motives, Abbey brought the Keats brothers' education to an end in 1811 and determined that they should move forward with their careers—John at fifteen, George at fourteen. Alice Jennings did not intervene. Tom, aged eleven, could have remained for an additional year, but he left school early to stay close to his brothers.

Clarke's School at Enfield, entrusted with the Keats boys during their formative years, succeeded beyond expectation. There can be no doubt that the school's progressive approach gave John's imagination the space it needed to grow. Charles Cowden Clarke's availability and literary encouragement helped John through the trials of his schoolboy years and pointed him inevitably toward the arts. George's experience was more traditional. He developed social and leadership skills and smoothed the path for his brothers. At the time, he was content to leave Clarke's School, but he later recognized that this premature departure denied him access to university, a profession, or even a higher-level trade position, all factors that contributed to his decision to emigrate.

The children's destiny was irretrievably determined by Thomas Keats's untimely death, which had momentous consequence for each of them. George, lacking an adequate inheritance to establish himself in London, was motivated to emigrate to America to restore his fortune. Fanny, after spending most of her childhood in Abbey's restrictive custody, married a Spaniard and resided for the next five decades on the Continent, never to return to England. John, hypochondriacal from childhood, matured in an atmosphere of growing financial and emotional insecurity. After George moved to London in 1811, John remained in Edmonton as apprentice to surgeon Thomas Hammond, and Charles Cowden Clarke stepped into the mentoring role that would profoundly redirect John's life toward poetry. Their stories would not have played out the same had Thomas Keats lived.

YOUTHS ABOUT LONDON

1811–1818

For the next eight years, John and George embarked on separate but overlapping lives. After being withdrawn from Clarke's School, George returned to the world of business in London, where he met his future wife, Georgiana. John trained in Edmonton as an apothecary, simultaneously discovering Spenser and poetry. It was a period in their relationship noted for their intense emotional codependence. As John wrote to George's mother-in-law, Ann Wylie, "My brother George has ever been more than a brother to me, he has been my greatest friend."[1] George's own recollection mirrored John's: "I claim being the affectionat[e] Friend and Brother of John Keats. I loved him from boyhood even when he wronged me, for the goodness of his heart and the nobleness of his spirit."[2]

George worked for Richard Abbey's tea wholesaling business,[3] training in the accounting department while he lived in a dormitory above the warehouse at 4 Pancras Lane, in the Poultry section of London.[4] Residing there was a matter of convenience, and it facilitated the supervision of a young boy in the city. Nothing suggests that George complained. Age fourteen and parentless, he probably saw the move as an opportunity to learn about business, live in the city, and get a start in life. Abbey may have seen his guardianship of George as an opportunity to employ a low-cost clerk. The Abbeys also lived part-time above the business, particularly during the winter. On certain nights of the week, year-round, if he had to attend business dinners, Abbey would remain in the city rather than making the six-mile trek back to his house in Walthamstow.

Fanny Keats, six years younger than George, lived with her grandmother until Alice Jennings died in 1814. Abbey and his wife then took Fanny (age eleven) in, and she remained in Walthamstow for more than ten years. Until she was fifteen, Fanny boarded at Miss Tuckey's School,[5] across Marsh Street and around the corner from the Abbeys' home.[6] Then she resided with the Abbeys for six more miserable years in their home. By her telling, Fanny hated every minute of it and disliked the Abbeys, calling Richard a "consummate villain."[7] However, because she had been kept away from London's pollution and exposure to tubercular patients during these years, Fanny was the only one of the four adult Keats siblings to survive past forty. Although neither recorded it, George and Fanny likely saw each other during the time George was involved at least tangentially in Abbey's London household.

George's employment was scarcely Dickensian. He enjoyed the work, never complained about the Spartan living arrangements, and lived within his income. Quickly approaching manhood, he prospered. He and John would visit occasionally, either in Edmonton, where John was apprenticed to surgeon Thomas Hammond, or in London. George collected a number of new friends in London. Tom Keats joined George in Abbey's business by 1814, and the two were rarely separated until George's departure for America.

Having shown such empathy and attention to detail while caring for his dying mother, John was indentured by Abbey to Thomas Hammond to be trained in surgery, diagnosis, and prescriptions.[8] Initially it was an agreeable arrangement all around. Hammond, who had treated John Jennings in his final months, was a friend of the family, as well as a neighbor in Edmonton.[9] In England's hierarchical medical system, apothecaries were the lowest rank—in effect, doctors to the poor. Surgeons such as Hammond were licensed to practice general medicine and dentistry. Physicians were university graduates, entitled to be called "Doctor."

Hammond charged John Keats more than £200 for the apprenticeship. This £200 fee—the same amount Hammond paid another surgeon to educate his own son—contributed to subsequent misunderstandings about John's finances.[10] After John quarreled with Hammond or his son, he decided to live in rental lodgings nearby, despite his obligation to continue to pay Hammond rent and board. He incurred these double living costs for about two years, from 1813 to 1815. Although Keats cut short his indenture by a year, his certificate from Hammond shows that he served the required five years. Abbey thought Hammond had failed to deliver all the training he had committed to and that he should rebate the unapplied room and board. Much later, Abbey wrote to Charles Brown that Hammond's charges summed more than £700, although Brown believed the total expenses actually approached £1,000.

According to Charles Cowden Clarke, John's five years with Hammond through the summer of 1815 were "the most placid period of his painful life."[11] John continued to see Clarke several times a month, and they would discuss Shakespeare and poetry. It was during John's tenure with Hammond that Clarke introduced him to Edmund Spenser's *The Faerie Queene,* infusing John with the spiritual fire that would drive him for the rest of his short life. Poetry was in fashion, and Clarke was attempting to establish himself as a poet. Clarke encouraged Keats's isolation in Edmonton, thinking it would soothe his moods.

George took the opposite tack. To deal with John's "nervous morbid temperament,"[12] George encouraged his brother to stay busy with friends. On their periodic visits, George showed John around the city, and the boys enjoyed such after-work activities as theater, card parties, billiards, cockfights, bearbaitings, and boxing matches.[13]

Passage of the British Apothecary Act of 1815, which attempted to clarify the three-level medical system and set standards for each, meant that John could not become a surgeon without first completing hospital training, in addition to his apprenticeship with Hammond. So John registered in 1815 at Guy's Hospital in London.[14] He hoped to apply for membership in the Royal College of Surgeons within a year. At Guy's he studied anatomy, chemistry, physiology, dissection, and botany, doing well enough in these studies to be appointed a dresser to one of the worst surgeons, Billy Lucas, after twenty-eight days (12 dressers were accepted from 700 applications).[15] He did not remain for a second year. George noted the yearly fees: "£30 *apprenticeship* fees, £50 *dressership* and £50 other *hospital* fees, £20 *books* and £20 surgical *instruments,* £160 per an."[16] Annual rooming costs were an additional £63.[17]

John lived that year with other medical students, including Henry Stephens (1796–1864) and George Wilson Mackereth, at 28 St. Thomas Street, Southwark, near the hospital.[18] On breaks from his intense medical studies, John socialized with them and also with George and Tom, who would cross the Thames for evening visits.

Stephens, writing three decades later to George Felton Mathew, noted his irritation at George and Tom's uncritical adulation of their brother.[19] John's roommates were startled by the brothers' closeness and by George's unrelenting praise of John's poems, which he submitted to George for first review. Another acquaintance, Henry Newmarch, critiqued the poetry (to Stephens's amusement), mostly to provoke the younger brothers into quarrels in defense of John. Stephens later wrote, "He had two Brothers, who visited him frequently, & they worshipped him. They seemed to think their brother John was to be exalted, & to exalt the family name.—I remember a Student [Henry Newmarch, a classical scholar] . . . who often came to see him, as they had formerly been intimate, but though old friends they did not always cordially agree. . . . I thought he was rather too fond of mortifying Keats, but more particularly his brothers, as their praise of their Brother John amounted almost to idolatry, & Newmarsh & they frequently quarreled."[20]

By 1816, George had left the dormitory and was living with Abbey's chief clerk, Mr. Swan. He reported either to Swan or to Cadman Hodgkinson, one of whom he nicknamed "wagtail."[21]

With their newfound independence in the city, the boys developed different groups of interlocking friendships. Two families welcomed George: the Mathews and the Wylies. The Mathews were wine merchants living northwest of the city, and there were two daughters, Anne Felton and Caroline. The family staged "at homes" for minor poets and poetical young ladies. A cousin with literary aspirations, George Felton Mathew, also visited.[22] George Keats introduced John into the Mathews' home, which offered a pleasant respite from the brothers' spare quarters. The boys wrote verse, contributing to the evening parlor games and songs. Both Keats boys wrote to the Mathew girls. Ultimately, John Keats distanced himself from the Mathews, whose young members were not up to his intellectual level.

The Wylies' matriarch was Ann Griffin Wylie, an older widow.[23] She had two sons, Robert Henry (known as Henry) and Charles Gaskell, and a daughter, Georgiana Augusta. In 1813, when Georgiana was fifteen,[24] Henry, who was fourteen years older than his sister, invited George to Mrs. Wylie's home at 3 Romney Street, just off Smith Square beyond Westminster.[25] Mrs. Wylie was an easygoing lady who encouraged her children's pursuits and quickly befriended their friends. Three years and many visits later, George and Georgiana announced their engagement.

George did some of the wooing with valentines and verse written by John. An 1816 valentine, later published as "To * * * *," began and ended as follows:

Hadst thou liv'd in days of old,
O what wonders had been told
Of thy lively countenance,
And thy humid eyes that dance
In the midst of their own brightness;
In the very fane of lightness.

Alas! thou this will never do:
Thou are an enchantress too,
And wilt surely never spill
Blood of those whose eyes can kill.[26]

Georgiana was not fooled as to the authorship, and she became a dear friend to John, as well as his sister-in-law.

Through the Wylies, George also met William Haslam, a solicitor,[27] and then the artist Joseph Severn, both of whom he introduced to John. Haslam and Severn would later prove to be fast friends and supporters of the poet and critics of George. As John wrote in a gracious 1818 overstatement, "I know not how it is, but I have never made any acquaintance of my own—nearly all through your medium, my dear Brother."[28]

Nevertheless, John soon met James Henry Leigh Hunt and, by extension, members of the Leigh Hunt circle through Charles Cowden Clarke. Leigh Hunt and his brother John were born in Southgate, where their Loyalist father had settled after being deported from Philadelphia. Both ended up working for the *Examiner,* and both were jailed for two years beginning in 1813, having written a scathingly accurate piece on the Prince Regent. While in jail, Leigh Hunt occupied two rooms so that his family could join him. He borrowed funds to decorate the rooms and also received funds from many liberals, who considered him a martyr. His jailer allowed guests until 10:00 PM, and Hunt's circle grew out of that list of visitors. Clarke, like his father, had always admired the *Examiner,* and he befriended the imprisoned Hunt by sending flowers and visiting him in jail.[29] Later, in 1817, while hanging out with the Hunts at their home in Hampstead, John Keats introduced George to Percy Bysshe Shelley and his wife, novelist Mary Godwin Shelley (daughter of Mary Wollstonecraft). Hunt was the first to publish anything written by Keats and continued to provide him, as well as Shelley, coverage in the *Examiner.* In addition to meeting the Hunts, John was introduced to Charles Brown, a schoolmate of Charles W. Dilke;[30] Brown would later supplant George as a surrogate brother. The poet was clearly establishing his own relationships, although he remained loyal to George and his future in-laws the Wylies.

The summer of 1816 was a turning point for the Keats boys. John and Tom took a vacation in Margate, aiming to cheer up Tom, who was unemployed and may have been showing the early signs of consumption. John returned from the school holiday to begin his final term at Guy's, living briefly alone at 8 Dean Street. Tom moved in with George, who by September 1816 had moved to 76 Cheapside, adjacent to the hat manufactory of Joseph Keats, a possible relation. The boys seemed to be in perpetual motion. In mid-November John joined them in Cheapside, just around the corner from Abbey's warehouse and within a reasonable walking distance of Guy's Hospital. Around that time, John wrote a sonnet to Tom to commemorate his seventeenth birthday:

> Small, busy flames play through the fresh-laid coals,
>   And their faint cracklings o'er our silence creep
>   Like whispers of the household Gods that keep
> A gentle empire o'er fraternal souls.
> And while, for rhymes, I search around the poles,
>   Your eyes are fix'd, as in poetic sleep,
>   Upon the lore so voluble and deep,
> That aye at fall of night our care condoles.
> This is your birth-day, Tom, and I rejoice
>   That thus it passes smoothly, quietly.
> Many such eves of gently whisp'ring noise
>   May we together pass, and calmly try
> What are this world's true joys,—ere the great voice,
>   From its fair face, shall bid our spirits fly.[31]

The Keats brothers enjoyed active social lives during this period. George was focused primarily on his fiancée Georgiana and spent a lot of time at the Wylie house.[32] All three boys played vingt-et-un, went to the theater in Drury Lane or Covent Garden, visited art galleries, and walked Vauxhall Gardens. Their correspondence tells of reading poetry, literary criticism, and travel books.

George used his spare time at Cheapside to copy John's poetry, which he then distributed to friends and other interested readers. John often revised his drafts, and their evolution provides a clear window into his poetic development. George also served as John's agent during this period, carrying copies to publishers, negotiating terms, proofreading, and monitoring the marketing and sales effort. John wrote several sonnets, including "On Looking into Chapman's Homer," and he apparently considered Georgiana the ideal woman. In December 1816 he penned a poem "To G.A.W.":

Nymph of the downward smile, and sidelong glance,
  In what diviner moments of the day
  Art thou most lovely? When gone far astray
Into the labyrinths of sweet utterance?
Or when serenely wand'ring in a trance
  Of sober thought? Or, when starting away,
  With careless robe, to meet the morning ray,
Thou spar'st the flowers in thy mazy dance?
Haply 'tis when thy ruby lips part sweetly,
  And so remain, because thou listenest:
But thou to please wert nurtured so completely
  That I can never tell what mood is best.
I shall as soon pronounce which Grace more neatly
  Trips it before Apollo than the rest.[33]

It could be that Keats liked Georgiana (as he writes in the tenth line) for her ability to listen.

That winter, in early 1817, George quit Abbey's employ. The reason may have been that Abbey's junior partner, Cadman Hodgkinson, had overstepped his authority and reprimanded George.[34] Uncharacteristically, George lost his temper and walked out, and Abbey did not intervene. John, completely loyal to George, used some of his best invective against Hodgkinson in letters over the next three years. An alternative reason, cited by Charles Brown thirteen years later, was that "George had been extravagant; it was Abbey's alleged plea for dismissing him from his counting house."[35] Because of Brown's longtime dispute with Dilke over George, his memory may have been skewed, given that Abbey and George continued to have a cordial relationship for seven years after George's exit from the business.

After leaving Abbey, George worked briefly for a man named Wilkinson, whose bona fides have never been clear, although he may have been an auctioneer.[36] John loaned Wilkinson £50 in support of the venture, perhaps because Abbey declined to release the funds to George. The sum was never repaid and contributed to later financial misunderstandings. Whatever the venture was, George soon gave it up and decided, at age twenty, to postpone any further employment. He would await his inheritance, trusteed by Abbey and coming due in February 1818, upon his twenty-first birthday. In the meantime, he would serve as a sort of house manager for his brothers and look after Tom, whose health was visibly declining. Later, went the thinking, he could establish a trade.

By this time, it was clear that George's strong influence over John, as his protective brother and best friend, was diminishing. Charles Cowden Clarke had introduced John to poetry, providing an entirely new and captivating dimension to his life. John's world continued to expand through Leigh Hunt, whose circle—a loose, informal affair—included writers, poets, artists, actors, solicitors, and even one enlightened businessman.[37] Hunt's literary coterie was dubbed the Cockney School by *Blackwood's Magazine,* and the taint of that word rubbed off on Keats as well. Old-school critics with Oxford or Cambridge degrees scoffed at the less-educated circle members, even suggesting that their rhyming reflected their Cockney accents. Keats was accused of "low diction" for rhyming *thorns* with *fawns* in "Sleep and Poetry," suggesting a working-class speech. The slur was not just an attack on the poets' aesthetics; it reflected a thinly disguised resentment of their barely middle-class backgrounds and their radical politics (non-Tory), which the boys indeed shared. In some circles, the definition of Cockney even stretched to those attempting to climb above their station.

No one really knows with what accent the Keats boys spoke. The epicenter of Cockneyism (facetiously, "Cockaigne")[38] was St. Mary-le-Bow Church, situated within steps of Abbey's establishment. Hackney and Shoreditch, where Frances and Thomas Keats lived, were part of the London Cockney environment.[39] However, the boys left London at an early age to live with their Lancashire grandmother in suburban Ponders End. It is hard to imagine that the tutors at Clarke's School spoke in a Cockney tongue; most likely they spoke with educated accents. It was also common for residents of Cockney London to have no trace of a Cockney accent.[40]

Among Hunt's group were Shelley, essayists William Hazlitt and Charles Lamb, and Dilke, who would later become a steadfast friend of George. William Wordsworth, a Cambridge-educated friend of poets Samuel Taylor Coleridge and Robert Southey and a man of shifting conservative views, mingled occasionally with Hunt and met John Keats at least twice. Also loosely included in the group, but not necessarily labeled Cockney, were poet Barry Cornwall (aka Bryan Waller Procter); Shakespearean lecturer and John's old friend Charles Cowden Clarke; parody writers Horace and James Smith; solicitor, poet, and early defender of *Endymion,* John Hamilton Reynolds; erstwhile friend Charles Jeremiah Wells;[41] painters Robert Benjamin Haydon and Joseph Severn; animal painter and engraver Edwin H. Landseer; surgeon Joseph Ritchie, who died while exploring Africa; publishers John Taylor and Augustus Hessey; Taylor's solicitor and reader Richard Woodhouse Jr.; actors Edmund Kean and William Charles Macready; editor James Elmes; poet and earlier friend George Felton Mathew; Benjamin Bailey, an Oxford scholar and friend of Taylor; theater critic Thomas Richards; solicitors James Rice and William Haslam; and writer-publishers James and Charles Ollier.[42] Others drifted into the circle later. In the 1820s Coleridge and poet-editor-humorist Thomas Hood joined the group. Membership was constantly shifting, although Reynolds, Rice, and Bailey were long-standing friends.

On 28 December 1815 Benjamin Haydon hosted the "immortal dinner" in his studio, overpowered by his enormous *Christ's Entry into Jerusalem* hanging on the wall.[43] Guests included Wordsworth, Keats, Reynolds, Lamb, and Thomas Monkhouse; Leigh Hunt, with whom Haydon was quarreling, was excluded. Involvement with this crowd was a heady experience for John. George lacked the artistic and literary credentials of these people, but he shared their values and tastes and was devoted to helping John gain exposure. At best, George was an outlier of the group, an occasional participant who helped John entertain his new friends. Many of these young men were impecunious, and with loans constantly being made back and forth, personal debts accumulated.[44] George kept track of John's financial affairs, for which John had neither the capability nor the desire.

Clarke introduced John to Charles Richards, an Enfield graduate and printer working on behalf of the publishing firm C. and J. Ollier. Richards typeset Keats's first book, *Poems,* which the Olliers published in late 1816. Sales did not meet expectations, leading George to critique the firm's insufficient advertising. He threatened to fire the publishers and offered to buy back the unsold copies. The Olliers accepted and wrote to George: "Sir—We regret your brother ever requested us to publish his book, or that our opinion of its talent should have led us to acquiesce in undertaking it. We are, however, much obliged to you for relieving us from the unpleasant necessity of declining any further connexion with it."[45] George did not serve John well in this imbroglio.

Abbey was no more encouraging than the Olliers. When John took his first published work to him, his reaction was, "Well, John, I have read your Book & it reminds me of the Quaker's Horse, which was hard to catch, & good for nothing when he was caught—So your Book is hard to understand & good for nothing when it is understood." Abbey told Taylor, "I don't think he ever forgave me for uttering this Opinion, which however was the Truth."[46]

Through an introduction by Bailey, John Keats established a relationship with Taylor and Hessey, who bought the unsold copies of *Poems* for remarketing. They went on to publish all of Keats's work, even representing him for years after his death. The Olliers went on to publish Shelley successfully.

The brotherly dynamic changed in several ways as 1816 passed into 1817. John made it clear that he was abandoning medicine for poetry. By March 1817, John found the ringing church bells of St. Mary-le-Bow and the environs of Cheapside depressing. Also, he wanted to be closer to Leigh Hunt, so he moved to the relative calm of Hampstead, leasing upstairs rooms from postman Bentley at 1 Well Walk. Because George had abandoned his job and no longer needed to be in London, he and Tom joined John in the semirural setting close to Hampstead Heath, about seven miles north of Cheapside. Tom, as sketched by Joseph Severn, was looking thin and pale and a bit pinched in the face, so the relocation may have been undertaken for health reasons as well, given that the Cheapside address was damp and smoky. Tom made no pretense at work, simply living off the income from his remaining assets.

John Keats made his objectives clear to Abbey, telling him of his decision to quit medicine. Abbey argued that John should move to Enfield and establish himself as an apothecary there while continuing to study surgery. As Abbey later recounted the conversation:

> Not intend to be a Surgeon! Why what do you mean to be?
> I mean to rely on my Abilities as a Poet—
> John, [are you Mad or Silly] you are either Mad or a Fool to talk in so absurd a Manner.
> My mind is made up, said the youngster very quietly. I know that I possess Abilities greater than most Men, and therefore I am determined to gain my Living by exercising them.

Abbey then called him a "silly boy & prophesied a speedy Termination to his inconsiderate Enterprise."[47]

Although John was twenty-one and entitled to the remaining inheritance from his grandmother's estate, Abbey created obstacles. Those funds had been depleted by the need to monetize assets during down markets for his tuition and living expenses. Inexplicably, John seemed to forget about the Chancery trusts from his mother and grandfather, perhaps thinking—erroneously—that they could not be released until after Fanny turned twenty-one in 1824 (by that time, John was dead, and his share equaled upward of £1,500). Alice Jennings's solicitor, William Walton, never notified John that he could apply for those funds, perhaps because he was no longer on retainer, or perhaps because he was elderly and simply forgot.[48] Had John requested his share at age twenty-one, as Fanny later did, the funds most likely would have been released.

The brothers' intentions clarified at this time. John would pursue poetry full time until his funds ran out; then he could take up some mundane occupation. Owing to Tom's questionable health and attitude of dependency, he did not work at all. By late 1817, John recognized the inevitable outcome of Tom's condition and made plans to take him to balmier Teignmouth for the winter;[49] Tom would die before the end of 1818. George's role in this limited-income scenario was to devise a means to restore the family's finances. Having actually had an earned income for six years, he was the most solvent of the three brothers and had not dipped into his capital.

Soon after moving to Hampstead, John left and spent six weeks on the Isle of Wight, where he wrote "On the Sea" and began *Endymion*. John returned to Margate, where Tom joined him, but by June they were back in Well Walk. John spent the month of September with Benjamin Bailey at Oxford, writing the third book of *Endymion*. During the same month, George and Tom went on holiday to rural France and to Paris, where they met the editor John Scott. The accounts of this trip are inconsistent and questionable. Reynolds noted that George and Tom may have frequented an expensive gambling hall and a notorious brothel. According to Brown, the brothers spent "far too much for their circumstances," and he rued "George's and Tom's pleasure jaunt to Paris, the trip to Lyons, and the money lost at the 'rouge et noir' table in the Palais Royale."[50]

When the brothers reassembled in Well Walk in October, it was John who was ill, and he prescribed mercury for himself. Mercury was used to treat venereal disease, depression, and certain respiratory ailments, and Keats biographers have debated which of these afflicted John. A few, including Sidney Colvin, concluded that he had an unfortunate sexual escapade while at Oxford.[51] By November, John had completed *Endymion*.

The relationships among the Keats siblings and their interdependencies have been described in many ways. Bailey disapproved of George and Tom; he saw the brothers as a distraction to John, who required solitude to write his poetry. John likely acquiesced in the living arrangement at Well Walk because he recognized Tom's need for care and to save on living expenses. The brothers, though orphans for seven years, were still very young, and they seemed to have an emotional codependency as well. Even

Fanny noted, much later, "I don't think it is easy to meet with a family more devoted to each other than we were. Perhaps it is owing in part to our being left orphans at an early age, and thus we clung closer to each other."[52]

Georgiana Wylie was an additional participant. The future Mrs. George Keats had a somewhat uncertain background. Her mother, Mrs. Wylie, had been married to an adjutant in the Fifeshire Fencibles but was widowed two years before her daughter's birth. Augustus Gaskell, a lieutenant in the North Gloucester Foot Regiment, may have fathered both Georgiana and her brother Charles, but he was not present when the Keatses came calling.

John was genuinely fond of his sister-in-law-to-be, calling her "disinterested"—a high compliment in his jargon.[53] Although she lived about eight miles away with her mother and aunt in Westminster, the group often met there for dinner. The subsequent John-to-Georgiana correspondence became an important window into the poet's views on women.

The year in Cheapside and Well Walk was a time of mutual convenience. George and John both looked after Tom. Tom copied John's poems, although not as carefully as George did. It was mostly John who looked in on Fanny, isolated in the Abbeys' house miles away in Walthamstow; the trail of correspondence between them reveals few strains. George helped John get his work published and assisted with his finances. He also furthered the process of introducing John, still a medical student, into poetic circles, including the aforementioned Mathew family, William Haslam, and Joseph Severn. Various gatherings of these people led to more connections, several of them in the Leigh Hunt circle.

A year later, the picture was not so simple with respect to John's artistic friends. Haydon's enormous painting, a speculation against future exhibition revenues, had been stopped by creditors. He and Leigh Hunt had fallen out. Haydon and John Reynolds also quarreled, and Haydon was badgering Keats for loans. Horace Smith was bored by Hunt's airs. By the end of 1819, the petty disputes and distrust would ultimately involve Charles Brown and Charles Dilke, with unhappy consequences for George Keats.

In November 1817, as the weather cooled, Tom's racking cough worsened. The brothers briefly considered the warmer clime of Lisbon, but Portugal was too far from John's publishers, too far from George's fiancée, and too big a strain on their finances. The compromise was Teignmouth, Devonshire, on the southwest coast of the English Channel. The initial plan was for John and Tom to spend the winter in Teignmouth, leaving George behind to handle business matters. However, having received the final manuscript of *Endymion*, Taylor and Hessey said it was too unfinished and required too much work for John to be away from London. So John, who had already left, turned around at Burford Bridge, Surrey, and stayed in London. George and Tom departed Hampstead in mid-December 1817 for Teignmouth.

George and Tom boarded with Mrs. Margaret Jeffrey and her daughters, Sarah and Marian. Mrs. Jeffrey cheerfully took up mothering Tom. George embarked on a friendship, or perhaps even a dalliance, with Sarah. She drew sketches that George promised to take up to London for review. Marian attempted to write poetry, so George coached her, using John's work as examples. He talked about his plans for emigration but never mentioned his engagement.

Tom was in good spirits but still hemorrhaged. This caused no great alarm, as the misguided medical wisdom of the time was that blood loss and regeneration were good therapy.[54] George wrote to John about Tom's improvement, but they both misunderstood that Tom's improved spirits masked his continued physical deterioration.

George's stay in Teignmouth distracted him from the primary issues of his life. Georgiana was in London, their wedding date having been set for 28 May 1818. George was planning how to use his inheritance, due in February. London was abuzz with emigration talk. George was greatly attracted to America, where he believed his limited capital could be invested with more effect than in London. However, he was unable to make plans from Devonshire. By February 1818, George wrote to John, hinting that he wanted to leave Teignmouth. John visited with Georgiana, who clearly expressed her desire for her fiancé to return to London. John agreed to trade places with George in Teignmouth and was surprised, immediately after posting his letter saying so, to see George walk in, having left Tom with Mrs. Jeffrey. John completed his work on *Endymion* in Teignmouth during March and April. George was concerned that John did not look so well himself, and he cautioned John not to burden Tom with his feelings.

Keats also wrote "Isabella, or the Pot of Basil" while in Teignmouth.[55] A year earlier Keats had met Isabella Jones while on holiday at Bo Peep, near Hastings. Although he was smitten by her, the feelings may not have been reciprocal. They kissed, but apparently that was all they did. She was pretty and intelligent, related in some undefined way to the titled Irish Whig family of Donat O'Callaghan. Whether the fair Isabella of the poem was modeled after her is not known; nor is it known whether George's naming of his second daughter Isabel had any connection. Keats himself regarded the work as popular, not serious. He thought it "smokeable," or that it could be "smoak'd,"[56] by which he meant it was not to be taken very seriously. Later, Isabella suggested the idea for "The Eve of St. Agnes," a night when girls could dream accurately of their true loves if they performed certain rites. Published in 1820, it was among Keats's best.

George, for his part, wrote a long farewell letter to both Jeffrey sisters a week and a half after his return to London. He made it clear that his Teignmouth visit had been a vacation; he did not tell them that he had decided to go to America or make any mention of Georgiana. He wrote, "I'll e'en entreat you Marianne to kiss Sarah and she must fancy it is from me, she must do the same and you must use your imagination in like manner."[57] Later he wrote to John in Teignmouth, lightly suggesting that he "give my . . . love to the Miss J's."[58] He also left it to John to tell the girls about his marriage (assuming that Tom had not already spilled the beans). John wrote to them on 4 June 1818, "George took unto himself a Wife a Week ago and will in a little time sail for America."[59] The Jeffrey family remained close to the Keatses, with Marian later advising John on the pros and cons of taking employment on an Indiaman.[60]

George emerged from his year of unemployment with a plan. He would claim his inheritance from Abbey, marry Georgiana in May, and leave for America as soon as practicable thereafter. George had committed to read the proofs of *Endymion* for Taylor and Hessey, but he found himself so caught up with his plans and with Georgiana that he asked Charles Cowden Clarke to take over. Given Tom's poor health and John's budding career as a starving poet, George had concluded that he had to be the family provider, and his chances of rebuilding their financial independence would be greatest in America. Georgiana, lacking a dowry and with sketchy social credentials, was equally intrigued by the idea of emigrating. Her Griffin cousins in Montreal were thriving. John concurred with George's thinking. He wrote to Bailey:

> You know my Brother George has been out of employ for some time, it has weighed much upon him, and driven him to scheme and turn over things in his Mind. the result has been his resolution to emigrate to the back settlements of America, become farmer and work with his own hands after purchasing 1400 hundred Acres of the American Government. This for many reasons

has met with my entire consent—and the chief one is this—he is of too independent and liberal a Mind to get on in trade in this Country—in which a generous Ma[n] with a scanty recourse must be ruined. I would sooner he should till the ground than bow to a Customer—there is no choice with him; he could not bring himself to the latter.[61]

Richard Abbey's role through these years was ambiguous. He attended to the Keats children's welfare as a guardian should, offering jobs and shelter to George and Tom, taking Fanny into his home, and providing John the wherewithal for an expensive medical education. His reward for these efforts was to be mocked and detested by John, thoroughly hated by Fanny, and distrusted by her advisers. Later literati took Abbey to task for just about everything, and few attempted to analyze events from his point of view. A notable exception was E. M. Forster (1879–1970), who inserted into *Abinger Harvest* a 1925 article titled "Mr. and Mrs. Abbey's Difficulties." Forster was critical of the Keats children, describing them as "restless," "always asking for money," and, in Mrs. Abbey's words, "idle."[62]

The Keats children, having grown up in London and Edmonton and experiencing the comfortable surroundings of their grandparents' home, doubtless felt a sense of entitlement. Being emotionally close to one another, as well as very young, they acted out their frustrations on the well-intentioned but hapless Abbey. Only George seems to have accepted the situation and made the most of it. In a letter to Fanny he wrote that Abbey is "a man upon whose integrity, and goodness of Heart the utmost reliance can be placed."[63] Abbey, in turn, favored George, distributing the funds from his grandmother's estate promptly and possibly investing £60 of his own in George's American adventure.[64]

Abbey, a Yorkshireman, valued prudence and practicality. He was a bluff, portly tea merchant who joined in chamber of commerce–type activities, such as the Patternmakers. Yorkshiremen as a group generally grow, manufacture, or sell the goods that are the necessities of everyday life. They are an outgoing lot and often describe themselves as "tighter than a Scot—why spend a pound when you can spend a penny?" Others say they are "meaner than a Scot, but lacking a Scot's personality."[65]

John Keats and his friends ridiculed Abbey. Taylor described him as having a lump, "a great Piece of Benevolence standing out on Top of his Forehead."[66] Abbey dressed in short breeches with white cotton stockings and half boots, although the fashion had changed to tight, high-waisted trousers with straps beneath the instep.[67] His thinking was illiberal. A businessman, he did not understand or appreciate poetry, but he did pursue numerous interests beyond the tea brokerage. For years he was a warden of the church in Walthamstow. He was a member of the Port of London Committee, the Committee for Improving the Navigation of the River Thames, and other committees as late as 1829, when he was a commissioner of sewers, lamps, and pavements. His career, in short, matched up with Taylor's description of him as stout and aldermanic.[68]

There is no record of Abbey's politics, but he was evidently going with the Tory flow in a Regency England marked by aristocratic excesses, widespread poverty, inflation, and the ever-present thought that a French-style revolution might sweep across the English Channel. John Keats and his friends were clearly to the left of this societal divide. Abbey, probably on the right, kept his head down.

As guardian of the Keats children, Abbey likely looked after their welfare consistent with Alice Jennings's wishes, as stated in her now-lost indenture. He assured that each child received an adequate education and subsequent career guidance, whether or not it was accepted. He properly trusteed the funds under his control from 1810 at least until his own difficulties in 1822–1824 swamped him. Abbey may have thought that the Keats siblings came from a modest social background, their father being a hostler. He had disparaged Thomas Keats, saying he "did not possess or display any great Accomplishments" and "thought it became him to act somewhat more the Man of Consequence than he had been accustomed to do."[69] Abbey may have been disinclined to enable the children to do much better. His decision to curtail their education in 1811, without mention of university attendance, was clearly uninspired.

The poet's friends, in contrast, were young and judgmental, with surprisingly casual attitudes toward parenting. Severn and Brown each had illegitimate sons, and Shelley had abandoned a child.[70] As far as anyone knows, none of them served as guardian for any children other than their own or included orphans in their households. Keats biographers from Milnes forward simply accepted Fanny's and John's characterization of Abbey without researching his story, unfairly turning him into a secondhand cartoon figure. Despite Abbey's well-meaning guardianship of the Keats children, it seems that his wife was less sympathetic, in particular to John Keats and his literary friends.

John had consumed £700 to £1,000 of his grandmother's trust during his years at Clarke's School, the Hammond apprenticeship, and Guy's Hospital, amounting to about two-thirds of his capital; these funds were often withdrawn during down markets. After leaving Guy's, John was in frequent travel mode and usually stayed in commercial lodgings: he went to the Isle of Wight, Margate, Canterbury, Oxford, Stratford, and Burford Bridge in 1817; Teignmouth and Scotland in 1818; and Chichester, Bedhampton, Isle of Wight, and Winchester in 1819, as well as other destinations. He was also caught up in the habit of lending money to his friends, although he never realized a shilling of income. These years probably consumed £200 to £300, or about half the remainder of his share of his grandmother's capital.[71] Abbey doled out the funds to John, often reluctantly, and he was clearly concerned that they would be completely diminished before John required start-up capital to embark on a career. It simply was not in Abbey's ken to imagine a self-supporting poetic career.

Abbey's mind-set, fixed in the tradesman atmosphere of the Poultry, led him to encourage John alternately to open an apothecary/surgery in Tottenham,[72] to become a hatter[73] or a bookseller,[74] or to join a tea brokerage.[75] John himself had considered returning to medical school in Edinburgh. Writing to George and Georgiana in March 1819, he stated, "I have been at different times turning it in my head whether I should go to Edinburgh & study for a physician; I am afraid I should not take kindly to it."[76] He discussed with Marian Jeffrey in Teignmouth the possibility of his becoming a surgeon on an Indiaman to benefit from the climate and the isolation from his acquaintances and to have the opportunity to write.[77] As late as May 1820 he wrote to Dilke, "I have a choice of three things—or at least two—South America or Surgeon to an I[n]diaman—which last I think will be my fate—I shall resolve in a few days."[78] Keats also considered a career in journalism to support himself, writing in August 1819 to John Hamilton Reynolds, "I feel it in my power to become a popular writer."[79] None of these mundane career alternatives ever eventuated.

A particular irritant to Abbey, perhaps representing his wife's point of view, was the remarkable volume of letter writing back and forth between Fanny and John. The Abbeys were trying to insulate Fanny from Keats and his circle, whom they regarded as Don Quixotes, yet his letters served to legitimize his activities and his friends in Fanny's eyes. In addition, John's letters often arrived in Walthamstow via the two-penny post, postage due.

The relationship between John and Abbey was a difficult one, exacerbated by John's repeated requests for funds. John thought Abbey was incompetent when it came to handling the Keats siblings' money. However, when two of John's friends, lawyers John Hamilton Reynolds and

James Rice, examined the records carefully in 1824—along with Charles Dilke and his brother William, an accountant—they found no malfeasance regarding the boys' accounts. Dilke, however, suspected that Abbey often intermingled the principal with the interest accounts and that he had, on occasion, borrowed from the principal, particularly Fanny's, for no explained reason. With respect to the boys, Abbey did nothing overtly wrong. Dilke believed, after the fact, that Abbey hid behind the threat of Margaret Jennings's lawsuit in Chancery Court when he felt disinclined to provide funds.[80] Despite the available resources, Abbey created an unnecessary sense of poverty and disenfranchisement that, ironically, may have stimulated some of Keats's best poetry.

Although Abbey entered into the guardianship arrangement with the best of intentions, and although he looked after the youths conscientiously, he clearly became frustrated toward the end, particularly with John. Aside from terminating their educations early, Abbey's other misjudgment was his failure to provide any of the children (with the possible exception of George) with a solid financial grounding. Had they been better prepared, they might have employed their resources far more wisely.

Georgiana Augusta Wylie was one of the youngest members of the Keats inner circle. She was just fifteen when her brother Henry introduced her to George, nineteen when they got engaged, and twenty on her wedding day. Standing five feet tall, Georgiana had a bright personality and a talent for easy hospitality, making her a magnet for George and appealing to John as well. Her mother, an army widow, was accustomed to independence and gave it easily to her children. In brief, Georgiana was older than her years and a force in her own right.

Georgiana was smart, with a strong interest in current affairs. She was not a gossip, conversing more about ideas than about people. Her ready wit included a flair for repartee. Evenings spent with Georgiana and John Keats were touch-and-go affairs. They bandied puns in person and traded arguments across the Atlantic. John cynically lumped women into three categories: the dressmaker, the bluestocking, and the most charming sentimentalist. *Bluestocking* was a term for an educated, intellectual woman; it originated with a literary society founded by Elizabeth Montagu in the 1750s, but by the end of the eighteenth century, it had become opprobrious. In 1822 William Hazlitt said, "The bluestocking is the most odious character in society . . . she sinks wherever she is placed, like the yolk of an egg, to the bottom, and carries the filth with her."[81] For Georgiana, John made an exception, stating that she belonged to none of these categories, writing, "forgive me little George you know I don't mean to put you in the mess."[82] His attraction to her was intellectual—and then some. Writing to his Oxford friend Benjamin Bailey after the wedding, John said of his sister-in-law, "I like her better and better—she is the most disinterrested woman I ever knew. . . . To see an entirely disinterrested Girl quite happy is the most pleasant and extraordinary thing in the world."[83]

No early image of Georgiana remains, except for a silhouette believed to have been made in New York on the occasion of a trip to London in 1828. It reveals small and regular features within an elaborate headdress. A photograph taken in about 1875 shows Georgiana in old age and nearly blind, but it reveals little of her character.

George wrote that Georgiana was "quick in her temper,"[84] an opinion echoed years later by her granddaughter Alice Lee Keats (1861–1948): "I saw my grandmother for the first time when I was about five years old [1866]. She awed me completely, and I was much scared of her. She liked children to behave properly, and I suppose I had terrible manners. Once she took me in her lap and taught me to sing 'God Save the Queen' and 'Ancient of Days.'"[85] George was always proud of his wife, taking care to introduce her to important friends on both continents. He also noted ruefully, after he had turned bald and somewhat wrinkled, that she had withstood the hardships of frontier life better than he had. As he wrote to Dilke in 1836, "she has a good flow of spirits is young in her feelings and fond of gaiety and cheerful amusement."[86]

George, who fell in love at such a young age, was less obvious than his brothers in craving affection. The boys' mother had been extremely affectionate, especially toward John; their grandmother had been kindly but reserved. Abbey sequestered their sister Fanny in Walthamstow, making it difficult for the boys to visit her. Despite his limited exposure to women, George seemed to understand them better than his brothers did. Georgiana was his perfect match. John, in contrast, idealized women, endowing them with fantastic virtues that were hard to find in real life.

George and Georgiana both had positive personalities. They seldom clashed, learning early the art of compromise. Mrs. Wylie had raised Georgiana to be skilled in all household tasks; she cooked well and excelled at needlecraft. Georgiana had definite opinions, however, leaving little doubt what they were. George later wrote that she was never dull, "she is the very spirit of candour, and generosity, a cheerful companion and persevering Freind thro' good and ill, she has considerable natural talents but is not overburthen'd with accomplishments . . . she thinks me better and wiser than I am, she is quick in her temper, and has not the talent to keep the children in good discipline leaving all the chastizing to their indolent Father, and interfering when I find chastisment necessary."[87] He had found an intrepid mate.

Charles Dilke, who hosted Georgiana and her children Georgiana Emily (Georgey) and John Henry on their 1828 trip to London, described Georgiana a bit differently. In his annotated copy of Milnes's *Life, Letters, and Literary Remains of John Keats,* he noted, "He [George] married a Miss Wylie. She was a pretty, lively, ignorant girl, unaccustomed to society—more need not be said. I believe she made him a good wife and even a good mother. She visited England some years after and staid some short time at my house, & brought with her a daughter as wild as a red indiana."[88]

A number of Mrs. Wylie's relations—in particular, two of her nephews, Henry and Frederick Griffin—had previously immigrated to Montreal, so the notion of her daughter's departure may not have seemed an untested, pioneering dream.[89] However, when Mrs. Wylie gave her assent to Georgiana's marriage as well as the move to America, her friends were amazed. One of them was outspoken in her disapproval. As George later wrote, "I frequently call to mind that Mrs. R immediately before I left England in 1818 expressed the utmost astonishment that Mrs. K was willing to go with me to America, or that her Mother would permit it."[90] Georgiana was scarcely out of her teens. George had shown no great prospects for business success and had a limited inheritance. Nothing in his background suggested that he would be at ease in backwoods America.

It is doubtful that anyone could have foreseen Georgiana's future: at the edge of the Illinois prairie, in the thick of Louisville society, widowed, then remarried to a civil engineer who traveled to such far-flung places as Havana, Cuba. She lived through the American Civil War and Reconstruction, dying in 1879 in Lexington, Kentucky. She returned to London only that one time, in 1828, to visit her mother and settle George's financial affairs.[91]

In the excitement of their departure for America, George and Georgiana probably failed to grasp that the deep psychological attachment between them and John would be broken. Dark clouds would gather over the relationship, with financial strains replacing the warm bonds of brother- and sisterhood.

Separation and Emigration

1818

The political and social cultures in England were difficult, but it was the economic opportunity that drove George Keats's decision to move to America. The Regency era commenced in 1811, just as the boys left school. It was a period of warfare, with the English twice defeating Napoleon, who had subverted the French Revolution. It was also a period of extravagance driven by the Prince Regent, later King George IV. While the warfare disrupted commerce, the excesses highlighted the dark side of London's squalor. The Tories, who dominated Parliament through much of the Georgian era, later found themselves stymied by the Whigs, thus preventing the development of good economic policy. In reality, the parties were similar, except that the Tories accepted the divine rights of the monarchy, whereas the Whigs believed those rights to be constitutional.

England was experiencing a postwar disinflation in 1818. Agricultural prices had risen during the wars but then dropped rapidly. Farmers were severely affected, as were landowners and others in the distribution chain. Soldiers returning from the wars on the Continent could not find employment. The Tory government was slow to stabilize the economy. There were price protests and antigovernment rallies, including the Manchester cotton spinners strike, but the expectation for change was not strong. The French Revolution had caused a reactionary political clampdown in England.

Emigration became the hot topic. In America, democracy was working. The White House, which had been burned, reopened in January 1818, the month John Keats wrote "On a Lock of Milton's Hair" and copied "When I Have Fears." The Stars and Stripes was approved as the U.S. flag, President James Monroe proclaimed disarmament of the Great Lakes, and General Andrew Jackson captured Pensacola, Florida. Importantly, America's western frontier was opening up, and seemingly endless land was available for the asking or dirt cheap.

George estimated his remaining inheritance to be about £1,600 to £1,700—insufficient to acquire a respectable trade in London. In modern terms, this meant that he could not act as an investor-owner of a business, with hired staff to do the work. He would have to be out on the shop floor, bowing to customers, just like his inner-city Cheapside neighbors. In the highly stratified London society, this would represent a lower-middle-class existence, throwing Keats back to his father's assumed Cockney origins. After the years in suburban Edmonton, and given the social standing of his friends in Leigh Hunt's circle, this would never do. Although George was likely liberal-leaning in his London days, there is no suggestion that he left England because of politics. His motivation was his and his family's economic situation. Initially, George's idealized solution was to emigrate to America, acquire property, make his fortune from the land, and then return to London solidly established as a gentleman. He thought he might lead a life of cultured ease or perhaps convert his American gains and become a British capitalist. He believed America offered the economic opportunity that had been denied him by his not attending Harrow.

Having read William Robertson's *History of America* at Clarke's School, George was captivated by Morris Birkbeck's agrarian scheme, which was actively being promoted in London and was attracting many investors. Birkbeck's pamphlet *Notes on a Journey in America*, published by Taylor and Hessey, was in distribution in 1818, just after George came up from Teignmouth. It ran through eleven editions in London and was translated into French and German.[1]

Morris Birkbeck (1764–1825), the agnostic son of Quakers, was a noted English agronomist. He was a tenant farmer on the property of Lord Arthur George Onslow (whose father was a minister to George III), paying an annual rent of £1,200. As a tenant farmer, Birkbeck was not entitled to vote, but he had to pay dues to the Church of England. So at age forty-five, with two daughters and four sons, he decided to try America. But Birkbeck was not simply a colonizer. His plan, formed with George Flower (c. 1780–1862), was to develop a proper English community there (eventually settling in southern Illinois). He intended to name his village Wanborough, after his hometown in Surrey. It would include a communal town center and would attract the better elements of society.[2] Educated beyond his station in life, Birkbeck cultivated a haughty manner, later calling himself "Emperor of the Prairies." Onslow bought out Birkbeck's lease for £2,000, and additional financing for the venture came from Flower's father, Richard, a former Hertford brewer and wealthy landowner.

Birkbeck and Flower initially acquired 16,000 acres (ultimately, 26,400 acres) and planned to subdivide it into sections to be sold for £1,350, or

US$3,000.³ Birkbeck claimed the investment would grow tenfold in ten years. The first wave of 100 emigrants departed in March 1818 for the "English prairie" in Illinois, located in modern-day Edwards County, about fifty miles northwest of Evansville, Indiana (which is across the Ohio River from Henderson, Kentucky).

The Birkbeck pamphlet reads like a personal letter, describing his travels. He had been to Virginia, Kentucky, and Tennessee but rejected them because of their pro-slavery attitudes ("that broadest, foulest blot" on the American landscape).⁴ He traveled through Ohio but dismissed it as an asylum of England's paupers; however, he carefully wrote about Cincinnati, leaving the impression that civilization would not be far away. Birkbeck described Indiana, the next state he visited, as a pleasant surprise. The Indians there were not savage, and the settlers were not barbarians; they were law-abiding, kind and courteous to strangers, and sober. Indiana's culture was not pronounced, but the people wore good clothing, kept their houses clean, and had plenty of food. The greatest evil in Indiana was sloth. Birkbeck's implication was that a hardworking Englishman would thrive by comparison. During his short stay in Illinois, he became head of the state's first agricultural society, dedicated to the scientific tilling of soil and raising of cattle. Birkbeck was appointed Illinois secretary of state by Governor Edward Coles, a London acquaintance; however, his tenure was brief because the pro-slavery legislature failed to confirm Birkbeck, who was an ardent antislavery activist.

The Keats circle was fully aware of the literature leading up to 1818, as well as the promotions, such as Birkbeck's, currently in circulation. George succumbed to the pitch but was unable to raise the funds in time for the first group's departure. Nor was he married yet. He asked the group to hold a lot for him, but the U.S. Federal Land Office in Shawneetown, Illinois, would not accept his promise of payment. The promoters agreed that George and Georgiana would come out to Illinois a few weeks later, settling up on site. This delay later proved to be a stroke of luck.⁵

Emigration fever was not limited to disenfranchised farmers and factory workers. Although the French Revolution had not overtaken England, it had attracted many English sympathizers who were frustrated by the Crown. These liberal English followers, disappointed by subsequent events in France, shifted their sights to seek an Arcadia in America.

Literary England, having earlier been intrigued by Jean-Jacques Rousseau's enlightened back-to-nature movement, was now swept up by the colony prospectuses and travel books. Wordsworth, in "Lines Composed a Few

Miles above Tintern Abbey," related human emotions to nature, as did Coleridge in "Dejection, an Ode." Later, Shelley picked up on the theme of nature's power and splendor being beyond man's capacity to comprehend. Both fiction and poetry embraced romantic settings, even introducing the "noble savage."

In the eighteenth century, America's landscape and Indians had become the essence of drama. Oliver Goldsmith, having "missed the ferry" to America himself, included (nonexistent) tigers in his descriptions of it. Thomas Gray and James Thomson, pastoral poets, believed that nature purified the morals and inspired creativity, as did poet William Collins. Artist and poet William Blake saw America as a place to free up not only the imagination but also faith and love. Fascinated by the strange American names, he wrote, "the Ohio shall wash his stains from me, I was born a slave but go to be free."[6] In 1794 Coleridge and Southey had dreamed up a colony scheme called Pantisocracy, a Utopian community along Pennsylvania's Susquehanna River. They eventually gave up the experiment due to a lack of funding. Lord Byron in *Don Juan*, Shelley in *The Revolt of Islam*, and Wordsworth in *Ruth* all wrote passionately about America as a land of promise. Byron's 1822 *Don Juan* devoted seven stanzas to Kentucky's Daniel Boone as an example of Rousseau's "natural man."[7] Thomas Campbell's 1809 poem "Gertrude of Wyoming"[8] pictures a life of leisure in a setting free from government.

Travel books also contributed to the fever. Some were honest reporting, but others were sponsored by promoters. Ship captains and American real estate developers hired propagandists to write glowing travel accounts. Even honest writers were carried away by their enthusiasm for freedom. English dissidents of various descriptions were setting out for the land of freedom and opportunity. Quakers, Moravians, Swedenborgians, Baptists, and many others were providing religious context for the emigration movement.

Few of these writers—and certainly not George—had the slightest training in agriculture, and their direct farm experience did not extend beyond walking down a country lane. George pictured himself as a country gentleman, hiring labor as needed. He could not foresee life on the prairie, with baked-hard soil to be turned, inadequate tools, and primitive living conditions. George may have initially planned on a large scale (at one point, John refers to 1,400 acres), envisioning a community with houses on five-acre lots and larger fields situated away from the town.[9] However, George never took title to any Illinois farmland.

Not everyone was so enamored. William Cobbett, a noted British essayist, published an article on 21 April 1818 in which he wrote, "Amongst all the publications, which I have yet seen, on the subject of the United States, as a country to *live in,* and especially to *farm* in, I have never yet observed one that conveyed to Englishmen any thing like a correct notion of the matter."[10] Cobbett, in a subsequent letter to Birkbeck published 15 December 1818, eviscerated the Wanborough plan over thirty-three pages. John Keats read Cobbett's letter in Leigh Hunt's *Examiner* and wrote to George about it in February.[11] Cobbett penned, "It has always been evident to me, that the Western Countries were not the countries for *English* farmers to settle in: no, nor for American farmers, unless under peculiar circumstances. . . . To invite men to go to the Illinois with a *few score of pounds* in their pockets, and to tell them, that they can become *farmers* with those pounds, appears to me to admit of no other apology than an unequivocal acknowledgement, that the inviter is *mad.*" Cobbett goes on to dissect the details of Birkbeck's book, from the cost of passage to the price of cows to the quality of Indian corn and the absence of easily drawn potable water: "I would sooner live the life of a gypsy in England, than be a settler, with less than five thousand pounds, in the Illinois."[12]

Cobbett enlisted the assistance of Thomas Hulme, an emigrant who had traveled to Birkbeck's Wanborough (Cobbett did not) before settling his family in Philadelphia. Although writing somewhat at cross-purposes to Cobbett, Hulme succinctly described the frustrations that propelled so many to cross the ocean: "I . . . looked seriously at the situation of England; and, I saw, that the incomes of my children were all *pawned* . . . to pay the debts of the Borough, or seat, owners. I saw that, of whatever I might be able to give to my children, as well as of what they might be able to earn, *more than one half* would be taken away to feed pensioned Lords and Ladies, Soldiers to shoot at us, Parsons to persecute us, and Fundholders, who had lent their money to be applied to purposes of enslaving us."[13]

Henry Bradshaw Fearon, a London doctor, published *Report on the United States as a Possible Future Residence* in 1818, following a one-year visit from August 1817 to May 1818. Fearon had been commissioned by thirty-nine English families to travel 5,000 miles throughout the United States and report on opportunities there. Though candid, his report was biased against emigration. Like Cobbett, Fearon took apart Birkbeck's pamphlet in a forty-one page critique, much of it challenging such basics as wages. Fearon chided Birkbeck: "The American character is, in one passage, (p. 74) represented to us as arrived at so high a state of perfection, that even national antipathies are annihilated. My judgment faltered upon the first perusal of this passage;—it so entirely contradicts every conclusion which I had come to upon the subject, that it caused me to hesitate as to the correctness of my own impressions: but surely Mr. Birkbeck here claims for the Americans a perfection, which is not only contrary to what they practise, but is superior to human nature itself."[14] Critics accused Fearon of writing the report, or having it ghostwritten, at the behest of the English government, which was eager to check emigration.

In any event, Birkbeck was persuasive. William Faux, another travel writer, said of Birkbeck in 1823, "It is true that no man, since Columbus, has done so much toward peopling America as Mr. Birkbeck, whose publications, and the authority of whose name, had effects truly prodigious; and if all could have settled in Illinois, whom he had tempted across the Atlantic and the mountains, it had been the most populous state in the Union."[15] Joseph Hanks, an Illinois settler interviewed by Faux in November 1819, added, "I was caught up by his fascinating writings; it was impossible to resist them. Who could?"[16] George Keats could not.

As George prepared to depart, John wrote to Benjamin Bailey, "I have two brothers; one is driven by the 'burden of Society to America.'"[17] Loosely translated, that "burden" included all the pressures brought to bear on George. The literary mind-set had been prepared by the Enlightenment and the pastoral poets. The media of 1817–1818 were filled with pamphlets and prospectuses breathing opportunity. The dominance of Tory politics in England was corrosive and disheartening. The state of the Keats family finances required action. Their ability to move upward in English society was hobbled by George's curtailed education and Georgiana's apparent illegitimacy. Likely underpinning all these factors was the simple force of a young married couple seeking something different, hoping for a better life. The decision was made.

Given John's financial misunderstandings with Abbey, George decided not to approach his guardian about monetizing his inheritance prior to his twenty-first birthday. He was so broke after a year of unemployment that when he returned to London from Teignmouth, he needed to borrow the coach fare from Mrs. Jeffrey. He arrived at Abbey's on his birthday to plead his case. This time, Abbey was prepared, having already freed up some cash for George. He agreed to monetize the remaining assets in his direct control and commenced advertising their sale immediately. It is possible that Abbey had heard about Birkbeck and Flower and saw an opportunity for profit. Evidently, after all the requests for living expenses from John and Tom, he was pleased that George actually had a plan to *make* money. Also, he may have been pleased to no longer be responsible for at least one of his wards.

George's positive outlook fed on the infectious enthusiasm of his friends. Dilke believed that the American experiment might save the world.[18] He pointed out to George the merits of having a part in such a cause. George later wrote, "*You* and poor *John* were the only ones who looked upon my American expedition as reasonable and proper."[19]

George and Georgiana's wedding at St. Margaret's Church, hard beside Westminster Cathedral, took place on 28 May 1818. The bride's mother and brothers attended, as did John Keats. Georgiana's recollection was that her dress was of a serviceable fabric but elaborately trimmed. She wore earrings and a pendant brooch of garnets set in gold. John gave her a heavy, beautifully fabricated gold bracelet.[20] The Abbeys unaccountably prevented Fanny Keats from attending the wedding or from seeing the couple at their house near Brunswick Square afterward. (George, thinking it might take a long time to receive his funds and make travel arrangements, had rented a house at 28 Judd Street, but to his surprise, Abbey produced the funds within twenty-four days of the wedding.) Georgiana left for America having never met her sister-in-law.

During one of the couple's evening entertainments before they departed, the guests included John Keats, John Taylor, and John Hamilton Reynolds, all of whom were interested in phrenology. George had written to Taylor, "Reynolds will be with me this Evening can you come, I think John likewise, you must see Mrs. Keats since you are physiognomist and discover if the lines of her face answer to her spirit."[21] Physiognomy is the assessment of a person's character or personality from his or her outer appearance, especially the face. The subject was taken seriously by Aristotle but then fell into disrepute; Leonardo da Vinci dismissed such character assessments as incorrect. In the 1770s Johan Kaspar Lavater published a series of essays on the subject that were embraced by Charles Dickens, Edgar Allan Poe, and others. The high point of physiognomy was perhaps Oscar Wilde's *The Picture of Dorian Gray*, published in 1891. Phrenology, a subset of physiognomy, is the belief that personality traits can be derived from the shape of the skull. German physician Franz Joseph Gall published a document in 1819, theorizing that the shape of the cranium represents the shape and relative development of the brain within.[22] George, like many, thought that physiognomy and phrenology were defensible and remained interested in the subject for years. By the end of the nineteenth century, it had all been debunked as pseudoscience.

George and Georgiana took their leave on 20 June. John agreed to travel with them to Liverpool, along with Charles Brown. Brown had invited John, who was in a gloomy mood, to accompany him on a 600-mile pedestrian tour to Scotland after seeing the newlyweds off.[23] Tom remained in London under the care of the Bentleys in Well Walk, but there were vague thoughts that he might spend the winter in Italy with John. William Haslam, George's classmate at Clarke's School, stepped in to look after Tom in the poet's absence. John was grateful to Haslam, called "our oak friend" by Severn; John wrote, "during my absence and since my return [Haslam] has endeared him to me for ever."[24]

The Prince Saxe-Cobourg coach started from the Swan with Two Necks Inn in Lad's Lane, near Poultry. The boys had lived close by, in their Cheapside apartment, and it was not far from Finsbury Pavement, where George was born. Boxes and barrels contained the couple's possessions destined for the New World. They had packed a few childhood mementoes, including a hunting scene of Georgiana's and some of the books awarded to John at Clarke's School.[25] George, wearing a suit and with a $5,000 letter of credit in his pocket, rode with John atop the coach to save money, even though, just ten days earlier, John had suggested to his friend Benjamin Bailey, "I am not certain whether I shall be able to go [on] my Journey on account of my brother Tom and a little indisposition of my own."[26] Georgiana had modified her hairstyle, piling it atop her head to look older, assuming the poise of a wife. The couple's composure reflected their ignorance of what lay ahead.

The brothers had not settled accounts prior to embarking, although George had left £500 of his funds (the so-called Abbey account) on deposit with Abbey for the benefit of John and Tom, as well as to pay his remaining bills. On the coach, George gave John £70 to £80 for the latter's trip, which was less than he required. Although John's request for cash was not a serious issue, it may have left a sour taste.[27] It also opened the door to Brown's edgy protectorate of the poet. Shortly thereafter Tom withdrew £170 of George's £500 for his room and board with Mrs. Bentley, for his medical expenses with Dr. Solomon Sawrey, and to pay George's miscellaneous bills of £20 to £30. Tom sent an additional £30 to John on his walking tour, leaving about £300 in the account.

Liverpool was thirty-two hours of hard coaching from London, with a stopover in Redbourne, Hertfordshire, where Henry Stephens was practicing surgery. Stephens, who had roomed with John Keats near Guy's Hospital, joined the party for dinner on 22 June 1818 at the Black Bull Inn.

Writing to George Felton Mathew about the event nearly twenty-nine years later, Stephens provides the only visual description of Georgiana from the period: "George's wife was rather short, not what might be strictly called handsome, but looked like a being whom any man of moderate Sensibility might easily love. She had the imaginative poetical cast.—Something singular & girlish in her attire, whether from her own taste, or whether she had accommodated herself to the taste of her husband, or to that of the Poet . . . I know not; but there was something original about her, & John seemed to regard her as a being whom he was delighted to honour, & introduced her to me with an evident satisfaction."[28] Stephens recognized that John Keats saw something of himself in Georgiana. John later described Georgiana: "she [Isabella Jones] and your George [Georgiana] are the only women à peu près de mon age whom I would be content to know for their mind and friendship alone."[29] At the time, John was unaware that his traveling companion, Brown, had just sublet his side of the Hampstead property to a family called Brawne, and that they had a daughter named Fanny.

After riding all night and the next day, the coach clattered to a stop at the Crown Inn on Red Cliff Street, Liverpool. Ocean passage was seldom booked in advance, due to the difficulty of communicating and the uncertainty of when ships would appear in the harbor. George had made no arrangements, expecting to catch the first ship out. The innkeeper informed them that it might be several days, as no ship was in port. Farewells were exchanged in the evening. The next morning John boarded a coach to Lancaster, having left a note for George. It is unknown whether or when John expected to see the couple again. The brothers had been nearly inseparable all their lives. Owing to their minor financial quarrel the day before, John might have believed that written words to George would mask his degree of upset. Another possibility is that Brown, impatient to begin his hike and wishing to avoid an emotional moment for his worn-out friend, convinced John to leave abruptly, taking the first available coach to Lancaster. At this point, Brown became John's surrogate brother. He would later become a harsh critic of George, and the brisk Liverpool departure may have presaged troubles to come.

Shortly thereafter, John wrote to George and Georgiana, "Your content in each other is a delight to me which I cannot express—the Moon is now shining full and brilliant—she is the same to me in Matter, what you are to me in Spirit. If you were here my dear Sister I could not pronounce the words which I can write to you from a distance: I have a tenderness for you, and an admiration which I feel to be as great and more chaste than I can have for any woman in the world."[30] John thus embarked on an extraordinary year of letter writing to George and Georgiana, even as he turned to other matters. These letters form an important body of thought that guides all Keats scholars as they interpret his meanings.

When John headed north to the Lake District and Scotland, he did not know the name of George's ship or its destination. He wrote a two-part journal letter to George; the first was posted to the Crown Inn in Liverpool, the second to Baltimore, where he assumed George and Georgiana would disembark. Both letters were returned to him, undeliverable. Surprisingly, George and Georgiana were able to leave the Crown Inn almost immediately, and Philadelphia was their destination. It turned out that the *Telegraph* was in port and completing its final manifests before setting sail. By 25 June, George had paid a £90 passage fee for one of the two cabins, and the newlyweds were aboard the packet ship, awaiting favorable winds. They also shipped their bundles, including books, clothing, cooking utensils, and letters of introduction.

The *Telegraph* was a fairly new American ship, built in Boston and owned by Wiggin and Whitney of Philadelphia. In *Gore's Advertiser* it was described as "coppered and copper-fastened, remarkable for making quick passages, and . . . always delivered her cargoes in good order." The average sailing time was eight weeks, although unseasonable and weak winds could stretch the voyage to eleven. The *Telegraph*'s mid-1818 voyage was only seven weeks. Its cargo capacity was 392 tons, consisting mostly of sheets of iron destined for American fabricators that would make implements requiring the higher-quality British raw material.

The newlyweds were surrounded by sights such as those described by William Amphlett, who had set sail out of Liverpool just a few weeks earlier on 21 May 1818: "The passengers running to and fro; some taking an affectionate, an everlasting farewell of their kindred and friends; others without a friend to take leave of, standing with a strange mixture of joy and grief in their countenances, looking a last adieu to the land of their fathers! Others arriving too late, are making to the vessel in boats, with their last articles of luggage hastily packed up—a strange medley of clothing and provisions—band-boxes, and bags of potatoes, legs of mutton, hampers of porter, salt herrings, and barrels of biscuit."[31]

George and Georgiana occupied a tiny cabin, or stateroom. Amphlett wrote, "nothing can be a greater burlesque upon the name [stateroom], than those hastily fitted up holes where you have but just room to turn yourself round, and barely height to sit up in bed. A person six feet high should never think of going to sea in small vessel."[32] George was just an inch shy of six feet, but the slight Georgiana may have been more comfortable. Ironically, because the cabins were well above water level, they were subject to more pitching and rolling, whereas the grim steerage quarters below had a more stable ride. George was seasick for the entire voyage.

The passengers remained onboard in port for nearly two weeks awaiting favorable winds, which did not arrive until 5 July. Captain Hector Coffin then set sail; the ship cleared the River Mersey and entered the Irish Sea on 7 July. Onboard were fifty-four passengers and an assortment of livestock.[33] The steerage passengers had paid £6, entitling them to makeshift cots belowdecks (the steerage level was five feet high, above the cargo level), rancid air, and horrendous sanitation. The shipping company's revenue model worked out about the same for cargo as for steerage passengers, and they were treated accordingly. The livestock on deck enjoyed better conditions. Passengers brought their own food, water, and utensils for cooking and eating, as well as blankets.

Captain Coffin was experienced with North Atlantic passages. On a subsequent trip from Liverpool to New York and Philadelphia, departing 26 November 1818, his crew consisted of two mates, a cook and steward, and a few rough-hewn sailors known as packet rats. The captain's role was to ensure safety and order onboard, while also maintaining a pleasant relationship with the passengers in the two cabins. Emotions must have run high as the handsome vessel left the Mersey, headed past Great Ormes Head into the Irish Sea, and sailed past the Welsh and Irish coasts down into the Atlantic. Most of the passengers would never see their native land again.

Unlike John in Scotland, George and Georgiana left behind no diary of their voyage, so we can only speculate on how they spent their days while the ship caught the wind and scudded through waves. Amphlett's account, written a month earlier, describes a sensory cacophony: wind whistling through the sails, waves rushing against the gunwales and sometimes onto the deck, migratory birds hitching a ride in the rigging, sailors constantly running about overhead, and the creaking and groaning of berths, many rigged by the passengers themselves. It took a while for the English landlubbers to adapt a Spartan sea diet, and those who ate heavily quickly "paid their tribute to Neptune." All those sensations occurred on a normal day.

North Atlantic crossings could take anywhere from three to eleven weeks. As the ships sailed north of the Gulfstream toward Newfoundland, seeking more favorable winds, they might encounter icebergs, sudden squalls, or heavy fog. Passengers with queasy stomachs and terrified children did not make the trip more pleasurable. Illness could spread quickly belowdecks, and the ship owners provided neither doctors nor remedies.

Although the *Telegraph*'s crossing to Newfoundland was relatively swift, it beat slowly southward to Cape May, New Jersey, without sighting land. Forty-nine days into the trip, and about twenty-five miles offshore from the entry to Delaware Bay, the ship came upon a flotilla of smaller vessels. Several raced toward it, competing for the opportunity to provide a pilot for the final two-day run up the bay and river to Philadelphia. Landfall, just a dark line on the horizon, was sighted shortly thereafter. Though not physically impressive, it was surely an enormous relief to the passengers. Their sea voyage was nearly over, and their escape from England's vexatious politics, taxation, economic stagnation, and class stratification was about to be rewarded—with great unknowns to come. Sailing up the Delaware with the tide was not a prepossessing experience either. New Jersey was flat, and Delaware was not much different. Wilmington, noted for its manufacture of gunpowder along Brandywine Creek, was a pleasant town of 5,000. Philadelphia, a clean, orderly city of 120,000, lacked the grandeur of European metropolises.

Fifty-one days after they sailed out of the Mersey River, on 26 August 1818, George and Georgiana set foot on American soil. The American authorities made two notations. File 5416-K reads: "Family name: Keats. Given name: Mr. George. Accompanied by: Lady and Mrs. Georgiana. Age: Not given. Sex: Male. Occupation: Not given. Nationality: Not given. Destination: United States." Georgiana's file, numbered 5417-K, was its mirror image.[34]

The couple made a somewhat greater impression on an anonymous correspondent to a newspaper back in Lincoln: "A native of this city has written from Philadelphia to his kinfolk here mentioning some of your townsmen who do not seem to have found the 'better life' they sought to gain by emigrating To America. . . . Mr. KEATS and his wife [arrived] from England to Philadelphia. They have gone westward to join BIRKBECK's settlement in the Illinois; they were a complete Bond-street Beau and belle, and shockingly unfit for their destination; for that is a miserable place of BIRKBECK's, who is a notorious Fibber."[35]

George never forgot the sight that welcomed him on the pier: a black man eating a watermelon. The fruit (also indigenous to Africa) was entirely unfamiliar to him, and according to family legend, he often joked about it, perhaps not realizing the image would become a stereotype for

African Americans.[36] He would see a few more of each during his time in Kentucky. George wrote to John, in a letter now lost, of their safe arrival in Philadelphia. John's reply was written in October 1818, which meant that George's letter had crossed the ocean in as little as seven weeks' time. John's response ended, "I hope you have a Son," indicating that Georgiana had arrived in America pregnant.[37]

George soon met Michael Drury, a Philadelphia merchant and cousin of John Taylor. Drury may have advised him on obtaining passage to Pittsburgh, as well as providing an introduction to his brother-in-law James Tallant, who later became George's agent in Cincinnati.[38] Drury also may have told Keats about Tom Bakewell, whose father, William, had immigrated from Staffordshire and lived on a farm named Fatland Ford, near Philadelphia. (William was also John James Audubon's father-in-law.) Tom Bakewell lived in Kentucky, and the Keatses may have met him on their way to Birkbeck's Illinois settlement.

The published books of Cobbett and Fearon, both critical of Birkbeck, had not yet appeared.[39] Nevertheless, as evidenced by the newspaper clipping about the Keatses, some people in Philadelphia were skeptical about Birkbeck's settlement. Eastern land speculators were bad-mouthing conditions on the western frontier in an attempt to lure immigrants to settle in the East. If George heard these negative opinions, he did not heed them; he decided to proceed with the original plan and judge Wanborough for himself.

His next project was to arrange the trek to Pittsburgh. There were coach lines, but the roads were bumpy, and carriage rollovers in the dark were not uncommon. With Georgiana pregnant, and having heard various horror stories about the trip over the Alleghenies, George elected to buy a low-slung wagon for the two of them, even if it diminished their capital. A carriage ride across Pennsylvania took six to ten days. The Allegheny and Laurel mountains were beautiful, but the crossings were hazardous. Many streams were not yet bridged. Tales abounded of animal attacks, rattlesnakes, and occasional Indian sightings. The roads were often rutted tracks of sun-baked clay or quagmires of mud. Inns were so far apart that travelers sometimes had to ride well into the night to reach one with rooms available.

After Pittsburgh, the couple booked passage down the Ohio River to Shawneetown, Illinois, where the federal land office completed arrangements for the sale of lots in Wanborough. The trip across Pennsylvania, identical to that of the Keatses, is best described by Amphlett. The words might have been George's, had he kept a journal:

Many emigrants purchase horses and wagons in Philadelphia, and take at once their families and their luggage, in order to be masters of their time, and travel on as suits their inclination or convenience.

I purchased two light covered Jersey wagons new for 150 dollars, and two useful horses for 165 dollars. I was told that I could sell them for prime cost at Pittsburg, or any place west of the mountains; this, however was not true. . . .

Waggons are rather a drug from the same cause; and if the traveller procures one-half for either, he must not complain. . . . Very probably the traveler may not be conversant with the management of horses; or, if he be, and come from Great Britain, it is impossible he can be acquainted with such roads as he will have to travel in this country. He must not only have the fatigue of driving his horses over such horrible sloughs, rocks, swamps, and precipices, as no English waggoner would allow to be passable, but when he puts up at night, he must be his own hostler.[40]

Amphlett described one overnight experience along the way, professing that he was not exaggerating:

A wet morning had delayed our departure from a tavern where we had passed the night, at the foot of one of the Alleghany ridges. The road was become very slippery and insecure, even for foot-travellers. The road itself was only a gullet of the mountain, down which a torrent poured after every shower. This circumstance, although it made the roadway cleaner than other parts, had caused such holes and abrupt declivities of the wheel-tracks, that the ascent would be often one, two, and three feet, all but perpendicular! The only way to enable a single horse to drag after him his load, was, at every one of these petty cascades, to form a temporary inclined plane of stones and wood, or whatever material was nearest at hand; and with all our ingenuity, thrice were we completely stalled, and obligated to unload half our luggage to get on a few yards, and then reload. Thus, in eight long hours of a summer's day, we climbed nearly two miles! It was now dark, when we approached the first tavern on the summit. We groped our way to the door, to behold our hostess sitting upon the ground, with her head in the lap of her daughter, who was hunting up her vermin

[lice] by fire-light! She did not attempt to rise on our entrance; and to our demand, if we could have beds and supper, after a dignified pause, she replied, "I guess so.—Bess, go and make some candles!—You should have come before sundown. The stable is behind the house.—Jack, get up, and give the movers some hay." We had now to attend to the horses in the dark as well as we could, and then wait about an hour and a half while our supper was procuring. The broiled chicken was alive long after our arrival; and the cakes unbaked, that we were to eat with our coffee. The coffee also was roasted in our presence, and the candle-making by the same hands that attended to it. Our supper-table was furnished with chicken, ham, cake, coffee, butter, sugar, eggs, apple-butter, apple-pye, cyder, cherry-bounce, milk, and whiskey.

Of these articles, the coffee only was not the produce of their own land! What people, therefore, can be more independent? To complain of delay, or express any kind of impatience, is not only futile, but impolitic. Patience is the only remedy, and complaisance your best recommendation.[41]

Amphlett's dispassionate journal of his trek, preceding George and Georgiana's by a month, provides a proxy for their own on-the-ground reactions to their new country. Amphlett also provides a backhanded compliment to the country's potential in his description of a typical Pennsylvania farm: "The appearance of the farm-house and yard, the implements of husbandry, and methods of using them, with the neglected state of the live stock and the corn-fields, will excite in him much wonder and disgust. . . . But he will see at once how much industry may accomplish in this country, when carelessness and inattention thrive so well. What most excites an Englishman's surprise, if not his contempt, is the slovenly-built log-cabins, which have all the outward appearance of wretched penury, and within but little show of cleanliness or comfort."[42]

George never recorded when he changed his mind about establishing a farming homestead in southern Illinois. On the one hand, the discouraging sights in Pennsylvania, which has always been a prosperous farming state, may have sown the first seeds of doubt. On the other hand, Amphlett's observations that a hardworking Englishman could accomplish much in a country that was well supported by sloth and indolence may have reflected exactly what was on George's mind.

The Keatses' arrival in Pittsburgh, at the head of the Ohio River Valley, was likely no more encouraging. Fearon, who was more cynical than Amphlett but more reportorial than Cobbett, wrote about Pittsburgh: "The published accounts of this city are so exaggerated and out of all reason, that strangers are usually disappointed on visiting it. . . . When I am told that at a particular hotel there is a *handsome* accommodation, I expect they are one remove from very bad; if '*elegant* entertainment,' I anticipate tolerable; if a person is 'a *clever* man,' that he is not absolutely a fool; and if a manufactory is the '*first in the world*,' I expect, and generally found, about six men and three boys employed."[43]

The couple disposed of their wagon in Pittsburgh. The horses, which might have become the nucleus of George's farm equipment, may have been entrusted to other settlers for overland transport. Georgiana was unfamiliar with horses and in no condition to learn. The newlyweds decided to travel down the Ohio River by keelboat, which proved to be the best part of the trip. Timothy Flint, a Harvard-educated Congregationalist, provides a description of the type of boats available:

> Next there is the keel-boat, of a long, slender, and elegant form, and generally carrying from fifteen to thirty tons. This boat is formed to be easily propelled over shallow waters in the summer season. . . . Next in order are the Kentucky flats, or in the vernacular phrase, "broadhorns," a species of ark, very nearly resembling a New England pig-stye. They are fifteen feet wide, and from forty to one hundred feet in length, and carry from twenty to seventy tons. Some of them . . . used by families in descending the river, are very large and roomy, and have comfortable and separate apartments, fitted up with chairs, beds, tables and stoves.[44]

George Keats retold his narrative so many times that his friend, Unitarian cleric James Freeman Clarke, was able to write it from memory:

> This voyage of six hundred miles down the river was full of romance to these young people. No steam boat then disturbed, with its hoarse pantings, the sleep of these beautiful shores. Day by day they floated tranquilly on, as through a succession of fairy lakes, sometimes in the shadow of some lofty and wooded bluff, sometimes by the side of widespread meadows, or beneath the graceful overhanging branches of the cotton-wood or sycamore. At times, while the boat floated lazily along, the young couple would go

ashore and walk through the woods across a point around which the river made a bend. All uncertain as their prospects were, they could easily, with the luxuriance of nature, abandon themselves to the enjoyment of the hour.[45]

Aside from their brief stay in Brunswick Square, the keelboat ride was the nearest thing to a honeymoon that George and Georgiana would experience.

The Keatses stopped in Cincinnati, where George visited Tallant. Then they proceeded by keelboat to Louisville, where, to his surprise, George met Charles Briggs, an old schoolmate from Clarke's in Enfield. Briggs was prospering—a good omen. Louisville, however, was not the Keatses' objective: Kentucky was a slave state. The early-autumn stop in Louisville was probably just long enough for the boatmen to off-load goods to be traversed around the rapids. In spring, when the water was high, the flat-boats could run the chute without off-loading. A canal with three locks would be built later, bypassing the obstacle and greatly facilitating Louis-ville's growth.

The last leg of the journey to Wanborough has been imputed from let-ters written by John to George, the latter's having been lost. George and Georgiana progressed by boat to western Kentucky and came to the town of Henderson, a section of which was previously called Red Banks.[46] They met naturalist John James Audubon, who was living in Henderson at the time. After crossing the Ohio River, it was a thirty-five-mile trek directly north to Princeton, in the southwest corner of Indiana. Birkbeck's head-quarters and staging area were there, twenty-eight miles from Wanbor-ough, over the state line in Illinois. Keats may have collected his first mail in Princeton.

It is possible that George left Georgiana with Birkbeck's daughters while he rode the remaining distance to see for himself the colony that had excited so many imaginations in London and so much despair among the returnees he had met in Cincinnati. It was late October 1818. From a dis-tance, the trees were in color, and the tall prairie grasses suggested fertile soil. The colony was attractively sited between the Great and Little Wabash Rivers. Up close, George found barely tillable soil, bad water, no labor, and squalid housing and came to the realization that he was not meant to be a dirt farmer.

The firmest indication that George actually visited Wanborough, with or without Georgiana, or that they made it as far as Birkbeck's staging base, is a line in John's 13 January 1820 letter to Georgiana: "There were very pretty pickings for me in Georges Letters about the Prairie Settlement."[47] Their doubts about the settlement had been developing ever since Philadelphia, and those doubts surely were not allayed by the countryside between Henderson, Kentucky, where they disembarked from the keelboat, and Princeton, Indiana. If George made it to Wanborough, he realized the naysayers were correct.

Construction at Wanborough was behind schedule, forcing several families to share each crude cabin. Furniture was nonexistent, other than makeshift beds. Food was scarce, and winter was approaching. Families who had invested all their assets did not have the means to leave. To add to the travails, Birkbeck and Flower had quarreled bitterly and decided to divide the settlement. Faux, writing just five years later, described the relationship as close to open warfare, and the split led to Wanborough's collapse.

In addition to his family, Morris Birkbeck had a ward, Eliza Andrews. Although he was old enough to be her father, he may have hoped to marry her. George Flower was twenty-nine and recently divorced. His family was prominent in Cambridge, where his father was a banker. Flower's father had encouraged his journey to America to seek out opportunities. His first move was to marry Eliza, perhaps frustrating Birkbeck.[48] Flower returned to England to recruit the first 100 families, leaving Eliza in Pennsylvania for the winter. Returning in the spring of 1818, Flower waited three days to meet with Birkbeck, who refused to speak with him for unclear reasons. The community was divided in half, and the principals never spoke again.

Birkbeck made several important agricultural innovations, including a method of ditch farming to drain and use stagnant water and a method of reusing native sod so as not to lose its nutrients. Birkbeck drowned in 1825, after which the Wanborough residents drifted away and the community disappeared.

Flower named his half of the community Albion. It grew slowly and eventually prospered, existing to this day in Edwards County. Both Birkbeck and Flower lacked overall organizational skills as well as the resources and infrastructure to make their communities an immediate success. Flower never saw a return on his investment. Both colonizers remained to the end; both lost sizable fortunes.

The most discouraging tale involved a man named Filder, a prominent member of Flower's party who had journeyed to the settlement three months ahead of Keats. The fifty-year-old Filder, who had invested £40,000, encountered foul weather and a series of accidents on the overland trip. Upon reaching Vincennes, Indiana, a mere two days from Wanborough, Filder turned back, despite having traveled more than 4,300 miles.[49]

The end story of the Birkbeck and Flower settlements is that the organizers were not con artists but Utopians, like the Pantisocrats Coleridge and Southey. Their promotions were not a fraud; each sincerely believed in the experiment. If they deluded others, they also fooled themselves. Unlike American frontiersmen who had crossed the Alleghenies thirty to forty years earlier, these Englishmen simply did not understand the soil. They had trouble digging proper wells to obtain decent water, and they had difficulty finding and organizing labor. They became discouraged and apathetic.

Down the Wabash River, in Harmonie, Indiana, Robert Owen and George Rapp had established a Utopian community on 30,000 acres in 1815. Peopled largely by German immigrants, the colony was a true communal experiment, with no individually owned land.[50] By 1824, this group splintered, and the Rappites moved back to Pennsylvania, where they preached the Second Coming of Christ. Owen, a British social reformer, resettled his followers in New Harmony, twenty-five miles south of Albion, in 1825. Within two years, his group of zealots, cranks, and authentic reformers had disbanded.

Having seen the confused governance and lack of facilities on the ground at Wanborough, George decided not to stay. He and Georgiana turned back, likely in late October or November 1818. George would not have migrated to the back settlements of America had he not possessed an early liberal predisposition, nor without Birkbeck's and Flower's financial come-on. Keats now recognized that he would have to do something else. The couple returned to Henderson but then appeared months later in Louisville.

John Keats subsequently described Birkbeck's book as one of a brace of "Decoy Ducks."[51] Charles Dickens's *Martin Chuzzlewit* tells the story of a young man with remarkable similarities to George Keats. Dickens's description of Chuzzlewit arriving at the fictional Eden might have been lifted from George's diary, had he kept one. The fictional Chuzzlewit, a more sympathetic character than his name implies, returned to London.[52]

As noted, all but one of George's letters to John from this time have been lost.[53] In his replies, John wrote, after reading Birkbeck's book but before hearing of the settlement's negatives, "Birkbeck's mind is too much in the American style—you must endeavour to infuse a little Spirit of another sort into the Settlement. . . . If I had a prayer to make for any great good, next to Tom's recovery, it should be that one of your Children should be the first American poet."[54] Earlier in this letter John mentioned nursing Tom through his deteriorating condition: "the tears will come into your Eyes."[55] John also wrote a poem in honor of Georgiana's unborn child:

'Tis the "witching time of night"—
Orbed is the moon and bright.
And the stars they glisten, glisten,
Seeming with bright eyes to listen.
For what listen they?
. . . .
Glisten, glisten, glisten, glisten,
And hear my lullaby!
Child, I see thee! Child, I've found thee,
Midst of the quiet all around thee!
Child, I see thee! Child, I spy thee!
And thy mother sweet is nigh thee!
. . . .
O' the western wild,
Bard art thou completely!—
Sweetly, with dumb endeavour,
A Poet now or never!
Little child
O' the western wild,
A Poet now or never![56]

William Haslam had taken on various chores with respect to Tom, in an earnest effort to relieve the poet of worry. He visited Tom in Hampstead several times during John's Scottish tour. And it was he who wrote to George, forwarded by Birkbeck, that Tom had died on 1 December 1818.[57] It had been a terrible fall for the poet.

Communications in the early nineteenth century were slow but surprisingly reliable. A letter crossing the Atlantic took about seven weeks, plus an additional three weeks to reach the frontier. Paper and postage were expensive, envelopes and stamps were not yet in use, and postage was typically not prepaid.[58] Postage would be calculated by the receiving post office, based on postmarks from the intermediate offices. John Keats used the prepaid two-penny post when he sent letters across London to Fanny Brawne—good etiquette at low cost.[59] However, his transatlantic letters arrived with postage due. The only revenge available to a recipient was to reply in kind.

Letters were often voluminous. Keats's first journal letter to George ran 8,000 words, a cross between a travelogue and a modern-day blog. Writing on extremely thin paper, one would use both sides of the sheet, leaving no margin except for the seal. The seal, consisting of a blob of wax, made it challenging to open a letter without tearing it. Some sheets were fourteen inches long. If a letter writer concluded before reaching the bottom of the page, a friend might add a separate message. If more space were needed, the writer would write perpendicular across the original, a method called crosshatching.

Before there was a government postal service, private companies handled the mail. They used stagecoaches, along with the personal trust of friends and ships' captains—a system that led to haphazard deliveries. The origination point indicated by the postmark might not be the place of the actual dispatch but somewhere along the way. Travelers were also sought out to hand-carry the mail as a favor to the sender. If George Keats heard of someone in the area—even an individual unknown to him—who was planning to leave for England, he would seek that person out, and ask the stranger to carry his letters all the way to their recipients in London. Charles Briggs, John P. Bull, Holliday W. Cood, Mr. Cuthbertson, Dr. Joshua B. Flint, Mr. Turner, Charles Whittingham, and others often served as his couriers.

HENDERSON AND AUDUBON

1818–1819

When George and Georgiana passed through Philadelphia in October 1818, they may have been introduced to John James Audubon's father-in-law, William Bakewell, by Michael Drury, their initial Philadelphia contact. In turn, as they passed through Louisville, they most likely met Bakewell's son Tom, either as part of a chain of letters of introduction or through Keats's Enfield schoolmate Charles Briggs.[1] Either way, someone probably suggested that they look up Audubon and his wife, Lucy, on their way through Henderson, Kentucky.

After opting not to purchase land at the Birkbeck settlement, the Keatses returned to Henderson. There, they became paying guests of the Audubons at their home on Second and Main Streets (on a lot now occupied by the Henderson National Bank), while deciding what to do next. In Henderson, Audubon had built a cabin with a veranda fronting a small pond he had dug. He kept wing-clipped wild geese and ducks, as well as turtles, as a convenient food source.

Audubon had prospered in Louisville from 1807 to 1810. His Henderson house was well furnished by frontier norms, with rugs, tables, mirrors, andirons, and candelabra sent out from Philadelphia or New York. Lucy played the piano, while Audubon played the flute and flageolet. She had a silver tea service, flat silver, and linens. By Henderson standards, the Audubons lived well. Many of the locals—including her sister-in-law, Elizabeth Page Bakewell—resented Lucy's upper-class mannerisms.[2] It is clear that either George or Georgiana wrote to John about her, given his response to Georgiana: "I have known more than one Mrs Audubon their affectation of fashion and politeness cannot transcend ours."[3]

George had his first experience as a forester under Audubon's watchful eye. Clumsily attempting to chop wood, George flailed away at the chore until he was finished. Audubon told George, "I am sure you will do well in this country, Keats. A man who will persist, as you have been doing, in chopping that log, though it has taken you an hour to do what I could do in ten minutes, will certainly get along here."[4] He then showed George how to use an ax gracefully, effectively, and swiftly.

Since arriving in Henderson in 1810, Audubon had mostly tended to his business. But he was prone to wander off for days or weeks at a time in pursuit of birds for his early sketches. George, freshly arrived from London, probably had no way of understanding the depth of Audubon's financial problems in late 1818. Audubon had invested more than $49,600 in various property and commercial enterprises. Henderson Circuit Court deed books show thirty-seven separate transactions, thirty-five of which were for real estate. He had also acquired seven mulatto slaves, a principal sign of wealth, for $10,500.[5] But in February of that year, Audubon's father had died in France. His cousins and half siblings successfully sued to void the will, which might have benefited him, on grounds that Audubon's mother had besmirched his father's name by publicly acknowledging his illegitimate birth.[6]

In 1815 Tom Bakewell had induced his brother-in-law to invest $15,000 in a steam-powered grist- and sawmill at the foot of Second Street and the Ohio River, where one of the original millstones remains on display. They leased property in 1816 from the Town of Henderson for $20 a year for ninety-nine years. The mill was an extension of a steamboat-building business organized by Bakewell and other partners, including Scottish engineer David Prentice and an English investor, Thomas Pears.

Unfortunately, Bakewell and Audubon had not analyzed the market need for such a mill, which was larger than the community of 200 could support at the time. In addition, its flour-milling potential, in a non-wheat-growing area, was excessive. They financed the mill almost entirely on credit, which the U.S. Treasury and Bank of the United States had greatly loosened after the War of 1812. Operationally, Prentice's mill mechanism, borrowed from shipbuilding, had many design flaws.

Pears, whose new bride, Sarah, was unhappy in Henderson, was the first to withdraw from the partnership. He took the balance of his equity and moved to Pittsburgh in 1816. In 1817, for much the same reason, Bakewell and his new wife, Elizabeth, decided to leave Henderson for Louisville. Bakewell wrote off $5,000 of his investment in the mill, transferring his remaining equity to Audubon in exchange for a $5,500 note, payable by Audubon at 20 percent interest. He also left Audubon with the debts of the enterprise. Audubon later wrote about the mill in his journal, describing it as "an enormous expense, in a country then as unfit for such a thing as it would be now for me to attempt to settle in the moon."[7]

Henderson and Audubon: 1818–1819

When Bakewell finally left in February 1818, he handed over to Audubon an asset of another of his entities, Prentice and Bakewell, in the form of a $4,250 note due from Henderson resident Samuel Adams Bowen, in exchange for the partial relief of Bakewell's debt to Audubon. Prentice and Bakewell had built the steamship the *Henderson* and sold it to Bowen and a group of partners, including his brother William Russell Bowen (a Henderson town trustee), Obadiah Smith, Bennett Marshall, George Brent, and Robert Speed, taking for payment a promissory note payable in April 1819.[8] In accepting this note, Audubon evidently failed to do due diligence with regard to its terms or to Bowen's capacity or motivation to pay it off. Bowen was also one of Audubon's creditors in the mill. Audubon wrote in his journal, "We also took it into our heads to have a steamboat, in partnership with the engineers who had come from Philadelphia to fix the engine of the mill. This proved an entire failure, and misfortune after misfortune came down on us like so many avalanches, both fearful and destructive."[9]

After it became evident that Bowen was not going to make the payment when due, Audubon sued him for physical recovery of the vessel as a means to ensure payment. But Bowen quickly removed the *Henderson* downriver to New Orleans. This imbroglio was unfolding just as George and Georgiana took up residence in the Audubon household.

George had a predisposition toward investing in a boat. As Clarke wrote in his 1843 "Memorial Sketch," the newly married couple had enjoyed a delightful trip down the river from Pittsburgh.[10] George's grandfather John Jennings had been the proprietor of a livery stable, and Thomas Hardy had noted a Keats family who were hauliers, so the transporting of goods may have been in George's blood. Further, the notion of investing in a boat, as opposed to operating it, may have appealed to his English sense of "property." In any case, George probably made his ill-fated investment, whether as a loan or as a share purchase, believing that he would end up with an interest in the *Henderson*. It is nearly certain that Audubon actually used George's money to pay off other creditors. Audubon had never put any cash into the *Henderson*. Thus, he gave George an ownership stake in a boat that Audubon had never owned outright and in which his title was uncertain. He expected to wrest the boat from Bowen as settlement for various debts and counterclaims. But with Bowen's departure and the ongoing credit disputes, it turned out to be a security that Audubon could neither monetize for himself nor deliver to George. That Audubon took the drastic action of pursuing the vessel to New Orleans to recapture it at least partially absolves him of any bad intent toward George.

Audubon's 1819 suit against Bowen was dismissed in Henderson when the boat disappeared, on its way to New Orleans.[11] According to his own journal, Audubon then set out in pursuit in a skiff with two slaves, rowing the entire way to New Orleans. Although such a trip, over 700 miles, seems implausible today, it was not out of character for Audubon to depart on extended sojourns with little notice. The journal states that he left Henderson on 8 May, but the first court date in New Orleans was 19 May, suggesting that his journal was inaccurate or his skiff made exceedingly good time.

When Audubon arrived in New Orleans, he posted notices at a church that Wilson Bowen and Company owed him $4,250 and was about to remove the underlying asset from Louisiana. He also sued for payment of the promissory note, claiming that Bowen had assets in Louisiana exceeding $10,000. After extracting an $8,000 bond from Audubon and a merchant friend named Eben Fisk that he had not wrongfully sworn to the facts in the case, Judge James Pitot issued an attachment. But he was too late. Bowen had already taken the boat from New Orleans.

Bowen's response to the suit on 20 August 1819 was that the *Henderson* had design flaws and was "supposed to have power to propel her as fast as the *Washington* and the *Vesuvius* and was delivered late and with a boiler and machinery wholly incompetent to propel said boat against the currents of the river on which she was to navigate. Wilson Bowen & Co. took cargo to New Orleans [on the *Henderson*] and picked up another cargo, which they had to abandon at Natchez due to the boat's insufficient power. The defects and deficiencies of said boat, the boiler engines, etc., have cost them damages of more than $10,000."[12] Bowen further claimed that Audubon did not have proper documentation to prove that he was the owner of the note originally assigned to Prentice and Bakewell. Audubon claimed to have another promissory note, also for $4,250, that was being sent to him by Prentice and Bakewell. The judge continued the case, without a decision.[13]

Audubon did not acquiesce to these events quietly. Outwitted, he denounced Bowen in the streets and in the taverns. Finally, he sold his slaves and returned north, sailing on the *Paragon* to the junction of the Mississippi and Ohio Rivers.[14] Audubon walked ninety-nine miles to Shawneetown, Illinois, then rode the last forty miles to Henderson.[15] Bowen, possibly after handing the *Henderson* off to his own creditors, had already returned to Henderson and was festering over Audubon's actions in New Orleans. In Audubon's own words:

As I was walking toward the steam-mill one morning, I heard myself hailed from behind, and I turning I saw Mr.—[Bowen] marching toward me with a heavy club in his hand. I stood still, and he soon reached me. He complained of my conduct toward him at New Orleans, and suddenly raising his bludgeon laid it about me. Though white with wrath, I spoke nor moved not till he had given me twelve severe blows, then drawing my dagger with my left hand (unfortunately my right hand was disabled and in a sling, having been caught and much injured in the wheels of the steam engine) I stabbed him and he immediately fell. Old Mr. [James] Berthoud and others, who were hastening to the spot, now came up and carried him home on a plank.[16]

Berthoud calmed the angry crowd, clamoring for instant justice against Audubon, by telling them to pursue the matter through legal channels. Berthoud died shortly thereafter, but his son Nicholas became a good friend of George's in Louisville.

The fight led to charges against Audubon for assault with a deadly weapon. Audubon pled self-defense, and Judge Henry P. Broadnax dismissed the charge. Anecdotally, the judge came down from the bench and said, "Mr. Audubon, you committed a serious offense, sir—in failing to kill the damned rascal."[17]

Next, Bowen sued Audubon for malicious intent relating to his actions in New Orleans. Audubon posted $10,000 bond and asked for a change of venue. He was concerned about receiving a fair trial in Henderson, home to many of his creditors, who had become increasingly restive. The case was moved to Owensboro, Daviess County. First it was postponed at Bowen's request; later the Bowen plaintiffs failed to appear, so the case was dismissed.[18]

George apparently wrote to John about the whole Audubon affair in a now-lost letter, likely posted between March and June 1819. John responded in his 17–27 September "Winchester" letter:

I cannot help thinking Mr. Audubon a dishonest man—Why did he make you believe he was a Man of Property? How is it his circumstances have altered so suddenly? In truth, I do not believe you fit to deal with the world; or at least the american world—But, good God—who can avoid chances—You have done your best— Take matters as coolly as you can, and confidently expecting help from England, act as if no help was nigh. . . .[19]

> Be careful of those Americans—I could almost advise you to come, whenever you have the sum of 500£, to England—Those Americans will, I am affraid still fleece you. . . . I know now [not] how to advise you but by advising you to advise with yourself. In your next, tell me at large your thoughts, about america . . . for it appears to me you have as yet been somehow deceived. I cannot help thinking Mr. Audubon has deceived you. I shall not like the sight of him—I shall endeavour to avoid seeing him.[20]

John's letter, sent from 4,300 miles away in London, is the first extant ink-on-paper notion that Audubon deceived George. However, the sentence construction suggests that *deceived* was John's word, not George's.

Litigation over the steamship matter continued until at least 1825. The summary of a case before the Kentucky Court of Appeals (the highest state court at the time) noted that Prentice and Bakewell had assigned a debt to J. Audubon against the steamboat the *Henderson*. Evidently, the company had taken the debt back from Audubon and was still trying to collect it from Bowen seven years later. In this case, one of Bowen's partners, James Wilson, had died, and his executor was attempting to insulate his estate from any liability to Prentice and Bakewell.[21] It is nearly certain that George Keats was aware of the litigation, as he became the executor of David Prentice's estate in 1826, while Bakewell and Berthoud remained his friends.

George Keats's grandson, John Gilmer Speed, provided the first published account of the incident in 1883, writing in a footnote, "Audubon, the naturalist, sold to George Keats a boat loaded with merchandise, which at the time of the sale Audubon knew to be at the bottom of the Mississippi River."[22] Speed's reference to the "bottom" may have meant that the vessel had sunk or that it was located in the remote lower reaches of the Mississippi, creating problems for reimbursement. His source would have been oral history passed down by Georgiana Keats and his mother, Emma Keats Speed. Given Georgiana's sharp tongue, it is unlikely she provided a fair and balanced version of events. There is no surviving record that George ever mentioned the incident again. Mrs. Speed, who was both well educated and well meaning, passed along other Keats family stories that subsequently proved inaccurate. John Gilmer Speed's casual reference to the lost boat has often been repeated as fact, despite the lack of evidence.

Tom Bakewell wrote a memoir in 1873, the year before his death, in which he acknowledged the *Henderson*'s underpowered design failure.[23]

Bruce Sinclair, a history professor at Kansas State University who edited the memoir, states that Bakewell convinced George Keats to invest in the *Zebulon M. Pike,* a hybrid half-keelboat–half-steamboat that sank in the Red River in 1818.[24] The Red River (of the South) is a tributary of the Mississippi, flowing from the Texas Panhandle along the Texas-Oklahoma border. The *Zebulon M. Pike* sank when it hit a sawyer—the submerged remains of a tree that had fallen into the water. Sawyers were the scourge of river pilots, who arranged for healthy trees to be removed from shorelines to prevent future problems. These removals led to serious erosion.

Although the sinking of the *Zebulon M. Pike* may have involved George Keats's investment, and although it explains the oral history of a sunken boat (the *Henderson* did not sink until later), it does little to explain George's broken relationship with Audubon while he continued his friendship with Bakewell. Alternative theories have been advanced.

Nicholas Roosevelt,[25] who had partnered with the Bakewells on various projects, built the steamboat the *New Orleans* in 1811. It sank in the fall of 1818 off Baton Rouge, was refloated, and sank again in February 1819. There is, however, no documentation that either Audubon or George had any investment in the *New Orleans,* although the timing of its sinking fits the Speeds' questionable oral history.

Some of his biographers have suggested that Audubon disliked the English in emulation of his father, who had been held as a prisoner of war by the English for more than six years.[26] This far-fetched version (Audubon's wife, Lucy, was born in Staffordshire) held that Audubon lay in wait for immigrant settlers heading through Shawneetown to the "English prairie," hoping to fleece them.

Louisville historian George H. Yater wrote, without stating a source, "George invested heavily in a flatboat load of merchandise with Audubon, but when the boat sank and the cargo was lost, relations between the men became strained."[27] When Audubon first settled in Henderson, he worked as a gun and fishing-tackle merchant and transported goods on river flatboats to his original partner, Ferdinand Rozier, in Ste. Genevieve, Missouri; however, there is no evidence that he was doing so in late 1818. Many flatboats did sink over the years, although Audubon never mentioned such an event in his otherwise detailed journal. Nor did Audubon even mention George Keats per se.

The only certainties are these: Audubon was insolvent during the Keatses' stay in Henderson, and George lost his capital in an investment scheme evidently proposed by Audubon. Although he had enjoyed some success as a merchant along the river, Audubon was clearly not primarily a business-man. Twenty-one-year-old George, having dropped out of Abbey's account-ing office at age nineteen, was hardly an astute investor. His money likely ended up in the hands of Audubon's creditors, not in any Keats-owned venture. History must judge whether this was a swindle or an unfortunate combination of Audubon's desperation and George's naiveté.

Meanwhile, the local citizenry of Henderson had reached much the same conclusions as had John Keats in London. Audubon needed to get out of town, so he liquidated his assets in a grand tag sale. In July, Nicho-las Berthoud—married to another Audubon sister-in-law, Eliza Bakewell—paid him $7,000 for all the household effects, leaving Lucy Audubon with nothing but her clothes. Berthoud bought the seven remaining slaves for $4,450 (Audubon had paid $10,500 for nine slaves), and he paid $14,000 for the mill, which had cost in excess of $15,000. Tom Bakewell, who had a $5,000 investment in the mill, loaned from his father, sued his brother-in-law Berthoud to prevent him from paying Audubon before Bakewell's own $5,000 was returned.[28] For his part, Audubon went to Louisville,[29] declared bankruptcy, and was jailed briefly.[30] It was an unhappy ending for all par-ties involved. Audubon biographer Stanley Clisby Arthur notes that "Audu-bon's treatment of George Keats was one of the reasons for the break of pleasant relations between Tom Bakewell and his sister's husband."[31]

It was time for George to start over. Tom Keats's death in December 1818, in the middle of the Henderson mess, created a new round of inher-itance issues that George felt could best be resolved by his going home. First, however, he and Georgiana moved upriver to Louisville, at the Bakewells' invitation, where he worked in the Prentice and Bakewell mill.[32] Then, leaving Georgiana and baby Georgiana Emily with the Bakewells, he set out in November 1819 for London via New York. Bakewell loaned him the £150 passage.[33]

Lucy Audubon retreated to the home of her sister, Eliza Berthoud, in Shippingport, just west of Louisville. Nicholas Berthoud, however, did not welcome Audubon, who briefly reinvented himself as a portrait painter and art teacher in Louisville to make ends meet. Although Audubon never referred to the Keats family in his Henderson journals, he did write about Georgiana on two later occasions. He wrote in 1826, upon visiting Liverpool:

> Dost thou remember the wife of George Keats, Esq., of London &c., &c., &c.? (I will write no more *et ceteras*, these dull my Ger-man quill.)

"Remember her? I am surprised thou shouldst put fresh questions to me," thou sayest.

Well if I did not see Mrs. Keats, the wife of George Keats of London, &c., &c. (confound the &c's, I say) I saw, undoubtedly, her ghost in Wales this afternoon.

"Why, is it possible?" thee asks. Yes it is possible, and I will answer thee *why* with,

"Because it was Sunday." Formerly ghosts walked at night. Now they walk on *Sun*-day. Pho! Pho!—what a poor pun. I do acknowledge that if I did not see Mrs. George Keats, the wife of George Keats, Esq., of London, &c., (damn the &c's), I undoubtedly saw her ghost, or a ghost very much like her ghost.[34]

Georgiana did pass through Liverpool on her way to London, but it was two years later, in 1828. Audubon's strange journal entry was probably written while he was intoxicated. That Audubon was disturbed by her image suggests that he felt remorse about the relationship; it also may have been a reaction to her probable outspokenness and negative commentary about him.

Audubon's second reference to Georgiana came during an 1843 visit to Louisville, after George's death. He reported that "Mrs. Keats is remarried with her 6 children tacked to her." Her handsome new husband, John Jeffrey, was quite a bit younger than Georgiana.[35]

Audubon's true interest was in neither the failed mill nor the phantom equity of the *Henderson*; rather, it was in his naturalist drawings. Audubon's work was published during the 1830s in an English magazine, the *Athenaeum*, edited by George's friend Charles W. Dilke.[36] Beginning in 1831, Audubon was also published in *Blackwood's*, edited by his friend John Wilson.[37] *Blackwood's*, and possibly Wilson himself, had earlier devastated John Keats with harsh reviews of his poetry. Yet George's library in Louisville included at least one Audubon title; it may have been *The Birds of America*, published by E. G. Dorsey in 1839, or his *Ornithological Biography*, published in 1831 by Adam Black in Edinburgh. A fair copy of either would fetch more than $1 million in the twenty-first century.

George Keats, after returning from England with fresh capital, embarked on a successful career that, ironically, mirrored Audubon's commercial efforts in Henderson. George's Louisville ventures included a steam-powered saw- and gristmill, timber purchases, multiple real estate transactions, and at least two investments in steamboats. Audubon's brother-in-law Tom Bakewell was an original backer in George's Louisville mill, although by 1827 he had pulled his capital out. On 27 April 1821 Prentice and Bakewell sold Keats a one-third ownership in the mill, in addition to granting him a managing fee of 20 percent of the profits.[38] Tom and his brother, William "Billy" Bakewell, serial entrepreneurs, alternately sued each other, made and lost fortunes, and declared bankruptcy. Tom's insolvency in 1841 would have disastrous consequences for George. Nicholas Berthoud, the other Audubon brother-in-law, made a success of the Henderson mill within a year of taking it over and became part of George's circle of friends in Louisville.

In a final twist of the Keats-Audubon relationship, Audubon's monument at Trinity Cemetery in upper Manhattan, erected after his 1851 death, is topped by a Celtic cross. The Keats monument in Louisville's Cave Hill Cemetery, erected by John Jeffrey in 1881, is also topped by a Celtic cross. There is no evidence that Audubon practiced any religion,[39] and George was a Unitarian, a faith that came to eschew the symbol of the cross.

LOUISVILLE

1819

Louisville was a settled town when George and Georgiana arrived in the first half of 1819. It was in the final decade of its frontier period, starting with the first pioneer settlement in 1778 and ending around the time the town became a city in 1828 and the Louisville and Portland Canal opened in 1830. The mercantile period lasted from 1830 through the Civil War. After getting established in the 1820s, George thrived during the mercantile era, when Louisville served as provisioner to the expansion of the United States' old Northwest.

When George and Georgiana moved upriver to Louisville, they may have stayed briefly at John Gwathmey's Indian Queen Hotel before living with the Peays.[1] London physician Henry Bradshaw Fearon had also stayed there in 1817 on his travels to Indiana. He wrote strictly as a sightseer, not staying long enough to become acquainted with Louisville's leadership, which was reputed to be warm and generous. The Keatses' first impressions likely mirrored those of Fearon, who wrote, "Louisville is said to be improving in health: the prevalent diseases are fever and ague; besides which, the common disorders of this State are consumption, pleurisy, typhus, remittent and intermittent fevers, rheumatism, and dysentery. Kentuckians . . . drink a great deal, swear a great deal, and gamble a great deal. . . . They also have [a] practice . . . called 'gander-pulling.' This *diversion* consists in tying a live gander to a tree or pole, greasing its neck, riding past it at full gallop, and he who succeeds in pulling off the head of the victim, receives the laurel crown." Fearon also wrote that "*Louisville*, at the falls of the Ohio, is daily becoming a most important town, being the connecting link between New Orleans and the whole western country." Importantly, he noted that "the capitalist could employ his money to much advantage in Kentucky."[2] One such capitalist whose enterprise bemused Fearon was Gwathmey. Fearon created a kaleidoscopic portrait of the Indian Queen:

A person desiring to put up . . . applies to the bar-keeper, and he must not feel disappointed should he be refused admittance from want of room [of which there were 140]. The place for washing is in the open yard, in which there is a large cistern, several towels, and a negro in attendance. The sleeping-room commonly contains from 4 to 8 bed-steads, having mattresses, but frequently no feather-beds; sheets of calico, two blankets, a quilt (either a cotton counterpane or made of patchwork); the bedsteads have no curtains, and the rooms are generally unprovided with any conveniences. The public rooms are—a newsroom, a bootroom, in which the bar is situated, and a dining room. The fires are generally surrounded by parties of about six, who gain and keep possession. . . . Smoking segars is practiced by all without an exception, and at every hour of the day. Argument or discussion in this part of the world is of very rare occurrence; social intercourse seems still more unusual; conversation on general topics, or the taking enlarged and enlightened views of things, rarely occurs; each man is in pursuit of his own individual interest, and follows it in an *individualized* manner.—But to return to the taverns: at half past seven, the first bell rings for the purpose of collecting all the boarders, and at eight the second bell rings; breakfast is then set, the dining-room is unlocked, a general rush commences, and some activity, as well as dexterity, is essentially necessary to obtain a seat at the table. . . . The breakfast consists of a profuse supply of fish, flesh, and fowl, which is consumed with a rapidity truly extraordinary; often before I had finished my first cup of tea, the room, which when I had commenced was crowded to suffocation, had become nearly empty. . . .

At table there is neither conversation nor yet drinking; the latter is effected by individuals taking their solitary "eye openers," "toddy," and "phlegmn dispensers," at the bar, the keeper of which is in full employ from sun-rise to bed-time. A large tub of water, with a ladle, is placed on the bar, to which customers go and help themselves. When spirits are called for, the decanter is handed, and you take what quantity you please; the charge is always 6 ¾ d. It is never drunk *neat,* or with sugar or warm water. The life of boarders at an American tavern, presents the most senseless and comfortless mode of killing time which I have ever seen. . . . I have not seen a book in the hands of any person since I left Philadelphia. Objectionable as these habits are, they afford decided evidence of the prosperity of that country, which can admit so large a body of its citizens to waste in indolence three-fourths of their lives, and would appear to hold out encouragement to Englishmen with *English habits,* who could retain their industry amid a nation of indolence.[3]

Fearon's last sentence could have had George in mind.

The full measure of the town was best described in 1819 by Dr. Henry McMurtrie, who published *Sketches of Louisville* that year. Its defining characteristic was the falls of the Ohio River, the only break in river traffic from Pittsburgh to New Orleans. Prior to the Keatses' arrival, there was discussion of building a canal; not all Louisvillians were in favor of this, as they profited from providing the portage labor. When Indianans proposed that the canal be built on their side, momentum built for the Louisville and Portland Canal, which opened in 1830. Without it, barge and steamboat traffic had to descend through one of three chutes, each more unsatisfactory than the next, depending on season and water flow. Louisville thus approached its mercantile era as an entrepôt, where goods were unloaded, carted downriver to the neighboring town of Shippingport (or vice versa, going upriver), then reloaded for further shipment. The town developed along the waterfront, gradually growing southward.

George and Georgiana were offered a place to live within the twelve-acre compound of Prentice and Bakewell, George's first employer.[4] The site, at First and Washington Streets, was one block removed from the waterfront and enjoyed a view downriver of the falls. Beargrass Creek, one of several navigable waterways emptying into the Ohio, flowed right past, parallel to the river, before entering it below Third Street. Years later the creek was rerouted to enter the river farther upstream, increasing the wharf area for commerce.

McMurtrie described "six hundred and seventy dwelling houses, principally brick ones, some of which would suffer but little by being compared with any of the most elegant private edifices of Philadelphia or New York." Lacking a census, McMurtrie guessed that the population was 4,020, at "six persons to each house." London's population at the time was about 1 million. "The theater, public and private balls, a sober game of whist, or the more scientific one of billiards, with an occasional reunion of friends . . . constitute the principal amusement." McMurtrie's description of the public buildings confirms that Louisville had matured from its early pioneer days: "The Court House is generally allowed to be the handsomest structure of the kind, in the western country, and was built in 1811, after a plan drawn by John Gwathmey, Esq."[5]

Louisville had three banks. The Louisville Bank, which became a branch of the State Bank of Kentucky, was capitalized in 1812 at $100,000. In 1817 a branch of the Bank of the United States opened. By 1819, the Commercial Bank of Louisville was also open for business, with $1 million capital.[6] There were also three churches: Methodist, Catholic, and Presbyterian.

McMurtrie described the local private school, called a seminary: "This is a tolerably capacious brick building, under the direction of the trustees of the town, wherein are taught the several branches of a regular and classical education. This institution is not, I am sorry to say, so well patronized as it deserves. . . . To know how to make money is the grand object, if he knows that, he knows every thing that needs to be learned, all else is deemed superfluous."[7]

The Hope Distillery, capitalized in 1816 at $100,000, was set up on 100 acres at Fifteenth and Portland Streets. Paul Skidmore set up Louisville's first iron foundry in 1812. Originally designed to supply blacksmiths, the foundry was sold twice, coming into the hands of David Prentice in 1817. Prentice brought in Thomas Bakewell as a partner and expanded the operation to build steam engines. By 1819, Prentice and Bakewell had sold ten steam engines—eight for steamboats and two for land manufactories—for a cumulative sum of $100,000. As McMurtrie's book went to press, they had orders for additional engines totaling $70,000. They forbade drunkenness on the job and reportedly had the best workforce in town.[8] It is nearly certain that George Keats participated in the Prentice and Bakewell operations, sited north of Main at First Street. The Bakewells would continue to figure importantly in George and Georgiana's lives thereafter.

Louisville also had a sugar refinery, a soap and candle manufactory, several tobacco processors, three bookstores, three printing offices, three drugstores, a nail factory, two hotels, four taverns, six bake houses, six brickyards, a brass foundry, and even a music repository. There were numerous blacksmiths, saddlers, harness makers, and carriage makers; eight tailors; a gunsmith; ten cabinetmakers; three watchmakers; a stonecutter; an upholsterer; one hundred fifty bricklayers; thirty plasterers; six shoemakers; twelve lawyers; and twenty-two physicians.

John H. Clarke and Company owned a steam-driven flour mill on Jefferson Street with a capacity to produce eighty barrels of flour per day. Directly in front of this was a steam-driven sawmill, owned by a man named Tunstall, capable of turning out 2,800 board feet of wood daily. A second sawmill of equivalent size was owned by Prentice and Bakewell, located next to their foundry.[9] With respect to the milling business, McMurtrie reported: "Timber is chiefly brought from the Allegheny mountains and the banks of the Kentucky (River), the former furnishing white pine the latter red cedar, which are both brought in rafts to the Falls, and there delivered to purchasers, at a moderate price. The principal woods used by the cabinet makers are cherry and maple, which are amply supplied from the surrounding country. Mahogany, however, which is superseding the two former, since the introduction of steam boats, is freighted up the river from New Orleans."[10]

McMurtrie's 1819 portrait illustrates that Louisville could no longer be called a frontier town. It had a nearly complete infrastructure, necessitated by the boom-like expansion. Even its moniker as a river town had changed. On 28 October 1811 Nicholas Roosevelt had arrived from Pittsburgh on the steamboat *New Orleans,* the first to navigate western waters. He had to wait until December to get the vessel through the falls, so he staged a series of excursions upriver to prove to the dubious local citizenry that the paddle wheeler could travel against the water's flow. In 1815 the *Enterprize* steamed from New Orleans to Louisville in twenty-five days. Louisville had turned into a city with a viable trading economy, and with the introduction of steamboat traffic to New Orleans, that economy was becoming international in scope.

Whereas McMurtrie's observations were those of a clinician, various writers showed Louisville's human face. In 1809 John James Audubon described a July Fourth celebration:

Each denizen had freely given his ox, his ham, his venison, his Turkeys and other fowls. Here were to be seen flagons of every beverage used in the country: "la belle riviere" had opened her finny stores, the melons of all sorts, peaches, plums and pears, would have sufficed to stock a market. . . . "Old Monongahela" filled many a barrel for the crowd. In a short time the ground was alive with merriment. A great wooden cannon bound with iron hoops was now crammed with home-made powder . . . and as the explosion burst forth, thousands of hearty huzzas mingled with its echoes. . . . You would have been pleased to see those who did not join in the dance shooting at distant marks with their heavy rifles, or watched how they showed off their superior speed of their high bred "Old Virginia" horses.[11]

It was during their early days in Louisville that a profound exchange of letters occurred between John and George and Georgiana. Their remoteness on the frontier spurred John to write five of his best letters (among those that were saved) during the fifteen-month period from October 1818 to January 1820. His first two letters, addressed to the couple while John was in Liverpool on his walking trip, were lost. Although the actual addressing of his letters to America was discarded, presumably the first was sent in care of Birkbeck's base in Princeton, Indiana, and was then forwarded to the couple in Henderson, Kentucky.

George's literary friend James Freeman Clarke wrote about the letters, with some understatement:

> These have not hitherto been published, but it appears to us, from the specimens which we have seen of them, that they are of a higher order of composition than his poems. There is in them a depth and grasp of thought; a logical accuracy of expression; a fullness of intellectual power, and an earnest struggling after truth, which remind us of the prose of Burns. They are only letters, not regular treatises, yet they touch upon the deepest veins of thought, and ascend the highest heaven of contemplation. . . . We feel a little proud that we, in this western valley, are the first to publish specimens of these writings.[12]

T. S. Eliot later wrote in the same vein: the letters "are what letters ought to be; the fine things come in unexpectedly, neither introduced nor shown out, but between trifle and trifle."[13]

John's letters, much like a composer's notes in the margins of his musical score, provide insights into his philosophy and poetry that guide critics and biographers to this day. George Keats's daughter, Emma Keats Speed, saved sixteen of the letters written during John's most productive years (1817–1819).[14] Her son, John Gilmer Speed, published all but one in 1883. George's serendipitous contribution to understanding John Keats and the evolution of Romantic literature was that he saved these monumental letters.[15]

The first of these letters was written to George and Tom while they were still in Teignmouth, in December 1817; it has been called the "negative capability" letter. The last of these letters, addressed to Georgiana (as his "sister"), was written 13–17 January 1820, in which he expounds on religion and humanity. Collectively, these letters reveal how intensely John missed George and Georgiana, a lasting testament to his love for them. Further, the letters serve as a coda to the burst of John's finest poetry, composed during 1819—his "living" year. It could also be argued that during this time, John ascended to a new creative plateau. Free at last of tiresome family issues, safely ensconced within the protectorate of Charles Brown, and, most important, deeply in love with Fanny Brawne, John made the absolute most of his living year.

A time line of the letters, intertwined with the completion of John's poetry, is included in the Chronology. Following here is a selected compilation of quotes from the letters to his siblings. They reveal much of the poet's character, entrusted to his closest relatives.[16]

John's 5 January 1818 letter, postmarked from the Featherstone Buildings in London, is basically a recounting of his activities. One theme that often bothered him was indolence, which he treats in an anecdote about Mrs. Abbey: "Mrs. Abbey was saying that the Keatses were ever indolent—that it would ever be so, and that it is born in them—Well, whispered Fanny to me, if it is born with us, how can we help it?"[17]

One of the most important letters (the "negative capability" letter) was written in December 1817 from Hampstead and addressed to the brothers in Teignmouth. John reports on a dinner-party discussion with Charles Dilke: "I had not a dispute but a disquisition with Dilke, upon various subjects; several things dove-tailed in my mind, & at once it struck me, what quality went to form a Man of Achievement, especially in Literature, & which Shakespeare possessed so enormously—I mean *Negative Capability*, that is, when a man is capable of being in uncertainties, Mysteries, doubts, without any irritable reaching after fact & reason."[18]

Keats scholar Aileen Ward has reflected on the meaning of "negative capability," writing that today it might be called a "tolerance for ambiguity." The capacity to suspend judgment also involves the "capability of submission" and the capacity for "annulling self." Yet the ability to "annul self" depends on a very firm sense of self.[19] It was a means for Keats to grow intellectually by putting aside one influence for another, followed by yet another.

Keats follows up his point two sentences later, writing, "with a great poet the sense of Beauty overcomes every other consideration, or rather obliterates all consideration."[20] Here he introduces the brothers to his evolving belief in an ultimate vision where truth and beauty become one and the same.

Keats, whose education had been cut short at age fifteen for a medical apprenticeship, was reading voraciously and attending the lecture series of William Hazlitt during this period. In a letter to Teignmouth dated 23 January 1818, he writes, "I think a little change has taken place in my intellect lately—I cannot bear to be uninterested or unemployed, I, who for so long a time have been addicted to passiveness—Nothing is finer for the purposes of great productions than a very gradual ripening of the intellectual powers."[21]

A favorite theme of Keats's was "disinterestedness." In a letter to George and Tom dated 21 April 1818, he notes, "that sort of probity and disinterestedness which such men as Bailey [John's friend from Oxford] possess does hold and grasp the tip-top of any spiritual honors that can be paid to anything in the world."[22]

After George and Georgiana left for America and John for Scotland, he wrote a lengthy journal letter, initially posted to brother Tom. In it, a number of his attitudes spill forth, including one, dated 3–9 July 1818, on the church: "I would sooner be a wild deer, than a Girl under the dominion of the Kirk; and I would sooner be a wild hog than be the occasion of a Poor Creature's pennance before those execrable elders."[23]

A month later, from Inverness, Scotland, Keats wrote to Georgiana's mother, describing his own view of Georgiana's emigration and evidently sympathizing with Mrs. Wylie about it: "I should like to have remained near you, were it but for an atom of consolation, after parting with so dear a daughter. . . . & I can never forget the sacrifice you have made for his (George's) happiness. . . . I wish above all things, to say a word of Comfort to you, but I know not how. It is impossible to prove that black is white; it is impossible to make out that sorrow is joy or joy is sorrow."[24]

After John returned to Hampstead, he wrote to George in America on 14 October 1818, posting the letter to Birkbeck's address. Although the letter starts out clearly addressed to his brother, it drifts into speaking to Georgiana directly (both Keats boys called her "George" from time to time):

> Your content in each other is a delight to me which I cannot express—The Moon is now shining full and brilliant—she is the same to me in Matter that you are in Spirit. If you were here my dear Sister, I could not pronounce the words which I can write to you from a distance:
>
> I have a tenderness for you, and an admiration which I feel to be as great and more chaste than I can have for any woman in the world. You will mention Fanny [Keats]—her character is not

formed; her identity does not press upon me as yours does. I hope from the bottom of my heart that I may one day feel as much for her as I do for you.

I know not how it is but I have never made any acquaintance of my own—nearly all through your medium my dear brother—through you I know not only a sister but a glorious human being.[25]

The letter goes on to describe John's travails with the critics: "This is a mere matter of the moment—I think I shall be among the English poets after my death . . . the attempt to crush me in the (Chro) Quarterly has only brought me more into notice."[26]

The letter is also important because it introduces the American Keatses to Fanny Brawne. After praising her virtues, Keats continues, in a sentence that confused biographers for 100 years: "You will by this time think I am in love with her; so before I go any further, I will tell you I am not."[27] Six months later, John had seriously upgraded his passion for Fanny.

The letter goes on to reveal John's disdain for the American character, and he challenges George to improve upon it:

Dilke, whom you know to be a Godwin-perfectibil[it]y Man, pleases himself with the idea that America will be the country to take up the human intellect where england leaves off—I differ there with him greatly—a country like the united states, whose greatest Men are Franklins and Washingtons will never do that—they are great men, doubtless; but how are they to be compared to these, our countrymen, Milton and the two Sidneys—The one is a philosophical Quaker full of mean and thrifty maxims the other sold the very Charger who had taken him through all his battles—These American's are great but they are not sublime Man—the humanity of the United States can never reach the sublime.[28]

Keats's historical references are not entirely clear. Benjamin Franklin was a lifelong Anglican who lived for sixteen years in Craven Street, Westminster. The fate of George Washington's horse, known as the son of Ranger, is uncertain: however, he retired Ranger to stud in Mont Vernon.

Keats then rambles back into his poetry, saying, "The only thing that can ever affect me personally for more than one short passing day, is any doubts about my powers for poetry—I seldom have any, and I look with hope to the nighing time when I shall have none."[29]

John suspended writing to George during the final weeks of Tom's life. After his death in December 1818, John wrote to George and Georgiana about it, then launched into another journal. Midway along, he reveals his thoughts about artistic individualism, quoting Edward Dubois (1775–1850): "In singing, never mind the music—observe what time You please. It would be a pretty degradation indeed if you were obliged to confine your genius to the dull regularity of a fiddler—horse-hair and cat's-guts—no, let him keep *your* time and play *your* time—*dodge* him."[30]

Two months later John began another journal, covering the period 14 February to 3 May 1819 and touching on many topics. While staying with Charles Brown in Bedhampton, he wrote an entertaining narrative that ended up as an anticlerical screed:

> The only time I went out from Bedhampton was to see a chapel consecrated. . . . This Chapel is built by a Mr. Way a great Jew converter—who in that line has spent one hundred thousand Pounds. . . .
>
> I begin to hate Parsons—they did not make me love them that day—when I saw them in their proper colours—A Parson is a Lamb in a drawing room and a lion in a Vestry—The notions of Society will not permit a parson to give way to his temper in any shape—so he festers in himself—his features get a peculiar diabolical self-sufficient, iron stupid exp[r]ession—He is continually acting—His mind is against every Man, and every Man's mind is against him—He is an Hippocrite to the Believer and a Coward to the unbeliever—He must be either a Knave or an Ideot—and there is no Man so much to be pitied as an ideot parson.[31]

Keats may have been hard on parsons, but he saved some of his best invective for a description of Henry Wylie's fiancée and Georgiana's future sister-in-law, Mary Ann Keasle. He calls her "a lath with a bodice—she has been fine drawn—fit for nothing but to be cut up into Cribbage pins. . . . one who is all muslin; all feathers & bone; Once in travelling she was made use of as a linchpin; I hope he will not have her, though it is no uncommon thing to be *smitten with a staff;* though she might be very useful as his walking stick, his fishing-rod, his tooth-pic—his hat stick (she runs so much in his head)."[32]

Having dispatched the future Mrs. Wylie, Keats continues his thoughts on disinterestedness: "Very few men have arrived at a complete disinterestedness of Mind: very few have been interested by a pure desire for the benefit of others—in the greater part of the Benefactors [of] & to Humanity, some meretricious motive has sullied their greatness—some melodramatic scenery has fascinated them."[33]

Next, John expounds on Dante and then bounces into one of his funniest writings, addressed to Georgiana:

> I want very much a little of your wit, my dear sister—a Letter or two of yours just to bandy back a pun or two across the Atlantic and send a quibble over the Floridas—Now you have by this time crumpled up your large Bonnet, what do you wear—a cap! do you put your hair in paper of a night? do you pay the Miss Birkbeck's a morning visit—Have you any tea? or do you milk and water with them—What place of Worship do you go to—the Quakers the Moravians, the Unitarians, or the Methodists—Are there any flowers in bloom you like—Any beautiful heaths—Any Streets full of Corset Makers. What sort of shoes have you to put those pretty feet of yours? Do you desire Compts to one another? Do you ride on Horseback? What do you have for breakfast, dinner, and supper? without mentioning lunch and bever, and wet and snack—and a bit to stay one's stomach—Do you get any spirits—Now you might easily distill some whiskey—and going into the woods set up a whiskey spop for the Monkeys! . . . for a whole day I tell you how you may employ it—First get up and when you are dress'd . . . give George a cold Pig with my Complements. Then you may saunter into the nearest coffee-house and after taking a dram and a look at the chronicle—go and frighten the wild boars on the strength—you may as well bring one home for breakfast serving up the hoofs garnished with bristles and a grunt or two to accompany the singing of the kettle—then if George is not up give him a colder Pig always with my Compliments.[34]

Keats concludes this letter by copying out "Ode to Psyche," one of his finest works, followed by an elemental discussion of his theory of poetry: "I have been endeavouring to discover a better sonnet stanza than we have. The legitimate does not suit the language over-well, from the pouncing rhymes—the other appears to elegai[a]c—and the couplet at the end of it has seldom a pleasing effect."[35]

The next letter to George is dated 17–27 September 1819. Following the familiar journal motif, Keats covers all topics. George had written to him about the Audubon fiasco, prompting John's reaction: "I cannot help thinking Mr. Audubon a dishonest man."[36]

Later, Keats includes a previous letter dated 23 July 1818, written by himself to brother Tom, in which he expounds more on his poetic theory: "You speak of Lord Byron and me—There is this great difference between us. He describes what he sees—I describe what I imagine. Mine is the hardest task. You see the immense difference—The great beauty of Poetry is, that it makes everything every place interesting."[37]

As the letter continues, Keats offers up both a premonition of his coming disaffection with George and a medical-based theory of personal reinvention: "From the time you left me, our friends say I have altered completely—am not the same person—perhaps in this letter I am for in a letter one takes up one's existence from the time we last met—I dare say you have altered also—every man does—Our bodies every seven years are completely fresh materiald. . . . This is the reason why men who have been bosom friends, on being separated for any number of years, afterwards meet coldly, neither of them knowing why—The fact is, they are both altered."[38]

With another of his frequent changes of tone, Keats quickly shifts back, expressing a willingness to do anything for George: "Feel with confidence what I now feel that though there can be no stop put to troubles we are inheritors of, there can be and must be [an] end to immediate difficulties. Rest in the confidence that I will not omit any exertion to benefit you by some means or other." John goes on to acknowledge that when Abbey distributes the proceeds from Tom's estate, his share must go to pay off debts: "What he [Abbey] has of mine I have nearly anticipated by debts, so I would advise you [George] not to sink it, but to live upon it in hopes of my being able to increase it."[39]

As John rambles toward a conclusion, he offers up several characterizations of their mutual friends that explain his own intellectual approach. About Charles Dilke, who would become Fanny Keats's trustee and George's lifelong friend, John says: "Dilke was a Man who cannot feel he has a personal identity unless he has made up his Mind about every thing. The only means of strengthening one's intellect is to make up ones mind about nothing—to let the mind be a thoroughfare for all thoughts. Not a select party. . . . All the stubborn arguers you meet with . . . never begin upon a subject they have not preresolved on."[40]

The last of the family letters to America was written to Georgiana while George was in London, dated 13–28 January 1820. It may also have been one of his funniest. Replying to a letter from his sister-in-law (now lost), John says:

Yours is a hardish fate to be so divided from your friends and settled among a people you hate—You will find it improve. . . . We
smoke [i.e., tease] George about his little Girl, he runs the common beaten road of every father, as I dare say you do of every
Mother—there is no Child like his Child so original!—original
foolsooth—However I take you at your words; I have a lively faith
that yours is the very gem of all children—Aint I its uncle?

The evening before yesterday we had a piano forte hop at Dilkes—There was very little amusement in the room but a Scotchman to hate—Some people you must have observed have a most
unpleasant effect upon you when you see them speaking in profile—This Scotchman is the most accomplish'd fellow in this way I
have ever met. The effect was complete.

I was surprised to hear of the State of Society at Louisville, is
seems you are just as ridiculous there as we are here—threepenny
parties, half-penny Dances—the best thing I have heard of is your
Shooting, for it seems you follow the Gun. Give my Compliments
to Mrs. Audubon, and tell her I cannot think her either good-look-
ing or honest. . . .

Were you in England I dare say you would be able . . . to suck
out more amusement for Saciety than I am able to do. To me it is
as dull here as Louisville could be.

If the American ladies are worse than the English, they must
be very bad—You say you should like your Emily brought up here.
You had better bring her up yourself. . . .

I know three people of no wit at all, each distinct in his excellence. A, B, and C. A is the [f]oolishest, B the sulkiest, C is a negative. A makes you yawn, B makes you hate; as for C, you never see
him though he is six feet high. I bear the first, I forbear the second I am not certain that the third is. The first is gruel, the Second
Ditch-water, the third is spilt—he ought to be wip'd up. . . .

Twang-dillo-dee. . . . This you must know is the amen to
nonsense.[41]

Keats expounds to Georgiana for another paragraph on the virtues of
Twang-dillo-dee. Those may be the last words he ever wrote to her. They
were also the last known words he wrote to anyone in America.

A Dismal Return

1820

Within a momentous twelve months spanning 1818 and 1819, George had turned twenty-one, received his initial inheritance from his grandmother, married, immigrated to America, and lost much of his inheritance. He left no record of his activities during 1819, but after moving up to Louisville, he likely attempted to complete a mill investment while working for Prentice and Bakewell in the fledgling mill operations at their iron foundry.

John had written of a premonition of brother Tom's death, based on his frailty and Dr. Sawrey's hopeless diagnosis.[1] William Haslam wrote to George and Georgiana to inform them of Tom's death on 1 December 1818 and his burial at St. Stephen's on 7 December. Haslam's letter likely arrived in Kentucky in late January or February 1819.[2]

Although George's job at Prentice and Bakewell provided a living wage, he lacked the wherewithal to make any investment for capital appreciation. He needed to augment his plans quickly, and Tom's residual estate would be the focus. Recognizing that Tom's remaining assets could be distributed to John and himself, George wrote to his brother, suggesting that he pursue the matter with Abbey. John received that letter prior to 7 July 1819, while on the Isle of Wight.[3] A second letter from George, dated 24 July, reached John in September, after he had returned to London.

John called on Abbey, who mentioned that their aunt, Margaret (Mrs. Midgley) Jennings, had also made a claim on Tom's estate.[4] It appears that the poet asked Abbey to send funds to George in America as a loan from Tom's estate. Abbey properly declined because of the uncertainty over Margaret Jennings's threatened action.[5] She claimed that a share of Tom's estate should go to her children because it contained funds that, upon Midgley's death, had reverted to his mother, Alice Jennings, and were then passed on to Tom upon her death (as specified in John Jennings's will, which had been approved by the Chancery). It is unlikely Margaret would have prevailed, but Abbey refused to clear Tom's accounts while there was a chance that her claim would succeed. John offered to loan funds to

George, writing, "If I cannot remit you hundreds, I will tens and if not that ones," but there is no evidence that he did.[6]

George persisted, through John, but to no avail. John wrote, "You urg'd me to get Mr Abbey to advance you money [from Tom's estate]—that he will by no means do—for beside the risk of the law (small enough indeed) he will never be persu[a]ded but you will loose it in America." The release of funds also depended on a man named Fry (perhaps Thomas Fry, a stock-broker and possibly a successor trustee to Sandell), who angrily agreed to do so prior to John's 12 November letter. As John described it, "For a bit of a treat in the heart of all this I had a most abusive Letter from Fry—committing you and myself to destruction without reprieve."[7] With Fry's approval, Abbey cautiously made £200 available in November, and John posted £100 of it to George on 19 November, perhaps mistakenly viewing this sum as a loan. In addition, there were problems with the law firm of William Walton (who had died during the summer), hindering the settle-ment of the estate. Stock prices were down, making Abbey reluctant to sell. By the time the £100 arrived in Louisville, through Philadelphia transfer agent John Warder and Sons, George had returned to London to sort out the various problems and conclusively settle the entire estate.

Meanwhile, Georgiana Emily Keats was born sometime before June 1819.[8] In her infancy they called her Emily, but later she became "Geor-gey." While George went to London, Georgiana and Emily stayed behind with the Bakewells. They both took seriously ill, but in the frontier spirit, Georgiana did not write about it, and both had recovered by the time he returned. George wrote, "My little Girl became so ill as to approach the Grave dragging our dear George [Georgiana] after her."[9] No one described their illness. However, McMurtrie observed in 1819 that the town had numerous undrained ponds that gave rise to near epidemic lev-els of a bilious fever. He wrote: "the most fatal complaint among adults (exclusive of small pox) is a bilious remitting fever, whose symptoms are often sufficiently aggravated to entitle it to the name of *yellow fever*."[10] Writ-ers sardonically called the city the graveyard of the West.

George arrived in London close to New Year's 1820. He found a changed John, consistent with the latter's premonitory letter of 21 Sep-tember 1819. John was in love with Fanny Brawne, and they had become secretly engaged. But he fatigued easily and did not enjoy parties as much, and his moods were of a different character than George had known dur-ing childhood. As their interests diverged, the two brothers had matured in different ways.

George was happy to see Mrs. Reynolds and her daughters. Jane and Marianne Reynolds had been hurt by John's coolness toward them, and they predisposed George to dislike Fanny Brawne, adding to the tension. George did not immediately warm to Fanny, which was a little unfair, as he later recognized. Late in 1820 he wrote to John, offering a backhanded approval of Fanny, "Marriage might do you good."[11] Charles Brown intercepted the letter and did not forward it to John, who was in Rome by then. George later wrote to Fanny Keats, "Knowing John's affection for that young Lady I feel very much disposed to like her, altho' I was informed by persons I very much respect that she was an artful bad hearted Girl, all I saw to object to in her was an appearance of want of affection for her Sister and respect for her Mother."[12]

After Margaret Jennings withdrew her lawsuit, Abbey agreed to accelerate an outright distribution of Tom's funds, although John may have continued to believe that the original transmittals were loans. No mention was made of their grandfather's estate or their mother's, both languishing in Chancery and unknown to either George or John.

The rest of George's stay in London was recounted in John's journal letter to Georgiana dated 13–28 January 1820. Having set in motion the release of funds, George embarked on a round of social calls. He met his new sister-in-law, Henry Wylie's wife, whom John described to Georgiana as homely and silent. On 10 January he took his mother-in-law to Shakespeare's *Comedy of Errors*. John's friends welcomed George back to London. Charles Dilke included him in a musical evening where a new waltz was played—the pianoforte hop, which was sweeping London. John did not dance. Political discussions fascinated George but bored John. For his part, George told tales of America, playing the traveled gentleman. After the strains of the previous eighteen months on the frontier, he felt like he was on holiday.

George went to Deptford in southeast London to see William Haslam, his best friend from Clarke's School. Haslam was spending time there with a girl (Mary) he planned to marry. John had grown temporarily remote from Haslam, so he stayed behind. Haslam propositioned George with the notion of a business venture in America, involving a friend named Kent and the export of upmarket goods to the frontier. He prevailed on George to return for a second evening, drawing him away early from a dinner arranged by the poet with the witty trio of James Rice, John Hamilton Reynolds, and Charles Richards. Later, when George returned to America and wrote to Haslam that his idea would not work, the letter went undelivered, and an annoyed Haslam turned into a fierce critic of George.

John and George dined with publisher John Taylor as well.[13] On 22 January John took George to a beefsteak dinner that Brown hosted in honor of Dilke, to whom Brown had lost a fairy tale contest earlier. George also found time to copy into a notebook John's poems completed in the intervening year—no small task. George was especially fond of "Ode to a Nightingale," written in April and May 1819, with Tom's last days in mind ("Youth grows pale").

Abbey succeeded in settling Tom's estate in a three-way division within a month of George's arrival. It had been reduced by a declining market to about £1,100, not including the unrealized sum in Chancery. Prior to George's arrival, Abbey had distributed £100 each to John, George, and Fanny. They divided the remaining £800 into thirds, or about £270 apiece. Fanny retained hers as a credit; George received his £270 and, in addition, claimed £170 from John, leaving the latter with only £100. George's claim evidently confused the poet and, by extension, Charles Brown and several others. George later explained that when he first sailed to America in 1818, he had left £500 of his own money in the "Abbey account," in part to clear his own debts, but mostly for the benefit of his brothers. John withdrew £70 immediately for his Scottish trip with Brown. After Tom's death, John withdrew another £176 and, although Abbey's records are inconclusive, probably an additional £46 before George's return to London. Thus, John's total withdrawals from the Abbey account were just under £300. Of this, George claimed the aforementioned £170. Abbey then added £60 to George's share, whether as a gift, a loan, or an investment in George's American venture.[14]

George's money-gathering exercise can be summed up as follows:

Recoupment of Tom's remaining share of the Abbey account left by George in 1818	£100
Abbey's initial distribution from Tom's estate	£100
George's one-third share of Tom's £800 estate	£270
Repayment of funds John withdrew from the Abbey account	£170
Gift, loan, or investment by Abbey	£60
Total	£700

The sticking point was the £170. Apparently, as noted earlier, John actually owed George £300 for his Abbey account withdrawals, or £130 more than George recouped. What is less clear is the sum of the intrafamily loans that preceded George's 1818 departure. In that year, he had written to John from Teignmouth, "I am about paying your's as well as Tom's bills, of which I shall keep regular accounts and for the sake of justice and a future proper understanding I intend calculating the probable amount Tom and I are indebted to you, something of this kind must be done, or at the end of two or three years we shall all be at sixes and sevens."[15]

Other letters suggest that John had loaned George's short-term employer, Wilkinson, £50. In addition, John may have footed the bill for George and Tom's 1817 trip to France. Dividing up their shared living costs must have been complex, due to John's continual stepping in and out of the arrangements. In any event, George was confident in the accounting and was later vindicated by Abbey, Reynolds, and the Dilke brothers.[16] But John, in early 1820, was indeed at sixes and sevens over the money.

Although the brotherly accounting was rational and fair, John was left with financial troubles of his own making. By the time he gave up his surgical career, John had consumed all but about £500 of his capital for his education. He evidently loaned upward of £200 of that amount to friends, including the painter Haydon.[17] There is no evidence that any of the loans were repaid, except from Haslam. Of the remaining £300, John used it for living expenses, such as rent paid to Brown, doctor's fees, and food and drink, as well as for travel. As a consequence, John was short of ready cash when George left for America in 1818 and also when he left the second time in 1820. On their second and final parting, George left John with about £60. John handed that over to Brown with his unpaid bills, which totaled £80, immediately putting him back in debt, where he remained for the rest of his life. John's financial issues were of his own making, but the question remains whether George was sensitive to John's perpetual financial plight, and what he could or should have done about it.

George's mistake was not being more rigorous in clarifying the intra-family accounts, in particular, distinguishing gifts from loans. Brown made no such mistakes during his co-occupancy with the poet. As George wrote to Dilke later, "John himself was ignorant of the real state of his funds, it was so painful a subject and in our private communications he was so extremely melancholy that I always had to shew him the pleasing side of things . . . it was always my intention to keep him under the idea I was in his debt."[18]

In any event, by the end of January, George was free to go with his £700 capital. He had spent two months in transit and one enjoyable month in

London, but it was time to return to his wife and small child. On 28 January 1820 he said good-bye to John and the Wylies and departed.

Fanny Brawne had asked the Abbeys if Fanny Keats might come and stay with her during George's visit, "an indulgence which was not granted me."[19] George saw his sister Fanny, sequestered in Walthamstow, at least once, although he did not venture back for a final farewell. Instead, he wrote to her on 30 January 1820 from Liverpool: "I considered not taking a final leave of you a misfortune, and regretted very much that constant occupation detained me from coming to Walthamstow; but now I look upon the pain attending the last good bye, and shake of the hand as well spared, and reflect on the pleasure of seeing you again at however remote a period: when you will be a *Woman* and I a '*bald Pate*.'" George never saw Fanny again. Their relationship was further strained by his urging her to respect Abbey, as he did:

> Mr. Abbey behaved very kindly to me before I left for which I am sure you will feel grateful. He is attentive in his commerce with his fellows in all essentials. He observes with pleasure, the pleasure communicated to others; he says you sometimes look thin and pale, but he thinks that you have been better since you have run about a little feeding chickens, attending your little Cat &c. A man of coarse feeling would never notice these things. He expressed surprise that neither you nor Miss A—(should not speak) spoke at meals; so you see it is not his wish that you should be moped and silent, therefore cheer up and look lively as nature made you.[20]

Fanny, then sixteen, likely did not appreciate George's admonishments. The exchange leaked to John as well, who wrote to Fanny days later about "Mr. Abbey's regret concer[n]ing the silence kept up in his house. It is entirely the fault of his Manner."[21] The trail of these letters delineated the battle lines: Fanny hated Abbey; John supported her, and George did not.

George had lightheartedly suggested that John should visit America. He also promised Mrs. Wylie that he would return with Georgiana within five years. In fact, when he left England this time, it would be forever. John accompanied George down to the coach, the *Royal Alexander,* scheduled to leave at a foggy six in the morning on 28 January. He walked away, leaving George atop the coach. There is no way to judge how disappointing the visit had been in brotherly terms.

From Liverpool, George wrote farewell letters to Dilke, Reynolds, Rice, Brown, and Haslam, as well as to Fanny and John Keats. On 1 February 1820 his packet, the *Courier,* with Captain Jonathon Eldridge, set sail.[22]

John remained in a confused state about the finances, in particular, mixing up all the loans and gifts that had gone back and forth. He confided in his housemate Charles Brown. Writing to Richard Monckton Milnes twenty-one years later, Brown said, "George left him for America, with more by £20 than Keats possessed, saying, which was repeated to me by himself;—'You, John, have so many friends, they will be sure to take care of you!'" His point was that George had given John £60, but John had £80 in unpaid debts at the time. Brown went on to write, "It was on the evening after that day, that his fatal attack took place, and the words were repeated with bitterness, and he added—'That was not, Brown, fair—was it?'"[23] In this decades-later missive, Brown misdated the poet's initial, nonfatal lung hemorrhage, which occurred five days after George's departure.[24] Nor did Brown explain why the poet, hemorrhaging and predicting his own death, would have chosen that moment to repeat his chagrin over £20. Larger issues were afoot among all the parties involved. Brown likely resented George's blithe departure, while he was left to handle John, who was seriously dependent on so many levels.

Fanny Brawne, even more intimate with the poet and writing to Fanny Keats just one year later, provided a more sane and balanced account, although it did not come to light until its publication more than a century later (in 1936). Brawne said a great deal about George:

> In a letter you sent me some time ago you mentioned your brother George in a manner that made me think you had been mislead about him. He is no favorite of mine and he never liked me so that I am not likely to say too much in his favor from affection for him, but I must say I think he is blamed more than he should be. I think him extravagant and selfish, but people in their great zeal make him out much worse than that—Soon after your brother Tom died, my dear John wrote to him offering him any assistance or money in his power.
>
> . . . He [George] had a wife and one child to support, with the prospect of another, I cannot wonder that he should consider them first and as he could not get what he wanted without coming to England he unfortunately came—By that time your brother

[John] wished to marry himself, but he could not refuse the money. It may appear very bad in George to leave him 60 pounds when he owed 80, but he had many reasons to suppose the inconvenience would not last long. Your brother had a book of poems nearly ready to come out (which his illness kept back till the summer) he had a tragedy (*Otho the Great*, which was unsuccessful) which Mr. Brown calculated his share of would be about £200. . . .

George could not foresee his illness—He might be a cause of the dreadful consequences but surely a very indirect and accidental one. . . .

The person who suffered most never thought so very badly of it, he used to say, "George ought not to have done this he should have recollected that I wish to marry myself[25]—but I suppose having a family to provide for makes a man selfish." . . .

. . . I am afraid whenever you have money in your own power you will find him troublesome but my dear girl be very cautious— be warned by what has already happened—and remember he is extravagant at least everyone says so.[26]

Remarkably, although both Fanny Brawne and Charles Brown viewed the discrepancy as £20, others, including John Taylor, apparently believed that George owed John the full £700. Taylor wrote to Michael Drury on 19 February 1821: "John Keats, the Poet, was at that time possessed of about 800£. . . . George borrowed so much of this from John as to leave him 70£ only."[27] Taylor was completely misinformed, and the source of his confusion was John's garbled accounting. Taylor later amended his version to state that earlier in the day John had given Brown £70 and a clutch of bills to pay—in effect, turning his finances over to Brown.

On an emotional level, the Keats brothers were changed persons. George's mind was in America, while John's became fixated on how he would live out his final days. They were separated from each other forever, and not simply by geography. A neurotic and despondent John Keats, unable to obtain any of the Chancery money, fell back into debt and dependency on his friends, who resented George.

Although George's trip to London was necessary, disillusionment set in immediately. These weeks remain the most controversial in George's life. His return to America became the basis of a curiously amoral hand-wringing by generations of Keats scholars who believed that George should have remained with John, oblivious to his wife and child on the frontier.

For his part, John wrote a cheerful postscript to his journal letter to Georgiana, indicating no strains. Then, just days later, after returning coatless from London to Wentworth Place in Hampstead, John had his first lung hemorrhage, foretelling his death one year later. He looked at his blood and remarked to Brown, "This is unfortunate. I know the colour of that blood. It's arterial blood. There's no mistaking that colour." As calmly as he could, he added, "That blood is my death warrant. I must die."[28] He wrote no more letters to George.[29]

Brown discovered that John was taking laudanum, an opium derivative, and forced him to stop, but the poet's depression had set back in.

Getting Established

1820–1826

While George was in London, a signal event occurred that would define Louisville's development and, indirectly, his opportunities over the next two decades. On Christmas Day 1819 a special canal commission established by five states bordering the Ohio River (Ohio, Indiana, Pennsylvania, Virginia, and Kentucky) voted to build the Louisville and Portland Canal. That action ended a rivalry dating to 1804 between factions in Indiana and Kentucky over which side of the falls should be canalled.[1]

Louisville was an entrepôt, a necessary evil for exporters from Pittsburgh, Cincinnati, and the agricultural inlands that had to transship their goods around the falls on their way to New Orleans and European markets. The advent of the canal, the widest such cut engineered in America up to that time, changed everything. Previously, there had been two choices: stevedores could off-load cargoes from upstream paddle wheelers and keelboats in Louisville, cart them a few miles west, and reload them onto downriver vessels; or experienced pilots could attempt to navigate through the chutes, water conditions permitting.

With the canal came two important new industries: commission merchants (wholesalers) and shipbuilders. They were followed by banking and insurance interests. The old frontier town was growing into a mercantile city.

When George left for London, the town was in the grip of the Panic of 1819. The panic—actually a recession, in modern terms—followed a boom period after the War of 1812. The government had eased lending restrictions; disbursed millions of acres of land to settlers who could not pay for it; and, in a classic monetary gaffe, suspended the issuance of specie (hard money—gold or silver). The government had borrowed heavily to finance the War of 1812, and repayments forced a contraction of the economy. The inability of Louisville's merchants and developers to arrange credit dried up business activity. President James Monroe's approval of the canal project, however, provided the stimulus the town needed. During its subsequent construction, the federal government's commitment proved inadequate, so private investment was brought in from Philadelphia and the East, as well as locally.

Having left Liverpool on 1 February 1820, George likely arrived in New York by the end of the second week of March.[2] By 1820 a six-day stage had been established between Philadelphia and Louisville, so he probably arrived back in Kentucky before 1 April. Coincidentally, George carried the first news of the death of King George III, which had occurred on 29 January, the day after he departed London.

Armed with his £700 capital, George was able to rejoin the firm of Prentice and Bakewell, this time as an equity partner, and continue its mill development. The company provided him with a house on the grounds, compensation of 20 percent of the profits, and a one-third ownership in the mill portion of the enterprise. His mill was due to come online just as the town's economy was perking up. A young Englishman, Holliday W. Cood, worked in the mill as a clerk. Daniel Smith became an additional partner.[3]

Within weeks of George's return, he received a letter (now lost), ostensibly from John but actually written by Charles Brown, requesting £200 for John's trip to Italy.[4] Brown's letter referred to the poet's hemorrhagic attack and was likely posted before the end of March. George replied on 18 June 1820, leading with: "Where will our miseries end?" Later he noted, "I have an offer for the Boat which I have accepted, but the party who lives at Natchez (300 miles only near New Orleans) will not receive information that I have accepted his offer for some weeks."[5] This illiquid investment in a boat continued to hang over George. Five months later he wrote to John, "Again and Again I must send bad news. I cannot yet find a purchase for the Boat, and have received no intelligence of the man who offered the price I accepted, it was only 500 dollars more than the sum she cleared me last year. If I lowered the price 500 dollars it would be as difficult of Sale. I hope to be able to send you money soon until I do I shall be fast approaching the blue devil temperament. Your inevitable distresses are subject of conversations to us almost every day."[6] This steamboat remains one of the unknowns in George's story. It was probably neither the *Henderson* nor the *Zebulon M. Pike,* his suspected investments made while in Henderson. Did it provide George with income during 1819, as he implies? Finally, why did John believe that the boat investment had been made with a loan from him?

There may have been one other letter between the brothers, also lost.[7] George, busily trying to set up in Louisville, was perplexed by the lack of correspondence from Haslam and his sister Fanny, but he had no way of knowing the terrible things they were saying about him in London, or that the poet's friends were not mentioning George in John's presence.

In addition to worrying over John's situation, George was having difficulty with the mill. As he wrote to John on 8 November 1820, "Had the Mill been finished within *a year* of the time agreed upon in my contract with the Builders you should not have wanted money now, it was not finished with 21 mos, such a disappointment driving me to every shift to live, [my] rent and servant hire unpaid, will weigh heavy upon me some time."[8] He did not anticipate being unable to live in his own home, on his own property, until the autumn of 1821.

George's letters about the boat and the mill lack a precise chronology. He likely invested in the boat in late 1818 or early 1819. Since a sale was pending in November 1820, this unnamed boat clearly had not sunk, as had been rumored of one of his other boat investments. If a sale did take place after November 1820, those proceeds likely went into the mill. Since the mill had been in construction for twenty-one months at the time of the November 1820 letter, the project must have begun by February 1819, which would be a reasonable guess as to the Keatses' arrival date in Louisville. That his contractor was running late may have resulted from George's inability to pay or perhaps to his absence while in London.

Upon his return to Louisville, George wrote to John, "Almost every day I am in the woods superintending the felling of Trees and cutting saw-logs, and the ground tinged [?] with leaves reminds me of your little prospect of breathing a milder air this winter."[9] John had included in his last remaining letter to Georgiana the line, "I hope while I am young to live retired in the Country."[10] In addition, there had been the now-lost correspondence about John's wintering in Italy.

Finally, on 27 April 1821, the Bakewells and Prentices sold George a bloc of land on Water Street, with buildings, for $6,000. The land was carved out from their twelve-acre foundry establishment and included the mill. The indenture deed, recorded with the Jefferson County Clerk, Worden Pope, was not delivered to Keats until 18 April 1822, suggesting that he did not make the initial payment for another year, while he got the mill up and running.[11]

George and Georgiana wasted no time expanding their family. Georgiana Emily was followed by Rosalind, likely named for Shakespeare's heroine in *As You Like It*, born 18 December 1820.[12] Next came Emma Frances, born 25 October 1823, named in part for her grandmother Frances Jennings Keats. The name Emma may have had literary origins: Wordsworth's noms de plume for his sister Dorothy were Emma and Emmeline, and there was Jane Austen's Emma Woodhouse in *Emma,* published in 1815.[13] Isabel Keats—likely named for Isabella, the heroine in "Isabella, or the Pot of Basil," who in turn was likely named for the poet's friend Isabella Jones—was born 28 February 1825.[14] Four more children arrived later. The Keatses bought an elegant leather-bound Bible, published in Philadelphia in 1821, which survives to the present day.[15]

George was ill in 1821, telling Fanny, "Last year I should have done *very well* but for the extreme sickliness of the season; besides being (ailing) positively confined to my bed 3 mos as well as my dear Wife and younges[t] child Rosaline, we were ailing 2 mos more, the child is still poorly. Extra of my *usual former* expenses and the loss attending the Mill's not working 3 mos (in consequence of the sickness of the hands, and mine) I spent £150."[16]

Although George did not identify his illness, Louisville was being swept with a form of yellow fever at the time.[17] The cause was a number of stagnant ponds dotting the city, festering in the summer heat. In 1823 the state sponsored a lottery to raise $40,000 to drain the ponds, as had been previously recommended by Henry McMurtrie. Also in that year, Coleman Rogers, who became George's personal physician, arrived in Louisville after separating his practice from that of the eminent Daniel Drake in Cincinnati.

George bemoaned his problems getting established in the community: "The goal to which we stretch is a future residence in England, and a communion once more with those who understand us and love us. . . . Here we are not understood if our conduct will bear two constructions, the worst is put upon it. Altho we have connections we have no genuine exercise of kindly feelings but between ourselves."[18] George continued this theme years later in a letter to his sister Fanny: "Our circumstances will not allow us to associate with what is called the first or in other words the richest people here." Yet he noted in that same February 1824 letter, "Last year [1823] was the first year that I realized more than my expense, and my prospects next year are I think better."[19]

He also wrote in 1824 that "Rosalind . . . is not so quick as Georgiana perhaps in consequence of having suffered so much sickness."[20] Rosalind died on 2 April 1826, at age five. According to family legend, she did not speak until age four. George wrote of her, "We think there was something *peculiar* in our child. . . . She had suffered so much sickness, had been so much indulged by us, she had no pleasure out of our society." He described her loss with some of the most tender and emotional words in all his assembled writings: "She was exquisitely beautiful, and the admiration of the whole town, whose sympathy justifies us in our opinion of her. I built much on her affectionate disposition being a Family link to hold her more volatile sisters together in bond of amity when we are no longer with them or when we are too old to influence their affections. She is however gone with all her charms real or imaginary."[21] Rosalind was buried in Louisville's old city graveyard, bounded by Eleventh, Twelfth, and Jefferson Streets. Six years later the city closed the graveyard, giving families thirty days to remove any remains and reinter them in the new Western Cemetery, located between Seventeenth and Eighteenth Streets, along Jefferson. There is no record that Rosalind's remains were moved.[22]

By 1825, George's first business venture, the sawmill, was throwing off sufficient profits to enable investment in a gristmill for the grinding of wheat, corn, and other agricultural produce brought in from surrounding farms and destined for distant markets. As he wrote to Charles Dilke on 20 April 1825:

> I have now the prospect of being more completely occupied in business than hitherto, being far advanced in erecting a Grist Mill (in addition to the Saw Mill) that will grind 75 Barrels of Flour every 24 hours, Of these establishments, when combined the most extensive in this country, I am the entire manager, viz, cheif engineer, cashier, clerk, without the interference or controul of the other owners except that I am bound to make settlement of the Books once a year. I own 1/3rd of the establishment, and receive 20 per Cent of the profits for my services, which of itself when the Grist Mill will be in operation will be sufficient to support my Family.[23]

George's last recorded mention of the gristmill was in an 1828 letter to Dilke: "I am now very busy, both mind and body, the new crop of wheat has commenced pouring in."[24] An 1829 notice in the *Louisville Public Advertiser* explained the dissolution of the business:

NOTICE.

THE PARTNERSHIP between the subscribers under the name of KEATS & ATKINSON is di-solved by mutual consent. All persons indebted to the concern are requested to settle their accounts with either partner without delay, and those to whom they are indebted will please present their accounts for payment.

GEORGE KEATS.
RICH'D. ATKINSON.

A second notice stated:

> STEAM FLOUR AND SAW MILLS.
>
> The business heretofore carried on by GEORGE KEATS and KEATS & ATKINSON will be continued by the subscribers, who will give the highest market price for WHEAT, delivered at their mill, on the bank of the river, corner of Eighth and Water streets. They are now prepared to execute orders for sawed timber of every description on the shortest notice.
>
> RICH'D. & JOHN ATKINSON[25]

Louisville's first city directory, published in 1832, listed four flour millers, suggesting that the field was too competitive for George.[26] His primary business going forward was the sawmill at First, Brook, Main, and Washington Streets.[27]

Despite all this activity, George continued to complain, writing to Dilke in 1825: "We seem liked as man and woman, but distrusted I may say disliked, as English People, we are still thoroughly English, and have not learnt with most foreigners the art of flattering the *egregious, excessive* vanity of the Americans . . . we are therefore kept a little out of society, which however from its extreme dryness, and insipidity, is no great deprivation; we are looked upon as proud, and treated with consideration, and respect, but not with kindness or familiarity." The same letter, however, presaged the beginning of his acceptance in the community. George noted, "We have a Philosophical Society here, not altogether uninformed, or unphilosophical, but certainly unpoetical, I am a lately elected member and in preference to many influential men who were at the same time refused. To night they will meet at my House and discuss 'whether the ancients or moderns are the greater.' We had the question of Phrenology warmly contested, what is thought of it now in England, I think well of it."[28]

An ever-present issue for Keats and for all proprietors in Louisville was the scarcity of labor. The "necessary evil" or "peculiar institution" of slavery was the solution. George had been sufficiently opposed to the institution to bypass the American South for Illinois, a free state north of the Ohio River. But Birkbeck's disheveled community, undeveloped due to the lack of labor, quickly disabused him of his free labor principles.

The conundrum in Louisville was that a plentiful supply of slaves, who were usually treated moderately well and accorded surprising levels of freedom and independence, often worked alongside unskilled whites, and both were paid poorly. This discouraged higher-skilled immigrants from Germany and central Europe from settling in Louisville; they refused to work for slave wages and chose to live in Pittsburgh or Cincinnati instead. Louisville's manufacturing development fell behind that of its northern neighbors precisely because those other cities attracted the skilled immigrant labor required.

Faced with an inadequate free labor pool, Keats advertised:

NEGROES WANTED

I want to purchase ten negro men between the ages of 16 and 25 years.

GEO. KEATS[29]

His advertisement was answered by Dr. Urban Epinitis Ewing, who owned slaves as a capital investment. Keats chose an intermediate alternative to outright ownership, hiring slaves from Ewing for about $70 per year, plus food and medical expenses.[30] Keats overcame his antislavery scruples and participated in the system because it was, in effect, his only choice.

The slaves working in the woodlots and in the mills often had the option of not returning to Ewing, or other owners, at night. They could remain downtown if they chose to spend their small cash incomes (granted in addition to the annual labor contracts, in which they did not share) on lodgings. Nevertheless, the cruelty of the system was evident when the children of slaves, as well as surplus slaves, were sold downriver, often to work on Mississippi cotton plantations under harsh conditions.

George's outlook shifted as time went by, and he assimilated. Writing to his brother-in-law Valentin Llanos in 1828, he opined, "I am stained . . . [as] an Englishman."[31] Ten years later, he wrote Dilke, "I am now a Kentuckian."[32]

Louisville's politics during George's early residency supported President James Monroe, a popular anti-Federalist. Monroe visited the town in June 1819 and was feted enthusiastically. As Ben Casseday wrote of the evening, "general hilarity and good feeling distinguished the occasion."[33] Keats hired as his attorney James Guthrie, a Jacksonian Democrat who was popular in the town because of his nonstop boosterism for civic improvements of all sorts. Guthrie was an early proponent of the canal and later became president of the canal company. He went on to serve as secretary of the treasury under President Franklin Pierce. The canal's completion in 1830 assured Louisville's commercial dominance in the region. George was picking his associates and friends well.

Keats had various thoughts on American government. In 1825 he wrote: "I . . . have attended enough to Politics to be able to see the bearings of our lax governments upon the morals of a People already sufficiently corrupt."[34] His outrage grew over the years, leading to an 1832 screed sent to Dilke:

> I am glad to see reform so prosperous in England, but I fear uni-versal suffrage; in this country where we have so much elbow room it is evidently a curse—we are getting blacker and blacker in political villainy, untill all is fair in politics—and all because the ignorant form a majority and can be easily misled by mean, art-ful, office seeking politicians. You would be astonished to see how shamelessly the press is carried on; lying, slandering blackguard-ing, changing opinion with every change of circumstan[ces], men are followed to the entire neglect of the interests of the country[.] . . . Demogoguism is the cause, and universal suffrage is the Demo-gogues staff. . . . Since I have taken an interest in American politics and written a few articles for the papers on prominent subjects, I am looked upon as a good republican, and in tolerable good odour with my townsmen. Altho' I consider the American repub-lic as the best possible for an intelligent and virtuous people . . . I do not consider the Americans either sufficiently virtuous or intel-ligent to perpetuate their institutions unimpaired to a very remote posterity.[35]

George's political transformation to a Kentucky Whig was complete. He was dependent on loans from the Bank of the United States, which Andrew Jackson closed. And he worried that the comportment of Jackson's follow-ers, who trashed the White House during inaugural events, augured poorly for the future of democracy. American politics was not as seemly as the workings of Parliament. Of course, William Pitt, who was to the left of the Tories in Parliament, described himself as an independent Whig. George's political journey to Whiggery was not all that far.

George Keats's circle of friends appears to have begun with the Bakewell brothers, Tom and Billy, who saved him from Henderson and provided employment, a loan, and a business plan in Louisville. Nicholas Berthoud, another Audubon in-law and resident of Shippingport, befriended George, later joining him on the Ohio Bridge Commission.

Keats partnered in 1829 with John P. Young to acquire twenty acres, plus a road, between Beargrass Creek and the Ohio River. This land was close to Keats's lumber mill, also situated between the creek and the river.[36] Young had his own mill, and in 1842, after George's death, he combined the two interests by buying out Keats's equity from the estate. The lumber merchants obviously both competed against and cooperated with each other.

Daniel Smith, a Catholic and a town trustee during the 1820s, joined the lumber firm in 1830. Smith posted a notice, suggesting that his was the majority position:

NOTICE.

DANIEL SMITH having taken GEORGE KEATS into partnership in the Lumber business, it will be conducted hereafter under the firm of SMITH & KEATS.[37]

For the next dozen years, Smith and Keats were coinvestors in multiple properties, notably the Louisville Hotel.

Community leader James Guthrie was George's friend as well as his attorney. Mann Butler, the principal of the Jefferson Seminary and a historian, was another early friend. Butler had spent eleven years of his childhood in Chelsea, so they shared London ties. After Christ Episcopal Church was chartered in 1822, it solicited 182 subscriptions, including one from Keats, for its construction. Rector James Craik later wrote of George, "He is described as a gentleman of fine address, literary in his tastes, like his brother of delicate sensibility, and commanding the respect of all who knew him, and the warm affection of all who knew him intimately."[38] The Keatses may not have been rigorous Episcopalians, however; they shifted their interest to Unitarianism after 1829.

Later, the circle continued to widen as George joined more and more boards. The appendix lists many of these acquaintances, gained as George's fortunes improved, his time available for community service increased, and his English attitude softened into an acceptance of Kentucky mores.

While George was laboring long hours throughout 1820–1821 to establish his sawmill, events in London were souring, unbeknownst to him. In a well-chronicled but swift succession of events, John's physical condition deteriorated. A month after his 3 February 1820 hemorrhage, he began having heart palpitations, possibly a consequence of the starvation diet imposed by his doctor, George Rodd. By May 1820 John had moved twice, Brown having leased out his house so he could visit Scotland again. In June the poet suffered from blood-spitting attacks and moved into Leigh Hunt's home for care. By July he was again advised to seek a better clime in Italy. His hemorrhages recurred in August, and on 17 September he boarded the *Maria Crowther* with Joseph Severn, bound for Rome. They arrived on 15 November, and John suffered a relapse on 10 December. From that date until his death on 23 February 1821, he was apartment-bound aside the Spanish Steps. None of these details were known by George.

John Keats's farewell letter was to Brown, dated 30 November 1820. He wrote:

> I am well disappointed in hearing good news from George,—for it runs in my head that we shall all die young. . . . Write to George as soon as you receive this, and tell him how I am, as far as you can guess;—and also a note to my sister—who walks about in my imagination like a ghost—she is so like Tom. I can scarcely bid you good bye even in a letter. I always made an awkward bow.
>
> God bless you!
> John Keats[39]

He wrote no more.

There is no evidence that Brown wrote to George as John had requested. It is unknown who notified him of the poet's death, although it may well have been Brown or Haslam. The news from Rome, transmitted through London, would have taken at least two months to reach Kentucky, making it late April or early May.

A wholly new and unwanted chapter was about to open in George's life.

WHO FAILED THE POET?

1820–1821

John Keats's death triggered three ugly sequences of events. First was an immediate and epic spasm of finger-pointing and guilt transference around the question of who failed the poet. Second was a ten-year slog to unravel and finally settle the poet's affairs in the broader context of his grandfather's and mother's estates at Chancery. Finally, there was the matter of who should take responsibility for the poet's legacy (not resolved until Richard Monckton Milnes's 1848 publication of *Life, Letters, and Literary Remains of John Keats*).

A number of John's contemporaries, particularly Charles Brown, followed by several Keats biographers, cast George in a harsh light. George's ability to defend himself from the attacks and to contribute to John's legacy was seriously disadvantaged by his remoteness in Kentucky.

To summarize the matter of who failed the poet, the blame falls into four realms. First were the conservative critics who demoralized Keats, sapping him of the creative energy to continue. Second were the doctors who provided abysmal care and the friends who encouraged him to take unwise health risks, including the final trip to Rome. Third were those, led by Brown, who blamed George for a lack of financial support. And finally there was the poet himself, whose disregard for his health amounted to a virtual death wish after repeated exposures to consumption.

Painter Benjamin Robert Haydon kept a journal, and his 1816 entries about meeting John Keats and hearing his childhood story constitute the best narrative of the early years. Haydon wrote: "He used sometimes to say to his brother he feared he should never be a poet, and if he was not he would destroy himself."[1] Four years later, in his final letter to Brown, John confirmed the point: "There is one thought enough to kill me—I have been well, healthy, alert &c, walking with her—and now—the knowledge of contrast, feeling for light and shade, all that information (primitive sense) necessary for a poem are great enemies to the recovery of the stomach."[2] To paraphrase, he was saying that he knew what was required for poetry, but he could not create it and also live. It was the classic death wish, uttered toward the end of his "posthumous" year.[3]

Before his death, Keats asked Joseph Severn to inscribe his tombstone simply with these words:

> HERE LIES ONE WHOSE NAME WAS WRIT IN WATER

However, Severn and Brown, on their own initiative, prefixed Keats's inscription with an angry addition:

> THIS GRAVE CONTAINS ALL THAT WAS MORTAL, OF A YOUNG ENGLISH POET, WHO ON HIS DEATHBED, IN THE BITTERNESS OF HIS HEART, AT THE MALICIOUS POWER OF HIS ENEMIES, DESIRED THESE WORDS TO BE ENGRAVEN ON HIS TOMB STONE

The "enemies" were the critics who had mocked Keats and his poetry, labeling him a "young apothecary" and a "Cockney." These attacks devastated the poet emotionally, sapping his interest in poetry and hastening his downward spiral to death. Severn's intemperate citation was probably a reflection of what he had heard from an overwrought Keats during his lucid moments.

First among the critical reviews was John Wilson Croker's in the *Quarterly Review*, a literary and political periodical edited by William Gifford and generally aligned with the Tories. Croker (1780–1857) was a graduate of Trinity College, Dublin; a conservative Irish statesman; secretary of the Admiralty; and an author with little patience for the younger school of poets. Writing unsigned in April 1818, he opined (while acknowledging he had not read *Endymion*):

> It is not that Mr Keats (if that be his real name, for we almost doubt that any man in his sense would put his real name to such a rhapsody) it is not, we say, that the author has not powers of language, rays of fancy, and gleams of genius—he has all these; but he is unhappily a disciple of the new school of what has been somewhere called Cockney poetry; which may be defined to consist of the most incongruous ideas in the most uncouth language. . . .
>
> [Mr Keats] is a copyist of Mr Hunt; but he is more unintelligible, almost as rugged, twice as diffuse, and ten times more tiresome and absurd than his prototype, who, though he impudently

presumed to seat himself in the chair of criticism, and to measure his own poetry by his own standard, yet generally had a meaning. But Mr Keats had advanced no dogmas which he was bound to support by examples; his nonsense therefore is quite gratuitous; he writes it for his own sake.[4]

A second review appeared in June 1818 in the *British Critic*, written from an establishment church point of view. Though negative, it had no serious impact. Then came the most damaging of the reviews. *Blackwood's Magazine* was the organ of the Scottish Tories; it had been launched in 1817 as a rejoinder to the Whigs' *Edinburgh Review*. Initially devoted to politics, *Blackwood's* brought in John Gibson Lockhart (1794–1854) as editor; he initiated a series of brilliant cultural reviews, first attacking the Cockney school in October 1817. The August 1818 issue of *Blackwood's* included a review, signed by "Z" (a common practice), that savaged Keats personally and rocked him emotionally. Some of the review's extracts are reproduced here:

The readers of [Leigh Hunt's] *Examiner* newspaper were informed some time ago, by a solemn paragraph, in Mr Hunt's best style, of the appearance of two new stars of glorious magnitude and splendour in the poetical horizon of the land of Cockaigne. One of these turned out, by and by, to be no other than Mr John Keats. The precocious adulation confirmed the wavering apprentice in his desire to quit the gallipots,[5] and at the same time excited in his too susceptible mind a fatal admiration for the character and talents of the most worthless and affected versifiers of our time. . . .

Mr Keats has adopted the loose, nerveless versification, and Cockney rhyme of the poet of Rimini [Hunt]; but in fairness to that gentleman, we must add, that the defects of the system are tenfold more conspicuous in his disciple's work than in his own. Mr Hunt is a small poet, but he is a clever man. Mr Keats is a still smaller poet, and he is a boy of pretty abilities, which he has done everything in his power to spoil. . . .

We venture to make one small prophecy, that his bookseller [Taylor] will not a second time venture 50 quid upon any thing he can write. It is a better and wiser thing to be a starved apothecary than a starved poet; so back to the shop Mr John, back to "plasters, pills, and ointment boxes," &c. But, for Heaven's sake, young Sangrado,[6] be a little more sparing of extenuatives and soporifics in your practice than you have been in your poetry.[7]

Lockhart, the son-in-law of Sir Walter Scott, never admitted responsibility for the review. Nor did John Wilson (1785–1854), who often used the pseudonym Christopher North and was *Blackwood's* principal writer; however, Wilson did acknowledge writing (anonymously) a vicious parody of the rival *Edinburgh Review*. Both Lockhart and Wilson were Oxford educated. Wilson kept a home in Windermere, where he socialized with the old-school Wordsworth.[8]

Keats's Oxford friend, Benjamin Bailey, faulted himself for revealing personal information about Keats to Lockhart at a July 1818 dinner party that included his future brother-in-law, George Robert Gleig, a staff member of *Blackwood's*. Bailey, in a series of letters to Taylor and later to Milnes, continued to believe as late as 1849 that Lockhart and Wilson were the Cockneys' antagonists.[9]

Haydon, contrarily, believed that "Z," whose reviews had been under way since 1817, was actor Daniel Terry and that his target was actually Leigh Hunt. As Haydon wrote, "Hunt had exasperated Terry by neglecting to notice his theatrical efforts. Terry was a friend of Sir Walter's [Scott], shared keenly his political hatreds, and was also most intimate with the Blackwood party, which had begun a course of attacks on all who showed the least liberalism of thinking, or who were praised by or known to the *Examiner*. . . . On Keats the effect was melancholy. He became morbid and silent, would call and sit whilst I was painting for hours without speaking a word."[10]

Keats wrote to Augustus Hessey in October 1818, "My own domestic criticism has given me pain without comparison beyond what Blackwood or the (Edinburgh) Quarterly could possibly inflict, and also when I feel I am right, no external praise can give me such a glow as my own solitary reperception & ratification of what is fine."[11] Later that month he wrote to George and Georgiana, "I do not know who wrote those in the (Quarterly) Chronicle—This is a mere matter of the moment—I think I shall be among the English Poets after my death."[12] The reviews festered, however. When Keats wrote to the couple again in February 1819, he lamented, "These Reviews too are getting more and more powerful and especially the Quarterly—They are like a superstition which the more it prostrates the Crowd and the longer it continues the more powerful it becomes just in proportion to their increasing weakness."[13]

Immediately after Keats's death, Percy Bysshe Shelley—who, along with his wife, Mary Godwin Shelley, had also been attacked by Croker— defended Keats against the *Quarterly* and Lockhart in his preface to *Adonais:* "The savage criticism on his Endymion, which appeared in the Quarterly Review, produced the most violent effect on his susceptible mind; the agitation thus originated ended in the rupture of a blood-vessel in the lungs; a rapid consumption ensued."[14] Neither Shelley nor Keats ever realized that Croker was the author of the review in the *Quarterly,* thinking instead that editor William Gifford was their nemesis. Lord Byron, who shared with Keats a mutual antipathy, then rejoindered, "'Tis strange the mind, that fiery particle, / Should let itself be snuffed out by an article."[15] Shelley went on to comment, perhaps obliquely referring to George, "[Keats] was exasperated by . . . those on whom he had lavished his fortune and his care."[16]

George Keats later wrote in frustration to Charles Dilke, "Blackwood's magazine has fallen into my hands, I could have walked 100 miles to have dirked him a l'Americaine, for his cruelly associating John in the cockney school, and other blackguardisms."[17]

William Hazlitt wrote repeatedly about the tragedy. His epitaph may have concluded matters as well as any: "To be a Reformer, the friend of a Reformer, or the friend's friend of a Reformer, is as much a man's peace, reputation, or even life is worth. Answer, if it is not so, pale shade of Keats."[18]

The second group of candidates to blame for the poet's shortened life was his own friends and a half dozen medical advisers. After John moved away from his initial physician, Dr. Solomon Sawrey, a venereal disease specialist, he came into the hands of George Rodd, a Hampstead surgeon, and then Dr. Robert Bree, an expert in asthma and psychosomatic illness. As John wrote to his sister, Fanny, on 21 April 1820, "The Doctor [Bree] assures me that there is nothing the matter with me except nervous irritability and a general weakness of the whole system which has preceded from my anxiety of mind of late years and the too great excitement of poetry."[19] Given the severe bleeding from the lungs, either the doctor was withholding the truth from Keats, or Keats was dissembling with Fanny.

Keats, who continued to hemorrhage, had consulted Dr. George Darling and Dr. William Lambe by the end of June. He got around to telling Fanny Brawne on 5 July, "They talk of my going to Italy."[20] Even George, in Louisville, had heard about the Italy trip prior to 18 June, when he wrote, "Since your health requires it to Italy you must and shall go."[21] Brown, who had alerted George, had obviously fixed on an Italian venue as early as April.

By August, the group of friends, including Taylor, Woodhouse, Reynolds, and Haslam (Brown was away, walking in Scotland), had made the decision, and Keats and Severn boarded the *Maria Crowther* on 17 September. Severn wrote toward the end of the voyage, "I am horror struck at his sufferings on this voyage,—all that could be fatal to him in air and diet—with the want [of] medicine—and conveniences he has weather'd."[22]

Keats was next attended by physician James Clark (his sixth), who wrote on 27 November, "Keats arrived here [in Rome] about a week ago. . . . The chief part of his disease, as far as I can yet see seems seated in his Stomach. . . . If my opinion be correct we may throw medicine to the dogs."[23] Clark also brought in an Italian physician for consultation, but by 3 January he had given up, writing, "His stomach is ruined and the state of his mind is the worst possible for one in his condition, and will undoubtedly hurry on an event that I fear is not far distant. . . . When I first saw him I thought something might [have been] done, but now I fear the prospect is a hopeless one."[24]

In retrospect, the decision by Keats's London doctors and friends to send him to Rome only hastened his death, due to the ordeal of travel. Clark, consistent with English medical practice, starved John, giving him a daily anchovy and piece of toast—certainly no way to cure a tubercular patient. These well-intentioned treatments made a gruesome death all the worse. Midway through the treatment, Clark said to Severn, "Keats should never have left England—the distance had made too great a progress to receive benefit from this Climate . . . nothing in [the] world could [ever] cure him when he left England—by this journey his life has been shortened—and rendered more painful."[25]

Keats had brought along a jar of opium to ingest when he decided that recovery was hopeless. Severn consulted with Clark, and they removed the opium, thereby depriving Keats of any vestige of control over the end of his life, heightening his excruciating pain, and prolonging death.

Brown's last communication to Keats began with a few self-centered lines: "And so you still wish me to follow you to Rome? . . . Little could be gained, if anything, by letting my house at this time of the year, and the consequence would be a heavy additional expence which I cannot possibly afford,—unless it were a matter of necessity, and I see none while you are in such good hands as Severn's."[26] Brown was busy in London, wresting his illegitimate son away from the child's mother.

In the most transparent of efforts to assign blame for John's death, Brown trained his sights on George. As early as 10 December 1820 he wrote to Haslam, "What is to be done with George? Will he ever dare to come among his brother's friends?"[27] This coincided with Haslam's 4 December note to Severn, advising him to "avoid speaking of George to him [John]— George is a scoundrel!"[28] Severn's first biographer, William Sharp, footnoted the quote with a comment: "Haslam wrote this remark about George under a misapprehension. He and Charles Brown were always harsh in their judgement of their friend's brother."[29]

Brown continued to express his pique in a 5 January 1821 letter to Haslam: "Should you hear news of that *money brother* pray let me know. —as for remittances from him,—we must dream about them.—Wait a month, and if George remains still silent, give him such a sting as he has had from me,—it will pierce deeper from you than from me."[30] With this passage, Brown introduced the term *money brother* into Keatsiana. Brown's wrath continued, and he wrote to Severn on 15 January: "Do you know how George has treated him? I sit planning schemes of vengeance upon his head. Should his brother die exposure and infamy shall consign him to perpetual exile. I will have no mercy."[31]

George, weeks behind in the communications, replied to Brown on 3 March, unaware of John's death: "The coldness of your [21 December] letter explains itself; I hope John is not impressed with the same sentiments . . . whatever errors you may fall into thro' kindness for my Brother however injurious to me, are easily forgiven."[32] George went on to explain patiently that his previous letters to Brown, Haslam, and John, in which he described the illiquidity of his finances, had all gone unanswered.

Severn made no contemporary complaints against George, although he later endorsed Brown's campaign of blame. Severn, in the vortex of events in Rome, was always very concerned about money, as was John. After first meeting Keats on 27 November, Dr. Clark had written, "I'm afraid the Idea of his expenses operates on his mind and some plan must be adopted to remove this if possible."[33] Clark wrote again on 13 January about expenses.

To help defray costs, John Taylor scrambled to raise a subscription totaling £150, which he relayed to Rome shortly after 3 February. He then promptly wrote to George on 17 February, invoicing him for the £150 and also observing that his losses on Keats's poems totaled another £110.[34] Taylor sent the original invoice to his relation Michael Drury in Philadelphia for collection. Knowing that Drury had no legal power to claim the £150, Taylor wrote a nasty memorandum in which he stated that George had left for America with a loan from John, taking all but £70 of the £800 possessed by the poet. Taylor's misunderstanding derived from John's confusion (caused by Abbey) as to whether the remittances to George from Tom's estate were loans or final distributions. Taylor went on, "But if he h[as a] greater Regard for Money than for his own Reputation, let [him] be made acquainted with the Consequences—his Brother is on his Death-bed; his life is a Subject of public Interest, and it will be written. These Facts will be therein stated . . . Georges Refusal to spare anything for the Relief of such a Brother will be—what I want to express & hope Language will not be necessary to make known."[35]

Taylor, whose solicitude toward the poet is unquestioned, was nevertheless writing four days before Keats's death, willing to slander George to ensure that his gift to John would be repaid. George eventually did reimburse Taylor the £150, and he dropped the issue. Taylor advertised within two months of the poet's death that he intended to write his biography, but the project never got off the ground; all the Keats materials held by George and by Brown were unavailable to him.

Brown did not let go of his anger so easily, and he made certain that the circle knew about it. His string of correspondence, growing into a vitriolic friendship-ending argument with Dilke, continued for seventeen years, until 1838. As Dilke wrote to George that year, "Brown & myself have never been friends since the discussions of which I sometime since [favored] apprised you—& our formal civility terminated lately because we did not flatter him about a silly book which he was pleased to publish."[36] Five years earlier, Dilke had written to George about Brown, "the correspondence about *your brother's* life has put a stop to all communication. . . . I regret this because our intimacy & friendship *was of five & thirty years standing.*"[37]

Twenty years after John's death, before sailing to New Zealand, Brown wrote a final blast to Milnes, accompanying his own flawed effort at a Keats biography. His 19 March 1841 letter concludes: "You will perceive, I have entirely spared Mr George Keats—not for want of proof. Without giving his name, he is included among those who borrowed *small* sums from Keats. Do you approve of my forbearance? The evidence against Mr George is incontrovertible, but does not lie in a small compass. Mr [Charles] Dilke, of the Athenaeum paper, denies the evidence, and, though he stands alone, has chosen to quarrel bitterly with me for my statement."[38] In other words, John had transferred his own misunderstanding of his finances to Brown, who garbled them further and caused a senseless twenty-year dispute with both George and Dilke—a dispute that deferred the publication of Keats's posthumous poems and, more importantly, deferred the poet's legacy. Brown's biographer, Eric Hall McCormick, assessed the preceding passage as follows: "Where they can be checked, the facts and dates are wrong, inspiring as little confidence as the conversations that accompany them, recalled in detail at a distance of more than two decades."[39]

Skeptical historians have noted that both William Dilke and Richard Abbey, as well as John Hamilton Reynolds, examined the accounts and fully exonerated George. When George left John the second time, in 1820, after divvying up accounts, he handed the poet £60, which proved to be £20 less than John's current debts. George likely believed that John had some royalty income headed his way from poetry volumes sold and from *Otho the Great*, although that proved not to be the case. Brown picked up the slack, plus paying a portion of Keats's expenses going forward. The £20 on which Brown fixated became his proxy for a deeper resentment and even hatred of George.[40]

George's own view, stated to Dilke, was characteristically straightforward: "If I did not feel fully persuaded that my motive was to acquire an independence to support us all in case of necessity, I never should forgive myself for leaving him, some extraordinary exertion was necessary to retrieve our affairs from the gradual decline they were suffering—that exertion I made whether wisely, or not, future events had to decide. After all Blackwood and the Qua[r]terly associated with our family desease Consumption were ministers of death sufficiently venemous, cruel and deadly to have consigned one of less sensibility to a premature grave."[41]

And to his sister, Fanny, George wrote, "When I heard of John's death I reproached myself for having left one so sensitive and hypochondriacal to the bare world, when I perhaps was the only person in it who knew him well enough, who was fitted to releive him of its friction, who was qualified to make things go easy with him. I cannot help thinking that he might now be living if I had remained with him, it is however no little consolation to me and honorable to his Friends that he should have met with so many perseveringly disinterested services at every point that he needed them."[42]

Finally, the poet himself may have presaged all this in a few gloomy lines about mankind written to Georgiana in January 1820: "The more I know of Men the more I know how to value entire liberality in any of them. Thank God there are a great many who will sacrifice their worldly interest for a friend: I wish there were more who would sacrifice their passions. The worst of Men are those whose self interests are their passion—the next those whose passions are their self-interest. Upon the whole I dislike Mankind."[43] A year later John was concerned about deathbed finances, but he heard nothing from George.

The answer to the question of who failed Keats is that they all failed him, and he failed himself. Severn and the Brawnes were the friends who unstintingly served his cause. Woodhouse and Taylor and, to a lesser extent, Haslam were always there for John. But Brown's relationship with the poet—the closest John had, other than with brothers George and Tom—was often compromised by his own unusual issues.

George was above the finger-pointing. He wrote to Dilke, "I hope to visit England . . . to express personally my gratitude and thanks to that Generous Fellow Rice, and those kind Friends Reynolds, Severn, Brown and particularly yourself."[44]

Aside from all these misguided decisions by the people around him, which germs killed the poet? Frances Jennings Keats may have initially infected her son with a tubercle that remained latent for eight years. John spent a year dressing the wounds of terminally ill patients at Guy's Hospital, resulting in constant exposure to primitive hygienic conditions. Tom Keats, desperately ill for two years before his 1818 death, was nursed by John at close quarters in Well Walk, another likely source of infection.

After returning from Oxford in October 1817, John took mercury for either a venereal disease or depression, commencing his three-year downward health spiral. On 6 June 1818 John was too ill to leave home, yet three weeks later he departed on an arduous and rainy walking tour in the north. On 22 July 1818 he was soaked on the Isle of Mull, slept on a shepherd's floor, and contracted such a sore throat (later determined to be laryngeal tuberculosis) that he had to terminate the trip and return home.

Following Tom's death, Keats traveled during much of 1819, with a drumbeat of references to sore throats, night coaches, and feeling rather unwell. In 1820, after the initial lung hemorrhage during which John self-diagnosed his impending death, he continued to record bitter days, high fever, heart palpitations, and then, unaccountably, a plan to repeat the Scottish walking tour (it was aborted, and Brown went alone).[45]

Throughout 1819 and 1820 Severn gave Keats commonsense advice that was ignored by the poet. Even Keats seemed to understand that consumption was not simply a family disease and might be contagious. In a final discussion with Severn, he asked, "Did you ever see anyone die? . . . well then I pity you poor Severn. . . . Now you must be firm for it will not last long." He cautioned his friend not to inhale his dying breaths.[46]

In the end, it was John's own indifference to his health, his reckless behavior, and an overarching death wish that hastened his demise. The efforts of his young friends to blame George were risible.

SETTLING AFFAIRS

1821–1828

Central to the relationship between George and John was their code-pendency, at the core of which were money issues. John was somewhere between oblivious and irresponsible when it came to financial matters, whereas George was solvent but a rather sketchy bookkeeper during his London years. Finances became contentious after the scrupulous, if poorly informed, Charles Brown came between the brothers. The cast of Keats advisers, including Abbey, Reynolds, Rice, Walton, and Gliddon, who could have clarified dealings for the boys, did not. The overwhelming irony is that their financial predicaments were unnecessary because the money was there, in a mix of Jennings trusts maintained for the Keatses, without their knowledge, by the Chancery Court.

No Keats biographer (all of them being poets or academics) has attempted to parse the substantial middle-class estate of John Jennings, with the exception of Robert Gittings. What follows is an effort to simplify and clarify the family finances, which lie at the heart of George's reputational problems among many Keats biographers. If, as Gittings claims, the Keats family history was akin to a Greek tragedy, then George was as much a victim of the tragedy as John. The poet believed he was impoverished during his most prolific writing years. Both brothers were the unknowing heirs to a substantial middle-class inheritance, but neither fully understood his financial affairs. Brown's ill-informed letter of 10 December 1820 to William Haslam blamed George for John's financial plight, even though George was also in the dark about the Chancery inheritance. Starting with Brown's 1820 missive and proceeding through numerous Keats biographies until 1964, when Gittings correctly interpreted the original John Jennings will, the misunderstanding persisted.[1]

The historical irony is that John Keats's impoverishment coincided with his finest poetry, giving the inheritance a signal importance. It took the lawyers seven years to unravel the situation, with long-distance prodding by George and the beneficial intervention of Charles Dilke. Another

130 years elapsed before scholars correlated the dysfunctional Jennings will, drawn up when George and John were eight and ten years old, to the equally dysfunctional Jennings family.

The original flaw was that John Jennings's estate was divided, following daughter Frances's ill-conceived lawsuit against it. After its division and the death of Midgley Jennings, about three-quarters of the remaining assets ended up with Alice Jennings. These ultimately flowed through her trust to the control of Richard Abbey for the support of the Keats children. But a major portion of the balance of John Jennings's 1805 estate ended up sequestered by the Chancery Court, not to be distributed until 1823–1825 and later—and, tragically, never for John's benefit. This would not have been the case were it not for Frances's suit.

The story backs up even further, to the 16 April 1804 death of Thomas Keats. Dying intestate, his assets were reportedly less than £2,000, over which Frances gained administration about a year later.[2] Whether the valuation was real or hypothetical, it went to Frances. It is possible that she ceded half the inheritance to her second husband, William Rawlings, upon their marriage (ten weeks after Thomas's death). Another possibility is that the £2,000 was an imputed value of the Swan and Hoop business. If the full nominal sum existed as cash, Frances could have run through upward of £300 a year before her 1810 death, affording a generous lifestyle. In any event, Joshua Vevers assumed the Swan and Hoop leasehold on 25 March 1806, ending Frances's business career and the need for capital. It is unknown what happened to Rawlings or his estate. When Frances showed up at her mother's house in the winter of 1809, she had no money. By the time of her death the £2,000 had been entirely dissipated, without explanation. Owing to Frances's financial incompetence, their father's estate was of no value to the Keats children.

The opening chapter of the family financial saga effectively started with the death of John Jennings on 8 March 1805. Nominally, his estate exceeded £13,600, but the stated nominal value was not the same as cash. Securities were described at their par value, even as their trading prices fluctuated dramatically. Business debts and mortgages also had stated valuations that were not readily convertible to cash. Based on a conservative conversion to 2012 currency values, the total value of the estate equaled about £517,000, or US$815,000.[3] In terms of equivalent buying power, adjusting for quality of life considerations, the estate's value would be considerably higher.

John Jennings's will, dated 1 February 1805 in anticipation of his death, was drawn not by his solicitor, Mr. Hall, but by Joseph Pearson, a land surveyor. Its wording was a bit obscure. The primary bequest was an annuity to his wife, Alice, valued at £200 a year, requiring capital of £6,667 at 3 percent. He owned bank annuities totaling £6,493, nearly covering the spousal bequest. Jennings also held £1,000 of East India stock at par, but its real market value fluctuated. He owned a £1,200 mortgage on an estate in Knightsbridge, as well as a number of debts, all denominated at par value. However, several of these debt instruments took years to collect. In sum, the assets behind his bequests were a mix.

Next he bequeathed to his son Midgley the East India stock at a par value of £2,000 (although he held only £1,000), plus £1,900 of "New Fives," a 5 percent government annuity introduced in 1797. Jennings did not provide for Midgley's children, as none had been born at the time the will was drawn. The will specified that Midgley's wife, Margaret, upon becoming widowed, could retain only £500, with the £2,400 balance of the capital returning to the "Family."[4] In other words, after Midgley died, the majority of his capital would revert to his mother, Alice, and presumably redound to the Keats children upon her death. However, Midgley had married on 12 March 1804, eleven months before the will was drawn, and his wife was expecting a child at the time of Jennings's death in 1805.

Jennings bequeathed £1,000 to the four Keats grandchildren, to be equally divided, with accumulated interest, when "they become of Age." The amount was funded by the payoff of the £1,200 Knightsbridge mortgage, which occurred five years later, in 1810. This sum ended up in Chancery, becoming known as the Infant Legatees Account.

Jennings's will provided a £50 life annuity for Frances, requiring £1,667 capital at 3 percent. After Frances's death, the capital was transferred to the Frances Keats Rawlings Life Account at Chancery. There was also a £30 annuity for his sister, Mary Sweetingburgh, requiring £1,000 of capital.

The family bequests totaled £13,234, in addition to another £25 of specific minor gifts. The identified assets totaled £13,192, although with the collection of additional debts, the assets finally exceeded the bequests by £535. Jennings named Midgley and Alice as coexecutors, with a neighbor, Charles Danvers, as the third executor. Early on, Danvers declined to serve.

Midgley immediately had problems with the will. First, his father had specifically left him all the East India stock, erroneously describing it as worth £2,000 when in fact its value was only £1,000. Second, his wife was pregnant, whereas the will assumed they were childless. Midgley, as coexecutor, acted primarily in his own interest, probably the result of preexisting family issues and his concern about providing for his children.

Viewed through the prism of two centuries, Jennings's will was flawed, just as the family structure was flawed. His widow initially inherited the use of half the assets during her lifetime, consistent with legal precedent. But the will did not specify what was to become of the principal upon her death. The same issue applied to the annuity for Mary Sweetingburgh. Jennings denied Frances all but a life interest in her capital, apparently not trusting her financial wisdom. Her £1,667 of principal underlying the annuity would roll over to the Keats children upon her death.

Using the nominal capital values, the rough split among the three main interests was 49 percent to Alice, 29 percent to Midgley, and 12 percent to Frances, with 7 percent for the Keats children and the balance of the immediate estate going to Mary Sweetingburgh and others. Midgley recognized that, upon his death, his 29 percent share could be reduced to about 4 percent remaining principal for his wife and (unborn) children. Frances, receiving the least in terms of current income, was equally unhappy. The unintended consequence of Jennings's oddly drawn will was to put the whole matter up for adjudication. Reasonable beneficiaries, with the help of competent solicitors, might have resolved matters, but it was not to be.

Within three weeks of Jennings's death, Frances and Midgley went to war. As executor, he properly asked her and her husband for the last quarter's rent for the Swan and Hoop. They counterclaimed that Jennings owed the business £41 for sundries. Then, on 6 April 1805, Frances and William Rawlings filed a bill of complaint in Chancery, noting the will's failure to reassign the capital underlying Alice's annuity after her death. The couple asked for a straight one-third of it (£2,222 of the £6,667), assuming that Alice and Midgley would also receive one-third apiece. Then they asked for half of Midgley's capital upon his death (£1,450 of the £2,900), assuming that Frances would outlive him.[5] Had they succeeded, the Rawlingses would have sealed a claim to outright ownership of £3,650, in contravention of Jennings's will, in addition to the £1,667 earmarked for Frances in trust. Their claim was an aggressive reach.

Midgley petitioned on the same day that he and his heirs be allowed to retain absolutely his £2,900 bequest, with no 50 percent reversion to Alice after his death. He also petitioned, mean-spiritedly, that he and Alice (as coexecutors) be permitted to divide the excess of assets over bequests (ultimately, £434) fifty-fifty, with none going to Frances.[6]

126

The Chancery judges ruled on 26 July 1806, mostly in Alice's favor. She retained absolute ownership of her capital. Frances won nothing, except her right to the £50 annuity. Midgley received a mixed verdict: he won the life right to his capital, but upon his death, it would be accessible to anyone who applied for it. In September 1805 Midgley began paying his mother's annuity, but not Frances's. While adjudicating the matter, Chancery held all the assets for two more years, until 2 August 1808. As a result of Frances's suit and Midgley's countersuit, Alice did not receive her principal share outright until 11 August 1808, three and a half years after her husband's death.

The Chancery action in August 1808 did not yield any cash to Frances, but it included an order that her capital be recalculated. By 11 August 1808, within nine days of Midgley's receipt of funds, Frances demanded payment of her back annuity. On 5 September he settled up with her. Having been coughing blood for a year, he likely suspected his own impending death. Midgley died 21 November 1808, at age thirty-one, having had the outright use of his funds for only about three months.

Midgley's death created yet another complication, since all his affairs were now in the hands of his solicitor, Charles John Wye. Frances petitioned Wye on 8 July 1809, before Chancery, for another two years' annuity payments. With Midgley out of the picture, payment was made fairly quickly, and the annuity's £1,667 capital was finally set aside for her.

On 8 December 1809 Midgley's widow petitioned Chancery on behalf of her three children, Margaret Alice, Midgley John Jr., and Mary Ann, for the entirety of the £2,900 allotted in Jennings's will. Under the will, Margaret would retain only £500, with the balance reverting to the family. However, the July 1806 Chancery decision had amended that to allow "with liberty upon his death for any party who is interested, to apply" for the capital.[7] Chancery replied to Margaret on 13 February 1810, awarding the Jennings children one-half, or £1,450, with the other half going back to Alice.

A final aspect of Wye's work in 1809 was to clarify the estate's residue as £535. Frances had claimed one-third of it in her unsuccessful suit, but the Chancery Court divided it equally between Alice and the estate of Midgley. Of this, Alice's £267 ultimately went to the Keats children. The lawyers received progress payments of £428 against their fees.

Because Jennings's will failed to specify when "each" Keats child came of age, a Chancery determination was required to revise the language to state: "on their respectively attaining their Ages of 21 years they are to be at liberty to apply to this Court for transfers of their respective shares."[8]

The £1,000 bequest to the Keats children was funded, at last, in 1810 as the Infant Legatees Account. This crucial determination by the court was not acted on by John Keats, who never understood the ruling, when he came of age in 1816, or ever in his lifetime. Nor did George Keats act on it when he turned twenty-one in 1818. Not until George applied in 1823 did the money in the Infant Legatees Account begin to be disbursed.

Compounding matters, Frances Rawlings died in March 1810, within weeks of Chancery's determination. Her annuity had been funded only a few months earlier, while she was on her deathbed in her mother's house. Her capital of £1,667 was then dispatched to Chancery as the Frances Keats Rawlings Life Account.

Mary Sweetingburgh, having been ignored for four and a half years, received her back annuity in 1810, with the underlying capital of £1,000. Mrs. Sweetingburgh died on 4 December 1813, and in due course her £1,000 principal was applied for by Midgley's executors, on behalf of his children, and by Alice's solicitor and then executor (Alice died in December 1814), on behalf of the Keats children. The amicable fifty-fifty split was approved 10 May 1815, with the Keatses' £500 share added to the Infant Legatees Account at Chancery. The sum of the several accounts grew, with interest accrued at 3 percent, and reached a value exceeding £4,500 by 1825.

At the time of Alice's death, John, age nineteen, was leaving his apprenticeship with Hammond for Guy's Hospital. George, seventeen, was working in Abbey's business. Neither was aware of the transfers to Chancery, although William Walton—their mother's solicitor and then their grandmother's—had arranged the whole matter.

A sixteen-year summary of the Chancery accounts is presented in table 1, based on the dates of the Chancery's orders, which did not coincide exactly with the dates of distribution to George and Fanny. The funds languished at Reynolds and Rice, and George did not receive the actual amounts shown. His accounts were not settled until Georgiana's 1828 trip to England, with various subtractions for legal fees and loans to his sister.[9] The amounts in the table have been rounded to the nearest pound, as the entries in the original documents included shillings and pence.[10]

George and Fanny each ultimately realized the return of £1,608.10 of principal, he starting after 1823 and she after 1825. George received an additional £523 of interest, all but £54.5 following the 1823 Chancery order. Fanny, whose funds remained in Chancery longer, accruing interest, received £782. Included in her receipts was £108.10 that George directed

Table 1. Chancery Accounts

	Infant Legatees Account	Frances K. Rawlings Life Account	Consolidated
Capital Funds into Chancery			
13 February 1810: J. Jennings bequest	£1,000		
3 July 1811: F. K. Rawlings Life Account		£1,666	
10 May 1815: Sweetingburgh capital	£500		
Accrued interest assumed	£52	£0	
Total	£1,552	£1,666	£3,218
Capital disbursements			
21 March 1823: George's share to him	£387	£417	
3 June 1825: Fanny's share to her	£387	£417	
3 June 1825: John's share to Fanny	£387	£417	
3 June 1825: Tom's share to George*	£387	£417	
Total	£1,548	£1,667	£3,215
Interest distributed			
Accumulated interest to 21 March 1823	£534	£620	£1,154
21 March 1823: disbursement to George (25%)	–£133	–£155	
Remaining	£401	£465	
Interest growth to 3 June 1825	£69	£75	£144
Available for further disbursements	£470	£540	
3 June 1825: Fanny's share to her	–£157	–£180	
3 June 1825: John's share to Fanny	–£157	–£180	
3 June 1825: Tom's share to George		–£180	
F. K. Rawlings Life Account closed out		£0	
Interest growth to 20 December 1825	£6		£6
Available for further disbursements	£162		
20 December 1825: one-third to George	–£55		
20 December 1825: two-thirds to Fanny	–£108		
Infant Legatees Account closed out	£0		
Total capital + interest			£4,519

Amounts are rounded; totals are nearly exact, even when the components do not add up to the total.
* This disbursement was made to Fanny as administrator of Tom's estate. George's 50 percent was remitted through their attorneys, Reynolds and Rice.

she receive from his share of Tom's interest in the Infant Legatees Account. In total, George was able to extract £2,131 from the Chancery accounts; Fanny received £2,390 (see table 2), which she brought into her marriage.

John Keats never realized a shilling from the Chancery accounts, which might have yielded him upward of £1,500, for the simple reason that he

Table 2. Distributions from Chancery

	To Fanny	To George
Infant Legatees principal	£ 774	£ 774
Frances K. Rawlings principal	834	834
Interest 21 March 1823		288
Interest 3 June 1825	674	180
Interest 20 December 1825	108	55
Total	£ 2,390	£ 2,131

did not apply. Several explanations are possible. John was only eight years old when his father died, nine when his grandfather died, and fourteen when his mother died. He was away at school most of this time, spending breaks with his grandmother. The families were torn apart by the litigation, which dragged on from 1805 to 1810, accompanied by the deaths of Midgley and Frances. In this environment, it is possible that no one told the boys the details of their inheritance. John referred to this period and the years preceding as ones of "earlier Misfortunes."[11] The brothers were aware that something bad was going on, especially when their cousins disappeared from their lives. Neither John nor George ever mentioned them again. One of the cousins, Midgley John Jennings Jr., achieved fame as an East India Company cleric, spending two decades in the subcontinent before being killed on 11 May 1857 in Delhi's Mughal uprising.[12]

William Walton, who was both Frances's solicitor and later Alice's, understood every aspect of the estate. After he drew his final fee in 1812, Walton bought a large house and property near Epping Forest and retired. His son, also named William, was part of the firm of Walton and Gliddon for many years. The firm did not notify John when he came of age in 1816 that he could apply for the funds, probably because its active representation of the estate had concluded.

Richard Abbey's role regarding the Chancery funds has never been clear. Some have speculated that Abbey did not know about the principal, which seems unlikely because he undertook at least one Chancery action. After Alice Jennings died in December 1814, coexecutors Abbey and John Nowland Sandell joined with Margaret Jennings and her sister Mary Maxwell, representing Midgley's estate, to petition Chancery for Mary Sweetingburgh's £1,000, which had been open for application since her death in December 1813. Their claim, undertaken 19 April 1815, was answered promptly on 10 May 1815, dividing the Sweetingburgh legacy between Midgley's and Alice's estates. Alice's £500 share was deposited into the Infant Legatees Account at Chancery, which already held John Jennings's £1,000 direct bequest to the Keats grandchildren, plus about £50 in accumulated interest. Abbey therefore knew about the Infant Legatees Account, and as Alice's close friend and guardian of the four Keats children, it seems probable that he also knew about the larger Frances Keats Rawlings Life Account, established for the children by the same law firm that represented Alice's estate. Abbey may have wrongly interpreted the distribution date of the principal, assuming it to be 1824, when the last of the children (Fanny) became twenty-one, even though Chancery had earlier amended the will to make it clear that "each" could apply upon attaining age twenty-one.

When John approached Abbey, at George's behest, regarding Tom's estate in September 1819, Abbey at first declined to release funds, referring to the possible claim by their aunt Margaret Jennings. However, such a suit would have been filed against Alice's estate (in Abbey's control), into which half of Midgley's capital had flowed after his death, not against the Chancery accounts, which held none of Midgley's capital. John wrote to George that since "Walton was dead—He [Abbey] will apply to Mr. Gliddon the partner."[13] Two months later, John wrote again, "I should [think] that Abbey from the delay of Waltons house has employed [another] Lawyer on our Business. Mrs. [Margaret] Jennings has not instituted [an]y action against us yet, nor has she withdrawn her claim I think I told you that even if she were to lose her cause we shold have to pay the expences of the Suit."[14]

At that juncture, Abbey had at least some contact with the firm that had initiated the Chancery accounts, and he was explaining at least part of the situation to John. He was not, however, an "interested party," because his trusteeship did not extend to the Chancery fund. Why he did not fully explain the Chancery accounts to John will never be understood. It could be that he was simply exasperated by John's unending applications for cash and grew evasive, deciding to communicate with John on a strictly "need to know" basis. Abbey suggested that John contact the Walton firm, but apparently, nothing constructive came of it.[15] Nor did Abbey explain matters to George during his 1820 visit, perhaps assuming that he knew. Or perhaps he believed that the boys should not receive the money until they had proved some financial competence.

Abbey told John Keats on 23 August 1820 that he had been severely affected by bad debts of his own for the past two years.[16] On 15 September 1821 the firm of Richard Abbey, John Cock, and William Johnson was dissolved, and Johnson removed himself. It is probable that Abbey then got caught up in the 1822–1825 speculative trade boom, followed by the Panic of 1825. He may have dipped into the £500 from Tom's estate held in trust for Fanny, and he may have used some of the spread between a 3 percent stock and a 5 percent stock held for Fanny when it was converted in 1822. Dilke and Rice sued Abbey on Fanny's behalf for £2,905 upon her twenty-first birthday, but Abbey did not pay in full for years, possibly not until 1831. Abbey maintained that Fanny was born in 1804, not 1803, based on his reading of her baptismal record;[17] nevertheless, he paid the balance of Fanny's share well after 1825. By 1830, Abbey was forced to mortgage his Walthamstow property for £2,500 and his chattels for £300 to Fanny and her husband to complete the payments and cover other business indebtedness.

John's public death notices jogged someone to act on the Chancery funds, perhaps a successor partner in the Walton and Gliddon firm, perhaps Abbey himself, or perhaps a clerk in Chancery. George was made aware of the funds and, having sent a power of attorney to Abbey, made a straightforward application through him, which Chancery approved on 21 March 1823. He applied only for his own inheritance, without invoking the legalities to become the administrator of either John's or Tom's funds. Nor, in the absence of such an administrator, did he make a claim for his share of his brothers' inheritance, to which he was entitled.

Nearly two years elapsed between Chancery's order and George's realization that additional cash from his brothers' shares was available. Having received £1,092 in principal and interest from his 1823 application, George then turned either £300 or £310 of his own money over to John's colleagues, at their demand, clearing all financial claims against the poet. In an 18 March 1825 letter, he asked Abbey to disburse the following:

Taylor and Hessey	£150
Haslam	£ 50
Brown	£ 70
and the Taylor	£ 30 or £ 40
Total	£300 or £310[18]

The first sum cleared Taylor and Hessey's losses on *Endymion*, *Poems*, and *Lamia, Isabella, The Eve of St. Agnes, and Other Poems*. The payment to Haslam was reimbursement for a loan he had made to enable the poet's trip to Rome. The Brown payment was to compensate him for housing the poet, at commercial rates, in Wentworth Place, as well as reimbursement for paying John's rent in Kentish Town during the summer of 1820. Brown claimed he had borrowed John's rent from his solicitors Skynner and Skynner, and he asked George to repay the interest as well. The additional sum to Taylor was not explained; it may have been to recoup actual publishing losses, aside from the copyright, or it may have been a repayment of Taylor's supposed gift to the poet in Rome. The moneys Taylor collected for John, such as £50 from Charles William Wentworth, the third Lord Fitzwilliam (1786–1857), and £10 each from Rice, portraitist William Hilton (1786–1839), and two or three others, were viewed as gifts and were not repaid.

The conclusion of the Chancery saga began on 3 June 1824, Fanny Keats's twenty-first birthday. Abbey had control of the funds from her grandmother's estate, but he was unable to produce them. Dilke, who was helping Fanny with her affairs, sued, with assistance from the law firm of Reynolds and Rice, and obtained the release of the funds from the Infant Legatees Account, including John's and Tom's shares, with half going to George. These were funds that their grandfather Jennings had set aside to support their mother but had sat in limbo from Frances's death in 1810 until the claim in 1824. Fanny ultimately realized about £2,344 from Chancery, including her share of her deceased brothers' shares, and later about £2,253 from Abbey.

On 21 May 1825 Fanny, on the advice of her legal counsel, obtained the right to administer her own accounts and Tom's and John's estates. Orders were handed down by 20 December 1825, giving her the capital and interest for her own account and, as administrator, for John's and Tom's estates. Although Chancery released the money to Fanny as administrator, it actually went into a Reynolds and Rice escrow account early in 1826.

Fanny wrote vaguely to George about the account status on 31 May 1826, telling him, "There is some property of yours in the Bank standing in my name, being your share of Tom's and John's property out of Chancery, after paying all debts. I cannot say the exact amount; but as Mr. Rice intends sending you a statement I shall refer you to him." It was only at this point that Fanny disabused George as to Abbey's stewardship: "I find he [Abbey] has deceived you shamefully respecting the sum of money you were to receive out of the Court of Chancery, would to God you had sent the power of attorney to Mr. Dilke or Rice."[19] The sum was a substantial £804 principal plus £188 accumulated interest, before deductions. Rice required a power of attorney from George to supersede the one sent to Abbey. The document George transmitted to Rice was flawed, lacking Rice's and Reynolds's Christian names and omitting the words "jointly and severally."[20]

Two years later, George's London affairs were still a mess. He wrote to Dilke on 25 March 1828 complaining that his authorized draft on the Reynolds and Rice firm had been refused. At his wit's end, George dispatched Georgiana to England, both to visit her family and to sort out his accounts. She, daughter Georgiana Emily, and infant John Henry sailed from New York shortly after 12 May 1828.

George stirred the pot further by involving his brother-in-law Charles Wylie on two matters. As a tag end to the Taylor and Hessey payback, Wylie wrote to Taylor on 17 August 1828, asking that he direct James Tallant in Cincinnati to give up Taylor's eight-year-old claim against George for £150,[21]—which George had directed Abbey to repay three years earlier. Instead, Tallant sent the claim to Brown in furtherance of the latter's slander campaign against George. Wylie also injected himself into the sinking affairs of the Reynolds and Rice law firm and into Dilke's own friendly representation of George with the firm. Wylie acted "roughly and injudiciously," but in any event, George wrote a year later, "I have not any claim whatever on the said Chars Dilke up to this 14 Nov. 1829."[22]

Due to the vagaries of the timing of John's and Tom's withdrawals from their grandmother's estate when the markets were down, Fanny received the largest share of the overall inheritance. Eight and a half years after John's death, the original Chancery accounts were wrapped up, but a separate matter—Alice Jennings's special bequest to Fanny Keats—would require Chancery's involvement for another five decades.

Back in 1810, after receiving from Midgley's estate the £1,450 capital and £267 residue of John Jennings's estate, Alice had created a separate £200 (or it may have been £300) bequest for the education of granddaughter Fanny, who had lived with her the longest. The bequest was never claimed or expended on Fanny's behalf by Abbey. Dilke, who was wrapping up the Chancery trusts in 1825, became distrustful of Fanny's husband, Valentin Llanos. Fanny was in danger of losing the bulk of her £4,600 inheritance, giving her dower share to Llanos and then lending him an additional £2,000 to invest in a bridle bit patent. Dilke later wrote to George, "As to advising Llanos about Spain, he is unfortunately not the man to take advice or to think he wants it—I believe him to be a very honorable man, but as weak as a child. There was never any speculation so silly as his patent bits."[23] Dilke wisely held back the special £200 bequest in a new Chancery account, from which Fanny drew interest over the years. When her dowery was lost on Llanos's speculations, George directed Dilke to assign his share of the loose ends of the trusts over to Fanny to help her remain solvent.[24]

Once they got past their initial financial problems, the Llanoses were well fixed in Spain for a long time. Dilke wrote to George in 1838, "As however I am yr Sister's Trustee I infer that money matters are not very urgent, as he draws at *wide* intervals only for her dividends."[25] Then, five decades later, Fanny found herself in financial straits and wrote to Ralph Thomas in London to retrieve the principal (the same Ralph Thomas whose 1885 analysis of the Chancery accounts forms the basis of this chapter).

Ultimately, the Keats children suffered from a series of misfortunes. Their family history was one of early death from tuberculosis. The surviving family was dysfunctional, with the members unable to resolve their differences while alive. John Jennings's flawed will mirrored these issues. Frances's reckless and futile challenge of the will ended with an exasperated Chancery sequestering the money for two decades. The death of solicitor Charles Wye and the apparent negligence of William Walton's law firm left the family members poorly advised. Not the least of their problems was that no one taught the Keats children how to manage their own affairs. The money was there; all they had to do was claim it.

Legal writers have joked that in most probate matters, when the court rules, the funds are distributed; however, when the Chancery Court ruled, it was only the beginning. That may be a little unfair to Chancery, for its rulings were fair and commonsensical, if somewhat slow in coming. Had John Jennings left a clear and proper will, and had there been no lawsuits, Chancery involvement would not have been necessary.

The second chapter of the family's financial story deals with Alice Jennings's indenture, or deed, dated 29 July 1810 and now lost, followed by her will, dated 31 July 1810. This saga was not destined to conclude until 1830–1831, after litigation between the Llanoses and Abbey.

Alice had endured the deaths of her son-in-law, husband, son, and daughter and had seen enough litigation to enrich several solicitors. To avoid a repetition of the wrangling over her husband's will, at age seventy-four she took the necessary steps to ensure that her estate would not be similarly bottled up in Chancery. She deeded her assets and the guardian-

ship of the Keats children over to Richard Abbey and John Nowland Sandell. Her counsel advised her that such a trust arrangement would bypass
the Chancery's probate procedures, making the funds readily available to
her beneficiaries. But Abbey would eventually have absolute authority over
Alice's estate.

Her £6,667 annuity capital had been augmented by the reversion of
Midgley's £1,450 and by her share of the £535 residue from her husband's
estate. Sometime between 1810 and her death in 1814, Alice apparently
gave £500 of East India stock to her Jennings grandchildren—the same
stock their father and mother had, on separate occasions, claimed should
be left to them. Her remaining holdings were about £8,000 capital valued
at par.

Upon Alice's death, Abbey distributed £60 annually to each of the
Keats children, which was their 3 percent right on par capital of £2,000
each. The boys, who were out of school and mostly on their own, used the
£60 for living expenses. Abbey probably kept Fanny's dividends to reimburse himself for housing her.

Three series of events caused John Keats's £2,000 principal to wither
away. First, there were school fees, for which Abbey paid out either £700
(his recollection) or £1,000 (Brown's) toward John's medical education
between 1811 and 1816. Second, the markets had been depressed by the
"Panic of the Hundred Days" in the summer of 1815, reducing the overall
value of his share to about £1,230, even before some of the medical tuition
was paid. Finally, John spent a great deal of money in the last two years of
his life. His peripatetic travels throughout England likely consumed £200
to £300, and he loaned upward of £200 to friends. In short, he ran through
his remaining funds and then some.

George's situation was different. He incurred no tuition costs after
Clarke's and resided over Abbey's warehouse or in shared flats with Tom,
living within his income. By 1818, the stock market had recovered. When
George applied for his capital from Alice's estate on his twenty-first birthday, Abbey was able to hand him £1,659. Of this, George left £500 in the so-
called Abbey Account for his brothers' use when he departed for America.

When Tom died in 1818, his total estate was valued between £1,300
and £1,400. No clear accounting of Tom's life survives, but his employment
was far shorter and less regular than George's. Tom had also traveled a bit,
including to France, and had incurred extensive medical bills in his final
years. Both George and Brown referred obliquely to a second trip Tom
took to Lyons when he was sixteen, but no other record survives, and the

journey seems unlikely.[26] After Tom's accounts were settled, the three surviving siblings each received £370, implying that this portion of his estate had a net value of £1,100.

After Abbey's guardianship of Fanny Keats terminated, the fair-minded Dilke became her trustee. She engaged in a busy social life in Hampstead and Chelsea, culminating in her 1826 marriage to Valentin Llanos. Fanny ultimately received £1,893 from her grandmother's estate on her own account, plus the £370 of Tom's.[27] These sums, added to the £2,390 she received promptly from the Chancery accounts of her mother and grandfather, provided Fanny with an inheritance totaling £4,600. On a currency basis, that sum is equal to £174,800 in 2012, and on a purchasing basis, it is equal to two to four times that amount—in other words, 100 times the nominal amount in 1818, or about £460,000.[28] Similar amounts either did or should have devolved upon George and John in a lengthy series of disbursements for tuition, living expenses, and the settling up of accounts.

Abbey administered the boys' trusts honestly, according to Dilke, whose telling was at odds with Fanny's. Abbey allowed his accounting office to serve as a bank for the Keats brothers. John even referred to it as "the bank," treating it as a cash till. When George was in America and in need of both a designee with a power of attorney and a remitting facility, Abbey continued to accommodate him.

When Fanny turned twenty-one, Abbey was caught up in the speculative trade boom-bust of 1822–1825. He evidently used Fanny's trust funds as collateral for his firm's business activities. He was caught short of liquid funds on her birthday, so Dilke and Rice sued him on Fanny's behalf. As late as 7 May 1830, the law firm of Reynolds and Rice had not completed the distributions to the Keats siblings. George wrote to Dilke that he wanted his sister to "get from it [Abbey's Walthamstow property] *all* her demands upon it, and if when she has been fully paid there is any left, I shall be well pleased to receive it."[29] Shortly thereafter, it appears that Fanny ran through her inheritance, because George wrote to Reynolds on 6 May 1832, instructing him to extract from the law firm the last £165, of which £100 was to be sent to Fanny and her husband as a loan.[30]

Another key element to understanding that George did not take John's money involves the back-and-forth loans and transfers between the brothers, the details of which can never be adequately reconstructed and, unfortunately, became the subject of invective by the uninvolved. For instance, Brown misunderstood, with some reason, the ownership of George's Abbey Account. He assumed it was either John's account or a family account.

When George returned to round up funds after the investment failure in Kentucky, Brown did not realize that George was simply repatriating his own funds. Brown thought George took £170 of Tom's inheritance from John and probably another £100 as well, not knowing that it was simply a brotherly payback of cash loans that happened to be funded by John's share of Tom's estate. John himself may not have been totally clear about the circumstances.

The source of William Haslam's annoyance was not related to the brothers' finances, but when he heard Brown's thirdhand account, he piled on. Trained as a solicitor, Haslam was not a creative member of the circle. He was more of a disciple, swept up by John's greatness, and he undertook some of John's correspondence duties. Originally, Haslam was closer to George, but he became annoyed when George failed to respond to his friend Kent's proposed merchandising scheme to sell expensive English goods in frontier America. Brown and Haslam then continually berated George to Fanny Keats, Severn, Dilke, and Leigh Hunt. It was Haslam who adversely influenced (temporarily) Fanny's opinion of George. He cajoled Charles Wylie on the same issue several years later. In 1825, after George repaid Haslam the £50 he had loaned John in 1820, Haslam went silent.

Severn's situation was different. He was simply wrung out by the experience in Rome, including daily worries about finances. Influenced by his friend Haslam, he joined in the chorus but had no real concept of the Keats family finances about which he lamented. Soon thereafter he dropped the issue, other than hoping for a handsome subscription from George toward John's grave marker. Severn remained in Rome through 1841, achieving respect as an artist, and he returned there as English consul from 1861 to 1872. At his death in 1879, friends arranged for Severn to be buried alongside John Keats, with a nearly identical headstone.

Fanny Brawne heard much of this story from Fanny Keats, who had picked it up from Haslam and Brown. Brawne wrote to Fanny in May 1824 that the Brown-Haslam version was incorrect: "I must say I think he [George] is more blamed than he should be."[31]

In retrospect, the misunderstanding should never have happened. In modern times, it would have been cleared up by a couple of telephone calls. In the 1820s, however, letter writing was the predominant means of communicating; some letters were saved, and some were not. For his part, George rarely spoke of it; he was guilt free in his own mind. His brother was dead, he was in Kentucky, and he had little to gain from Brown.

Table 3. George Keats's Transfers to America

Year	Amount	Source
1818	£1,100	George's inheritance from grandmother
1819	100	Sent by John from Tom's Abbey account
1820	370	Balance of Tom's estate
	100	Remainder of Tom's Abbey account
	170	John's settlement of his debts to George
	60	Gift from Abbey
1825	1,088	Withdrawal of George's funds from Chancery, partly to pay off John's debts (£300–310)
1828	333*	Share of Tom's Chancery funds sent by Rice
Total	£3,321	

* An approximate value, as the Reynolds and Rice accounts were muddled. After fees and transfer costs, the amount received in Kentucky was likely less.

George ultimately transferred as much as £3,321 to America, in several sweeps (table 3). His 1819–1820 restart in America was financed by the £370 realized from Tom's estate and the settling up of the approximately £170 debt from John, as well as the £60 from Abbey. This £700 capital was the same sum Taylor referred to as if it were all John's. From America, George ultimately settled all of John's debts. He paid Brown's £72 invoice, including interest. He also repaid Taylor and Hessey's £150 advance. At the same time, he attempted to acquire the copyright to Keats's last poems to prevent Brown from obtaining it. It is not clear how much of the gift money, organized by Taylor, George repaid or whether he reimbursed Taylor's claimed losses of £110 on *Endymion* and £100 on *Lamia*. But with Abbey's help, George settled all of John's other sundry debts out of his own pocket.

When Dilke and Rice arranged the release of John's inheritance from Chancery, including his portion of Tom's residual estate, in 1825–1826, the John Jennings saga was over. The Alice Jennings saga was wrapped up in 1832.

The central theme here is that George's financial dealings were always above reproach. He unknowingly left John short of funds in 1820, three days before John's first hemorrhage and the start of his "posthumous" year, which George had no way of knowing from the frontier. John's confused reaction was that George "ought not to have done this," which Brown escalated into a smear campaign lasing two decades. Fanny Keats Llanos received the largest share of the inheritance but did not contribute to paying John's debts; she was also given or loaned about £265 by George. Nevertheless, she allowed her resentment of George's support of Abbey to color her feelings against her brother. Fanny Brawne—who was not a party to the finances, other than taking John in, without charge, during his worst moments of 1820—saw the issue clearly and supported George. A Shakespearean summary of George's financial culpability might simply be that it was "much ado about nothing."

A poetic grace note was attached to George's last known letter to his sister Fanny, dated 6 May 1832. It dealt with her straitened circumstances and her need for the above-mentioned £100. He also included two poems, each of them undated but closed with his initials "G. K.," so presumably were penned by him:

The Influence of Tea upon the *Ladies*
Dear Tea, that enlivener of Wit and of Soul,
More loquacious by far than the draughts of the Bowl
Soon unloosens the tongue, and enlivens the mind,
And enlivens the eyes to the fault of mankind,
It brings on the tapis their neighbours defects,
The faults of their Friends, or their willful neglects,
Reminds them of many good-natured tale,
About those who are stylish, or those who are frail;
In harmless Chit Chat an acquaintance they roast,
And serve up a friend, as they serve up a toast,
The Wives of our men of inferior degree,
Will sip up repute in a little *Bohea*,
With *Hyson* a beverage still more refin'd,
Our Ladies of fashion enliven their mind.
But the scandal improves (a refinement in wrong)
As our Matrons are richer and rise to *Souchong*,
And by nods innuendoes and hints and what not
Reputation and Tea send together to Pot,
While Madam in Cambrics, & Laces array'd
With her plate and her liveries in splendid parade.
Will drink in *Imperial* a friend at a sup,
Or in *gunpowder*, blow them by dozens all up.
                    G. K.

On Woman
Happy a man may pass his life,
If freed from matrimonial chains,
If he's directed by a Wife,
He's sure to suffer for his pains.

What tongue is able to unfold
The falsehoods that in Women dwell,
Virtues in Women you behold,
Are almost imperceptible.

Adam could find no solid peace,
When Eve was given for a mate
Till he beheld a Woman's face,
Adam was in a happy state.

For in this sex you'll see appear
Hypocrisy, deceit, and pride,
Truth, darling of a heart sincere
In Women never can reside.

Distraction take the men, I say,
Who make the Women their delight.
Who no regard to Women pay;
Keep reason always in their sight.

Ceux qui sont plus favorablement enclin vers les dames, qu'ills lisent la première
& troisième line & ensuite la seconde & quatrième de chaque Vers.
G. K.

Valentin Llanos, upon reading these lines in French (translated loosely as "those who are favorably inclined toward women should read the first and third lines and then the second and fourth in each verse") noted, "I think George Keats must be a perfect divine if he made these Lines for I am sure he meant to have the first and second line read so—as nothing could proceed from his angelic lips not bearable with respect to the fair sex."[32]

George's poeticizing, though less than stellar, certainly softens his image as the "business brother."[33]

THE LEGACY DEFERRED

1821–1848

The most vexing and lasting issue was how best to define John Keats's legacy. George fretted over it until his death. Everyone in the poet's circle shared the belief that they had been touched by his greatness. But not one of them succeeded in capturing and memorializing it, especially not George. The biographical genre was typically described as the life, letters, and literary remains of the subject. In John's case, his life in the decades after his death was mostly a blank, shrouded in a veil of nondisclosure that George was best qualified to explain.

Other members of the circle possessed various Keats letters, although many of his best were in George's hands. With the poet's death, his publisher John Taylor held most of the copyrights to the published poems. Charles Brown, as self-appointed "literary executor," possessed many of the "literary remains," the evolutionary drafts that revealed how the poetry developed, as well as the draft play *Otho the Great*. George, Brown, and Taylor needed to cooperate with one another to achieve a biography, but it was not to be.

Percy Shelley and Leigh Hunt published incomplete vignettes about the poet. Taylor had the desire to do a biography but never pulled it off. John Reynolds would have liked to be asked to write one, but he was not. Charles Cowden Clarke also had the desire from the beginning, and although he wrote a few articles, he did not pull all his thoughts together until his *Recollections of Writers* appeared posthumously in 1878. George Keats, as represented by Charles Dilke, played more than a passive role in creating his brother's legacy. It is worth looking at what each accomplished to understand George's point of view. In the end, Brown's selection of Richard Monckton Milnes, who had never met the poet, proved to be as good a solution as any.

The first to jump at the opportunity was John Taylor, who advertised on behalf of Taylor and Hessey in the *New Times* on 29 March and 9 April 1821, "Speedily will be published, with Portrait, Memoirs and Remains of John Keats."[1] He believed that a swift vindication from his Tory critics would benefit the poet's reputation and perhaps help sales. In April Taylor asked Severn to forward the poet's papers from Rome, but Severn sent them to Brown instead. Brown thwarted Taylor, writing to Severn: "I shall always be the first to acknowledge Taylor's kindness to Keats; . . . however . . . I fear Taylor may do Keats an injustice . . . from the want of knowing his character . . . I am afraid it will be made a job—a mere trading job—and *that* I will lend no hand to." Brown also noted, "I heard yesterday that [Charles Cowden] Clark[e] is thinking of writing a memoir—to tell the truth I would rather join him."[2]

Taylor had led Brown to believe that he wanted the Keats materials but not Brown's editorial contributions. Taylor's efforts were assisted by Reynolds, whom Brown disliked and who was also feuding with Leigh Hunt. Dilke and Thomas Richards believed that Taylor's effort showed indecorous haste. Nevertheless, Taylor announced in the June 1822 edition of his *London Magazine* the proposed "Memoirs of . . . [Keats'] life. . . . To be accompanied with a selection from his unpublished manuscripts."[3]

Within months of John's death and his receipt of Taylor's invoice, George responsibly sent a note of indebtedness to Taylor and Hessey for the £150 advance made to the poet against unrealized revenues from *Endymion* and *Lamia, Isabella, The Eve of St. Agnes, and Other Poems.* In 1825 George repaid the £150, as well as another £30 to £40 to cover what Taylor may have loaned to John. However, Taylor had seriously irritated George in 1821 by asking James Tallant in Cincinnati to collect the publishing losses and encouraging him to gossip that George had appropriated £700 of the poet's funds the year before.

In 1825 George wrote to Dilke, "I am not competent to write a life and shall be happy to communicate any materials I am in possession of to any person to whom I have no positive objection as the author of John's life. Reynolds and yourself [are] I think every way Competent to execute it with truth, feeling, and good taste."[4] George clearly omitted Taylor, as well as Brown, from his preferred list of biographers. Claiming the copyrights (by means of a threatened injunction) on the poet's unpublished works, including his inherited half interest in *Otho*, George held a strong veto power.

Only Benjamin Bailey cooperated with Taylor, sending him his correspondence from Keats, but his collection was not nearly enough to complete a volume. Taylor transcribed the Abbey Memoir on 20 April 1827, but his counselor Richard Woodhouse argued against publication, as it demeaned the Keats family's origins and early years. As late as 1835, Taylor wrote, "I should like to print a complete Edition of Keats's Poems, with several of his Letters, but the world cares nothing for him—I fear that even 250 copies would not sell."[5]

The second one out of the gate was Shelley, who published *Adonais* in June 1821 and later that year wrote a prose piece in honor of Keats for the London *Literary Gazette*. Having been stung himself by the Tory critics, Shelley wrote an elegy that portrayed Keats as a fragile figure, an unappreciated genius unable to survive his critics. Blazingly written, Shelley's lines have endured even as they misportrayed his friend. William Hazlitt also joined in the anti-Tory fray, describing Keats as "a bud bit by an envious worm."[6]

Loosely, the Tory poets included Samuel Taylor Coleridge, Robert Southey, and William Wordsworth—sometimes called the Lake school. They were urbane and university educated, but they were also truly of the countryside. They, along with Walter Scott, generally sided with the government. The Tories characterized the Cockney school, which included Hunt, Hazlitt, and Keats, as being antinational, less well educated, from a lower social stratum, and prone to sickliness and effeminacy; they also accused the Cockneys of exhibiting an overdone sensuality in their poetry. But Southey had supported the French Revolution, and both Byron and Shelley had upper-class backgrounds, so the distinctions were not black and white.

The next effort to honor Keats came with Leigh Hunt's 1828 sketch in *Lord Byron and Some of His Contemporaries;* another appeared in John Gorton's *General Biographical Dictionary,* which came out the same year. Some of John's difficulties with the Tory critics were traceable to his having been befriended, published, and patronized by Hunt, whom many believed to be the focal point of Cockneyism and the critics' real target. Hunt's article noted:

> He was a seven months' child: his mother, who was a lively woman, passionately fond of amusement, is supposed to have hastened her death by too great an inattention to hours and seasons. Perhaps she hastened that of her son.
>
> Mr. Keats's origin was of the humblest description: he was born at a livery stables in Moorfields, of which his grandfather was the proprietor. . . . He never spoke of it, perhaps out of a personal soreness which the world had exasperated.[7]

Hunt continued at great length to deconstruct, critique, and generally compliment the poetry. However, when Hunt's article made its way to

America, George's reaction was immediate and hostile. Writing to Dilke on two occasions, he opined in an overwrought manner, similar to his self-defense on finances:

> Meeting with Hunt's Lord Byron and his contemporaries has raised in my mind a crowd of old associations, it reminds me that you had some idea of writing a life of John, and of the materials that I am able and willing to furnish for that purpose to you or any one who is competent to do it well—Hunt's sketch is not altogether a failure but I should be extremely sorry that poor John's name should go down to posterity associated with the littleness of L. H., an association of which he was so impatient in his Lifetime. He speaks of him patronizingly, that he would have defended him against the Reviewers if he had known his nervous irritation at their abuse of him . . . the fact was he more dreaded Hunt's defence than their abuse—
> . . . He then tells you that he lived with him, that he lived with Brown, that it was a pleasure to his friends to have him at their Houses &c.
> . . . [John] misled me himself if he did not divide with Brown the expences of House Keeping at Hampstead. . . . It is not the thing to hand down to posterity that John was *born in wretchedness* and lived with spiritless carelessness on Messrs Hunt and Brown.[8]

> Hunt entirely mistook his character. . . . Hunt has not told exactly the truth in saying—"Mr Keats and I were friends of the old stamp, between whom there was no such thing as obligation, except the pleasure of it."[9]

Brown, who by 1829 was living in Florence with his son Carlino, was also put off by Hunt's sketch. Brown began to organize his thoughts for a Keats biography, writing to Severn, Dilke, and others for their support. Severn was willing, but Dilke was reserved, particularly because Brown seemed determined to make an issue of the finances between George and John. Brown then wrote to Dilke, "I hate him [George] more than ever, and feel tempted to put these documents to a vindictive use."[10]

Dilke kept George informed of Brown's plans, leading George to respond from Kentucky on 7 May 1830:

> The threatened life of poor John by Brown, involving the sacrifice of my good name is most unwelcome. The very nature of Brown's

mind is such that however he may intend to honor his memory, he will hurt him as much by false painting as he will me from obstinacy, and misinformation—He has no impulsive instantaneous love of goodness or beauty, his judgement says this is vice, and that is virtue. . . . He is nothing if he is not critical. It would give him dissatisfaction to find me blameless, and I doubt if he would confess it, altho John admitted he had good points, he would not much relish his general opinion of him. . . . He is the antipodes of John, he is close, painstaking and calculating, John was open, prodigal, and had no power of calculation whatever.[11]

George respected Reynolds as a possible biographer, despite the unresolved legal problems that Fanny and her husband attributed to the law firm of Reynolds and Rice. George continued his thoughts:

I am perfectly willing to put you in possession of my recollections of John's early life, of his inward mind and his letters to me which are very long and numerous, and think with you, that Reynolds and not Brown is the man to write it. If [it] were not for the claims my family have upon my time and industry I would come to England. . . . I will commit to paper my recollections, and take the first safe opportunity to send them, and the letters, to do with them as to you may seem good. . . .

It seems to me *now,* that I have a great deal to communicate altho' it is more than likely, that when I sit down, to put it on paper, I shall be as a Flint, that requires a Steel, yourself or Reynolds, to come in contact with me to strike a light.[12]

George thereupon asked Dilke to enjoin the use of John's various unpublished, or "posthumous," manuscripts, many of which were in Brown's possession.[13] Thus, the thirty-year Dilke-Brown relationship unraveled, and Brown set aside the project sometime after 1830. The good-hearted Severn, wearied by Brown's maneuvers, wrote to him on 14 March 1834: "I remember you said 'the public should never have the Tragedy until they had done justice to Keat's other works'—*The time has come,* AND I FEAR THE TIME MAY PASS. . . . If you will not, I mean to defy you and try and write his life myself which I am sure will make you look about you."[14]

Brown met Richard Monckton Milnes in Florence during 1833, striking up the relationship that would, eight years later, break the gridlock over a Keats biography. In May 1835 Brown returned to England, choosing to live in Laira Green, near Plymouth. On 27 December 1836 he delivered a three-hour paper on Keats to the Plymouth Athenaeum. Brown handed elements of this paper over to Milnes on 19 March 1841.[15] Milnes showed it to Hunt and Dilke, who advised him the material was unpublishable. Brown was never destined to be Keats's biographer, although his flawed paper was finally printed in 1937.[16] Brown wrote of having a severe headache sometime after his lecture, likely one in a series of minor strokes (sometimes described as apoplexy or epilepsy), the last of which felled him in New Zealand in 1842.[17]

Meanwhile, Keats's artist friend, Benjamin Robert Haydon, was writing a remarkably lucid autobiography that first appeared in 1853. He wrote sparingly but productively about Keats, repeating tales from the poet's childhood and his reactions to the critics. Brown, who detested Haydon, would never have cooperated with a larger Haydon effort. Likewise, Charles Cowden Clarke took umbrage at Haydon's characterization of Keats as a heavy drinker. But Haydon, whose writing was as good as his art, was a credible storyteller.

Despite observing these events with a sort of frustrated eagerness, George never assembled his recollections for anyone. Even his grandchildren said that he never spoke about the family or its origins. However, he wrote to Dilke in 1836, noting that he expected to cover any losses resulting from a biography:

> Had I better publish a complete edition of all John's works or a selection of the best of those published and unpublished, or only the latter? Do I pray you *think out* this to me most important affair. It is useless for *me* to dwell on the minutia of this undertaking *to you* who will at a glance see more into it, than I have been able to imagine after years of study. At what season had I better be in London. Give me some idea of the cost of collecting materials, writing biography and the terms on which the work can be published in handsome style, the publisher to keep the whole impression; I take it as a matter of course that the sale would not pay expences, at what sum would a publisher risk the publication?[18]

Then he admitted in 1838:

> I have reflected a great deal about publishing the life, and works of my brother, but not having the slightest idea what quantity or

description of materials can be got in the shape of letters, post-humous poems &c whether "Otho" can be obtained from Brown, and whether a competent writer among his old friends will undertake the work. I am altogether at a loss what to calculate on. . . . If I should come to England, I could not remain there long enough to collect, assort, arrange, and publish, and besides I am entirely incompetent, wanting talent and experience in such matters.[19]

Dilke relayed George's thinking to Brown, who told Severn in 1838, "Moxon [Milnes's publisher] told me that Taylor, like a dog in a manger, will neither give a second edition, nor allow another to give one. But now, I believe, his copyright is out. George Keats threatened anyone with an injunction who should publish the posthumous poems; this indeed stopped me in the intended publication of the memoir. Dilke, George's agent, however, told me, when I was in town, that George wished to obtain from me those posthumous poems, by purchase, if they could not otherwise be obtained."[20]

The memoir matter lingered, unresolved, for two more years. In the fall of 1840 Brown proposed that Milnes be involved in publishing Brown's own journal of the tour to the Highlands. By March 1841, this unfulfilled proposal (part one was published in an independent journal) morphed into Milnes's taking on the entire Keats project.[21]

The copyright ownership trail leading up to this resolution is thinly documented. Under the 1709 Copyright Act, or the Statute of Ann, authors sold their materials to booksellers. In this case, John Keats sold his work to the firm of Taylor and Hessey, which became the copyright owner. The Copyright Act of 1814 established a term of twenty-eight years from publication or until the death of the author, whichever was later. Taylor and Hessey thus owned the copyright to Keats's legally published materials (the French A. and W. Galignani edition of 1829 was pirated)—specifically, to *Endymion; Lamia, Isabella, The Eve of St. Agnes, and Other Poems;* and "Hyperion." Taylor also claimed, by dint of possession, "other Miscellaneous Poems and Poetical Compositions and . . . Manuscript Letters and copies of Letters [written by Keats]."[22] In 1840 Taylor sold William Smith the rights to publish the first subsequent English edition.

George initially directed Abbey to ascertain whether his £150 reimbursement to Taylor entitled him to ownership of the copyrights. Not receiving an answer, he then asked Dilke to inquire into the ownership of John's posthumous papers.[23] Eleven years later, George was still fretting over Taylor's ownership of the copyright, suggesting to Dilke that he pay Taylor an additional sum to gain possession: "I am willing to buy them of him [Taylor] if he is so mean as to require it."[24] George also acknowledged that Brown possessed a perfect copy of *Otho the Great* and perhaps a one-half ownership of it.

Dilke discussed with both Brown and Taylor the notion of George buying the rights necessary to prepare John's biography. Brown answered obliquely that he would hand over all papers, except for those he might choose to use in his own biography. Taylor responded similarly, saying that he was agreeable but would have to undertake "calculations" to set a price, which he never did.[25]

The way to prevent the publication of noncopyrighted material was to seek an injunction from the Chancery Court. It is unclear whether George and Dilke ever obtained such an injunction. More likely, it was George's threat of noncooperation and the failure of the others to coalesce around an alternative plan that stymied Brown.

Before departing for New Zealand in June 1841, Brown set the Keats biography project in motion by handing over all his materials, and presumably the right to copyright them, to Milnes. This included his diatribe against George as well as Brown's own flawed biography, which had been rejected by several publishers. He noted that "George's *veto,* as I was told by his forbidding friend, Mr. Dilke, . . . no longer exists."[26] Word had arrived in March 1841 that George had waived his legal rights and agreed to the publication of a memoir and literary remains.[27]

Despite Milnes's activity beginning in 1841, Taylor did not give up until 1845. At that time, he sold for £50 to Edward Moxon (1801–1858), Milnes's publisher, a half interest in the Keats copyrights that would be expiring in 1848.[28] Thereafter, Taylor cooperated with Milnes, to the annoyance of his former cohort Reynolds, in producing the first Keats biography.

Milnes, with circumspection, wrote: "George Keats paid a short visit to England . . . and received his share of the property of the youngest brother. He probably repaid himself for moneys advanced for John's education or liabilities and thus the share which John received was not above £200. . . . After John's death . . . George offered, without any obligation, to do his utmost to discharge his brother's engagements . . . it was only just to acknowledge that they [John's creditors, George's critics] had been deceived by appearances and that they [subsequently, after repayment] fully acquitted him of unfraternal and ungenerous conduct."[29]

At the time, Dilke was recommending Reynolds, rather than Brown, as the best biographer—an opinion that George accepted. But in 1846 Reynolds resignedly turned his materials over to Milnes. The free-for-all struggle as to who would write and publish the first biography of John Keats had an ironic outcome: Milnes, fourteen years younger than John, had never met him. George would have preferred Reynolds or Dilke, but among George, Dilke, Brown, Reynolds, and Taylor there was simply too much schadenfreude.[30] Dilke cooperated with Milnes, but it is clear from his reviews and fact-correcting notes in the volumes' margins that he would have been the better biographer.

Richard Monckton Milnes (1809–1885) was a curious but apt choice to take on the assignment. A grandson of the fourth Lord Galway, he had been educated at Cambridge, where he befriended Tennyson. After university he toured Greece and Italy, where he met Brown. In 1837 Milnes was elected to Parliament as a conservative from Yorkshire, and he interested himself in copyright law and reform schools. When he undertook the Keats assignment, he had published three small books and was working on another, a book of verse called *Palm Leaves*, published in 1844.

Milnes's Keats project was a seven-year effort, culminating with publication in 1848. He methodically contacted members of the Keats circle, seeking their correspondence from and recollections of the poet. A partial collection of their replies occupies more than 200 pages in the second volume of *The Keats Circle*. Had Milnes not undertaken this task during the 1840s, it is likely that major portions of the Keats story would have been lost.

The twist in the story, with respect to George, is that when he died on 24 December 1841 he had not yet written to Milnes, who was just getting started on the project. George's widow Georgiana married John Jeffrey on 5 January 1843. Jeffrey wrote to Milnes in 1845:

> I have recently seen in the public newspapers that you are about to publish a new & correct Life of John Keats, the poet; & such information afforded me much pleasure, as I am fully satisfied that such a task could not have been undertaken by a more appropriate person, yourself a poet & an Englishman. By my recent marriage with the widow of the late George Keats, who resided in this City; I have become possessed of papers & information relative to the poet Keats, without which, it is impossible in my opinion to give his complete life. . . . It is earnestly desired by the children of the late George Keats, who are now living here, that full justice,

so long withheld, should be done to the memory of their Uncle &
that the garbled life [Hunt's sketch] of him now before the public
be corrected & made complete if possible.[31]

Milnes responded immediately, and Jeffrey began the tedious task of
transcribing Keats's letters. When he sent the transcripts to Milnes in September, he noted, "I am rather disappointed with it [the correspondence].
. . . I have copied nearly all the letters for several reasons; in the first place
I think you are the proper judge as to what ought & what ought not to
be published; in the second place I could scarcely comprehend the letter until I had copied it, as they were almost all miserably illegible & badly
dated; in the third place I suppose there are many things mentioned in the
letters which though unfit for publication may yet be of considerable service to you."[32]

Jeffrey's transcripts were enormously helpful to Milnes, but they were
incomplete.[33] The Keats letters remained in Louisville for decades thereafter. When George's grandson, John Gilmer Speed, published *The Letters
of John Keats* in 1883 after working with the same materials, he noted, "Mr.
Jeffrey evidently exercised his own discretion in making selections from
the letters, and just as evidently did not exercise a very wise discretion."[34]

So ended the saga of George Keats's involvement in defining the legacy of
his brother John. The primary deterrent was his remoteness in Louisville.
Although he could have, and should have, squared up his accounts with
John in 1820, his failure to do so left him exposed to Charles Brown's ven-
detta. If George had devoted the time and the means to travel to London
sometime between 1828 and 1840, he might have resolved the dispute and
begun the task of rounding up the materials and recollections that it later
took Milnes seven years to accomplish.

Because George was prosperous during the 1830s, even offering to
underwrite the expenses of a biography, one must assume that there were
other things on his mind. As he wrote to Dilke in 1838, "I am now a Kentuckian."[35] Perhaps he did not want to confront all the old issues—the
family origins, the abandonment, the Cockney label, the early financial
setbacks, hostility from the poet's friends who believed he had failed John,
and the intractable Brown. The passage of time, the distance, and his busy
life in Louisville were factors as well. So George left the Keats legacy to be
defined by others—notably, Milnes.

After publishing *Life, Letters, and Literary Remains* in 1848, Milnes continued to serve in Parliament but switched from Tory to Liberal. In 1863 he was made the first Baron Houghton by Lord Palmerston, who had made the same political journey. Harry Buxton Forman's four-volume set *The Poetical Works and Other Writings of John Keats* appeared in 1883, overshadowing Speed's trilogy of the same year. William Michael Rossetti (1829–1919) and Sidney Colvin (1845–1927) both published Keats biographies in 1887. Amy Lowell's blockbuster two-volume *John Keats* was published in 1925. Numerous biographies followed, including Dorothy Hewlett's in 1938 (Marie Adami's *Fanny Keats* was published a year earlier, in 1937), Walter Jackson Bate's and Aileen Ward's in 1963, Robert Gittings's in 1968, Andrew Motion's in 1997, and Nicholas Roe's in 2012. In addition, many other works usefully peeled away specific layers of the story, such as Gittings's *Keats Inheritance* in 1964. The monumental collections of letters published by Hyder Edward Rollins between 1948 and 1955, as well as a posthumously corrected 1965 edition, define Keats as well as any biographer might. Other compilations by Maurice Buxton Forman and Jack Stillinger also serve valuable purposes. More such efforts will appear over time.

PROSPERITY

1828–1841

Georgiana and the two children returned from England in November 1828 aboard the *Britannia,* arriving in New York's South Street Seaport evidently much refreshed by their stay. George wrote to his sister Fanny, "I was on the beach ready to receive her, and was happy to see her and the children look so well, they are certainly improved by the journey." Although Georgiana may have expedited the settling of the estate matters, she made little headway in warming relations with Fanny Llanos. George went on to tell his sister, "The main drawback . . . is that circumstances prevented you from becoming so well acquainted with her as might reasonably have been expected."[1] In other words, Fanny had ignored Georgiana in London.

Aside from the troublesome matters in England, George had found his bearings in Louisville by 1826. The following decade and a half would lead him to real prosperity, both intellectual and financial. Because so few writings by or about George remain, the development of his character is best framed by the type of friends he kept and by the community of which he became an important part.

The community was gradually being built up, particularly as travel and communications became easier. Stage routes had been added to Washington, Philadelphia, and New York. The trip from New York to Louisville took seven days, with a fare of $50, as George noted in a letter encouraging the Dilkes to visit.[2] A stage line had been opened in 1824 linking Maysville, Kentucky, on the Ohio River above Cincinnati, to Louisville through Lexington and Frankfort, a two-day journey.[3] Nightly passenger steamboat service to Cincinnati was also in place.

The population of Louisville had risen to 7,503. An 1826 visitor, the Duke of Saxe-Weimar, described the city in his *Travels through North America:* "I . . . found an extremely numerous and, contrary to my expectations, even an elegant society. It [a wedding] was a real English rout. . . . [Louisville] consists of three streets running parallel to the Ohio, of which only the first or front one [Main Street] is built out completely and paved. . . . It has several churches, tolerably well built; . . . to the north side of the town [are] several respectable country-houses . . . all built of brick; and then a handsome wood, through which a causeway runs, which is used by the inhabitants as a pleasure walk."[4]

The building boom continued for a number of years, fueled by population growth (there were 10,341 residents in 1830 and 21,210 in 1840)[5] and by calamity. The flood of 1832 was described by historian Ben Casseday: "An unparalleled flood in the Ohio [rose] to the extraordinary height of fifty-one feet above low-water mark. . . . Nearly all the frame buildings near the river were either floated off or turned over and destroyed. . . . This calamity . . . could have but a temporary effect on the progress of the city. . . . There were built during the summer of this year [1836] 110 stores and 114 dwelling houses and as for dwellings it would be impossible to rent one, finished or unfinished."[6] Four years later, the so-called great fire engulfed thirty buildings along Main, Market, and Third Streets. The opportunities for construction and the demand for timber were boundless.

The trail of George's business dealings consists of 114 land transactions in Louisville (as well as timber lots elsewhere) between 1822 and 1845 in which he was the principal grantor or grantee or had a partnership interest, recorded in deeds in the Jefferson County Courthouse. The first of these, filed 18 April 1822, was for the sale of a half interest in the land under the sawmill at Water Street; the sellers were David Prentice and Thomas W. Bakewell and their wives, and the sale price was $6,000. The filing was an indenture recording a mortgage from Keats to the sellers.[7] He paid it off ten years later. This transaction was emblematic of many that followed: an exchange between friends that involved a going-forward debt. Keats bought another lot on Water Street from Prentice on 1 February 1826 for $2,000, by this time owing him $8,680. For the next two decades, this property served as home base for Keats's various enterprises.

Prentice died in 1826, about the time Daniel Smith became George's partner, presumably having bought out the residual Prentice and Bakewell equity. George and Joseph Middleton were named executors to Prentice's will.[8] Smith and Keats remained partners, in multiple arrangements, for fifteen years. Deeds suggest that Smith usually provided the majority of the capital, while George described himself as the managing partner.

During this period, George's philosophical society was gathering steam. The society's formal name, membership, and agenda were unrecorded. Others have noted that there were discussions of Thomas Carlyle and transcendentalism, and George surely would have suggested a discussion of phrenology. Louisville, it turned out, had a cultured elite who were happy to put business aside in the evenings. The philosophical society was the second of fourteen known civic and business groups that George became involved in as his friendships and his reputation grew. Although his activities list is punctuated by business and governmental endeavors, it also illustrates his abiding interest in ideas and education, such as his trusteeship of Louisville College, a precursor to the University of Louisville. George's activities included the following:

1824	Water warden, Preservation Engine Fire Company[9]
1825	Philosophical society
1827	Ohio Bridge commissioner
1830	Incorporator, Merchants Louisville Insurance Company
1830	Unitarian Church
1831	Curator, Louisville Lyceum
1832	Director, Bank of Kentucky
1832–1841	Director and president, Louisville Hotel Company
1836	Trustee and treasurer, Kentucky Historical Society
1836	Mechanics Savings Institution
1836	President, Louisville Charitable Society
1837	Chairman, Harlan Museum
1839	Director, Lexington and Ohio Railroad Company
1840	Trustee, Louisville College
1841	Member, Louisville City Council

At the end of 1827, the Ohio Bridge Commission was formed. In addition to Keats, the commissioners included James Guthrie and John Jeremiah Jacob, both of whom would figure importantly in George's circle. Also on the board was George Wood Meriwether, treasurer of Louisville before and after its incorporation and a future fellow Unitarian.

Guthrie served as Keats's personal attorney in numerous real estate transactions and assisted George in drawing up his will in 1841. During the years of their friendship, Guthrie served as chairman of the Finance Committee of the City Council and in the state legislature—in both the house and the senate. He drew George onto the boards of the Lexington and Ohio Railroad and the Bank of Kentucky and encouraged his involvement with the Louisville Medical Institute. After George died, Guthrie went on to become secretary of the treasury (1853–1857) under President Franklin Pierce, head of the Louisville and Nashville Railroad during the Civil War, and a member of the U.S. Senate in 1865. George, like much of Louisville, was a Whig, while Guthrie was a Jacksonian Democrat, but their political differences did not impede their friendship.

John Jacob became the first president of the Bank of Kentucky when it was organized in 1835, with George as a founding director. Jacob owned a large swath of land just south of the original city center, known as Jacob's Wood, bounded by Fifth, Preston, Prather (Broadway), and Breckenridge Streets. George may have bought timber from him.

The Ohio Bridge Commission completed its recommendations by the end of 1829, leading to discussions about expense. The city's charter, which had been drafted at the same time, was amended in 1830 to prevent the City Council from borrowing or appropriating money without a majority vote, and there was a fear that the bridge might be too lavish.[10] Another six years passed while architect Ithiel Town (1784–1844) designed a wooden structure and the financing was organized. The cornerstone was finally laid on 7 September 1836 at the foot of Twelfth Street, with Wilkins Tannehill orating.[11] However, the Panic of 1837 intervened, and the contractor did not proceed with the project. Finally, in 1867, following an act of Congress, the Louisville and Nashville Railroad financed the first bridge spanning the Ohio River at Louisville, known as the Fourteenth Street Bridge. After forty years, the commission's dream was finally realized when a train passed over the bridge in 1870.[12]

Keats advertised his business discreetly, including a notice in four issues of the *Focus* in 1828: "Builders are informed that my Saw mill is now in operation, and will continue cutting so long as there are bills wanted."[13] George expanded the sawmill's scope by vertically integrating his timber sourcing. Logs were transported to Louisville from the Appalachian foothills, down the Kentucky River, then to the Ohio River, and finally to his mill. On 1 January 1830 he entered into a five-year timber concession, giving him a supply advantage over his competitors. He also cleared timber stands closer to Louisville, out on the Bardstown Pike,[14] requiring more leased slave labor from Dr. Ewing. Leaving aside the moral issues surrounding slavery, the arrangement was typical in the pre–Civil War period and in some ways was analogous to modern union-hall hiring practices.

The Bank of the United States opened a new branch at 45 East Main Street in 1831.[15] George had been borrowing from it since 1828 to develop his real estate holdings, which became an extension of the sawmill or a second line of business.[16] However, he was subject to the bank's political fortunes. As he wrote to Fanny in 1832:

I intend to continue my present timber business untill I have built homes enough to yield an annual rent sufficient to support my family in a liberal manner. . . . [One day] I shall retire from my present engrossing occupation, and visit the country of my youth. Upon my real estate rests my credit, which has hitherto enabled me to extend my business to any extent, by paying an Interest of about 6 ¾ per Cent. . . . However the U.S. Bank has been withdrawing its loans, thereby reducing my business capital, and . . . making the collection of debts more difficult than heretofore, and causing me considerable trouble, and a general stagnation.[17]

The Unitarian Church of Louisville was established in 1830, shortly after the 1825 founding of the American Unitarian Association in Boston.[18] Hobbled by Congregationalist resistance to the faith in Massachusetts, and driven by young Harvard graduates determined to spread their enthusiasm to the West, Unitarianism first arrived in Louisville in 1829, when Francis Goddard welcomed the Reverend John Pierpont (1785–1866) into his schoolhouse to hear about the rational theology. Mann Butler, George Meriwether, Henry Pirtle, Samuel S. Nicholas, and Fortunatus Cosby, all friends of Keats, were there. Some were likely members of his philosophical society, considering that its interests were similar to the tenets of Unitarianism, but the only proclaimed member was Samuel Osgood, an associate of Clarke. Osgood said, "We used to be often together at a Club of the choice men of Louisville Ky.—scholars, men of the learned professions, judges, statesmen, &c. There George Keats was well received."[19]

The founders of the church quickly raised an edifice at Fifth and Walnut Streets, loosely patterned after New England churches. The front was in Greek Revival style, with Doric columns supporting a pediment frieze and entablature, while the exterior was coated with marbled stucco. Inside were 74 pew boxes (for sale) and gallery seating for 650. Finished in 1832, it was the westernmost outpost of the Unitarian Church.[20] Francis Parkman (1788–1852) came out from Boston to dedicate the building. In 1833 twenty-three-year-old George Chapman was installed as the church's first minister.

Keats, nominally an Episcopalian, did not join immediately. The following anecdote was relayed by his great-granddaughter, Emma Keats Speed Sampson: One Sunday, the community's churches were hosting a combined picnic for the young families in their congregations. George came across a few children playing by themselves and asked why they were not at the picnic. "Oh, we are Unitarians and we weren't invited," one of them responded. After that, George looked into the church to find out what Unitarians stood for and what they believed. He was so impressed by their doctrine that he became a member. This was before James Freeman Clarke came to Louisville.[21]

Within a year, Chapman, who was dying of tuberculosis, returned to Massachusetts. He was replaced by Clarke, an 1833 Harvard Divinity School graduate. He arrived having no place to live, so he stayed with the Keats family during a portion of his 1833–1839 tenure in Louisville, perhaps in an earlier home or perhaps on Walnut Street, just two blocks from the church. Clarke was a popular figure in Louisville, admired for his intellectual underpinnings, and an indefatigable proselytizer of the Unitarian faith.

The Keatses welcomed Clarke into their home, and the friendship that blossomed resulted in the most important surviving description of George and the most persuasive written defense of his character. From 1835 to 1837, Clarke was assisted by Samuel Osgood, who was also an admirer of Keats. When Clarke returned to Boston in 1839, he retained his interest in the Keats family, having arranged for Emma Keats to study with his cousin Margaret Fuller at the Greene School in Providence and later at Miss Tilden's in Jamaica Plain, Boston.[22]

While in Louisville, Clarke launched the *Western Messenger,* a liberal magazine of religion, abolitionism, and national duty targeted to readers in the Mississippi Valley, who were generally "hard-shelled Calvinists" and anti-Unitarian.[23] His cousin, Ralph Waldo Emerson, contributed his earliest poems to the *Messenger;* transcendentalist Margaret Fuller's writings appeared in the magazine as well. George Keats contributed "Winander Lake and Mountains and Ambelside" by John Keats,[24] the work's first publication, along with John's "Ode to Apollo," which had been included in a letter to Tom Keats dated 25–27 September 1818.[25] Hyder Edward Rollins commented about these contributions, "Without doubt George Keats did everything possible to advance his poet brother's reputation, the growth of which he watched with almost pathetic eagerness."[26]

George was also one of the founders of the Merchants Louisville Insurance Company, incorporated in 1830. His friend William Gifford Bakewell was a fellow incorporator, as was Nicholas Berthoud. James Hughes, president of the Bank of the United States, and William Prather, whose father Thomas headed the first Bank of Kentucky, were also involved in the insurance group. Guthrie was the company's counsel. As the city grew into its mercantile phase, there was an increasing need for marine insurance to protect against losses during river transport and handling. With few insurers west of the Alleghenies, individual merchants took to covering the liabilities of their colleagues, usually for a 6 percent premium. In 1818 Keats's friend Thomas Bullitt had chartered the Louisville Insurance Company to address the need.[27] Later, the Merchants Louisville Insurance group insured a steamboat that was blown up on the Red River and was involved in a precedent-setting case resolved by the U.S. Supreme Court in 1837.

In 1831 the Louisville Lyceum was organized, possibly as an outgrowth of the philosophical society, and George was one of its seven original curators. Its purpose was to support public education: "Its objects are simply to promote popular improvement, by the diffusion of useful knowledge: its means of executing these objects are, 1st. Written Essays; 2d. Oral Addresses; and 3d. Discussions. A small library has been commenced."[28] According to the *History of the Ohio Falls and Their Cities:* "The Louisville Lyceum, which was established this year [1831], under the encouragement and with the more direct aid of some of the most intelligent and prominent citizens of the place, [sent] $100 to Governor Metcalf . . . to be offered as a premium [for] 'the best theory of education, to be illustrated by the examination of two or more pupils who have been instructed in accordance with its principles.'"[29]

Among the other curators was educator Edward Mann Butler, principal of the Jefferson Seminary (a precursor of the University of Louisville) and of Louisville's first public grammar school. Another curator was the above-named George Wood Meriwether, a retail merchant and friend of Audubon's in-laws, the Berthoud family. The *History of the Ohio Falls and Their Cities* goes on to note that "the Lyceum . . . was evidently ahead of its time, and did not last more than a few years."[30] In 1840 another of the original lyceum curators, Simon S. Bucklin, founded the Louisville Franklin Lyceum, which became the Mercantile Library, housing 3,000 volumes.[31]

Flush with successes, George assembled a development tract between Sixth and Seventh Streets on the south side of Main Street by completing thirteen separate transactions, most of them in 1830, for a cumulative $7,741. The majority of the transactions were in the name of Smith and Keats, the entity that went on to invest $10,000 cash in the Louisville Hotel, an investment that equaled 10 to 12 percent of the company's capital.[32] Construction of the hotel began in 1832, and local architect Hugh Roland modeled the structure, with a colonnaded limestone front, after Boston's Tremont Hotel. The city directory noted that the "edifice . . . will surpass in elegance and arrangement, any in our Western Country, and in extent will exceed most in the United States."[33] The 124-foot frontage on Main Street opened back to a 22-foot-diameter rotunda that led to wings of bed chambers on the upper floors and a large dining room on the main floor. In the basement were "Rooms for Servants, Shoe Blacks, &c. . . . In the back are situated Bathing Houses and every other convenience."[34]

Guests were likely happy to arrive at the hotel after a ride down Main Street. Caleb Atwater (1778–1867) described the scene: "Main St., for the distance of about one mile, presents a display of wealth and grandeur. . . . The stores filled with commodities and manufactures of every clime and every art, dazzle the eye."[35] J. S. Buckingham (1786–1855), a later English traveler, saw Louisville with a somewhat more jaundiced eye: "The streets have brick pavements at the side ways. . . . The central parts of the streets are paved with narrow slits of limestone, standing on their edges; and the roughness of a ride over these in one of the hackney coaches of the town, is equal to the punishment of a corduroy road, and makes riding more fatiguing than walking."[36]

Competing with the nearby Galt House, the Louisville Hotel provided visitors with a thoroughly up-to-date guest experience. The hotel was opened in 1833 and survived in its original form to 1853, when it was architecturally altered. A successor hotel remained open until 1938; the building was razed in 1949.

The hotel board elected Keats president in 1841. Guthrie was a director, as was Dr. Theodore Samuel Bell, who was also the board's secretary and one of George's closest friends. Another director and friend was Louisville notable Leven Lawrence Shreve, who later founded the Louisville Gas Company with John Jacob. Shreve and Keats were also Bank of Kentucky directors and fellow Unitarians. Shreve lived in an enormous double house on Walnut Street, just a few blocks from George; it was the first residence in the city to be lit by gas. Jacob Beckwith also sat on the hotel board. He was a former captain of the 109-ton steamboat *Velocipede,* co-owned with Thomas W. Bakewell, and was a successor owner of the Prentice and Bakewell foundry.

Completion of the Louisville Hotel cemented George's reputation, even in his own mind, as a builder. He then turned his energies toward building a new residence for himself, his final one, on West Walnut Street. He bought two lots in 1831 between Walnut and Chestnut Streets, near Third and Fourth Streets, paying Ann E. F. Smith $3,735 and Frederick and Ellen Ernst $3,400 for the adjoining property.[37] Completed in 1835 adjacent to Jacob's estate, George's new home was quickly dubbed the "Eng-lishman's palace" by locals. Constructed of limestone and brick, it included an extensive library, where George operated his cultural salon and entertained visiting dignitaries.[38]

The family that filled the Englishman's palace was expanding in proportion to it. In addition to the "Georges," there were seven surviving children and at least three household slaves: Jesse, Hannah, and Lucy.[39] George described Georgiana to Dilke in 1825 as "cheerful and contented."[40] The same year he told his sister Fanny, rather candidly, "You could not fail to love her; for she is the very spirit of candour, and generosity, a cheerful companion and persevering Freind thro' good and ill, she has considerable natural talents but is not overburthen'd with accomplishments."[41] In a reflective moment eight years letter, he acknowledged to Dilke, "It is true she endured many grievous privations in my adverse circumstances, in fact she offered to assist me with her needle, and by her noble behaviour showed me the best side of her character which under uninterrupted good fortune would never have been developed."[42]

Georgiana was often sick with bilious fever and rheumatism, and she gave birth to eight children during these years. In addition to the first four (Georgiana, Rosalind, Emma, and Isabel), there was John Henry, named for his uncles John Keats (despite the poet's request not to; he preferred the name Edmund) and Henry Wylie, who was born in 1827. He was followed by Clarence, a popular name,[43] who arrived in 1830; Ella, in 1833; and Alice Ann, named for her great-grandmother Alice Jennings and her grandmother Ann Wylie, in 1836. George wrote of them to Dilke, describing Ella as "a pretty blue eyed Baby."[44]

Also commencing in 1831, Keats and Smith bought about thirty-five properties and developed residences on several of them, which they either rented out or resold. These properties were scattered from Floyd Street to the east to Twelfth and Jefferson to the west, mostly running along Main, Market, and Jefferson Streets. Two—one at Fifth and Jefferson, and another at Eighth and Water—were on a scale with the hotel property. They also acquired 213 acres along Bardstown Pike, which was most likely a woodlot used to supply the mill. That transaction, with Richard Porter, included one "negro boy." Among the parties to these transactions were Andrew Buchanan, Dr. Theodore Samuel Bell, Charles Whittingham, Billy Bakewell, John Bull, Samuel Gwathmey, James Rudd, John Wenzel, Fortunatus Cosby, Isaac Stewart, and others who constituted a who's who of both Louisville and the boards George would eventually sit on.

John Howard Payne (1791–1852), the American actor-poet-author, visited the Keatses on 11 December 1834, after returning from a successful two-decade theatrical stint in London. There, he had composed the song "Home! Sweet Home!" for the opera *Clari or the Maid of Milan,* which sold more than 100,000 copies. Payne was attempting to raise funds for a weekly international literary periodical to be titled either *Jam Jehan Nima* (translation: the goblet wherein you may behold the universe) or the *Journal of Two Hemispheres,* so he looked up Keats. Also, Payne had been involved in an unreciprocated romance with Mary Godwin Shelley, providing a link to John Keats. George promised to subscribe to Payne's journal, to find other subscribers, and perhaps to invest. He also turned over four of John's poems to Payne for first-time publication in the *Ladies' Companion,* to which Payne was contributing. These included the sonnets beginning "Fame like a wayward girl will still be coy" and "Hither, Hither, Love" and the poem beginning "'Tis the witching time of night."[45]

Meanwhile, George's recognition in the community propelled him onto the board of the Bank of Kentucky. The original Bank of Kentucky had been an amalgam of branches assembled after its charter was issued on 27 December 1806. It then ran into the headwinds of economic crises, competition, currency confusion (with other state banks and the U.S. Bank all issuing their own specie), and finally political interference. By 1822, the state let all the branches go their own way, with the last of them separated by 1830. In this diminished environment, it was very difficult for business-people like George to obtain credit or even to conduct cash transactions.

The U.S. Bank, where Keats did business, provided a measure of financial stability. However, when Andrew Jackson became president in 1829, he made it clear that he would not renew the bank's charter. In 1832 he vetoed its charter renewal past 1836, and in 1833 he withdrew all federal funds, effectively destroying the bank. Nervously anticipating these events, the state incorporated a successor Bank of Kentucky on 22 February 1834. Guthrie, by then a state senator, arranged for Keats to be one of fifteen "commissioners to open books and receive subscriptions for the capital stock, and to superintend the selection and induct in office the first Board of Directors."[46] Other commissioners included Keats's friends Jacob and Shreve. The bank's charter divided its eleven directors into two classes: George was one of three named by the commonwealth, while Jacob and Shreve were among eight representatives of the shareholders. On 26 January 1835 Jacob (previously a director of the Bank of the United States branch in Louisville) was named president of the rechartered bank.

George Clark Gwathmey, who had been a teller in the Bank of the United States, became the first cashier. Gwathmey's son Alfred later married Georgey Keats.[47] Other directors were William Garvin, Angereau Gray, Robert J. Ward, Ariss Throckmorton, and others—a list that included many of Louisville's leaders and major characters (see their biographical sketches in the appendix).

The Bank of Kentucky soon moved into the former U.S. Bank building on Main Street between Second and Third, whose construction had barely been completed in time for its dissolution. The building was given "a handsome Tetrastyle Ionic stone Portico . . . [whose] proportions . . . are those of the Temple of Bacchus at Teos."[48] In the rear was a residence occupied by the Gwathmey family, where Georgey Keats Gwathmey would later live.

The bank did not enjoy a smooth start. Jackson's suspension of the federal banking system augured in a period of wildcat banking supervised by each state under inconsistent regulatory standards. Eastern financial interests may have hoped that Jackson's replacement by Martin Van Buren of New York would bring a policy change; however, he retained Jackson's cabinet (with one exception), and his efforts to create an independent Treasury policy did not succeed until 1840, when he was voted out of office.

The bank had planned to deputize George for a capital-raising trip to London in 1836, but the markets proved too unsettling. In 1836 he informed Dilke, "I was applied to by the B of Ky and afterwards by the Governor [James Clark, in office from 1836 to 1839] and the Corporation of Llle to undertake the commission to sell a large amount of Scrip in London belonging to the respective parties. I was for 2 mos in daily expectation of starting for London . . . various circumstances have crea[ted] delays until the price of the securities is so fallen as to induce all parties to wait for a more favorable time, only at present making occasional efforts at the Eastern Cities."[49] A year and a half later, his venture to London was still under consideration, but it never happened. His last mention of the trip was to Dilke in 1838: "If it were possible for me to leave my business, I might accept an appointment which has been suggested to me to negotiate a loan in London for the City of Louisville, and perhaps for the State & B of Kentucky."[50]

In a remarkable coincidence, George Keats's friend from Enfield, Charles Briggs, played a significant role in creating the Panic of 1837.[51] Briggs had moved to New Orleans in 1824 to establish himself as a cotton broker and dealer in Mexican specie. On 4 March 1837, the date of Van Buren's inauguration, the firm of Hermann, Briggs and Company, which was overextended on cotton loans in a falling market, defaulted.

Its losses, totaling between $4 million and $8 million, immediately caused its New York backer, J. L. and S. Joseph and Company, to fail, triggering an East Coast bank crisis. Van Buren declined to intervene, and with no federal safety net, banks throughout the United States froze their liquidity and watched their asset values plummet, hastening a deep recession.[52] Economic recovery came in fits and starts but did not take hold until 1840, when Van Buren was replaced by Whig William Henry Harrison, followed by John Tyler.[53]

The Lexington and Ohio Railroad was originally chartered on 27 June 1830 with the intent of linking Lexington to the Ohio River (but not at Louisville) to get its agricultural goods to eastern and European markets via the river system. By 1834, its managers had succeeded in laying about twenty-five miles of track into Frankfort, using stone sills from a quarry in Lexington and iron rails acquired in Liverpool, shipped via New Orleans and Louisville.[54] The train's first run from Lexington to Frankfort was completed in two hours and twenty-nine minutes in 1835. The railroad, however, endured constant financial crises,[55] and the organizers reluctantly turned to Louisville for capital assistance, adding Guthrie and Keats as directors. A short segment of track was laid along the center of Main Street, starting at Sixth Street and extending about three miles west to Portland. Using a steam engine, the trains were extremely noisy, dirty, and unpopular. In 1842, after yet another financial reorganization, the Louisville trackage was sold to a street railway system that used less intrusive horse-drawn carriages that could accommodate twelve passengers each. Finally in 1851 the line connected Frankfort to Louisville, terminating at Jefferson and Brook Streets.[56]

A large group of investors, including Keats, incorporated the Mechanics Savings Institution in 1836. Capitalized at $100,000, it was a distant fourth among the city's banks, behind the Bank of Kentucky ($5 million), the Bank of Louisville ($2 million), and the Louisville branch of the Northern Bank of Kentucky ($600,000).[57] Its president was Samuel Gwathmey, brother of George C. Gwathmey. Keats's role was passive.

The Kentucky Historical Society was organized on 22 April 1836 and settled in Louisville in 1838. George Keats, an incorporator, became one of its trustees when the society created a library and began functioning in the Telegraph Building at Third and Market Streets. The society's goal was to collect and preserve items of historical interest pertaining to Kentucky. Judge John Rowan, recently retired from the U.S. Senate and living at Federal Hill ("My Old Kentucky Home") in Bardstown, was elected president.

George Mortimer Bibb, also recently retired from the U.S. Senate, was vice president. Dr. Edward Jarvis, a Harvard-educated physician from Concord, Massachusetts, was librarian; he was responsible for the gifts of books by Ralph Waldo Emerson, Henry David Thoreau, and John Quincy Adams. Serving as trustees were Keats's close friend Clarke, also with transcendental connections, and Humphrey Marshall Sr., yet another former U.S. senator, brother-in-law of Chief Justice John Marshall (Humphrey had married his own cousin, Mary Marshall, sister of the chief justice), and author of the 1812 *History of Kentucky*. Among Marshall's accomplishments was fighting a pistol duel with Henry Clay in 1809 in which each was slightly injured. Another trustee was Benjamin O. Peers, a former president of Transylvania University who had recently removed to Louisville to serve as rector of St. Paul's Episcopal Church. Leonard Bliss Jr., who reported for George Dennison Prentice's *Louisville Journal,* was another trustee, but his term did not last long. After Bliss wrote a critical article on a political speech by Henry C. Pope in 1842, Pope's cousin Godfrey hunted Bliss down and shot him dead as he emerged from the Galt House.[58]

Probably the most colorful of the society's trustees, however, was Prentice himself, the *Louisville Journal*'s Whig editor and a close friend of the Keats family. Prentice's paper sparred editorially and libelously throughout the 1830s with Shadrack Penn's *Louisville Public Advertiser* in one of the great American newspaper wars. One of Prentice's milder retorts to a Penn editorial was this: "We prefer that they should accept our hand open and ungloved, but if they would rather have it in the shape of a FIST it is still at their service."[59] A subsequent sketch of Prentice stated, "Next to being a good writer, it was also useful to be a good shot."[60] Prentice was both. In 1838, the year the Historical Society opened in Louisville, it was reported: "Mr. Prentice, of the Journal, fought another pistol battle August 14th—this time with Major Thomas P. Moore, at the Harrodsburg Springs, both parties coming out of the conflict without physical injury."[61]

The Kentucky Historical Society's trustee meetings must have been some of the most entertaining George attended. After Judge Rowan died in 1843 and Dr. Jarvis returned to Massachusetts due to his distaste for slavery, the society became inactive and turned its collection over to the Louisville Library. In 1876 the society was revived with state sponsorship in Frankfort, where, after some lapses, it remains a vibrant institution.[62]

The Harlan Museum's predecessor, the Louisville Museum Company, was chartered on 20 February 1835,[63] three years after James Reid Lambdin moved the artifacts from his first museum in Pittsburgh, the Museum of

Natural History and Gallery of Paintings, down to Louisville.[64] It was modeled after Philadelphia's Peale Museum—in modern parlance, a curiosity cabinet. Very few records remain. It appears that Samuel Casseday was the museum's landlord on Main Street. A letter from an 1836 visitor, James R. Robertson, provides a sense of the museum's contents: "I paid 25 cents and went into the museum, where I saw near 3,000 natural curiosities consisting of animals, vegetables, and minerals, together with a splendid gallery of painting, both ancient and modern."[65]

By 1837, the entity was in need of reorganization, including new shareholders. George Keats's friend Dr. Urban Epinitis Ewing, along with several other stockholders, proposed that the new funds be paid to Casseday to obtain title to the museum.[66] Subsequently, in October 1837, a somewhat different group, this time including Keats, met to continue with the reorganization; Keats was elected chairman. On 1 February 1838 the legislature rechartered the museum, this time as the Harlan Museum Company. Casseday remained a trustee. The reason for rebranding the museum "Harlan" has been lost. One possible explanation involves Dr. Richard Harlan, a naturalist from Philadelphia and a longtime colleague of John James Audubon. Harlan, born 19 September 1796 into a Quaker family, completed his medical degree at the University of Pennsylvania in 1818. At that time, he had already been elected (in 1815) to the Philadelphia Academy of Natural Sciences, where he showed an interest in paleontology and comparative anatomy. By 1821, he was professor of anatomy at Peale's Philadelphia Museum Company. Over the next twenty years, he published more than sixty works on a variety of subjects ranging from herpetology (the study of reptiles) to *Fauna Americana,* a zoological survey of North America, to an *Inquiry into the Functions of the Brain in Man.* His writings were controversial, and he was sometimes accused of plagiarism, but his works were also regarded as anticipating Darwin.

Harlan was an indefatigable collector of mammals, reptiles, and human skulls. Many came from Audubon, who would ship extra alligators and birds back to Philadelphia for Harlan's use. The two had met in 1824, beginning a seventeen-year period in which Harlan helped raise subscriptions for Audubon's printed volumes.[67] In 1829–1830, when Audubon was on one of his extensive travels, he parked his two sons in Louisville with his brothers-in-law: Victor G. stayed with Billy Bakewell, and John W. stayed with Nicholas Berthoud.[68] Harlan was well aware of Audubon's deep ties to Louisville, and in early 1830 the latter visited the city on his way north from New Orleans. Harlan and fellow Philadelphia Academy member McMurtrie (who had written the first history of Louisville in 1819) were jointly involved in preparing an Audubon folio for publication.[69] In 1832, when that publication did not succeed, all the parties were left mired in debt. Another Philadelphia acquaintance, Jane Bachman, noted Harlan's "unreliability in business matters."[70] That same year he came into possession of the partial remains—the snout—of an ichthyosaur, described as an "alligator animal of about seventy feet in length."[71] He gave the relic to the Museum of Natural History in Paris. Also in 1832, Harlan absented himself to join a cholera commission in Montreal and then took several trips to Europe. He moved to New Orleans in 1842 and died of apoplexy there on 30 September 1843.[72]

Lacking documentation, it is reasonable to assume that Bakewell knew about Harlan's artifacts and arranged for a number of them to be displayed in Louisville in 1835 under Harlan's imprimatur. Harlan, perennially stressed for funds, was likely not an investor in the museum, and although Bakewell did not serve as a museum trustee, his fingerprints on the project seem evident.[73] The trustees of the Harlan Museum were generally downtown businessman types who would have joined the Chamber of Commerce; they lacked university or curatorial training. Trustees Dr. James C. Johnston and Dr. U. E. Ewing had medical training, but both were more interested in their investments than in their medical practices. After the museum failed, date uncertain, Harlan's artifacts disappeared.[74] When Peale's Museum in Philadelphia failed following his death in 1827, its curiosities were acquired by promoter P. T. Barnum (1810–1891).

George also continued to be involved in public education. The Louisville Medical Institute was chartered in 1833 and opened in 1837, the same year the Louisville Collegiate Institute (LCI) was chartered. LCI was renamed and rechartered as Louisville College on 17 January 1840. The college, a lineal descendant of the old Jefferson Seminary (1813–1829), was devised as an extension of the free school system, which by that time had fourteen public schools.[75] The City Council, of which Keats was a member, voted in 1841 to make the schools tuition-free.[76] John Hopkins Harney, a former mathematics professor at Hanover College, was president of Louisville College. As a practical matter, LCI and then Louisville College competed with the Medical Institute in a sort of tug-of-war for support. In 1844 the college inherited the old Jefferson Seminary estate, but it was having difficulty staying open. The Medical Institute was more successful, and in 1846 they were consolidated to form the University of Louisville.[77]

Many of the college trustees came from George's circle, drawn largely from the Louisville Lyceum, the Kentucky Historical Society, and the Unitarian Church. They included judges John Rowan, Henry Pirtle, William Fontaine Bullock, and Samuel Smith Nicholas; educators Mann Butler and Francis Goddard; publisher John P. Morton; Keats; and his close friend Dr. Theodore Samuel Bell. But George was also vitally interested in the Medical Institute. His friend Joshua B. Flint was a professor of surgery there, and in 1838 the institute gave Flint $15,000 for a trip to England and Europe to gather books and medical instruments to equip the school. George provided Flint with a letter of introduction to Dilke, writing, "My friend professor Flint visits England for the purpose of buying books and apparatus for the medical Institute of Louisville."[78] The buying spree was a success, and Flint returned home with 3,000 volumes. The institute's 1838–1839 circular referred to "several thousand volumes" and noted, "in consequence of the unparalleled continuance of low water in the Ohio River, all the purchases made in Europe by one of the Faculty, during the past summer, have not been received until very lately."[79]

As the 1830s wrapped up, a few events helped define the city. Daniel Webster, at the height of his oratorical powers, visited in 1838 and was treated to a barbecue with 4,000 citizens. Gas lighting came to the downtown area in 1839—a great relief to citizens, who had been subjected to nightly attacks by robbers. And the Oakland Race Course staged a match race for the unheard-of purse of $20,000. A Kentucky horse, Grey Eagle, raced a Louisiana horse, Wagner, in a best two-out-of-three contest of four-mile heats. Even though Wagner won, Kentucky's reputation as the preeminent horse racing state was established that year.[80] It is possible that the losing owners repaired to Jim Porter's tavern to commiserate. Porter, a former jockey who had been living around Louisville since 1811, had grown to seven feet eight inches tall. When Charles Dickens met him in 1842, he described him as a lighthouse among lampposts.[81] The Louisville Jockey Club included Keats's friends Robert J. Ward and Major Ariss Throckmorton as judges, while Billy Bakewell and John Jacob served on its Ladies' Committee.[82]

Dickens did not encounter any of the George Keats circle during his one-night visit to Louisville in 1842. His unhappy view of the citizenry was framed in the bar of a steamboat: "There was a magnetism of dullness in them which would have beaten down the most facetious companion that the earth ever knew. A jest would have been a crime, and a smile would have faded into a grinning horror. Such deadly leaden people; such systematic plodding weary insupportable heaviness; such a mass of animated indigestion in respect of all that was genial, jovial, frank, social, or hearty; never, sure, was brought together elsewhere since the world began."[83]

Meanwhile, George's intellectual curiosity had moved well beyond phrenology. He became a devotee of Scottish essayist Thomas Carlyle's *Sartor Resartus* (the "tailor retailored"), published in 1832 and republished in Boston in 1836 with a preface by Ralph Waldo Emerson. Like George, Carlyle (1795–1881) was a Unitarian who had flirted with transcendentalism. Coincidentally, he had been born about five weeks after John Keats. Carlyle's work marked the literary transition from the Romantic period to the Victorian. The sartorism philosophy, loosely interpreted as an attempt to find the truth behind appearances, became an element in existentialist thinking. It was also viewed as an attack on the utilitarianism and commercialization of Britain.

Clarke wrote to Emerson in 1838: "My chief companion in the study of Carlyle is Geo. Keats—a brother of the poet John—a merchant of great intelligence & literary taste. . . . He is a man of great energy and activity here, & has built up an estate & influence, without losing a single moral feeling or literary taste. He has kept his literature for the love of it, all alone—for he has few to sympathize with him." Clarke also told Emerson that "'Sartor' he [George] likes much, and says that when debating with the other bank-directors about discounting, etc. he is puzzling himself to find out the meaning of what they are all doing by the application of the Sartor philosophy, to tear off the shows of things, and see their essence."[84]

Clarke had encouraged Emma Keats to study in Providence and in Boston. Upon her return, Emma, who was not yet eighteen, married Philip Speed in the Unitarian Church on 9 June 1841. Thirteen years later, her sister Ella married Speed's nephew George N. Peay. Little did they know that over the next two centuries they would spawn more than 500 issue, representing 90 percent of all Keats descendants, including those of Fanny Keats Llanos.

During the first year of their marriage, Emma and Philip Speed lived at Farmington, the plantation home of the late Judge John Speed, about eight miles outside the city center along the Bardstown Pike. One of Philip's brothers was Joshua Fry Speed, who invited his friend, a young Illinois legislator named Abraham Lincoln, to visit during August 1841. When Lincoln wrote a thank-you note (his so-called bread-and-butter letter) to Philip's older half sister Mary, who had served as hostess, he sent his "affectionate regards to all your sisters (including 'Aunt Emma')."[85] Emma Keats Speed was seventeen at the time.

There is no record of Lincoln and Keats having met, but Lincoln journeyed several times into the city to visit with James Speed, another of Philip's brothers who had also developed a lawyer-client relationship with George. Given that both held elective office, there may have been a gathering. If so, Keats probably would have been the more eminent of the two as the poet's brother and a city leader, versus an obscure Illinois legislator.

George had taken the plunge into elective politics late in 1840, earning a seat on the City Council from the Fourth Ward, along with his next-door neighbor and friend John Jacob. His term began in 1841 and ended upon his death on 24 December 1841. Keats was succeeded by William Neville Bullitt.

Dickens's contemporary description of Louisville remains a classic: "The buildings are smoky and blackened, from the use of bituminous coal, but an Englishman is well used to that appearance, and indisposed to quarrel with it. . . . Here, as elsewhere in these parts, the road was perfectly alive with pigs of all ages; lying about in every direction, fast asleep; or grunting along in quest of hidden dainties."[86]

Leaving Dickens aside, the mercantile city that George left behind when he died in 1841 was very different from the frontier town that had welcomed him in early 1819. The population was 21,210, including 8,554 slaves and 764 free blacks.[87] Steamboat construction, tobacco handling, large butchering and packing houses, and sawmills such as Smith and Keats were thriving. In 1840 William B. Belknap founded a hardware and manufacturing company, providing farm implements to the West, at the site of George's original sawmill.[88]

The slavery issue, which retarded Louisville's economy compared with that of Cincinnati and Pittsburgh, was twenty-four years short of resolution. German immigrants, arriving with education, skills, and, in some cases, radical ideas about freedom from government, were not readily accepted. After the Civil War, it was primarily the Germans who built Louisville's late-blooming industrial base. George Keats's partner in the Louisville Hotel was a German, John P. Wenzel. Another travel writer, Prince Maximilian of Wied, arrived in Louisville in 1832 with an introduction to Wenzel, who gave him a tour of the city.[89] Wenzel was virtually the only German American member of George's group.[90]

George's adopted city, having matured from its frontier phase and developed its mercantile character in fits and starts, was poised for a greatness that it never quite realized. George's own fate mirrored that of the city.

RUIN AND DEATH

1841

The last year of George's life was not carefully chronicled. He entered 1841 at the apex of his career in Louisville, having been elected to the City Council and continuing on several business and civic boards. He had become a member of the establishment, a term coined by Emerson just two weeks before George's death.[1] His last saved letter, to James Freeman Clarke on 4 July 1841, dealt with transcendentalism and mentioned his happiness about his daughter Emma's marriage to Philip Speed. It revealed no troubles.

It appears that Keats had earlier guaranteed the indebtedness of Tom Bakewell, who coinvested with his brother Billy over several decades, to the Portland Dry Dock Company for the construction of a hull of a large passenger steamboat. Portland Dry Dock was a hybrid entity, serving as an insurer (and perhaps financier) of riverboats as well as a maintenance and repair shop under both its own name and that of the Louisville Dry Dock Company. The officers and directors came mostly from the Louisville and Portland Canal Company, including president James Marshall and directors Simeon S. Goodwin and Billy Bakewell, among others. George provided surety for Tom despite his own misgivings about asking for such personal guarantees from others. Earlier he had explained to Dilke, "not being a scheming financier, [I do not like] . . . to ask my acquaintances to endorse for me."[2] When economic conditions made the boat's completion impractical, Portland Dry Dock demanded payment. Tom, who was residing in Cincinnati, pled insolvency, leaving $125,000 in unpaid loans. George scrambled to cover his portion of the guarantee by arranging numerous personal loans and mortgaging many of his properties.

Audubon's biographer Alice Ford, writing about the naturalist's visit to Louisville on 19–23 March 1843, stated, "William [Bakewell] implied that Thomas Bakewell's dependence on George Keats had helped bring the latter to his death, but not until after William's involvement in their affairs made his own ruin certain."[3] Billy Bakewell and his wife, Alicia, signed over their brick home on Market Street to a coffee and spice dealer named John Brand on 10 January 1842. Unable to pay off the mortgage, they vacated it on 4 April 1842, having lived there since 1829.[4] Billy, a wholesale grocer and river trader of means,[5] left Portland Dry Dock's board and shortly thereafter left Louisville. He moved to New Orleans, where his finances gradually recovered. Tom Bakewell, however, never fully rebounded. He died in 1874 after clerking for a decade for a Cincinnati paper merchant.

During the second half of 1841, George became ill, by one account having caught a cold on an arduous timber-buying trip. By 20 December 1841, Mildred (Mrs. William C.) Bullitt wrote to her son John, "Dr. Rogers thinks he [Keats] will not live long."[6] The family's oral history is garbled; one version says he died of a stomach ailment, and another attributes his death to intestinal tuberculosis.[7] George, whose symptoms likely included severe diarrhea and dehydration, wrote his will on 21 December with a firm hand and clear intent.[8] Three days later, on 24 December 1841, he died. It was less than twenty-five weeks from his "all is okay" letter to Clarke.

On Christmas Day, Keats's friend George D. Prentice penned an obituary that appeared in the *Louisville Journal*. It read in part:

> Mr. Keats was a younger brother of John Keats, the distinguished British poet, and possessed much of the genius, and all of the philosop[h]y, benevolence, and enlarged philanthropy, of the lamented bard. The suavity of his manners and the charm of his conversations endeared him to all who knew him, and his enterprise and public spirit rendered him an inestimable member of society. There is not a man in our community whose death would be more deeply and universally mourned. When such a one passes away from among us, every heart feels a mysterious chill, as if touched by the awful shadow of the tomb.[9]

Georgiana did not feel the tomb's chill for long. As Martha Bell Bullitt (daughter of Mildred) described to John less than a month after George's death, "Mr. Bakewell was broke; and it has been found that Mr. Keats died a bankrupt. But notwithstanding all that, they still continue to give parties and dash about; I believe there is a party in the City almost every evening."[10]

George's will had been witnessed by James Guthrie, who likely helped dictate its terms, and by Holliday W. Cood,[11] his sawmill colleague. The will contained somewhat unusual language, directing first that all his debts be paid, then that Georgiana receive a life interest of one-third of the residue, with the balance going outright to his children. The terms regarding the bequest to Georgiana were remarkably similar to those employed by his grandfather John Jennings with respect to George's mother. George appointed Georgiana the executrix, along with son-in-law Philip Speed and Speed's brother James (who later became attorney general of the United States). George was buried in Western Cemetery, where he remained until 1879, when John Jeffrey and Philip Speed arranged for his remains to be moved to Cave Hill Cemetery to rest with the then-deceased Georgiana.

The details of the estate reveal much of George's character. He had worked hard to build an enterprise and a portfolio of real estate interests, yet he never accumulated a solid, independent capital base. He was prone to borrowing and to working with partners who were often better capitalized. He and Georgiana lived somewhat ostentatiously, with frequent entertainments, in the Englishman's palace. George's high-profile existence led to his membership on many important community boards and yielded a distinguished circle of friends. As his clerical admirers noted, George was always willing to set aside the ledger book to discuss philosophy. However, going back to his departure from school at age fourteen and the inadequate financial grounding offered by Richard Abbey, it turned out that he was a hard worker but not a great businessman.

Two weeks after George's death, Georgiana, realizing that the debts would zero out the estate, began the process of amending the will to protect her interest. On 10 January 1842 she and Cood filed a statement, along with the will, declaring that she would renounce all the benefits due her and take her dower instead. In effect, she was claiming outright a share of the house and the real estate on which it sat as a dower. And as events unfolded, this would roll over to her second husband, John Jeffrey, when they married less than a year later, on 5 January 1843.[12] George's noncollateralized assets were sold, his remaining debts were paid at twenty cents on the dollar, and the children, to whom George had bequeathed his entire residuary estate, received nothing.[13]

George's intent, which was to deny Georgiana a half interest, was unexplained. Her comportment after his death, including the parties and her hasty remarriage to a man twenty years younger than she, suggests that their relationship was not perfect at the end. He may have suspected her future actions and worried that his estate would benefit those outside the family. From Georgiana's point of view, she may have been concerned that the creditors would seize everything, leaving her one-third share and the children's residuary shares worthless. She may have thought it was better to grab her one-half dower first and then let the creditors squabble over the balance. The Speeds, as coexecutors, did not contest Georgiana's and Cood's actions, even though Emma Keats Speed lost her inheritance as a result.

On 7 February 1842 the commonwealth ordered an appraisal of the estate to be conducted by George's old friends: educator Francis Goddard, lawyer-educator Fortunatus Cosby Jr., sawmill colleague Felix Smith,[14] and Billy Bakewell. Bakewell recused himself from the proceedings, possibly due to his own financial discomfiture or the conflict of interest due to his membership on Portland Dry Dock's board. The remaining appraisers' work was completed in five days and was returned to the court by Georgiana as correct on 17 February. The appraisement listed $38,950 in real estate, $2,175 in personal estate, $1,250 in slaves,[15] and $1,627 in bank stock. Aside from the real estate, no value was given to George's interest in the Smith and Keats sawmill, which had been used to guarantee Bakewell's debt to Portland Dry Dock. These assets totaled $44,002.[16] Seventy years later, John Henry Keats told a newspaper interviewer that his mother had realized "about $30,000" from the estate.[17]

The liquidation got under way quickly, following a 9 March 1842 notice in the *Louisville Journal*:

> Public Sale—On Thursday the 10th day of March, commencing at 10 o'clock, will be sold at public auction at the residence of the late George Keats on Walnut Street, the Household and Kitchen Furniture, together with a select collection of Books, also two female slaves. Terms: for all sums of twenty dollars and under cash, over that amount a credit of six months, the purchaser giving a note of security, payable in Bank.

Much of the furniture was bought by Cood, likely for Georgiana's continuing use. After the sale was complete, including that of the male slave, Jesse,[18] Georgiana sent a sale record to the court, noting: "P.S. Bank of Kentucky stock is mortgaged to its full for a debt of Smith and Keats to the Portland Dry Dock Co. The other stocks had been offered for sale equal to their value. Georgiana Keats—Adm. March 10."[19]

Daniel Smith was nearly caught up in his partner's bankruptcy. On 26 May 1842 he filed indentures, prepared by attorneys James Speed, William H. Field, James Guthrie, and Levi Tyler, to sequester $8,700 into his (second) wife's name to protect her against his debts. The document noted

George Keats (1797–1841) as depicted in a watercolor miniature by Joseph Severn, c. 1817.

T. Chew and Son Livery and the King's Arms Tavern in Little Moorfields, similar to the Swan and Hoop. Drawing by Charles Bigot, c. 1840–1850.

Swan and Hoop layout, filed 1 November 1786.

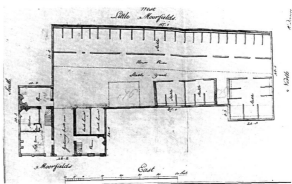

The Keats family lived in a Craven Street, City Road, row house, photographed here c. 1900. Craven Street was called Craven Place in 1801 and is currently Cranwood Street.

George was baptized at St. Leonard's, Shoreditch. Drawing by Thomas Hosmer Shepherd, c. 1820.

Tom Keats (1799–1818) in a drawing by Severn, c. 1817.

Thomas Keats (1774–1804) died in a riding accident at the entrance to Bunhill Fields when his head smashed against the gate.

An Edmonton house that may have been similar to the Jennings home. Unfinished watercolor by George Scharf, 1824.

Southwark High Street in Edmonton Center, by Edward Pugh, 1806.

Enfield marketplace, by William Ellis, 1806.

Clarke's School at Enfield,
by Mario Gigliucci.

Charles Cowden Clarke (1787–1877),
Keats's tutor, c. 1825–1830.

The Reverend Midgley John Jennings Jr.
(1806–1857), Keats's cousin, c. 1855.

John Keats (1795–1821) in a watercolor by Joseph Severn, c. 1818–1819.

Joseph Severn (1793–1879). Pencil drawing by John Partridge, c. 1825.

Maria Dover Walker Dilke (died 1850) miniature, c. 1820.

Fanny Brawne (1800–1865) watercolor, c. 1833.

Charles Brown (1787–1842). Miniature watercolor self-portrait, c. 1805–1810.

Charles Wentworth Dilke (1789–1864), c. 1820.

St. Mary-le-Bow Church, the epicenter
of Cockneyism, by Thomas Malton.

John Hamilton Reynolds
(1794–1852),
by Severn, c. 1820.

Hampstead Heath,
1840 engraving by
William Westall.

James Henry Leigh Hunt
(1784–1859), line engraving
by Henry Hoppner Meyer,
c. 1815.

Percy Bysshe Shelley
(1792–1822),
oil by Severn, c. 1822.

Benjamin Robert Haydon
(1786–1846), by Georgiana
Margaretta Zornlin, c. 1836.

Lord George Gordon Byron
(1788–1824), oil by
Richard Westall, c. 1813.

John Taylor (1781–1864)
in an 1817 sketch.

Richard Monckton Milnes
(1809–1885), later
Lord Houghton, in a chalk drawing
by George Richmond, c. 1844.

George and Georgiana were married at St. Margaret's Church. Image published in 1822 by Richard Holmes Laurie.

The Keatses last sight in England was Great Ormes Head, Wales.

The Keatses traveled to America in a packet similar to the *Antarctic*, painted by Duncan MacFarlane in 1851 off The Skerries, North Wales. Like the *Telegraph*, it plied the Liverpool–to–New York route.

The Keatses floated down the Ohio River in a keelboat or perhaps in a flatboat (foreground). Image by Clarence E. McWilliams, 1939.

John James Audubon (1785–1851) in an 1822 self-portrait in Feliciana Parish, Louisiana.

Thomas Woodhouse Bakewell (1788–1874), by Audubon, 1820.

James Berthoud
(c. 1760–1819),
in an 1819 oil by
Audubon.

Nicholas Berthoud (c. 1790–?),
in black chalk by Audubon, 1819.

View of the Ohio rapids
from Clarksville, 1820.

John Gwathmey's
Indian Queen Hotel.

The Bank of Louisville, designed
by Gideon Schryock and built in
1837, is the only extant structure
from Keats's time.

Map of
Louisville,
1819.

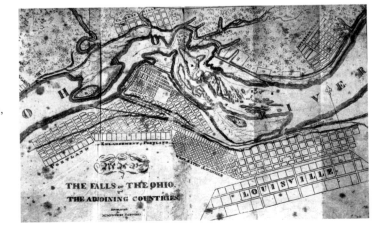

Louisville from the Indiana shore, by T. A. Evans, c. 1825.

Beargrass Creek joins the Ohio River, 1840. The perspective is from the site of George's original sawmill.

Fourteenth Street Bridge, the eventual result of George's service on the 1827 Ohio Bridge Commission. The bridge was designed by Albert Fink and built in 1867.

The Louisville and Portland locks, shown in 1870, were under construction when George served on the Bridge Commission.

Steam Boat For Sale.

ONE fourth of the Steam Boat George Madison, is offered for sale; she is now lying at the mouth of Cumberland, and is on her way to Shippingport by the first rise of water; she is a substantial well built vessel in good repair, and has the reputation of being as good a running boat as any on the river. Terms of sale will be made easy to the purchaser. For further particulars apply to

BARCLAY & WILSON.

A typical advertisement for a steamboat in the *Louisville Public Advertiser*, 3 May 1820.

FIFTY DOLLARS REWARD.

NEGRO man CHARLES, a slave for life, who belongs to the Louisville Foundry, and to the estate of David Prentice, deceased; left Louisville on the 24th June, after dinner, with his wife and their son, about 10 or 11 years old. Charles was purchased of R. Woolfolk, up the river, by Prentice & Bakewell, in 1818. He is of a pure black complexion, about 40 or 45 years old, about 5 feet 8 or 9 inches high; has large broad feet, walks slow, and stoops a little; he has rather a down look, and when spoken to, is modest and respectful. He is supposed to wear a white fur hat, nearly new, which cost ten dollars—he had two suits of summer clothes; supposed to have a large bundle. His wife DILLY is perhaps 35 years old, nearly 7 months gone in pregnancy. Their son, JESS, is a fine looking boy; both black, and both slaves belonging to the estate of A. Pope, dec'd of Louisville. It is supposed they have gone up the river, and crossed into Indiana, with an intention to make their way to Ohio or Pennsylvania. Any person who will deliver Charles at the Louisville Foundry, or secure him in any jail in Kentucky, so that he can be recovered, shall receive a reward of thirty dollars if caught in this state, or fifty dollars if out of the state, and all reasonable expenses paid.

GEORGE KEATS
JOSEPH MIDDLETON
Executors of D. Prentice, dec'd.

jun28.

As executor of David Prentice's estate, George placed an advertisement for the return of a runaway slave in the *Louisville Public Advertiser*, 28 June 1827.

Silhouettes of Georgiana (1798–1879) and George Keats, 1828.

Emma Frances (1823–1883), Isabel (1825–1843), and Georgiana Emily Keats (1819–1855), c. 1828.

George built the "Englishman's palace" in 1837.

Georgiana and John Jeffrey moved to Green and Sixth Streets briefly after they were married in 1843, before moving to Cincinnati.

George headed the board of the Louisville Hotel, c. 1840 lithograph by Drake and Haskell.

View of Main Street, wood engraving by Eastman, c. 1840.

Oakland House and Race Course, c. 1840 oil by Robert Brammer and Augustus A. Von Smith.

George served on the board of the Lexington and Ohio Rail Road, 1838 letterhead by Finnell and Zimmerman.

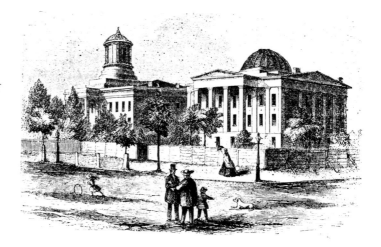

George served on the board of a precursor of the University of Louisville, pictured in the 1840s.

Farmington, 14 April 1820 gouache by John Rutherford.

Lucy Gilmer Fry Speed (1788–1874), Emma Keats Speed's mother-in-law, by Joseph Bush, c. 1825–1835.

Judge John Speed (1772–1840), by Bush.

Philip Speed (1819–1882), c. 1876.

Emma Keats Speed (1823–1883), c. 1876.

James Speed (1812–1887), 1833.

Ella Keats Peay (1833–1880), photograph by Edward Klauber, c. 1880.

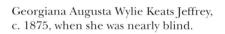

Isabel Keats's grave marker in Cave Hill Cemetery. She died in 1843, a likely suicide.

Georgiana Augusta Wylie Keats Jeffrey, c. 1875, when she was nearly blind.

Valentin Maria Llanos y Gutierrez
(1795–1885), 1861.

Fanny Keats Llanos (1803–1889),
charcoal drawing by her son, Juan
Enrique Keats y Llanos, c. 1861.

Fanny Keats Llanos in Rome, 1863.

Dr. Theodore Samuel Bell (died after 1882), one of George's best friends.

Senator George Mortimer Bibb (1776–1859), c. 1820.

John H. Brand (1775–1849), coffee and spice dealer, c. 1820.

William Christian Bullitt (1793–1877), engraving by Alexander Hay Ritchie, c. 1840.

Judge William Fontaine Bullock (1807–1889), engraving by Henry Bryan Hall, c. 1870.

Edward Mann Butler (1784–1855), c. 1820.

Samuel Casseday
(1795–1876),
c. 1860.

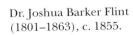

James Freeman Clarke
(1810–1888), oil by
William Morris Hunt,
c. 1870.

Dr. Joshua Barker Flint
(1801–1863), c. 1855.

William Garvin (1795–1868),
1860 photograph by J. C. Elrod.

James Guthrie (1792–1869), c. 1840.
He was George's personal attorney,
chaired the Louisville City Council's
Finance Committee, and later served
as secretary of the treasury.

Richard Harlan (1796–1843),
Audubon's friend and the impetus
for Harlan Museum, whose board
George headed.

Jacob Keller (died 1880), by Philip Davenport.

Senator Humphrey Marshall (1760–1841), c. 1800.

George Wood Meriwether (1789–1864), c. 1830.

Samuel Osgood (1812–1880), engraving by Capewell and Kimmel, c. 1835.

Judge Henry Pirtle (1798–1880), who was James Speed's partner, c. 1855 engraving by Henry Bryan Hall.

George Dennison Prentice (1802–1870), by Godfrey Frankenstein, c. 1845. The controversial newspaper editor befriended George and wrote a postmortem poem to Isabel Keats.

Dr. Coleman Rogers (1781–1855), George's physician, c. 1840.

Judge John Rowan (1773–1843), owner of Federal Hill ("My Old Kentucky Home"), by Matthew Harris Jouett, c. 1835.

James Rudd (1789–1867), c. 1840.

Leven Lawrence Shreve (1793–1864).

Willis Stewart (1799–1857), encased
daguerreotype, c. 1843–1851.
Stewart founded a Masonic Lodge.

Robert J. Ward Sr. (1800–1862),
c. 1855 engraving by Henry Bryan
Hall.

that his wife, Margaret, was twenty-nine and that Smith was fifty-one and had been prone to "violent attacks of illness."[20]

During the same time frame, the Chancery Court master, Thomas P. Smith (not known to be related to either Daniel Smith or Felix Smith), was pushing along the sale of assets to contribute to creditors' claims. The 21 June 1844 sale of the house for $7,700 was recorded on 9 July 1844, along with a lot adjacent to the Louisville Hotel at Seventh and Main Streets for $900, a lot across the street from the hotel for $2,656.50, as well as two smaller lots for $390 and $300.[21] On 26 July 1844 a lot on the east side of Seventh Street at Main Street, adjacent to the Louisville Hotel, sold for $550.[22] Between 21 June and 13 September 1844 John Jeffrey acquired two lots between Jefferson, Green (now Liberty), Third, and Fourth Streets for $950 and $1,312.50.[23] Keats's one-third interest in the sawmill and the ten acres on which it sat was sold to John P. Young on 26 July 1844 for $2,850.

The proceeds from the house went to Georgiana as her dower. Of the other sales, a bit less than $10,000 was divided up by a list of creditors that resembled George's circle and his business ties. The institutions included the Bank of Kentucky, the Bank of Louisville, the Northern Bank of Kentucky, the Mechanics Savings Institution, the Louisville Savings Institution, the Louisville Hotel Company, the State Bank of Indiana, and D. A. Sayre and Company. In addition to his partner Smith, the individuals listed were James Rudd, Willis Stewart, John Brand, and fellow lumber merchants John P. Young and Edward V. Bunn. Other miscellaneous creditors included Daniel B. Leight, John P. Bull, William C. Bakewell, Dr. Coleman Rogers, Holliday W. Cood, Felix Smith, Jacob Beckwith, Elijah Gray, John P. Young, pharmacist Arthur Peter, and twenty-six others, all of whom had waited nearly three years for partial settlements of George's debts.[24]

The family vacated the Englishman's palace after its mid-1844 transfer to the Bank of Kentucky. They may have moved to the property purchased from the estate by Jeffrey on Green Street between Third and Fourth, or perhaps they lived in a hotel.[25] James Trabue, a wholesale dry goods merchant, was listed as living in the big house in 1848.[26] After 1846, Georgiana and Jeffrey reestablished themselves in Cincinnati, where he was general superintendent of the gas works.

The final word on the estate came on 17 September 1844. An indenture recorded the estate's sale of a "sawmill and two acres" to John P. Young.[27] On the same date, another indenture was entered into among the children:

September 17, 1844. Indenture made and entered into between: Georgiana E. (Emily) Keats, Emma Speed and Philip Speed, her husband, Isabella Keats, John Keats, Clarence Keats & Alice Keats, children and heirs—The administrator and administratrix filed bill in Chancery against heirs—said estate was largely indebted and possessed of a large real and personal estate and dower had been assigned to widow.

Life estate in parcels of land
Sold one lot to John Jeffrey for $950
Sold one lot to John Jeffrey for $1,312
Personal estate insufficient to pay off and discharge debts.

Louisville Court of Chancery, Children of Geo. Keats
Thomas P. Smith, Master in Court of Chancery 1844–47
John Love
E. W. Craig[28]

With this indenture, Georgiana, as administratrix, notified the court that there was nothing left for the children and that George's debts would never be fully paid (unless the creditors sued the children, of whom only Georgiana and Emma were over twenty-one). It was a practical outcome to a messy estate. The legal maneuvers provided Georgiana and the minor children with some wherewithal, but the distribution was in contravention to the provisions of George's deathbed will, specifying that the creditors be paid first.

George's books, letters, and furnishings that were not sold after his death to Cood and others were scattered widely throughout the Keats family. Some of these are still in the hands of various family members in the twenty-first century. The titles in George's library, serving as an insight into his mind, are included in the appendix. Some of his favorite authors were Chaucer, Ben Jonson, Wordsworth, Scott, Coleridge, Hazlitt, Beaumont and Fletcher, Byron, Gibbon, Goldsmith, Audubon, and Webster. He also had sets of *Blackwood's* magazine and his brother-in-law Valentin Llanos's published books. Interestingly, given the gastrointestinal nature of his death, he owned a book by Andrew Combe (1797–1847) entitled *Physiology of Digestion*, published in 1837. For an orphan who dropped out of school at age fourteen, George assembled an impressive book collection.

George's posthumous reputation fared better than his balance sheet.

Clarke wrote to his cousin Margaret Fuller in November 1834, "George Keats is one of the best men in the world."[29] He continued in this vein when he wrote an 1843 sketch in Emerson's *Dial:*

> His appearance and the shape of his head arrested my attention. The heavy bar of observation over his eyes indicated the strong perceptive faculties of a business man, while the striking height of his head, in the region assigned by phrenology to veneration, was a sign of nobility of sentiment, and the full development behind marked firmness and practical energy. All these traits were equally prominent in his character. He was one of the most intellectual men I ever knew. I never saw him when his mind was inactive.
>
> It was strange to find, in those days, on the banks of the Ohio, one who had successfully devoted himself to active pursuits, and yet retained so fine a sensibility for the rarest and most evanescent beauties of early song.
>
> It needed a longer acquaintance before you could perceive, beneath the veil of a high-bred English reserve, that profound sentiment of manly honor, that reverence for all truth, loftiness and purity. . . .
>
> In the prime of his life and the midst of usefulness, George Keats passed into the spiritual world. The city of Louisville lost in him one of its most public-spirited and conscientious citizens. . . . We cannot hope to find many such in this world. We are fortunate if we find any.
>
> The love of his brother, which continued through his life to be among the deepest affections of his soul, was a pledge of their reunion again in another world.[30]

Clarke's five paragraphs in the *Dial* constitute the best and virtually the only comprehensive description of George's fully matured character. As a young man, George's letters to his sister Fanny were patronizing, and his letters to Dilke were often more descriptive of events than revealing of his character.

More than thirty years later, Clarke continued his defense of Keats. In *Life, Letters, and Literary Remains of John Keats,* Richard Monckton Milnes had sided with George in the controversy among him, Brown, and Dilke, yet the debate must have continued privately. Clarke sent his *Dial* sketch to Milnes on 31 October 1845.[31] When Milnes (by then Lord Houghton) was preparing the 1876 *Aldine Edition of British Poets,* he wrote to Clarke, asking for a contribution. Clarke replied immediately:

> In thinking over what you told me of the charge made by some persons in England against George Keats, of having improperly used money of his brother—I am more than ever convinced that such a charge must be wholly unfounded. Of all men I have ever known he was the man least capable of such an act. He was not only a strictly honest man—but high minded & honorable in a high degree. All those who knew him while he lived in Ky. would say the same thing. More than this, his love and reverence for his brother John amounted to a sort of worship.[32]

Milnes accepted Clarke's appraisal of George and amplified his original commentary by stating in his preface to the *Aldine Edition,* "His voluntary payment of his brother's debts, after his death, including what had been advanced by Mr. Brown, certainly showed no niggard spirit; and in America he bore the highest character for uprightness and generosity."[33]

Samuel Osgood, Clarke's assistant, described George in the *Knickerbocker Gallery:* "The brother of one of the most ideal and gifted poets, he did not lose sight of the ideal world in the prosaic business of a lumbermerchant. He was always ready for a literary conversation, and took delight at any time in turning away from his ledger to his library. . . . [He] never ceased to prove that he was of kindred blood to the author of 'Endymion' and 'The Eve of St. Agnes.'"[34] Osgood, who was also privy to the Clarke-Houghton discourse, wrote to Houghton from New York, "They [the Keatses] were most kind and pleasant to me, & the husband's serious sense went well together with the playful volatility of the buxom wife. He was decidedly an intellectual man, & we talked much of literary subjects, not infrequently upon his brother's poems."[35]

Georgiana, not prone to writing, left no remembrance of George, nor did any of the children. While ensconced in Matanzas, Cuba, for an extended period, John Jeffrey wrote to his brother, "I have no letter from my wife yet . . . the Keats name has a reputation for writing, but that is not my experience."[36] John Henry's September 1911 interview with the *Maysville Herald* provided a few facts but none of the eloquence of Prentice, Clarke, and Osgood. Emma Keats Speed acknowledged the poet, his letters, and his reputation, but she never memorialized her father. Neither did her son, John Gilmer Speed, a journalist who published a few articles on the poet as well as a three-volume set of his poetry and letters.

The paper trail of George's legacy has thus been unfairly compressed into a few sound bites. John termed him "selfish" for returning to his wife and child on the frontier. Fanny Brawne described him as "extravagant," which subsequent events proved to be fairly insightful. Haslam and Brown tried to peg him as the "business brother" and a "scoundrel," based on misinformation. Audubon correctly noted that "a man who will persist, as you have been doing . . . will get along here." If Emerson had known George personally, he would have described him as an "establishment" figure, which was a long way from his Cockney London origins. Mildred Bullitt posthumously labeled him a "bankrupt." Several twentieth-century biographers of John Keats implied that George was self-centered. George's own letters revealed his maturing: from a snippy 1821 comment that his wife had "good taste enough to dislike this country"[37] to his 1832 letter to Dilke praising the American republic and his election to public office in 1841. Clarke, Osgood, and Prentice would have the last words, however, calling George "honorable," "intellectual," and "an inestimable member of society."

George's innate humanity remains somewhat hidden behind his list of accomplishments. His love of his brother, wife, and children is amply demonstrated in the correspondence with Dilke, Clarke, and sister, Fanny. He was obviously a proud man, having built the Englishman's palace as a statement proclaiming his arrival. He credited Georgiana for sticking out the hard times, even volunteering to take in sewing, but he did not dwell on earlier misfortunes. He cared deeply about educational opportunities, and not simply for his own children. Throughout it all, he was an inveterate punster, betraying a quick sense of humor.

George's capacity for personal growth continued to the end. His library evinced an intellectual curiosity that was exceptional in mercantile Louisville. New cultural ventures always attracted him. He was something of a workaholic, even to the detriment of his own health. It is noteworthy that Georgiana wished to be interred next to him, as did a number of his children and descendants. His good character was as lasting as the poet's transcending brilliance.

Fifty years after George died, the City of Louisville named a mundane residential street in Crescent Hill, filled with modest homes and apartments, Keats Avenue, the only civic reminder of his community stature.[38]

AFTERMATH

1842–

The next two years were eventful. Georgiana, aged forty-five, married twenty-five-year-old John Jeffrey. Their motivations, aside from the possibility of real love, are lost to history. Some have speculated that his initial interest was in seventeen-year-old Isabel, before her mother stepped between them. Jeffrey moved into the Keats home on Walnut Street after their marriage on 5 January 1843. Georgiana may have been propelled to remarry by the memory of her own mother, a single parent living in shared lodgings with relatives under straitened circumstances. Jeffrey was a handsome, industrious Scottish engineer with good prospects.

Shortly after their marriage (likely in 1843 or 1844), Jeffrey and Georgiana were caught up in an ugly marital spat. While Georgiana was pregnant with Jeffrey's child, he traveled to Nashville, where he met a woman named Mrs. Barrow, presented her with a gift, and returned home with a warm thank-you note that Clarence Keats discovered. Georgiana confronted Jeffrey, who described Mrs. Barrow as "beautiful" and "pure." Georgiana wrote a threatening letter to Mrs. Barrow, whose name she thought was "invariably coupled with some tale of scandal," and this infuriated Jeffrey. He told her that if she ever visited Nashville, she would be "shuned by every person there, and if I [Georgiana] went into public I should be insulted." A few weeks later, Mrs. Barrow wrote again to Jeffrey, who unaccountably and mistakenly handed the envelope to Georgiana. Mrs. Barrow had written some vaguely erotic and inarticulate prose about her love for him. After reading it, Georgiana miscarried and was bedridden for three weeks. Given that Georgiana's last child, Alice Ann, had been born in 1836, when Georgiana was forty, hers was an at-risk pregnancy, and her emotional state was such that her doctor said "he could not 'minister to a mind diseased.'" She wrote about all this in a bitter complaint (undated) to Jeffrey's brother Alexander.[1] Evidently, Jeffrey's travels kept him away from Nashville thereafter, and the affair died down.

Isabel's heart-rending death on 20 October 1843 added to the family's trauma. She died in the library from a self-inflicted gunshot wound, having aimed her brother John Henry's shotgun at a spot between her heart and her neck. Isabel was described by the family as the brightest and most similar in appearance to the poet, and her death was a tragedy. Georgiana portrayed the event as an accident. George Dennison Prentice penned a poem to her:

To a Poet's Niece
I know a little girl
With spirit wild and free,
And it ever seems a blessing
With that pretty one to be—
To mark her ringing shout
And her ever joyous words
Like anguishing of a fountain
Or the cadence of the birds.
That joyous little girl
Is wild as a gazelle,
Yet a poet's name and lineage,
Are thine, sweet Isabel.
And although thy wild heart seemeth
All heedless of the lyre,
Within that young heart dwelleth
The poet's gift of fire.

But 'twas a fearful gift
To that noble child of song,
Whose glorious name and lineage
To thee, bright one, belong:
For it turned his heart to ashes
Where its centered light was flung,
And he perished in his morning—
The gifted and the young.

Ay, he perished in the morning,
That child of light and gloom,
But he left a flame that glitters
Like a star above a tomb;
And I dream thou hast a genius

Like that which *won* his fame;
Thou hast his name and features—
And why not his soul of flame?[2]

Perhaps to make amends, Jeffrey took an interest in the Keats children, establishing decent relationships with John Henry and Ella and a trusting partnership with Clarence. And he was genuinely fond of Georgey.

In Louisville, John Jeffrey read about Milnes's plan to publish a Keats biography. Although George had abandoned his objections to Brown's publishing a biography, Georgiana still had letters and several poems that were essential to Milnes's work. Jeffrey wrote to Milnes on 13 May 1845 and again on 26 July 1845, providing a list of all the materials he was prepared to copy. Jeffrey noted at the conclusion of his July letter: "As to the profits arising from the sale of the work you are about to publish in my opinion, they belong undoubtedly to yourself; but if relinquished by you, I should by all means claim them for the children of George Keats, who are legally the heirs of the Poet, being descendants of the oldest Brother & are in such circumstances as to render such a thing very acceptable.[3] Jeffrey sent Milnes his copying efforts on 8 September 1845, which scholars have criticized as careless; he himself acknowledged, "I am rather disappointed with it."[4] Nevertheless, Jeffrey's contributions enabled Milnes to publish the first reasonably complete version of John Keats's works.

Georgiana and Jeffrey's marriage churned for a few more years. By 1846, the family had moved to Cincinnati for a fresh start. Jeffrey became general superintendent of the gas works there and simultaneously established a base from which he organized and built municipal gas works in other cities as far-flung as Springfield, Illinois, and Matanzas, Cuba. He traveled extensively and often lived apart from Georgiana, who visited her children for lengthy periods, paying them board. Georgiana and her youngest child, Alice, returned to Louisville in 1852.[5] This precipitated an anxious letter from Ella, aged nineteen, to Jeffrey, focusing on the problems between him and her mother: "There are two things which would conduce toward my happiness and the first is to see you and my mother happy. I know you can be so, do not all of your stepchildren love you as a father?"[6]

Considering Georgiana's midlife impoverishment, her six dependent children, a twenty-year age gap,[7] and her volatile personality, juxtaposed with Jeffrey's relentless travels, it is remarkable that the young Scot entered into the union at all and then finally made it work. But the marriage calmed down, and after 1862 the couple settled peacefully into an apartment in Lexington's Phoenix Hotel.

Georgiana died in Lexington on 3 April 1879. Jeffrey and her son-in-law Philip Speed arranged for her to be buried adjacent to the Speed family plot in Louisville's Cave Hill Cemetery. They then exhumed George from Western Cemetery and interred him next to her. Jeffrey designed a rustic monument consisting of a small pyramid engraved with the words "The Keats Family in America" and topped with a Celtic cross. Two years later, on 18 February 1881, Jeffrey died in Lexington. He was buried on the opposite side of the Keats monument, adjacent to Isabel Keats, who had also been moved from Western Cemetery.[8]

Georgiana never attempted a rapprochement with Fanny Keats Llanos, although in his 1845 letters, Jeffrey encouraged Milnes to seek her out. As late as 1847, Fanny seemed to be unaware of George's death. According to her biographer Marie Adami, "So absorbed had she [Fanny] been in her life in Spain that she had not known of George's death for at least five years after it took place." Fanny did not require remittances from England during the 1840s, so she may not have been in contact with Dilke, who would have given her the news about George.[9]

The Keats children began a matriarchy of sorts, in which the daughters showed strength of character while the sons and sons-in-law often struggled for success. John Henry and Clarence had only daughters, so the immediate Keats family name died out with George's grandchildren. The lives of George's eight children spanned the following:

Georgiana Emily	June 1819–1855 (sometime before 17 June)
Rosalind	18 December 1820–2 April 1826
Emma Frances	25 October 1823–10 September 1883
Isabel	28 February 1825–20 October 1843
John Henry	November 1827–7 May 1917[10]
Clarence George	February 1830–19 February 1861
Ella	2 March 1833–12 March 1888
Alice Ann	1836–15 June 1881

Georgey was the beneficiary of John Keats's poem "'Tis the witching time of night / . . . / A Poet now or never / Little child / O' th' western wild / A Poet now or never." She saw England as a child and later married Alfred Gwathmey, son of George Clark Gwathmey, cashier of the Bank of Kentucky, of which George Keats was a board member. Jeffrey wrote in

August 1850, "Young Gwathmey who married my wife's eldest daughter has been frightened by the cholera into the habit of getting drunk every day and when he comes home he abuses his wife so badly that I suppose I will have to go down [from Cincinnati] and thrash the rascal into good behavior."[11] Three months later, Gwathmey abandoned his wife and their child, George Keats Gwathmey, born on 10 August 1850. Alfred went to New Orleans, where, ironically, he died of cholera in the Charity Hospital on 24 November 1850. Bullitt cousins took Georgey and her child into their estate at Ox Moor for a year or so while a favorite slave nursed the boy, who was sickly, back to health.[12] Georgey died at age thirty-six in an 1855 flu epidemic, causing Jeffrey to write, "Poor Georgey Gwathmey is also dead. What a gentle good spirit has gone to heaven . . . she never imagined harm to anyone."[13] Orphaned at age five and placed in the care of the semifunctional family of Georgiana and John Jeffrey, George Keats Gwathmey ran away to sea at age fourteen. He returned seven years later and ultimately became a newspaper editor and then the postmaster in Lathrop, Missouri.

As noted earlier, Rosalind Keats died at age five after a series of illnesses.

Emma Frances Keats and Philip Speed had ten children, forming the largest core of Keats descendants (more than 250 by 2012). Speed was a merchant, served as a tax collector for Kentucky during the Civil War, and concluded his career superintending the Western Cement Company, owned by his nephew J. B. Speed. Emma later struck up a correspondence with her aunt Fanny that lasted until 1878, but the two never met.[14] She subscribed to the 1876 renovation of the Keats tombstone in Rome. Emma achieved minor literary note when in 1882 she invited Oscar Wilde to spend a day perusing the Keats letters and papers entrusted to her. She gave Wilde an original of "Sonnet on Blue."

The Speeds' second child, George Keats Speed, married Jane Butler (Jenny) Ewing, daughter of George Keats's friend Dr. U. E. Ewing. They lived on a sixty-five-acre estate called Chatsworth in Louisville's Crescent Hill section. Emma's fifth child, Alice Speed McDonald, assisted Naomi Kirk in assembling the family's oral histories. Her sixth child, John Gilmer Speed, became a journalist, editing *Harper's Weekly* and *American* magazines. He wrote several articles about John Keats and edited a three-volume set of his letters and poetry, published in 1883. Emma and Philip Speed arranged for the cluster of plots in Cave Hill Cemetery to which they moved George, Georgey, and Isabel Keats and in which many family members are interred.

Isabel Keats, who may have shared facial features with the poet, was considered the brightest in the family, having attended the Sisters of Charity convent school in Nazareth, Kentucky. As noted earlier, her death in 1843 was a family tragedy.

John Henry Keats, the poet's namesake (despite his wishes that no one be named for him), followed in his uncle's footsteps with pharmacy training. He eventually joined his stepfather's gas works enterprise instead, working in Havana and Matanzas, Cuba, and in Springfield, Illinois. John Henry found that he disliked the work, however, and he became a schoolteacher in Missouri. He worked as a hospital steward in a Union army hospital during the Civil War and then took up teaching again, followed by farming. Emma Keats Speed described him to Fanny Llanos as "an eccentric, unbalanced genius [who] wanders we know not whither."[15] At age fifty-three he married Kate Bartholomew. His last job was as a county surveyor and bridge inspector. In 1911 John Henry gave an interview to the local newspaper, the *Maysville Herald,* providing a trove of family information not recorded elsewhere.

Clarence George Keats was eleven when his father died. He got along well with John Jeffrey, who had enormous confidence in his stepson and counted on Clarence to handle a series of troubleshooting assignments at gas works from Cleveland, Ohio, to Vicksburg, Mississippi. While in Cincinnati, he married Mary Ann James, a niece of lawyer-banker-politician John H. James, who owned the bank of which Thomas W. Bakewell was president. Clarence and his wife moved to Evansville, Indiana, where he became president of the local gas works at age twenty-two. Clarence developed a case of consumption that progressed rapidly, and he died at age thirty-one, the last Keats known to have died of the disease.

Ella Keats married George Nicholas Peay (1833–1881), grandson of John Peay (1775–1838), with whom the Keatses lodged in Louisville in 1819, and a nephew of Philip Speed (his mother was Peachy Speed Peay, 1813–1891). Ella's life took a troubling turn when her husband defalcated the funds of various family members and those of a business acquaintance; he later turned up in Montreal as a faro dealer in a gambling house.[16] With enormous fortitude, she kept the household intact, including several former Peay family slaves who had nowhere to go. Three of Ella's daughters "married north" to successful men. Two of her granddaughters helped authors Amy Lowell and Aileen Ward with their Keats biographies; a third, Ella Keats Whiting, served as acting president of Wellesley College during World War II. Ella Keats Peay's issue, numbering more than 200, constitutes the second-largest cluster of Keats descendants.[17]

George and Georgiana's last child, Alice Ann, married Edward Morton Drane, a tobacco and grain dealer in Frankfort, Kentucky. Alice died at age forty-five. Four of her five children never married. The fifth, Clarence Keats Drane, disappeared after Alice's 1881 death and reemerged in Melbourne, Australia, by the end of the decade with a new name: Keats Clarence Courtenay. In his possession was George Keats's leather copy book from his 1819–1820 trip to London. The copy book changed hands numerous times. In Melbourne, Drane sold the book in 1891 to Professor Edward Jenks, who in turn sold it on 11 April 1893 to Bernard Quaritch, a rare book dealer. It was subsequently sold by Sotheby's on 23 June 1947 to the British Museum, which on 21 May 1968 turned it over to the British Library—just a couple of miles from its original place of purchase. It has never been satisfactorily explained why Drane disappeared from America to form the Australian branch of the family.[18]

George Keats's progeny numbered more than 525 by the twenty-first century. Although the surname died out, at least 67 used Keats as a given name or a middle name. They married foreign nationals from more than twenty countries, including China and Japan. Nine became writers, and seven others were journalists. Yale, Harvard, and Princeton claim nineteen, eighteen, and ten Keats alumni, respectively. Their careers have included finance, manufacturing, and medicine, among many others. An incidence of alcoholism and suicide, perhaps within statistical norms, has also been observed, along with several bankruptcies and a couple of jail sentences. The Keats descendants appear to be a fairly normal collection of souls—though not a single poet among them—and many share a great pride and interest in their forebears.[19]

APPENDIX A

The George Keats Circle of Friends and Acquaintances

George Keats's character developed in keeping with his times and his community, as well as his friends and acquaintances. George was intimate with men who were U.S. senators, cabinet members, judges, state legislators, editors, educators, doctors, clergy, and a host of businessmen. In many respects, George's circle of acquaintances was more distinguished than that of his brother John, many of whose friends ended their lives in oblivion.

The following sketches of those who influenced George's life draw on the earlier compilations by Harry Buxton Forman and Hyder Edward Rollins of those individuals who impacted John Keats. New information has been assembled for Richard Abbey and the Wylies, and the other sketches have been rewritten to be more George-specific. The Kentucky sketches are fresh, although certain individuals, such as James Guthrie and James Speed, are well known.

ENGLAND

Richard Abbey   Keats scholars have parodied Richard Abbey as, in Fanny Keats's words, a "consummate villain," without learning much about the man. Abbey was born in 1765 in the Vale of York, Yorkshire,[1] the county to the east of Lancashire, where the Keats children's grandmother, Alice Whalley Jennings, was born in Colne. He appears to have arrived in London at age twenty-one with significant funds. Abbey lived in the parish of St. Benet Sherehog in the Poultry. He immediately established a tea brokerage called Abbey, Cock and Gullet in Pancras Lane and bought a membership in the Patternmakers, a city company, as well as his Freedom of the City. The firm's named changed several times and was often referred to as Abbey, Cock (or sometimes Cocks, suggesting a second Cock partner).

Abbey parlayed the tea brokerage into an importing house, known by the same name.

On 5 February 1786 he married Eleanor Jones, an illiterate from St. Stephens, Walbrook. They lived onsite at the business, around the corner from the church of St. Mary-le-Bow, and also set up a comfortable country house called Pindars on Blackhorse Road near Marsh Street in Walthamstow. Upon the death of her husband, Alice Jennings asked her friend Abbey to be a guardian for her Keats grandchildren. He served in this capacity from mid-1810 until Fanny Keats came of age in June 1824.

George Keats, having worked for Abbey from 1811 to 1817, used him as his agent in London until about 1825, when problems with Fanny's accounts disillusioned the siblings. Abbey's business partnership with John Cock and William Johnson prospered until setbacks occurred sometime prior to 1824.[2] Johnson withdrew from the firm on 15 September 1821. The remaining entity of Abbey Cock and Company dissolved on 25 September 1827.[3]

In April 1827 Abbey dined with John Keats's publisher, John Taylor. The two men talked about the Keats family, and the interview was recorded by Taylor as the so-called Abbey Memoir, which remains the most detailed description of the Keatses.

After settling up with Fanny's lawyer, James Rice Jr., by mortgaging his business and the Walthamstow house, Abbey moved back to London in 1831. He was variously engaged as a coffee dealer in Size Lane and a wholesale tea dealer at 5 Barge Yard and, in early 1837, at 22 Budge Row.[4] Business reverses followed him to his death. Abbey was buried 27 January 1837 at St. John of Jerusalem in South Hackney; his last known address was Mare Street.[5] The Patternmakers Company advertised on 17 March 1837 to fill a vacancy in the Court of Assistants caused by his death. He left no will, perhaps indicating that his assets had been dissipated.[6] No record survives with regard to his wife or adopted daughter.

Frances "Fanny" Brawne Fanny Brawne, betrothed to John Keats from mid-1819 until his death in February 1821, was involved with the poet during his most prolific writing period, notably resulting in "The Eve of St. Agnes" and "Lamia." She was viewed with suspicion by several of the poet's group, including Charles Brown, John Hamilton Reynolds, and Charles Dilke. They were variously concerned that she was a distraction to his writing, that she lacked intellectuality, or perhaps that her mother was interested in fashion, a métier that Fanny was pursuing as well. History proved them wrong, as her chain of correspondence with Fanny Keats revealed a sensitive and loving young woman whose interests were absolutely linked to the poet's.

Born 9 August 1800 in Hampstead, she was ten when her father died of consumption. Six years later an uncle, John Ricketts, died, leaving the Brawnes a livable income. Fanny learned French and German as a child and became a serious student of fine embroidery and historical dress. Living in Hampstead, the Brawnes subleased Brown's portion of Wentworth Place in the summer of 1818, until Brown returned from Scotland; they later moved to Dilke's half of the house in April 1819. In November 1818 the Dilkes introduced Fanny to John Keats.

Tom Keats was also living, and dying, in Hampstead, boarding in nearby Well Walk with the family of the postmaster, Bentley. Tom's demise in December 1818 greatly depressed John, but Fanny's cheerful demeanor pulled him through. He first mentioned her in a letter to George and Georgiana in which he described Fanny as "beautiful, elegant, graceful, silly, fashionable and strange."[7]

After spending Christmas Day 1818 together, Fanny wrote, "It was the happiest day I had ever then spent." Her mother was amenable to the relationship but somewhat skeptical, given John's lack of prospects. The parties kept their engagement, perhaps occurring in mid-1819, under wraps.[8]

Keats composed "Bright Star" on the Isle of Wight during the summer of 1819, likely with Fanny in mind: "Bright Star! Would I were stedfast as thou art."[9]

When Keats departed for Rome in September 1820, he believed he would never see her again. According to Joseph Severn, until his death, Keats often held in his hand a polished white cornelian that Fanny had given him.[10] Upon receiving word of his death, Fanny cut her hair, donned black clothing, and grieved for six years. The Brawnes hosted Fanny Keats when she left the Abbeys in 1824. The Brawnes suffered more sadness when Fanny's brother Samuel died of consumption in 1828, followed by the gruesome death of her mother in 1829 when her dress caught fire.

Fanny Brawne moved to Boulogne, France, in 1833, where she met and married Louis Lindo. They later lived in Heidelberg, Germany, and ultimately returned to London in 1859, changing their name to Lindon (he was a Sephardic Jew). She virtually never referred to Keats. Shortly before her death, she entrusted all the remains of the romance, including Keats's letters, to her children. She died 4 December 1865 and was buried in Brompton Cemetery.[11]

Fanny's son, Herbert Lindon, published *Letters of John Keats to Fanny Brawne*, edited by Harry Buxton Forman, in 1878, after the 1872 death of his father. The letters set off a firestorm of criticism at the time, yet from a historical perspective, they added an important dimension to understanding the poet.

Another volume, Fred Edgcumbe's *Letters of Fanny Brawne to Fanny Keats*, appeared in 1934. Fanny Brawne's reputation was considerably enhanced by these publications, as well as by Joanna Richardson's 1952 biography. She emerged as a thoughtful and supportive woman whose time with John was a great benefit to him.[12]

Charles (Armitage) Brown   Charles Brown was born 14 April 1787 in Lambeth, south London, where he was one of six sons. At age fourteen he was a clerk in a merchant's office, and at eighteen he joined a Petersburg, Russia, merchant house that was partly owned by his London-based brother John. After taking on a large inventory of pigs' bristles, used in combs in Russia, the firm was swamped by the English innovation of split whalebone combs. Another brother, James, an India merchant, reestablished Charles in London, and upon his death, "left him the competence (about £3,333) which allowed him to lead a life of literary leisure afterwards."[13]

Brown's comic opera *Narensky or the Road to Yaroslaff* was produced in Drury Lane in early 1814, earning him £300 and a silver ticket, good for life, which Keats occasionally borrowed. After 1816, Brown and schoolmate Charles W. Dilke occupied the double house in Hampstead now known as Keats House. Through Dilke, Brown met John Keats in 1817 and invited him to share his smaller side of the house in 1818. The two-year period in which he acted as John's surrogate brother began in July 1818 and included on-and-off shared living arrangements.

Brown absented himself in the late summer of 1819, and beginning in October of that year, he briefly cohabited with a housekeeper, Abigail Donahue, described as "a handsome woman of the peasant class . . . a bigoted catholic, and Irish."[14] A child, Charles (Carlino) Brown Jr., was born in July 1820. Carlino's memoir of his father rather explicitly states that Brown viewed the coupling simply as the means to conceive a child. Brown leased out his portion of the house for the summer of 1820 when he left on another Scottish tour. He sent Keats over to Kentish Town, near Leigh Hunt. Abigail went elsewhere to deliver Carlino alone. Brown's 7 May 1820 parting from Keats proved to be final, as he had not yet returned from his trip to Scotland when Keats and Severn left for Italy on 17 September

1820. In fact, Brown returned the day they sailed, and their ships may have passed in the dark.

By August 1822, Brown had wrested Carlino from Abigail and departed for Italy, where he spent the next twelve years, settling in Florence to fashion himself as a man of letters. During this period, he contributed articles to Leigh Hunt's journal and added a middle name, Armitage, drawn from a maternal relation. Brown and Carlino returned to Plymouth, England, in 1835, where he desultorily discussed writing a Keats biography. He held a public reading of a sketch of Keats on 27 December 1836 but was subsequently unsuccessful in getting it published.

Brown served as guarantor of a friend's loan, just as George Keats had, and lost a portion of his principal when the loan was called. In 1841 he and his son set out for the North Island of New Zealand, hoping to find a less expensive environment. Ironically (given George's career), Brown took with him a steam engine and the necessary parts to establish a sawmill to be run by his son. However, he was disillusioned by the one acre assigned to him on the outskirts of New Plymouth (Taranaki) and immediately protested his fate. Possibly the last words written about Brown were those of John Tyson Wicksteed, resident agent of the New Zealand Company, who recorded, "He was a pestilent madman. I kept on good terms with him, but peace could not have lasted long, he was so abusive."[15] Before he could arrange a return to England, Brown died of apoplexy[16] on 5 June 1842, less than six months after George Keats's death in Kentucky.[17]

Charles Wentworth Dilke　Dilke was born 8 December 1789. Employment in the Navy Pay Office until its 1836 closure did not prevent him from having an active life in literary circles. From 1814 to 1816 he published a useful six-volume set of Old English plays.

In 1815–1816 he and Charles Brown, a former schoolmate, occupied a double house in John Street, Hampstead. Little did he know that John Keats would do some of his best writing there and that the house would eventually become known as Keats House, a literary shrine and tourist attraction. William Woods, a local builder, had constructed the house in 1814–1816. It was acquired in 1838 by retired actress Eliza Jane Chester, who significantly changed its appearance to the elegant Regency villa that is often pictured in Keats biographies and is preserved to this day. However, the buildings in which Keats, Brown, the Dilkes, and the Brawnes lived were two rather boxy town houses with a common wall.[18]

Dilke was friendly with James Henry Leigh Hunt, editor of the *Exam-*

iner, and his circle of friends, which came to include Keats. Dilke's house served as a gathering place for Reynolds, Hunt, Severn, Taylor, the Brawnes, and other acquaintances.

In 1808 Dilke married Maria Dover Walker, and she became a charming focal point for family and friends. Being a few years older than the Keatses, Maria was in some respects a stand-in mother or at least like an older sister to the boys. Dilke and Maria later took an interest in Fanny Keats, introducing her to society after she left the Abbeys' home in Walthamstow. He was helpful in obtaining her inheritance from the trusts that Abbey had mismanaged. Dilke also served well into the 1830s as George Keats's proxy in London on numerous financial and artistic concerns. George wrote, "[Dilke is] the best Friend I have in the world."[19]

While continuing with his day job in the Navy Department, Dilke purchased an interest in and became an editor of the *Athenaeum* in 1829. He took control of the literary weekly in 1830 and remained with it until 1846. He succeeded Charles Dickens in managing the *Daily News* (1846–1849) and afterward devoted himself to writing books and articles on literature.

Maria Dilke died in 1850. Their son, Charles, became a Whig politician and was granted a baronetcy for his support of the Great Exhibition. When Sir Charles's wife died, the elder Dilke moved in with his son and continued writing. He died 10 August 1864.[20]

William Haslam   Haslam may have been born in 1795, the same year as John Keats. Brown believed that Haslam had attended Clarke's School with the Keats boys. He was a solicitor and later succeeded his father as a wholesale grocer with Frampton and Sons. He endeared himself to John Keats by looking after the sickly Tom during the poet's Scottish walking tour. His solicitude continued until Keats left for Rome, including various correspondence duties for the poet, such as writing to George to inform him of Tom's death.

He witnessed the copyright assignment of *Endymion,* which produced £100 for the poet's last trip, and he helped gather additional funds for Rome. Haslam persuaded Severn, who called him his "oak friend," to accompany Keats to Rome.

George and Haslam's good friendship lasted through January 1820, after which Haslam turned into a fierce critic, accusing George of financial improprieties against John.

Haslam had married in about 1820, but his wife, Mary, died in 1822, leaving a daughter named Annette Augusta. He remarried and dropped from view after the poet's death, although he was in casual contact with Brown and assisted Milnes with the Keats biography. He died 28 March 1851, apparently after experiencing business failures.[21]

Frances "Fanny" Keats Llanos   Fanny Keats was born 3 June 1803, just ten months before the death of her father. She was barely a year old when her mother remarried and gave her over to her grandmother, Alice Jennings. George and John were away at Clarke's School while Fanny grew up in the Jennings household in Enfield. In 1810, following John Jennings's death, Alice entrusted Fanny's guardianship to Richard Abbey. It is unclear whether she remained in her grandmother's house until the latter's death in 1814, but her happiest childhood memories revolved around Alice Jennings.

Fanny attended Miss Tuckey's School in Marsh Street in Walthamstow, near Abbey's home, and remained there until 1818. After leaving school at fifteen, she lived full-time with the Abbeys. Fanny had a lonely existence punctuated by infrequent visits from John Keats. Her relationships with George and Tom were primarily via the post.

As John Keats prepared to depart for Rome, he sent Fanny a farewell note, which she received 12 September 1820. He never mentioned Fanny Brawne to his sister, although he had mentioned Mrs. Brawne in a letter, saying that he hoped Fanny might visit her in Wentworth Place. Fanny Brawne wrote to Fanny Keats on 7 October, introducing herself and thus commencing a friendship that continued until Fanny Brawne's marriage in 1833. After John's death, Mrs. Brawne and Maria Dilke called on Fanny Keats in Walthamstow, drawing her out of her sulkiness and inducing her to visit Hampstead.

Fanny Brawne introduced Fanny Keats to Valentin Maria Llanos y Gutierrez, an exiled Spanish liberal, in the summer of 1821. They married 30 March 1826 at St. Luke's, Chelsea. The Llanoses' financial affairs were never straightforward. With Charles Dilke's help, they realized £4,600 from Fanny's trusts by 1833. As the money became available, they consumed most of it for living expenses and in his failed bridle bit patent investment. Llanos wrote three books, *Don Esteban, Sandoval or the Freemason,* and *The Spanish Exile;* the last was never published. They lived for five years in London, departing first for France and then arriving in his father's home in Valladolid, Spain, by 1833.

In 1835 Llanos became secretary to Spain's lead minister, Juan Alvarez Mendizábal, a fellow former exile in London. Llanos later became Spanish consul in Gibraltar, worked to deaccession church properties, and managed the canals in Castile (aqueducts to Madrid). After Llanos's retirement in 1861, the couple journeyed to Rome to be with their daughter and son-in-law, Leopoldo Brockmann, who was building the Roman railway (streetcar) system. There Fanny met Joseph Severn and became active in the city's English community. Frederick Locker-Lampson provided the only written description of Fanny as an adult: "She was fat, blonde and lymphatic" (meaning lazy).[22]

After they moved to Spain, the Llanoses were comfortable until about 1880. Fanny cooperated with Harry Buxton Forman in arranging for the publication of certain Keats letters. He became aware of her financial plight and arranged for a £300 grant from the Queen's Bounty Fund. Dilke's grandson, working with solicitor Ralph Thomas, cleared out the £200 set up in Chancery fifty years earlier, remitting it to Fanny in Madrid.

From the 1860s until the 1880s, Fanny conducted a correspondence with George's daughter Emma Keats Speed and her son John Gilmer Speed. Fanny's son, Juan Enrique Llanos y Keats, painted her somewhere between 1875 and 1880. The original painting, with a lock of hair attached, is now at Keats House, Hampstead.[23]

Llanos died 14 August 1885. Fanny followed on 16 December 1889.[24]

John Hamilton Reynolds   Reynolds was born 9 September 1794 in Shrewsbury, the only son among five children, and attended school there and at St. Paul's in London. He met John Keats at Leigh Hunt's house in 1816, and it was he who introduced the poet to Brown, Taylor, Hessey, and Bailey, as well as James Rice and likely Dilke. Like many in the circle, Reynolds aspired to be a writer and poet and had several works published. However, by 1819 he shifted to the law and eventually partnered with Rice. Reynolds later served as attorney for both Fanny Keats Llanos and George Keats.

The Reynolds family played a significant role in the lives of all the Keatses. For instance, Reynolds's sister Marianne (1797–1874) was a favorite friend of George's in the interval between her being jilted by another Keats friend, Benjamin Bailey, and her marrying H. G. Green. His sister Jane Reynolds married poet and humorist Thomas Hood.

Reynolds did not support John Keats's trip to Rome, likely because of the fissure over Fanny Brawne. After the poet's death, he drifted away from the circle. By 1847, Reynolds was an assistant clerk in a county court on the Isle of Wight. His bright prospects forever diminished, he descended through "brandy and water" and died there on 15 November 1852.[25]

Joseph Severn Severn was born 7 December 1793 in London. During his early years, he was apprenticed to an engraver while practicing miniature portraiture. His 1817 miniature of George Keats is the only surviving image of him. John Keats retained it when George and Georgiana sailed for America, positioning it aside his writing desk.[26]

Severn met John Keats in 1816 while he was busy advancing his artistic career. In 1819 he was awarded a gold medal from the Royal Academy, allowing him to apply for a three-year travel grant. Although he was not an intimate of the poet, other friends, including Haslam, determined that Severn was, in the absence of Brown, the best-suited (i.e., most available) to accompany John to Rome. Against his father's wishes, he did so. Severn's letters from Rome form the definitive narrative of the poet's last months.

Severn organized the grave site for John Keats at the Acattolica Cimitero in Testaccio, Rome. Severn, unlike Brown and Taylor, did not ask George for reimbursement of his expenses related to John. Although he was hoping for a large subscription from George for the cemetery monument, it is not clear that George was aware of the need.

Severn remained in Rome after the poet's death, enjoying a successful painting career through the 1830s. Owing to a misconception about Severn's supposedly straitened circumstances in Rome, George asked Dilke to commission a painting in 1832, but evidently, nothing came of it.[27]

Severn returned to England in 1841, and although he had exhibited fifty-three paintings at the Royal Academy in London, his artistic career began to flounder. He was appointed British consul to Rome in 1861 and continued in office until 1872. He died 3 August 1879 and is buried alongside John Keats in the Protestant cemetery in Rome.[28]

John Taylor Taylor was born in East Retford, Nottinghamshire, on 31 July 1781. In 1806 he and James Augustus Hessey established the publishing firm of Taylor and Hessey at 93 Fleet Street. On 15 April 1817 they agreed to become John Keats's publisher. Taylor and Hessey advanced £100 that enabled Keats to travel to Rome. However, when it appeared that *Endymion* would not earn its advance and that Keats was dying, they quickly petitioned Richard Abbey and George Keats for the return of their funds. Abbey refused; George later reimbursed them.

Taylor and Hessey also published Morris Birkbeck's 1817 *Notes on a Journey in America,* the book that helped influence George Keats's emigration. Taylor was a cousin of Michael Drury in Philadelphia, who in turn was a brother-in-law of James Tallant in Cincinnati. Taylor armed George with letters of introduction to each.

Taylor, who never married, retired in 1853 and died 5 July 1864 in Kensington.[29]

Ann Griffin Wylie   Mrs. Wylie was George Keats's mother-in-law. Her parents were likely Robert Griffin and Elizabeth Russell, married 8 January 1754 at St. Martin Outwich, London.[30] The Griffins baptized six children at St. Thomas Apostle, including Ann in 1761 and (Mary) Amelia in 1764.[31]

It is unclear who Georgiana's father was. Her scrapbook, at Harvard's Houghton Library, includes two separate commissions for a man named James Wylie, both dated 20 October 1794 and signed in the name of George III. The first commission names James Wylie a lieutenant in the Fifeshire Infantry Fencibles; the second names him a captain and adjutant. It is likely that this James Wylie was born 28 November 1762 in Dumfernline, Fifeshire, across the Firth of Forth from Edinburgh.[32] The Fencibles were a form of voluntary National Guard, raised to defend the borders of England but not to go to war against another country unless all the regiment's members voted to do so. The Fifeshire Fencibles were active from 1794 to 1803 and served against the United Irishmen in County Antrim, Ireland, in 1797 until being disbanded.

A War Office record indicates that a man named James Wylie was on half pay in the 127th Foot in July 1795, while another record shows that James Wylie activated his commission as captain with the Loyal Fifeshire Volunteers on 22 July 1795. His unit was under the command of Andrew Durham from Largo, which is a bay in the Firth of Forth, south of St. Andrews, Scotland. The Fifeshire Fencibles muster roll for June–September 1795 indicates that Wylie died 18 October 1795; the roll was signed by commanding officer James (not Andrew) Durham. This James Wylie may have been Mrs. Wylie's husband, brother-in-law, or father-in-law. A listing for a different James Wylie than the man in Georgiana's scrapbook, perhaps the adjutant's son, described him as a quartermaster on half pay until 1803, when the records cease.

Also contained in Georgiana's scrapbook is a commission for Augustus Thomas Garskill, gentleman, as lieutenant to the 1st Company for North Gloucester, commanded by General Robert Prescott of the 28th Regiment of Foot, dated 26 July 1804. The name Garskill (though spelled Gaskell) occurs several times in the Wylie family: Frederick Gaskell Griffin (born 16 May 1816), the son of Ann's brother William, and Georgiana's younger brother Charles Gaskell Wylie. Likewise, there is the connection between

Augustus Garskill and Georgiana's own middle name, Augusta. Garskill's identity is not otherwise confirmed. The muster roll for the 28th Foot describes a Charles Thomas Carskell (the difficult-to-read spelling may be Carskill or even Garskill) serving in Lord Robert Kerr's company from 1804 to 1810.[33] The spelling inconsistencies are more pronounced than usual, as officers' names were generally transcribed correctly.

The adjutant James Wylie may have been the father to only Henry Robert Wylie, born in 1783. Mrs. Wylie gave birth to Georgiana Augusta in 1797 and to Charles Gaskell in 1800, likely fathered by someone else to whom she was not married. Augustus Thomas Garskill is an obvious paternal candidate.

Ann Wylie was buried at St. John the Baptist, Hoxton, on 13 March 1835 (also where Charles was buried four years later).[34] Her residence was recorded as Great James Street in the Gray's Inn area, so she likely lived with Charles at the time of her death. Her burial in Hoxton, somewhat distant from Gray's Inn, might be explained by the existence of a family plot or vault at St. John the Baptist. Her age was recorded as seventy-three, indicating her birth sometime after 14 March 1761, consistent with her baptismal record.

Charles Gaskell Wylie   Georgiana's brother Charles's birth year of 1800 is verified both in a French visa application and in his June 1839 death record.[35] When Charles and his wife, Margaret, baptized their son, George Keats Wylie, on 4 March 1829 in West Hackney, he stated his occupation as a warehouseman. George Keats Wylie died at age two and was buried at St. Ann's, Blackfriars, on 22 January 1831. A sibling, Edward Henry Wylie, aged three months, was also buried there a week earlier, on 13 January. Possibly they succumbed to an infectious disease or to cholera, which was epidemic in London at the time. In 1833 Charles was bankrupted. In 1834 he was listed in the Sun Fire Office insurance records as an artificial flower manufacturer at 39 Great James Street, in the Gray's Inn area.[36] He died of delirium tremens at 28 Dorset Crescent, Hoxton, New Town, on 5 June 1839.

Charles Wylie was mentioned in George's correspondence, when he complained to Dilke that Haslam had tried to persuade Charles that George was a "scoundrel."[37]

Henry Robert Wylie   Georgiana's older brother, Henry, was born in 1783.[38] He married Mary Ann Keasle[39] at St. George's Church, Bloomsbury, on 23 December 1819, witnessed by John Keasle, Mary Waldegrave, and Mary Amelia (illegible, but possibly Millar).[40] Their daughter, Augusta Christina Wylie, was baptized in 1820. John Keats, who was not especially fond of Wylie's wife, skewered her:

> Her gown is like a flag on a pole; she would do for him if he turn freemason; I hope she will prove a flag of truce; when she sits languishing with her one foot on a stool, & one elbow on the table, & her head inclined, she looks like the sign of the crooked billet— or the frontispiece to Cinderella or a teapaper woodcut of Mother Shipton at her studies; she is a make-believe—she is bon a fide a thin young—'Oman—But this is mere talk of a fellow creature; yet pardie I would not that Henry have her—Non volo ut eam possideat, nam for, it would be a bam, for it would be a sham.[41]

The Latin translates: "I would not that [Henry] have her," while "bam" was slang for "travesty." Later, John went on: "I am sorry he [Henry] has not a prettier wife: indeed 'tis a shame: she is not half a wife. I think I could find some of her relations in Buffon, or Captn Cook's voyages, or upon a Chinese Clock door, the sherpherdesses on her own mantelpiece, or in a *c(rue)l* sampler in which she may find herself worsted, or in a dutch toy shop window, or one of the Daughters in the Ark, or in any picture shop window."[42]

Henry Wylie played a role in preserving George's miniature portrait by Joseph Severn. According to Fanny Keats Llanos, John Keats gave her the miniature, which she loaned to Wylie so that it could be copied. It was not returned to her, despite her request,[43] but it ended up with George in Louisville, along with one or both of Severn's sketches of Tom Keats. George deflected Fanny's request, not knowing her whereabouts at the time.[44]

George makes numerous references to Henry Wylie in his correspondence with both Fanny and Dilke. Wylie evidently made a real effort to stay in touch, although none of the correspondence survives.

Wylie died 23 October 1846 at 17 Bedford Terrace, Trinity Square, St. Mary Newington. His wife, Mary Ann, registered the death, caused by heart disease and dropsy (edema). She listed his occupation as a merchant's clerk.

KENTUCKY

George's circle of relationships in Kentucky is encapsulated in the following sketches, which reveal the connectedness of the leadership community of which he became a part (see table 4). A few of his more interesting friends are included, although many were omitted if the individual's story did not reflect back on George.

Table 4. Fellow Directors, Trustees, Board Members, and Other Associates

Ohio Bridge Commission Members: 1827
James Guthrie
John Jeremiah Jacob
George Keats
George Wood Meriwether
D. R. Poignard
John S. Snead
J. H. Tyler

Incorporators, Merchants Louisville Insurance Company: 1830
Col. Thomas Anderson (insurance)
William Gifford Bakewell
Nicholas Berthoud
Brown Cozzens (insurer of slaves)
James McG. Cuddy (merchant)
H. B. Hill (merchant)
James Hughes (president, U.S. Bank branch)
John Jeremiah Jacob (president, Bank of Kentucky)
George Keats
E. H. Lewis (grocer)
William H. Pope (merchant)
William Prather (with H. B. Hill)
John S. Snead (cotton manufacturer)
George Starkey (auctioneer)
J. C. Wenzel (insurance)
Daniel Wurts (merchant)

Curators, Louisville Lyceum: 1831
J. W. Palmer, president
George Wood Meriwether, vice president
Simeon Samson Goodwin, treasurer
Simon S. Bucklin, secretary
Napoleon Bonaparte Buford

Edward Mann Butler
George Keats

Directors, Louisville Hotel Co.: 1832
John C. Wenzel, president
George Keats, president (1841)
Dr. Theodore Samuel Bell, secretary
Jacob Beckwith
James Hewitt (Shreve's partner)
Leven Lawrence Shreve

Directors, Bank of Kentucky: 1832
John Jeremiah Jacob, president
William Anderson
William Bell
Capt. David S. Benedict
William C. Fellowes
William Garvin (also in 1838)
Angereau Gray (landowner)
James Guthrie
George Clark Gwathmey, cashier
George Keats (also in 1838)
William H. Pope
William Riddle
Leven Lawrence Shreve
Thomas Steele, teller
James Stewart
Wilkins Tannehill, discount clerk
Ariss Throckmorton (also in 1838)
Robert J. Ward

Stock Commissioners: 1834
Edward J. Bainbridge
William Bell (dry goods)
George Buchanan
John D. Colmesnil
William C. Fellowes
Henry Forsyth
John Jeremiah Jacob
George Keats

William H. Pope
Leven Lawrence Shreve
James Stewart

Directors, Lexington and Ohio Railroad: 1832–1839
E. J. Winters, president
Benjamin Cawthorn
George Keats

Trustees, Harlan Museum: 1835–1838
George Keats, chairman
James Reed, president
Dr. James Chew Johnston, secretary
Evans U. Beard (silversmith)
Robert Buckner (ship chandler)
Samuel Casseday
Thomas Coleman (insurance)
Dr. Urban Epinitis Ewing
Nathaniel Hardy
John Hawkins
Jacob Keller (merchant)
James Marshall
Joseph Metcalfe
Shadrack Penn Jr.
Robert Puck
James Rudd
Samuel S. Spence, custodian
James Stewart
Willis Stewart

Louisville Charitable Society: 1836
William Bell, president
George Keats, vice president (president in 1838)
John P. Bull
Samuel Dickinson (school superintendent)
William Garvin
Simeon Samson Goodwin
Samuel Russell
Willis Stewart
John C. Wenzel

Trustees, Kentucky Historical Society: 1836

John Rowan, president

George Keats, treasurer (1838)

Sen. George Mortimer Bibb

Leonard Bliss Jr.

Dr. Edward Jarvis

Judge Henry Pirtle

Wilkins Tannehill

Additional Trustees: 1837

Rev. James Freeman Clarke

Simeon Samson Goodwin

Sen. Humphrey Marshall

Rev. Benjamin Orr Peers

George Dennison Prentice

Trustees, Louisville College: 1839

John Hopkins Harney, president

Dr. Theodore Samuel Bell

Judge William Fontaine Bullock

Edward Mann Butler, historian

Francis E. Goddard

George Keats

John Price Morton

Judge Samuel Smith Nicholas

Judge Henry Pirtle

John Rowan

Louisville City Council, 1841

John Jacob

George Keats, Fourth Ward

Portland Dry Dock Company

James Marshall, president

William H. Bacon

William Gifford Bakewell

Simeon Samson Goodwin

John Hulme

Unitarian Church Members
Rev. James Freeman Clarke
Rev. Samuel Osgood
Simeon Samson Goodwin
George Keats
Judge Samuel Smith Nicholas
Leven Lawrence Shreve
James Speed

Witnesses to Keats's Will
Holliday W. Cood
James Guthrie

Executors of Keats's Will
Georgiana Wylie Keats
James Speed
Philip Speed

Keats Estate Inventory Appraisers
William G. Bakewell (did not serve)
Fortunatus Cosby Jr.
Francis E. Goddard
Felix Smith

Friends Noted in Ella Keats Peay Obituary
Dr. Theodore Samuel Bell
James Freeman Clarke
Fortunatus Cosby Jr.
George Dennison Prentice

John James Audubon   Audubon was born 26 April 1785 in Aux Cayes, Sainte Domingue (Haiti). The city was a principal harbor for the exportation of sugarcane. Import officials in New York generally reweighed shipments, not trusting the original waybills. However, the French officials who transshipped at Aux Cayes were so precise that their waybills were marked with an "OK" (Aux Cayes), thus giving rise to the term.

The slave rebellions of 1788 convinced Audubon's father to return to Nantes, France, where the son spent the next fifteen years. In 1803 he migrated to the Philadelphia area, where his father owned property. There he met the neighboring Bakewell family and married their daughter Lucy in 1808.

That same year, Audubon moved to Louisville, establishing a general store that did not succeed. In 1810 he moved downriver to Henderson, where he opened a store specializing in hunting and fishing gear. His affairs there began to unravel by 1819, when he met the newly married George and Georgiana Keats, who had decided against settling in Morris Birkbeck's Wanborough village in Edwards County, Illinois. Audubon invited the Keatses to be paying guests in Henderson during the winter of 1818–1819. In 1819 his gristmill failed, coincident with investment losses in a steamboat scheme, so Audubon declared bankruptcy and was temporarily jailed in Louisville. The experience galvanized his interest in naturalist drawings, leading to a lifetime of travels in pursuit of birds and other wildlife.

The Audubons ultimately settled along the Hudson River in Upper Manhattan, where he died 27 January 1851.[45]

Thomas Woodhouse Bakewell   Born 28 April 1788 at Burton-on-Trent, Staffordshire, Bakewell migrated with his parents to America in 1802. After a variety of farming, mercantile, and manufacturing experiences, Bakewell ended up in Henderson, Kentucky, in 1818, where he invested with his brother-in-law John James Audubon in an ill-fated gristmill. Bakewell married Elizabeth Rankin Page, whose parents had emigrated from England at the same time as the Bakewells and had settled in Pittsburgh, where they operated a glassworks in partnership with Bakewell's uncle Benjamin Bakewell. With the 1819 failure of the gristmill in Henderson, Tom and Elizabeth decamped for Louisville, where he developed a steam-powered sawmill and gristmill with David Prentice, a Scottish engineer. Shortly after, George Keats became its managing partner.

Bakewell also partnered with Jacob Beckwith in the construction of several steamboats; Beckwith handled the hulls, and Bakewell handled the machinery. In 1824 the Bakewells moved to Cincinnati. Tom also developed machinery to convert Kentucky hemp into cotton bagging, operated an iron foundry, and laid out much of Covington, Kentucky, for development, while continuing with mercantile interests.

Tom Bakewell and his brother Billy, like many others, were caught up in the Panic of 1837. They had ordered steamboat hulls from a Louisville boat builder, the Portland Dry Dock Company, and George Keats had guaranteed their notes, ultimately bankrupting himself because of it. Immediate members of the Keats family averred, without proof, that Tom Bakewell sheltered funds in various family members' accounts that he could have used to pay down the debt. Nevertheless, Bakewell never fully recovered financially. He sold his foundry interests, resumed mercantile activities, and from 1851 to 1857 was president of the Mechanics and Traders Bank branch in Cincinnati.[46] The Depression of 1857, triggered by an Ohio bank failure, finally wiped him out. Disdaining help from his family, the seventy-year-old Bakewell worked for the next ten years as a clerk for the Cincinnati paper merchant Chatfield and Weeds. He died 6 April 1874 in Allegheny City, Pennsylvania.[47]

William Gifford "Billy" Bakewell   Billy Bakewell, Tom's younger brother, was born 17 February 1799.[48] He was a close friend of George Keats throughout their respective stays in Louisville. His older sister Lucy was married to John J. Audubon, while his younger sister Eliza married Nicholas Berthoud of Shippingport. Billy married Alicia Adelaide Matthews of Philadelphia in November 1828.[49]

In 1829 the Bakewells boarded his nephew, Victor Gifford Audubon, then twenty, while Victor's naturalist father was on a trip to Europe. Billy Bakewell guaranteed his brother Tom's 1837 investment in a paddle wheeler for $125,000. He was forced to sell his home in Louisville in 1842 to cover the debt.

Alicia Bakewell died in 1847, and by 1848, Billy had moved to New Orleans, where his business interests were centered. He died there of heart disease on 21 March 1871.[50]

Jacob Beckwith   This Jacob Beckwith, a director (with George Keats) of the Louisville Hotel Company, may be the same Jacob Beckwith who was captain of the 109-ton steamboat the *Velocipede* for a number of years. This was the first steamboat engaged in regular commerce between Louisville and Pittsburgh and was owned in partnership with Thomas W. Bakewell.[51] Beckwith was a follow-on successor to the Prentice and Bakewell foundry, which built steam engines between 1817 and 1826. After Prentice died, Bakewell dissolved their partnership and sold the foundry to Jacob Keffer, who failed at the business in 1831 and subsequently turned the opportunity over to Beckwith.

Theodore Samuel Bell   Dr. Bell was cited by Ella Keats Peay as one of her father's best friends after moving to Louisville in 1832.[52] Bell was born in Lexington in about 1810, to humble circumstances. Working fourteen hours a day as a tailor's apprentice, he saved $10 to buy a ticket to the local library. Professor Mann Butler, then at Transylvania, discovered him there and guided him to an education that concluded at the Louisville Medical Institute.[53] Bell also had an interest in writing, so he worked with Wilkins Tannehill's periodical and later George D. Prentice's *Journal*. His articles spanned topics from the absence of a railroad in Louisville to the need for public education. He also served as substitute editor for the Whig *Journal*.

Bell, working with James Guthrie, succeeded in luring important faculty from Transylvania to Louisville, strengthening its medical school. He became an editor of the *Louisville Medical Journal* and of its successor, the *Western Journal*. He wrote frequently on issues of public health and hygiene while advocating that Louisville address its sanitary problems, in particular, poor drainage from stagnant ponds. Bell served with George Keats on the Louisville Hotel Company board and on the Louisville College board.[54]

During the Civil War, Bell headed the Kentucky branch of the Sanitary Commission. As such, he doctored wounded soldiers, both Union and Confederate, from the skirmish at Harrodsburg and battle at Perryville. He also was president of the board of the Kentucky State Institution for the Blind for eighteen years.[55] Finally, Bell wrote a book about Cave Hill Cemetery, including extensive horticultural information and guidance.[56] He died in late 1884.

David S. Benedict   A Bank of Kentucky director, Benedict was also a partner in Benedict, Carter and Company, a mercantile house. Benedict was a heavy investor along the river, owning upward of twenty steamboats over the years. He was also president of the Louisville Fire and Marine Insurance Company. Benedict played an active role in Louisville's relationship with New Orleans and was later appointed the Bank of Kentucky's agent in New Orleans. In the Mexican-American War, the "Louisville Legion" of 500 to 700 men joined U.S. troops to fight in small engagements; Benedict handled the finances. Born in 1797 in Westchester County, New York, Benedict died in Louisville on 15 July 1874.[57]

James Berthoud and Nicholas Berthoud   James Berthoud, a native of Neuchâtel,[58] was born in about 1760, left France by 1794, and arrived in Shippingport in 1803 to join his in-law Louis Anastasius Tarascon. They were part of the small but enlightened French community that thrived in Shippingport, making it a sort of Bois de Boulogne adjacent to Louisville, where Berthoud became a boat builder. He was a member of the failed Ohio Canal Company in 1804. One faction favored the canal route past Shippingport (still in use), whereas competing interests in Indiana favored a route on their side of the river, bypassing the falls. Neither side could raise the necessary investment capital, largely because of their failure to agree. Two decades passed before a new organization undertook the project. Berthoud was a trustee of the City of Louisville from 1805 to 1807 and a charter subscriber to the Bank of Kentucky.

A long-standing friend of John James Audubon, it may have been Berthoud who saved Audubon's life when Samuel Bowen and a group of aggrieved investors attacked the naturalist in Henderson in June 1819. After Audubon stabbed Bowen, an angry crowd of Bowen's friends went to his cabin to demand retribution. Berthoud, applying good manners and French logic, though armed with a gun and supported by knife-wielding slaves, encouraged the crowd to leave and let the law handle the contretemps. Berthoud died shortly thereafter, on 19 July 1819.[59]

James's son Nicholas Berthoud joined the partnership when brothers Louis and John Tarascon bought Audubon's Henderson mill, which afterward became profitable. Nicholas and Keats were original subscribers in 1830 to the Merchants Louisville Insurance Company, whose formation was counseled by James Guthrie.

George Mortimer Bibb   Bibb was one of seven directors, with George Keats, of the Kentucky Historical Society. They were likely not close friends, however. Bibb, born 30 October 1776 in Virginia, moved to Lexington in 1798, where he was elected to the state house of representatives in 1806, 1810, and 1817; he was also appointed judge of the Court of Appeals in 1808 and then chief justice in 1809–1810. He was elected as a Democratic-Republican to the U.S. Senate and served from 1811 to 1814. He served again as chief justice of Kentucky in 1827–1828 and was then reelected to the U.S. Senate as a Jacksonian, serving from 1829 to 1835. During his shared term in the Kentucky Historical Society with Keats, Bibb was chancellor of the Louisville Chancery Court from 1835 to 1844. In 1844 President John Tyler appointed Bibb secretary of the treasury (1844–1845). Bibb remained in Washington thereafter and died in Georgetown on 14 April 1859.[60]

Leonard Bliss Jr.   Bliss was born 12 December 1811 in Massachusetts. He attended Brown University, where his classmate Elias Nason wrote of him, "He was a great leader and his brain was full of literary schemes. His scholarship was good, but he had rather spend time in reading and writing poetry than over the pages of LeCroix's Algebra."[61] Bliss found his way to Louisville in 1837, after a bout of consumption in his lungs, and was appointed professor of history and general literature at the Louisville Institute, which did not survive.

He became editor of Louisville's *Literary News Letter* and reported for George D. Prentice's *Journal*. After writing about a political speech by Henry C. Pope, Bliss was hunted through the streets by Pope's cousin, Godfrey Pope, who shot him as he was coming out of the Galt House on 26 September 1842. Godfrey Pope was tried for Bliss's murder, but in light of his family's money and influence, he was acquitted. Pope was subsequently ostracized and enlisted during the Mexican-American War; he was shot dead by an American sentinel when he failed to provide the correct countersign. Politician Henry Pope was killed in a duel, as was his brother William Fontaine Pope. William H. Pope, another relative, served on the Bank of Kentucky board with George Keats.

Charles Briggs   George Keats was surprised and delighted to find his Enfield schoolmate Charles Briggs, who was born in 1794 or 1795, when he first passed through Louisville in 1818. Briggs was involved in trade with England and traveled back and forth periodically. He often carried correspondence for Keats, both ways.

Briggs settled in New Orleans in about 1824, where a city directory listed him as a *négociant*.[62] He was destined to play on a large stage. In 1836 he joined Samuel Hermann in founding Hermann, Briggs and Company, a bank specializing in the exchange of specie, with an emphasis on Mexico. Hermann was a member of a large, prominent Jewish family in the New Orleans community. The firm, also involved in financing cotton transactions, became overextended and failed on 4 March 1837 (coincidentally, the date of Martin Van Buren's inauguration as president), involving losses of between $4 million and $8 million. Its New York backer, J. L. and S. Joseph and Company, immediately collapsed, triggering a bank credit crisis on the East Coast. President Andrew Jackson had shuttered the Bank of the United States, and Van Buren's refusal to intervene led to the panic and depression that ensued throughout the country.[63]

During the same period, Briggs joined with Charles A. LaCoste and Louis Hermann in a firm called Briggs, LaCoste and Company in Natchez, Mississippi. The firm (though not Briggs individually, because he was not a resident of Mississippi) was involved in a jurisdictional lawsuit that was finally resolved in the U.S. Supreme Court in 1841.

Briggs recovered from these setbacks and by 1850 was an agent for the General Mutual Insurance Company. Subsequently he became an agent for the Liverpool and London Fire and Life Insurance Company and then president of the Louisiana Mutual Insurance Company. In 1858 he was elected president of the Chamber of Commerce.[64] Briggs built a Garden District house in an unusual Gothic style; it is still standing. Disapproving of slavery, he employed Irish servants in his home.[65]

Briggs died in New Orleans on 1 April 1874 at age seventy-nine; his funeral was held at Trinity Church.[66] Although an 1834 property transaction listed his wife as Louise C. Wood, a 1903 *New York Times* obituary reported the death of an Amelia Cruger Briggs, aged ninety, described as the "wife of the late Charles Briggs of New Orleans, LA." Her family was from Cruger's Island in Dutchess County, New York.[67]

George Buchanan   Born 24 March 1790, apparently in Scotland, George Buchanan arrived in America in 1816 and settled in Louisville. He operated a commission and forwarding business for many years, then converted the business to a wholesale grocer specializing in sugar, molasses, and coffee.[68] Buchanan became a Whig Party loyalist.

Buchanan bought land to the east of downtown, where he developed the stockyards. In the 1850s the city relocated Beargrass Creek, which formerly entered the Ohio River between Third and Fourth Streets, to a new egress farther east and through his property, which proved ideal for dumping animal remains. Buchanan had the neighboring streets named for Federalist leaders Washington, Adams, and Franklin, as well as for the Whig Webster. Democrats were not included.[69]

Buchanan served in 1834 with George Keats in a fund-raising capacity for the Bank of Kentucky to "Open Books for Subscription of Stock."[70] Later, Buchanan moved to New Orleans and then to St. Louis, where he died on 13 January 1854.[71]

Simon S. Bucklin   The 1832 *Louisville Directory* lists S. S. Bucklin as a curator and secretary of the Louisville Lyceum, a literary organization founded by several distinguished citizens.[72] Little is known of Bucklin, although John Carpenter Bucklin, probably his brother, was Louisville's first mayor. J. C. Bucklin was a Unitarian, as was Keats and many of the other intellectuals of the community; S. S. Bucklin belonged to St. Paul's

Episcopal Church and served on the Committee of Accounts of the State Diocese.[73]

Napoleon Bonaparte Buford Born 13 January 1807 on his family's Woodford County, Kentucky, plantation, N. B. Buford was an 1827 graduate of West Point; he later studied law at Harvard and also taught at West Point. Because his active military service lasted eight years, he was likely stationed with the army in Louisville during the time he served as a curator of the Louisville Lyceum with Keats. During the Civil War, Buford rose to the rank of brevet major general. His younger half brother, John Buford, was a general in the Union army and served heroically at Gettysburg. A cousin, Abraham Buford, was a general in the Confederate army. The Bufords may have descended from the Beauforts, who fought in the War of the Roses with the Lancastrians (red rose). If so, it would seem that they were genetically predisposed to fight in civil wars.

After the war, N. B. Buford was a government inspector for the Union Pacific Railroad and a special commissioner of Indian affairs. Later he moved to Peoria, Illinois, and became president of the Rock Island and Peoria Railroad. He died on 28 March 1883 in Illinois.[74]

John P. Bull Bull was a wholesaler with Bull, Rankin and Leight on East Main Street in Louisville. During one of his trips to England, he carried a letter from George Keats to Charles W. Dilke. Not much else is known, except that George memorialized him in an 1828 letter to his sister Fanny:

> I am obliged to stop with requesting you to pay more than common politeness, civilities to him, whose name if he were otherwise without recommendation should be a passport to your good offices. He is a plain straightforward, worthy, uneducated, sagacious, slow-minded, spirited, brave native born Kentuckian, bred a builder. He was once my traveling companion. . . . The Steam Boat in which we traveled was detained by ice about half way up the Mississippi, and we went out a gunning; after we were tired out with unsuccess, we desired to strike straightaway for our boat, in our course we got entangled in a cane break, so high and (almost) so nearly impenetrable that we almost despaired of getting out of it; we were confident of our direction but the thickets almost made our progress in the right course impossible; I mounted a tree about 25 or 30 Feet to look out and distinguished a somewhat

less obstructed way. . . . When it was Bull's turn to climb which did not prove to him so easy as it had done to me, for he lost his wind, and for a time could neither ascend or descend, while he was in momentary fear of falling it struck me what an odd thing it was to see a Bull up in a tree . . . when in the very midst of his trouble I cried out to him that I had heard of Bears climbing trees but I never expected to see a Bull at such an altitude. He reserved his laugh untill a short residence on terra firma had restored his breath: this was good nature.[75]

John P. Bull is not to be confused with a slightly younger John Bull in Louisville, who made a fortune selling patent medicines.

William Christian Bullitt   William C. Bullitt was born 14 February 1793 at Oxmoor (sometimes spelled Ox Moor), the family estate where he lived most of his life. He was a great-nephew of Captain Thomas Bullitt (1730–1778), who first surveyed Louisville in 1773. Although Bullitt was trained as a lawyer and served in Kentucky's 1849–1850 Constitutional Convention, he practiced law in Louisville only briefly.[76] He married Mildred Ann Fry, a sister-in-law of Judge John Speed. They entertained frequently at Oxmoor. Bullitt died 28 August 1877.[77]

Mildred Bullitt wrote about George's impending death on 20 December 1841, and her daughter Martha wrote on 12 January 1842 that George had died bankrupt; Martha also wrote critically of Georgiana Keats. They were clearly in close touch with events. In 1849 Georgiana Emily Keats, her husband Alfred Gwathmey, and their infant George Keats Gwathmey stayed at Oxmoor for a period, where a Bullitt family slave nursed the child back to health. William Bullitt's sister-in-law, Diana Gwathmey (Mrs. Thomas) Bullitt, was George C. Gwathmey's sister and Alfred Gwathmey's aunt.[78]

William Fontaine Bullock   Born 16 January 1807 in Fayette County, Kentucky, Bullock attended rural schools before entering Transylvania University at Lexington. He moved in 1828 to Louisville to establish a law practice. From 1838 to 1841 he served Jefferson County in the state legislature, where he introduced and was instrumental in passing the act creating the common school system in Kentucky. In 1839 he served with George Keats as a trustee of Louisville College. In 1841 Bullock convinced the legislature to create the Kentucky Institution for the Education of the Blind in Louisville. Likewise, he led the legislature in creating programs for the mentally ill, resulting in a progressive "Lunatic Asylum."[79] From 1846 to 1856 he served as judge of the Fifth Judicial Circuit Court. Judge Bullock was a Whig and a devoted disciple of Henry Clay.[80] He was also one of the primary founders of the Louisville and Nashville Railroad. He died 9 August 1889.

Edward Mann Butler   Butler was one of Louisville's most prominent educators of the early nineteenth century, as well as the author of the respected *History of the Commonwealth of Kentucky,* published in 1834. Although born in Baltimore in July 1784, he lived from age three to fourteen in Chelsea, London, with his grandfather. After earning degrees in medicine and law from St. Mary's College in Georgetown, D.C., Butler was in Louisville by 1815 and became the first principal of the Jefferson Seminary, one of the precursors to the University of Louisville. In 1829 the City of Louisville made him the principal of its first public grammar school. During this period, he also served as a curator of the Louisville Lyceum with Keats.

Butler left Louisville in 1834, following an instructional dispute, and moved to St. Louis.[81] He died there from injuries received in a train accident on 1 November 1855.

Samuel Casseday   Casseday was born 6 August 1795 in Lexington, Virginia. His widowed mother moved the family to Kentucky in 1813. By 1822, Casseday had settled in Louisville, working initially as a carpenter and then as a store clerk. He impressed John S. Snead, who in 1824 set Casseday and John Bull up as dealers in queensware, glass, and china goods. After several successions, the store remained in business past 1870 as Casseday and Sons.

In 1836 Casseday invited a British potter, James Clews, to set up an earthenware manufactory. They decided on a site in Troy, Indiana, about seventy miles downriver from Louisville. Casseday, teamed with John Bull and William Garvin, bought fifty-six acres with an abundance of clay, marl, flint, and spar, as well as access to coal. Clews sent to Staffordshire for thirty-six potters. By 1838, due to the Panic of 1837, the British potters had largely left rural Indiana for home, and replacement American workers were unsatisfactory.[82] The project failed.

Casseday was an early landlord of the Louisville Museum Company. The museum, which was incorporated 20 February 1835, had failed by early 1838. A group of civic leaders, including George Keats and Casseday himself, reincorporated the collection as the Harlan Museum Company on 1 February 1838.[83]

Casseday had ten children, including Ben Casseday, who in 1852 wrote the *History of Louisville*, the city's most comprehensive documentation up to that time. Samuel Casseday died 6 July 1876.[84]

Benjamin Cawthorn   Cawthorn, who operated a brick foundry, served on the Lexington and Ohio Railroad board as a public director with George Keats. As public directors, they were appointed by the government to look after its interests and were in a different class from the private director-shareholders. Later, Cawthorn invested in real estate in a section now known as Old Louisville, south of Broadway.[85]

James Freeman Clarke   James Freeman Clarke was born 4 April 1810 in Hanover, New Hampshire. He graduated from Harvard College and Harvard Divinity School, after which he was appointed to his first active ministry at the Unitarian Church in Louisville. For part of his 1833–1839 stay in Louisville, he lived in the Keats household. Kentucky was a slave state, and Keats owned three household slaves. Clarke quickly threw himself into the national movement to abolish slavery.

While in Louisville, Clarke launched the *Western Messenger,* a magazine of liberal religion, abolitionism, and national duty targeting readers in the Mississippi Valley, who were generally "hard-shelled Calvinists" and anti-Unitarian.[86] His cousin, Ralph Waldo Emerson, published his earliest poems in the *Messenger*, and transcendentalist Margaret Fuller contributed writings as well. George Keats contributed "Winander Lake and Mountains and Ambelside" by John Keats, its first publication.[87] Clarke later influenced Emma Keats to study under Fuller in Providence and Boston.

Returning east in 1839, Clarke founded the Church of the Disciples in Boston and served as its minister (with one break in 1850–1854) until his death. He also held a Harvard professorship in Christian doctrine. During this period, he published twenty-eight books and more than 120 pamphlets. His "Memorial Sketch of George Keats," written for the *Dial* in 1843, became the primary source for the Keatses' arrival in Kentucky and for defining George's character.

After a long and distinguished theological career, Clarke died in Boston on 8 June 1888.

John D. Colmesnil   Joining Keats and Buchanan in raising capital for the Bank of Kentucky was John D. Colmesnil, born in Haiti on 31 July 1787. His father owned two plantations—one cultivating sugar, the other cotton and indigo—and a total of 2,500 slaves. Caught up in the early slave rebellion of 1791, his mother, three sisters, and two brothers were all killed. Colmesnil and his father managed to escape to New Jersey with a few loyal slaves, although they later settled near Savannah, Georgia. At age eighteen, Colmesnil returned to Haiti on a coffee-buying venture. At the old plantation, he unearthed two tons of silver and other treasures his family had buried before the uprising. He hid the silver in 450 coffee bags and got them as far as St. Marks, Haiti, where his scheme was discovered and all was lost. When Colmesnil's father died, his will freed the remaining Haitian slaves, who were transported north.

Colmesnil's next adventure was a trip to sell flour in Havana. To circumvent an exceedingly high import duty, he bribed the Cuban customs agent, but he was discovered and imprisoned in Moro Castle for thirty-one days, until the island's captain-general, a family friend, released him. Colmesnil restarted his enterprise after visiting his in-laws, Louis and John Tarascon, in Louisville, with whom he went into business. On another trading mission, he happened to be in New Madrid, Missouri, on 16 December 1811, when the first of four earthquakes measuring over 8.0 struck. The shock was felt as far away as New York. People in New Madrid, who watched the Mississippi River briefly reverse course (it was actually a large wave moving upstream), thought it was the end of the world.[88]

Over the next thirty years, Colmesnil ran an active river-trading enterprise, as well as a dry goods store in Louisville. He owned one of the largest warehouses near the docks. He served as a trustee for the Town of Louisville in 1826–1827. Colmesnil made and lost several fortunes, although in 1834 he was on top of his game and, along with George Keats, helped raise funds for the Bank of Kentucky.[89] He died in 1871.

Holliday W. Cood   Englishman H. W. Cood was a low-profile person who acquired most of George Keats's possessions after his death in an auction process. Most likely he made friendly bids for the items in order to preserve them for Georgiana. Her brother, Henry Wylie, referred to Cood in an 1837 letter to Dilke, noting that Cood was traveling in Yorkshire but would return to Louisville through Liverpool and bring mail back with him.[90] Cood and Felix Smith were partners of Smith and Company and then Smith and Cood, the successor enterprise to Keats and Smith Lumber Merchants. Cood lived onsite during his early tenure with George and later moved to an apartment in the Galt House.[91] Little else is known about him, other than that he was buried in Cave Hill Cemetery on 10 January 1881.

Fortunatus Cosby Jr. Born 2 May 1802 at the family plantation on Harrods Creek, Cosby studied at Transylvania and then took a law degree at Yale. After college, he was director of a private girls' school. In 1829, when Louisville's first free public school opened, Cosby was appointed to its Board of Trustees. He served intermittently as superintendent from 1839 to 1849. A friend of George D. Prentice, he contributed poetry and prose to the *Louisville Journal* and was a "gradual emancipation" editor of the *Louisville Examiner.* Cosby was a frequent visitor in the Keats household and later served as a court-appointed appraiser of George's estate. In 1848 he wrote an ode that was recited at the dedication of Louisville's Cave Hill Cemetery.

In 1850 Cosby moved to Washington and worked in the Treasury Department. President-elect Lincoln nominated him in 1860 to be consul in Geneva. With a son and son-in-law serving in the Confederate army, Cosby raised suspicions in Congress and was not confirmed in his post until February 1863. By the end of that year he was ousted, having been visited by former Kentucky governor Charles Morehead, who was suspected of being an overseas Confederate agent. Cosby returned to Louisville and died there on 14 June 1871.[92]

Urban Epinitis Ewing U. E. Ewing was for many years a prominent physician and surgeon in Louisville. Born in 1800 in Russellville, Kentucky,[93] he studied medicine in Lexington. There he met Sarah Moore, his first wife, granddaughter of a Pennsylvania governor. Sarah's aunt had married the French minister to the United States, and her cousin married the Duke DePlaisant. Following a chain of deaths with no heirs, Sarah and Ewing came into possession of a French fortune.

An early Keats acquaintance, Ewing lived on Market Street between First and Second Streets, about two blocks away from Keats's lumber mill.[94] Ewing was a slave owner and leased his men to Keats for mill work. Surviving documents outline how Ewing acquired slaves as an investment, paying between $200 and $700 each, depending on their age, gender, and condition. He would then enter into agreements with third parties, such as Keats, assigning a slave for about $70 per year, with the assignee responsible for costs such as food and medical care.[95] In Louisville's atmosphere of reasonable treatment, slaves were sometimes free to line up their own work and give a portion of their earnings back to their master. The slaves could either return home at night or choose to stay in a black quarter for entertainment. Ewing provided good medical care for his slaves.

Ewing served as a trustee of the Harlan Museum with Keats. His second wife, Jane Hawkins Butler, gave birth to Jane (Jenny) Butler Ewing in 1848. Jenny married George Keats Speed, a grandson of George Keats, in 1866. Dr. Ewing was buried in Cave Hill Cemetery on 24 December 1874.

Joshua Barker Flint Joshua Flint, born 13 October 1801 in Cohasset, Massachusetts, was an 1820 graduate of Harvard College and an 1825 graduate of its medical program. After 1832 he became a professor of surgery at the Louisville Medical Institute. He was the first surgeon in the West to use ether during procedures. When Flint went to England on an 1838 buying trip, seeking surgical instruments, George Keats provided him with a letter of introduction to Dilke.[96] There were medical schools in Cincinnati, Louisville, and Lexington and an insufficient number of qualified instructors, as well as intense academic rivalries. In 1840 Flint was dismissed from the Louisville Medical Institute, probably unfairly, and took up his practice in Lexington.[97]

Flint's wife was Nancy Trimble, daughter of Justice Robert Trimble of the U.S. Supreme Court and resident of Louisville.[98] His cousin Timothy Flint authored *Recollections of the Last Ten Years in the Valley of the Mississippi*.[99] Timothy Flint's enthusiastic chapter on Lexington included a half paragraph about Louisville as a place where steamboats put in. Joshua Flint died on 19 March 1863 and was buried the following year adjacent to what later became the Keats lot in Louisville's Cave Hill Cemetery.

Henry H. Forsyth Forsyth, a fellow director of the Bank of Kentucky, operated steamboats along the Ohio and Mississippi Rivers and served on the Board of Managers of the Galt House.[100] Forsyth was also a commission merchant and factor in the firm of Forsyth and Limerick. Forsyth filed for bankruptcy prior to January 1844, having sold 150 bales of cotton on behalf of one John Chapman, whom he did not pay. Chapman, claiming that his commission relationship was outside Forsyth's bankruptcy, sued and won in a case decided in the U.S. Supreme Court. Forsyth's activities thereafter were not chronicled, other than his 26 March 1870 burial.

William Garvin Born in Londonderry, Ireland, in 1795, Garvin migrated to Philadelphia in 1816. By 1827 he was in Louisville and opened a dry goods store, Garvin, Bell and Company, which continued in various iterations until 1861. He invested with Samuel Casseday in an ill-fated queensware operation in Troy, Indiana, and served as a director, with George Keats, of the Bank of Kentucky in 1838.

Garvin died in a spectacular accident on the Ohio River on 4 December 1868. Two steamboats, the *United States* and the *America*, collided almost head-on. Between fifty and sixty passengers perished, all but two of them with Garvin on the *United States*. The better staterooms were generally in the stern of paddle wheelers, farther from the danger of snags, bow-side collisions, and fire.

Garvin had served for many years as a principal of the Board of Trade and an elder in the Presbyterian Church. The funeral procession up to Cave Hill Cemetery was more than a mile long.[101]

Francis E. Goddard A New Englander by birth, Goddard headed the Jefferson Seminary from 1826 to 1829. The Unitarian movement in America, having first been defined in 1819 by William Ellery Channing, was expanding westward by 1829. A group of mostly "literary men" gathered in Goddard's schoolroom to form a Unitarian Society; they included Mann Butler, Samuel S. Nicholas, Henry Pirtle, and Fortunatus Cosby Jr., along with businessmen Simeon S. Goodwin and George Meriwether.[102]

The University of Louisville, considered by some the successor institution to the Jefferson Seminary, credits Goddard as being its fourth head. Goddard participated in itemizing George Keats's household inventory in early 1842. He died 15 September 1845 at age fifty-four.

Simeon Samson Goodwin Born in 1782, Goodwin was an insurance agent specializing in maritime matters. He was a director of the Louisville and Portland Canal Company and a fellow incorporator of the Merchants Louisville Insurance Company. There were some unspecified political issues, as James Guthrie wrote to George W. Meriwether, "Mr. G[oodwin] is so very unpopular that if he takes stock you can't get the stock taken."[103] His role on the Louisville and Portland Canal board may have been controversial. Goodwin was active with Keats in the Kentucky Historical Society and in the Unitarian Church. He died in 1847.

James Guthrie Born 5 December 1792 in Nelson County, Kentucky, Guthrie began his education in a log schoolhouse, followed by several trips as a laborer on flatboats headed downriver to New Orleans. Disliking the work, Guthrie decided to study law under Judge John Rowan and was admitted to the bar in 1817. In 1827 Guthrie was elected to the state legislature, where in 1828 he succeeded in passing the act that made Louisville a city and created the Ohio Bridge Commission, of which George Keats was a member. This permitted more self-government, and Guthrie soon joined the City Council as chairman of the finance committee. Guthrie remained active in state politics through the 1849–1850 Constitutional Convention.

As a civic booster for Louisville, Guthrie was a director of the Louisville and Portland Canal Company from its inception in 1825 and pushed for the first bridge across the Ohio River to Indiana to be built in Louisville. He was also involved in the Lexington and Ohio Railroad, on whose board George served. After various financial setbacks, the railroad pushed through to Frankfort by 1851. It was ultimately consolidated into the Louisville and Nashville Railroad. Guthrie initiated work on the Jefferson County courthouse, as well as laying the foundation for the first waterworks. In 1836 he implemented an ordinance to establish the Louisville Medical Institute, which was later folded into the University of Louisville. Guthrie served as board president of the University of Louisville from 1847 to 1869. Guthrie also helped draw up George Keats's will in 1841.

In 1853 President Franklin Pierce appointed Guthrie secretary of the treasury, a post he held until 1857. Guthrie had been a Jacksonian Democrat, and he ran briefly in 1860 for the presidential nomination as a Democrat. Following his return to Louisville, he devoted himself to completing the Louisville and Nashville Railroad, which he ran during the Civil War. In 1865 he was elected to the U.S. Senate, from which he retired due to ill health in 1868. He died in Louisville on 13 March 1869. The city was indelibly framed by Guthrie's boosterism.[104]

George Clark Gwathmey   Gwathmey was born in 1790. His uncles were the celebrated George Rogers Clark, a founder of Louisville, and William Clark, of the Lewis and Clark Expedition. His father-in-law was James Garrard, Kentucky's second governor.[105] Another uncle, John Gwathmey, was proprietor of the Indian Queen Hotel, Louisville's first. George Gwathmey was cashier of the Bank of Kentucky while Keats was a director. His oldest child, Alfred, married Georgiana Emily Keats. Another connection was his sister, Diana "Missy" Gwathmey, who married Thomas Bullitt, a prosperous merchant. Gwathmey died in 1850.[106]

Nathaniel Hardy   Hardy was born 24 May 1795 in Bradford, Massachusetts. He left for Indiana in 1814, riding on a mule and with a fiddle slung over his shoulder. Hardy initially settled in Indiana, where he purveyed goods to the paddle wheelers. After 1823 he moved to Louisville, where he became a hardware dealer. He was a founding incorporator, with George Keats, of the Mechanics Savings Institution, chartered by an act of the legislature in 1836.[107] He was likewise a founder of the Louisville Savings Institution. Keats and Hardy were fellow trustees of the Harlan Museum. He died 3 May 1848.[108] A son, James, married Lucy Gilmer Davis, a niece of Philip Speed.

On slavery, Hardy wrote to his sister, Caroline:

> Respecting slavery, as I have said before, I am as much opposed to it as any of the New England people, yet I can not view it in the light that many of them do, nor can I blame my present generation for an evil which was entailed upon them by their ancestors. Almost every one will admit that it is an evil in our country and would be glad to get clear of it, if some safe plan could be adopted. As to the situation of the slave, he is far more happy than the poor whites. . . . He has every thing that is necessary for his comfort. . . . As to freedom he cares very little about it and not one in ten would accept it were it offered to them.[109]

Richard Harlan   The reason for the Louisville Museum's rebranding as the Harlan Museum has been lost. The most plausible explanation involves Dr. Richard Harlan, a naturalist from Philadelphia and a longtime colleague of John James Audubon. Harlan, born 19 September 1796 into a Quaker family, completed his medical degree at the University of Pennsylvania in 1818. He had already been elected in 1815 to the Philadelphia Academy of Natural Sciences, where he showed an interest in paleontology and comparative anatomy. By 1821, he was professor of anatomy at the Philadelphia Museum Company. Over the next twenty years, he published more than sixty works, including *Fauna Americana,* a zoological survey of North America, and *Inquiry into the Functions of the Brain in Man.* Harlan was an indefatigable collector of mammals, reptiles, and human skulls. In 1832 he came into possession of the snout of an ichthyosaur, described as an "alligator animal of about seventy feet in length."[110] Harlan gave the relic to the Museum of Natural History in Paris. Because Europe and America were competing over dinosaur finds, his gift to Paris was a form of bragging.

Harlan died in New Orleans on 30 September 1843.

Appendix A

John Hopkins Harney   Harney was born 20 February 1806 in dirt-poor circumstances in Bourbon County, Kentucky. He never attended school but educated himself as a surveyor; this led to his becoming a schoolmaster in Paris, Kentucky. He eventually saved enough money to study belles lettres and theology at Miami University in Ohio. Thereafter he taught at Indiana University and Hanover College, where he began work on an algebra textbook. Harney was named president of Louisville Collegiate Institute, of which George Keats was a trustee, in 1839. When Harney published his algebra textbook in 1840, it was the first such endeavor by an American. After the institute merged into the University of Louisville, Harney began publishing the *Louisville Daily Democrat,* which he did until his death on 26 January 1868. In later years, he headed the Louisville School Board and was a pro-Union legislator during the Civil War. He was married to Martha Rankin Wallace, a cousin of General Lew Wallace (1827–1905).[111]

John Hawkins   Hawkins operated a chair factory on Third Street, between Market and Main. When it burned in 1840, it was one of the worst fires in Louisville.[112] He served on the Harlan Museum board with Keats.

John Jeremiah Jacob   Jacob was born 20 October 1778 in Baltimore. After moving to Louisville, he purchased large real estate holdings, including "Jacob's Wood," an area just south of downtown bounded by Fifth, Preston, Broadway, and Breckenridge Streets. His home was a lot bounded by Third, Fourth, Walnut, and Chestnut Streets. It was within this large residential plot that George Keats built his "Englishman's palace," on property immediately abutting Jacob's.[113] Several of the ten Jacob children were playmates of the Keats children. Richard, Tom, and Mary Jacob (Tyler) were especially close, with Tom being exactly the same age as Isabel Keats.[114]

　　Long after Isabel Keats died in 1843 (a likely suicide), a rumor began that in 1890 an elderly, refined-looking stranger appeared several times at the Keats house (by then the Hampton Institute for Girls) and asked to be left alone in the library, where Isabel had died. When pressed for an explanation by school head Alice Hegan Rice, the stranger said, "I parted from her in there, and have returned from California to visit the scene once more." His implication was that a broken love affair had triggered the tragic event. However, a letter written by Mary Jacob Tyler to her half brother Tom Jacob, a student at Hanover College, immediately after Isabel's death formed the basis of the Keats family's contention that it was an accident, not suicide. Thomas Prather Jacob went on to become a diplomat, serving in Lisbon, among other places. The "refined gentleman" of 1890 may have been Tom Jacob, but I cannot speculate about any love issues.

J. J. Jacob served with George Keats on the Ohio Bridge Commission in 1827. He was a director and then president of the Louisville branch of the Bank of the United States. When the Bank of Kentucky was formed to succeed it, Jacob became president and Keats became a public director. Jacob was also an advocate for a railroad to Frankfort and served for a time on the board of the Louisville and Frankfort Railroad, which was subsumed into the Lexington and Ohio.[115] Both Jacob and Keats were elected to the City Council representing the Fourth Ward in 1841.[116] Jacob died in 1852, one of the wealthiest men in Louisville.

Edward Jarvis   Given his brief tenure in Louisville, Dr. Jarvis was a somewhat unlikely trustee of the Kentucky Historical Society. Born 9 January 1803 in Concord, Massachusetts, he graduated from Harvard College and Boston Medical School, then practiced in Northfield and Concord, Massachusetts, until 1837. He lived in Louisville from 1837 to 1842; then, disapproving of slavery, he returned to Dorchester, Massachusetts. Throughout his career he published a large number of reports on public health, mortality rates, education, insanity, and other subjects. For thirty-six years he was president of the American Statistical Association.[117] He died 31 October 1884 in Dorchester.

John Jeffrey   Jeffrey, born 2 June 1817 in Edinburgh,[118] was a twenty-five-year-old assistant city engineer in Louisville when he married Georgiana Keats on 5 January 1843, barely a year after George's death. He had helped design the jail and installed gas lights up and down Main Street, including in front of the Louisville Hotel. From Georgiana's viewpoint, Jeffrey was a handsome Scot, a competent engineer, and perhaps a stabilizing influence for her children, who ranged in age from eight to twenty-five.

Jeffrey's obituary notice, furnished by his brother Alexander, claimed that he began his engineering career working for Robert Napier in Glasgow, building engines for the first oceangoing steamers. He had previously volunteered, at the age of twelve, to accompany George Stephenson's *Rocket* during its 1829 trial run from Liverpool to Manchester, in which the rail locomotive achieved an unheard of twenty-nine miles per hour, traveling light. He worked on the deepening of the Clyde River in Glasgow and the construction of the Thames Tunnel, the first underwater tunnel. The obituary, which included some inaccuracies, is the only source of Jeffrey's work experience in England.[119]

Jeffrey, upon establishing his own firm, installed gasworks in numerous cities from Springfield, Illinois, to Matanzas, Cuba. Although the firm was called John Jeffrey and Company, he worked with his brothers, particularly Alexander Jeffrey, throughout his lifetime. Alexander, living in Canandaigua, New York, served as the senior partner and financial officer of a consortium of family entities that included John's development firm and the individual shareholdings in the gasworks. More than 100 John-to-Alexander letters detail the operations, issues with outside investors, and even engineering drawings of the various coal-to-gas facilities.[120] John Jeffrey handled the organization, construction, and initial operations of the gasworks. He was continually on the road, especially after 1850. While he traveled, he retained his position as general superintendent of the Cincinnati Gas Works.

While Jeffrey took extended trips in the South and to Cuba, Georgiana would often leave Cincinnati and stay with her children. John noted to Alexander that she paid board to the children and that Alexander should send her whatever funds she required.[121] Georgiana returned to Louisville in December 1853, joining the Unitarian Church there with her youngest daughter, Alice Ann.

The Civil War created challenges for the enterprise, although Jeffrey evidently traveled freely from North to South. The family lost its investment in a Montgomery, Alabama, iron foundry and machine shop but retained ownership of a Vicksburg, Mississippi, gasworks until Jeffrey's death in 1881. In their later years, he and Georgiana lived peacefully in an apartment at the Phoenix Hotel in Lexington, Kentucky.

When the Jeffrey family first emigrated from Scotland, an uncle, Willie McConnell, set them up in business in America. Shareholdings in each of the gasworks generally included various Jeffrey and McConnell family members. When Jeffrey died on 18 February 1881, less than two years after Georgiana, his estate included the gasworks shares in Vicksburg and in Maysville, Kentucky, worth about $55,000 but appraised at $41,292. These were left to various nieces and nephews, some in Scotland.[122] The dower portion of George Keats's estate, which was legally assumed by John Jeffrey upon his marriage to Georgiana, was thus ultimately distributed to Jeffrey relations.

James Chew Johnston Johnston was born 31 July 1787 at Cave Hill Farm, his father's summer place outside of Louisville. After studying at Princeton, he received a medical degree from the University of Pennsylvania, where his thesis was titled "Nourishment of the Fetus." After returning to Louisville, Johnston gave up medicine to tend to his investments, including an interest in the Mechanics Savings Institution. He was secretary of the board of the Harlan Museum, of which George Keats was chairman. Johnston died 4 December 1864, having previously sold his farm to the city to become the new Cave Hill Cemetery.

James Reid Lambdin Born in Pittsburgh on 10 May 1807, Lambdin established the first museum west of the Alleghenies there in 1828. Originally called the Museum of Natural History and Gallery of Paintings, it was renamed the Louisville Museum when Lambdin moved it there in 1832. The collection was modeled after Peale's Museum in Philadelphia, put together by Charles Willson Peale. It included a diverse collection of botanical, biological, and archaeological items. Louisville historian Benjamin Casseday wrote, "The collection of objects of natural history, of curiosity, and of vertu was extremely good."[123]

Trained as an artist by Thomas Sully, Lambdin continued to travel, accepting portrait commissions from Pittsburgh to Mobile, while the Louisville entity floundered in his absence. In 1837 he returned to his home in Philadelphia. Lambdin painted every president from John Q. Adams to James A. Garfield. He died on a train while returning home to Germantown, a suburb of Philadelphia, on 31 January 1889.[124]

Humphrey Marshall Eminently qualified to serve in the Kentucky Historical Society, Humphrey Marshall had written *History of Kentucky* in 1812; it was republished in 1824 as a two-volume set. Marshall, born in 1760 in Fauquier County, Virginia, served in the U.S. Senate from 1795 to 1801 as a Federalist. His brother-in-law and cousin was Chief Justice John Marshall (Humphrey married his own cousin, Mary Marshall). He also served numerous terms in the Kentucky legislature, where he opposed Henry Clay's proposal that all Kentucky legislators should wear domestic homespun rather than English broadcloth.

In 1809 Marshall and Clay fought a duel in which each man suffered slight wounds. Clay had defended Aaron Burr, facing a treason trial in Marshall's cousin's court. In the heat of debate, Marshall called Clay a liar, and the latter charged at him. Clay subsequently apologized, but Marshall refused to accept, calling it the "apology of a poltroon." They dueled across the river in Indiana near present-day New Albany. After three rounds, the seconds stopped the fight, declaring both men "cool, determined, and brave in the highest degree."[125]

Living as a public figure in Frankfort, Marshall was stridently antireligion. He died 3 July 1841.[126]

James Marshall   A director of the Harlan Museum with Keats, Marshall was president of the Portland Dry Dock Company and a major creditor at the time of George's death. He also partnered with Hew Ainslie, a brewer on Seventh Street between Water and Main. He died sometime before 13 August 1863.

George Wood Meriwether   Born in 1789 and descended from a prominent Virginia family, Meriwether was a retail merchant in Louisville, as well as a founding member of the Unitarian Church and an officer of the Louisville Lyceum. He served as treasurer of the City of Louisville, both before and after its incorporation. He also served on the Bridge Commission and the City Council. During the Andrew Jackson administration, he was the Kentucky agent for the payment of naval pensions; he performed the same function for army pensions during the Martin Van Buren administration. Meriwether died 23 March 1864.[127]

Joseph Metcalfe   Metcalfe, an Englishman, operated a brewery on Market Street between Sixth and Seventh Streets that grew to be Louisville's largest, producing upward of 6,000 barrels a year before closing in 1859. The beer was top-fermented, producing ale, beer, brown stout, and porter (a dark, London-style brew). He was a trustee of the Harlan Museum.[128]

John Price Morton   Morton, who served with Keats as a trustee of Louisville College, was born 4 March 1807. After studying at Transylvania University, he came to work for the Louisville Book Store on Main Street. Out of the bookstore emerged a pro-Clay newspaper, the *Focus,* with Morton in charge. After selling the *Focus* to George D. Prentice of the *Louisville Journal,* he founded a printing and binding business, John P. Morton and Company, which became a large supplier to schools and colleges throughout the South and West. As one of Louisville's wealthiest residents, the childless Morton established the Morton Home with a gift of $100,000. Under the auspices of the Episcopal Church, it helped care for the aged and invalid and continues to do so today. He died 19 July 1889 in Louisville.

Samuel Smith Nicholas Born 6 April 1797 near Danville, Nicholas, the youngest of thirteen children, had to leave school after only three or four years. When his parents died, Nicholas entered the employ of an uncle, a merchant in Baltimore. On his uncle's behalf, Nicholas sailed to Peru and China, educating himself in Latin, French, and Spanish. He returned to Kentucky and studied law under George M. Bibb. In 1829 he married the wealthy Matilda Prather, which brought him financial independence. The large Prather family had marital connections with Henry Clay Jr. and with the Pope, Hardy, Churchill, and Jacob families, providing Nicholas excellent social connections as well.

Nicholas was an appointed member of the Court of Appeals from 1831 to 1836 and chancellor of the Louisville Chancery Court from 1844 to 1850. Nicholas served in 1846–1847 as the first president of the newly chartered University of Louisville, a result of the merger of Louisville College and the Louisville Medical Institute. He had served with Keats as a trustee of Louisville College.[129] President Andrew Johnson offered him a seat on the Supreme Court, which he declined due to his age and his concerns over Reconstruction politics. Nicholas died 27 November 1869.

Samuel Osgood James Freeman Clarke's replacement at the Unitarian Church was another young man, Samuel Osgood, born 30 August 1812 in Charlestown, Massachusetts. After graduating from Harvard College and Cambridge Divinity School, Osgood embraced Unitarianism. He was sent west, including his 1835–1837 stay in Louisville. While there, he assisted Clarke in editing the *Western Messenger,* a literary and faith-based journal. By the mid-1840s, he had become the acknowledged leader of the church, moving his pastorate to New York City. A prolific writer, Osgood contributed "Eighteen Years: A Reminiscence of Kentucky" to *Knickerbocker Gallery, a Testimonial to the Editor of Knickerbocker Magazine* in 1855, including a sketch of George Keats.[130] In 1869 Osgood retired and, remarkably, converted to the Episcopal faith. He died 14 April 1880 in New York City.[131]

Benjamin Orr Peers Peers was born 20 April 1800 in Virginia and moved to Kentucky at age three. After graduating from Transylvania and studying a year at Princeton Theological Seminary, Peers became an Episcopal minister and returned to Lexington. From 1833 to 1835 he was the president of Transylvania, after which he moved to Louisville and became the rector of St. Paul's Church.[132] He edited the *Journal of Christian Education* as well as church school publications while serving as a trustee of the Kentucky Historical Society. He died in Louisville on 20 August 1842.[133]

Shadrack Penn Jr. Journalist Shadrack (sometimes spelled Shadrach) Penn was born in 1790 in Frederick, Maryland. He served in the War of 1812 and then settled in Louisville in 1818. He launched the *Louisville Public Advertiser*, a Jacksonian Democratic journal. During Kentucky's bank crisis and economic meltdown of 1819–1823, Penn opposed chartering the Commonwealth Bank.

The bitter, decade-long rivalry between Penn's paper and George Dennison Prentice's *Louisville Journal* was without parallel in the newspaper industry. By 1841, Penn had tired of the rivalry and departed for St. Louis, where he died 15 June 1846.[134] Keats was a close friend and political sympathizer of Prentice's, but he likely maintained a proper relationship with Penn, with whom he served on the Harlan Museum board.

Henry Pirtle Born 5 November 1798 in Washington County, Kentucky, Pirtle was a lawyer and an eminent judge. After the Revolutionary War, Kentucky had been settled by a mix of early pioneers and land speculators, as well as veterans who received land grants in lieu of back pay. The process of taking a land grant and receiving a legal deed of ownership involved endless property line disputes. This litigation arguably created more lawyers per capita in Kentucky than in other states, and many of Kentucky's brightest youth decided to learn the law.

Pirtle studied under Judge John Rowan in Bardstown. By 1825, he moved to Louisville and became a Jefferson County circuit court judge the following year. Pirtle resigned his judgeship in 1832 to boost his income as a private attorney, and that year he and George Keats helped found the Kentucky Historical Society. In 1835 he partnered with James Speed in a lifelong friendship and in a law practice that continued on and off for years. Both men named sons after the other. Pirtle served in the Kentucky senate for two terms between 1840 and 1843. He then accepted a professorship at the University of Louisville Law School in 1846, where he taught until 1873 and was a trustee for twenty years. In 1850 he was elected to a six-year term as a chancellor in the Louisville Chancery Court; he served again in that position in 1862. He was also a director of the Louisville Water Company.

During Pirtle's several terms as a judge, he wrote numerous opinions spanning contract, property, and constitutional law. In 1842 he was chairman of the Committee on Federal Relations, which rendered an anti–states' rights ruling on the treatment of runaway slaves, an opinion that formed the basis of the Supreme Court's decision in *Prigg v. Pennsylvania.* He was a Whig and a Unionist throughout his life. Pirtle died 28 March 1880.[135]

William Hamilton Pope Jr.   Pope, born in 1803, was a partner in the mercantile house of Pope-Davis Company. His father had been in the salt business with Judge John Speed, at Mann's Lick. (A lick is a well, or spring, with a high mineral content. The water is boiled off, leaving behind salt.) Pope served with Keats on the Bank of Kentucky board.[136] His cousin Worden Pope was Jefferson County clerk during the 1830s and 1840s, appending his name to countless civil documents, including George's estate settlement. Pope's partner, Benjamin O. Davis, was a Boston native who married Susan Fry Speed. Joshua Fry Speed, Judge Speed's son, worked for Pope in the early 1830s before moving to Springfield, Illinois, to set up his own general store, where he met Abraham Lincoln. Pope died in 1866.

William Prather   Prather's father, Thomas, was an early leader in Louisville, serving as first president of the Bank of Kentucky. Broadway was originally named Prather Street in his honor. William was born 8 February 1804 and married his cousin Penelope Pope. He partnered in business with H. B. Hill. His sister Matilda married Judge Samuel Smith Nicholas; another sister, Maria, married Henry Clay Jr., son of the Great Compromiser. Prather was an incorporator, with George Keats, in the Merchants Louisville Insurance Company. He died 27 August 1876.[137]

David Prentice   Prentice, a Scottish engineer, partnered with Thomas Bakewell in opening Louisville's first steam engine shop in 1816. Prentice was christened 18 April 1781 in Scotland and moved to America in 1805.[138] Initially a millwright on William Bakewell Sr.'s farm, Fatland Ford, outside Philadelphia, Prentice became intrigued with steam engines and steamboats. By 1817, he had partnered with Thomas Bakewell in a Louisville iron foundry, called Eagle Works, to make engines for mills and boats.

It was Prentice who designed the *Henderson,* the steamboat that was too underpowered to make the return trip up the Mississippi and led to Audubon's suit with Samuel Bowen and to Audubon's inability to repay George Keats for his first investment in America. Prentice also designed the gristmill that was Audubon's final undoing in Henderson. A separate entity, Prentice and Bakewell, began as a gristmill in Louisville. When Keats returned from his London fund-raising trip, he became a one-third partner and manager. Prentice died in 1826; his will was probated 2 October 1826, with George Keats as executor. By 1827, the gristmill had apparently been succeeded by a sawmill, and Bakewell and Prentice had been replaced by Daniel Smith as Keats's partner.

Thomas Bakewell later wrote to his brother, "There was no better man to plan than D. Prentice but he either would not or could not execute his plans to make them work well—when we were together I was the merchant, he the mechanic . . . and there has been too much just cause for complaint with his [engineering]."[139]

George Dennison Prentice   Possibly the most controversial of George's friends was George Dennison Prentice, the Whig editor of the *Louisville Journal*. Born 18 December 1802 in Connecticut, Prentice graduated from Brown University, where he studied under Horace Mann, the proponent of public education. Although he studied law and was admitted to the Connecticut bar, Prentice chose to edit the *Hartford New England Review*. His writings were so pro–Henry Clay that Clay's partisans invited him to Kentucky to write a campaign biography, which was published in 1831 and sold 20,000 copies.

In 1830 Prentice established the *Louisville Journal* to rival Shadrack Penn's *Louisville Public Advertiser*. Among Prentice's quotes about Penn was the following:

> We assure the editor of the Advertiser that we shall never under any circumstances covet a personal controversy with him. We do not believe that his readers would be willing to pay him $10 per year for dissertations upon our private character, however bad it may be; and we are quite sure that ours would be loth to pay that sum for daily disquisitions on him, whatever may be his excellencies. . . . We believe he (Mr. Penn) had not had an article since we came here that was not made up of hints taken from the Journal. Well, we have one consolation—"*he that giveth to the poor lendeth to the Lord.*"[140]

Prentice, as a close friend of the Keats family, wrote a gracious obituary for George in the *Journal*.[141] When Isabel Keats died a year and a half later, Prentice composed a poem for her. Although twenty years her senior and married, he was obviously quite taken by Isabel.

By 1855, the Whig Party had splintered, and Prentice drifted into the Know-Nothing Party, espousing its nativist, anti-immigration views. On Bloody Monday, 6 August 1855, at least twenty-two Irish and German immigrants were killed, and their sections of the city were partially burned. Although the *Journal* had fanned the hysteria, Prentice later publicly regretted his role. He was always an ardent pro-Unionist, although he objected to what he believed to be the radical excesses of Reconstruction. A statue of Prentice stands in front of the Louisville Free Public Library, symbolizing his journalistic ability, although many still regret his anti-Catholic and anti-immigrant rhetoric.[142] He died 22 January 1870.

William Riddle William Riddle was born 8 October 1810 in Pittsburgh. He served on the Bank of Kentucky board with George Keats. Riddle was active in founding the Louisville and Nashville Railroad, having been a member of the initial 1851 survey party that devised a route over the formidable Muldraugh Hill north of Elizabethtown.[143] The success of the railroad cemented Louisville's role as an entrepôt between North and South. Riddle also served as president of Louisville's Board of Aldermen in 1851–1852. He was buried in Cave Hill Cemetery on 15 December 1855.

Coleman Rogers Born 6 March 1781 in Culpeper County, Virginia, Rogers studied medicine at the University of Pennsylvania. In 1817 he partnered with Dr. Daniel Drake in Cincinnati and worked with Drake to establish the Medical College of Ohio, where Rogers was vice president and professor of surgery. The college started off well, receiving a state charter and enrolling many students. However, Drake and Rogers disagreed over the recruitment effort, which led Drake to push Rogers out of the college and Rogers to challenge Drake to a duel, which he declined. Rogers moved to Newport, Kentucky, and then to Louisville in 1823.[144]

Rogers served as surgeon of the Marine Hospital for ten years. After helping to form the Louisville Medical Institute and serving one term as professor of anatomy, he declined any further role in it. Rogers was George Keats's personal physician, attending him on his deathbed. Rogers's daughter Jane Ann married Henry Pirtle; his son, Lewis Rogers, became a successful doctor.

After practicing medicine for thirty-two years in Louisville, Rogers died on 17 February 1855.[145] A group of his medical colleagues, including Joshua B. Flint, Theodore Samuel Bell, and Urban E. Ewing—all close friends of George Keats—prevailed upon Dr. Henry M. Bullitt to prepare a commemorative testimonial for the Kentucky Medical School. Bullitt complied with a thirty-six-page address.[146]

John Rowan Judge Rowan, who was twenty-five years older than George Keats, was the president of the Kentucky Historical Society, of which Keats was treasurer. They were also trustees of Louisville College. Rowan, born 12 July 1773, moved from Pennsylvania as a child, settling near Bardstown. After studying law in Lexington, he set up a private practice in Louisville in 1795. He was an ardent Jeffersonian, espousing supremacy of the legislature over the judiciary and the executive branch. Representing Nelson County in Kentucky's second Constitutional Convention, he advocated the direct election of the governor and state senators.

In 1801 Rowan killed Dr. James Chambers in a duel near Bardstown. Purportedly, the duel was the result of an argument over which of the two men was the better scholar of dead languages. Judge George M. Bibb was Rowan's second on the "field of honor." Rowan, a Latin scholar, was charged with the murder of the Greek scholar Chambers, but he was released owing to insufficient evidence.[147] The episode did not harm his future career. An 1849 act forbade legislators from dueling, and the practice slowly came to a halt thereafter.

Rowan served in the U.S. House of Representatives, the Kentucky house, the Kentucky Court of Appeals (its highest branch), and the U.S. Senate (1825–1831). Between 1795 and 1818 Rowan constructed Federal Hill, now known as "My Old Kentucky Home," in Bardstown.[148] Stephen Collins Foster (who, according to tradition, was Rowan's nephew) composed "My Old Kentucky Home," Kentucky's state song, after a visit. Rowan died on 13 July 1843 in Louisville and is buried at Federal Hill.[149]

George Keats's great-great-granddaughter, Amelia Harrison Bingham, married John Rowan Boone, a descendant of Judge Rowan, in 1929.

James Rudd Rudd was a founder of the Louisville Gas and Water Company, along with John J. Jacob, L. L. Shreve, and John Tyler. Born 13 June 1789 in Maryland, Rudd first came to Springfield, in Washington County, as a child and then moved to Louisville in 1808, having had a cumulative education of just six months. He began working as a carpenter and then became a crockery merchant and real estate investor. He was known as Captain Rudd for having raised a rifle company to support Andrew Jackson at the Battle of New Orleans in 1815. Like George Keats, his fellow Harlan Museum trustee, Rudd often guaranteed the notes of his friends. He too was wiped out following the Panic of 1837 when he honored other people's debts. Unlike Keats, he was able to recover.

Rudd participated in Kentucky's 1849–1850 Constitutional Convention, where he gave a spirited defense of his Catholicism against a speech by Garrett Davis (later a U.S. senator), who had attacked foreigners and Catholics. Rudd was also a director of the Bank of Louisville and a founder of Cave Hill Cemetery. He died 8 May 1867; his wife, Anna (Nannie), died in 1880. He had a large funeral, which his daughter Anna did not attend because she was studying in Rome at the time.[150]

The Rudds' home was demolished in 1884. In 1995, when excavation got under way for the Kentucky Convention Center, bounded by Second, Fourth, Market, and Jefferson Streets, the Rudd's privy pit (outhouse) was discovered in near-perfect condition. The debris around the pit included medicine bottles, smoking pipes, and china. The medicines indicated that family members were dealing with dysentery, hair loss, and lung problems. It remains one of Louisville's most remarkable archaeological finds.[151]

Leven Lawrence Shreve   Shreve was born 27 August 1793 in Maryland. His father moved to Kentucky and became a prosperous farmer near Nicholasville. The father gave Shreve and his brother $5,000 each, which they used to start an iron-mongering business that eventually had branches in Louisville and Cincinnati.

L. L. Shreve was an across-the-street neighbor of the Louisville Hotel, on whose board he sat with George Keats. They also served together on the Bank of Kentucky's board and were members of the Unitarian Church. Shreve and his brother Thomas built an enormous house on Walnut Street, a few blocks from George's; it was the first in Louisville to be lit by gas.

In 1838 Shreve founded the Louisville Gas and Water Company with John J. Jacob and others. He was the first president of the Louisville and Nashville Railroad and was instrumental in the creation of Cave Hill Cemetery. Shreve died in Louisville on 3 April 1864.[152]

Daniel Smith   Daniel Smith, George Keats's partner in operating the lumber mill, maintained a lower community profile. Smith, an Irish Catholic, was born in 1786. He was a Louisville trustee from 1823 to 1827 and served as a councilman in 1828, representing the Second Ward. Keats's ownership interest in the Louisville Hotel was recorded as a Smith and Keats investment, with Daniel Smith's name appearing in the corporate records. Very few accounts of Smith remain, but one is a 30 December 1828 notice in the *Focus* recounting the meetings of the "Friends of Ireland." Samuel Bell, Worden Pope, and James Rudd were also members.

When Keats's estate was inventoried, one of the appraisers was Felix Smith, Daniel's son. He succeeded his father and continued the Keats and Smith lumber house under the name Smith and Cood.

John S. Snead   Born in 1784 in Accomack County, Virginia, Snead and his family moved to Winchester, Kentucky, in 1815 and to Louisville by 1818, arriving at about the same time as Keats. He operated a series of mercantile businesses with several partners, including James Anderson, selling everything from blacksmiths' anvils to silk dresses to wholesale groceries. Snead served with Keats on the Ohio Bridge Commission. In the 1830s he built a large cotton mill that occupied an entire city block; he later removed it to a different community with better access to power. He was also president of the Bank of Louisville.[153] Snead died in November 1840.

James Speed   Another of Keats's personal attorneys was James Speed, a member of the large family whose patriarch had created Farmington, a hemp plantation outside of Louisville. Born 11 March 1812, Speed was educated at St. Joseph's College in Bardstown and later at Transylvania's law school. Returning to Louisville in 1833, he established a law practice that he continued, with interruptions, until his death.

Speed's politics were ardently Whig and antislavery. After serving in the Kentucky house of representatives for one term (1847–1848), he ran as an Emancipation Party candidate for the 1849–1850 Constitutional Convention but lost to James Guthrie, who was pro-slavery but nevertheless argued for the state to emancipate its slaves. As the Whig Party dissolved in the 1850s, Speed joined the Republicans and was elected to the state senate in the 1861 Unionist landslide. He worked to keep Kentucky in the Union, serving as a mustering officer for Kentucky volunteers and commander of the Louisville Home Guard.

President Lincoln appointed Speed U.S. attorney general in December 1864. Speed's bona fides as an emancipationist attracted Lincoln, as did the president's desire to have a border state Kentuckian in the cabinet. In addition, Lincoln had known him for years through his association with Speed's brother, Joshua Fry Speed. Speed became increasingly affiliated with the radical faction in the Republican Party and resigned his cabinet post in July 1866, reflecting disagreements with President Andrew Johnson.

In 1868 the Kentucky delegation proposed Speed as Ulysses S. Grant's vice-presidential nominee; however, no other state supported him. Returning to Louisville, Speed practiced law and taught it at the University of Louisville.[154] He died 25 June 1887.

John Speed John Speed, the proprietor of Farmington, was born 17 May 1772 in Virginia and crossed the Wilderness Road into Kentucky at age ten. In 1808, as a widower, he married Lucy Gilmer Fry, with whom he had eleven of his thirteen children. A son, Philip, married Emma Keats, George's daughter, in June 1841. A grandson, George Nicholas Peay, married Ella Keats, another of George's daughters. Another grandson, John Gilmer Speed, married Mary Clark Poindexter, whose first cousin Alfred Gwathmey had married Georgiana Emily Keats. (Alfred's father was George C., cashier of the Bank of Kentucky during Keats's directorship.) The issue from the Keats-Speed marriages constitute about 90 percent of all the Keats family progeny.

Although John Speed lived several miles outside of Louisville on the Bardstown Pike and devoted himself to his 554-acre hemp plantation, he certainly knew George Keats. Both James Freeman Clarke and Samuel Osgood, the Unitarian ministers, had visited with Speed and written short articles about him. Clarke's autobiography included the following passage:

> We next drove to the house of my dear old friend, Judge Speed, who took me about his plantation, and showed us the negro cabins, having in them various comforts and ornaments. My [Bostonian] companion [Osgood] said, "Judge, I do not see but the slaves are as happy as our laboring classes in the North." "Well," answered the Judge, "I do the best I can to make my slaves comfortable, but I tell you, sir, you cannot make a slave *happy,* do what you will. God Almighty never made a man to be a slave, and he cannot be happy while he is a slave." "But," continued the Boston visitor, "what can be done about it, sir? They could not take care of themselves, if set free." "I think I could show you three men on my plantation," replied Judge Speed, "who might go to the Kentucky legislature. I am inclined to believe they would be as good legislators as the average men there now."[155]

"Judge" Speed was a lay judge, appointed as a sort of arbitrator to handle local cases in his part of Jefferson County. Two of the slaves he mentioned,

Cato and Morocco, were favorites. Morocco was later Abraham Lincoln's coach driver during his 1841 visit to Farmington. After Speed's death and the piecemeal sale of the farm, several of the slaves remained with family members as retainers, one of them as late as 1895.

Speed died 30 March 1840, shortly before the first of the Keats marriages. After a succession of private owners, his home, Farmington, became a museum in 1959, providing an extensive picture of life in Louisville during the first half of the nineteenth century.[156]

Philip Speed   George Keats named his son-in-law, Philip Speed, an executor of his estate; he had a limited role, however, as Georgiana and John Jeffrey acted as administrators. Speed, born 12 April 1819, had married Emma Keats on 9 June 1841 in the Unitarian Church. He was the tenth of Judge John Speed's thirteen children. The newlyweds lived for a year at Farmington.

Before the Civil War, Speed worked with his partner, J. O. Campbell, in the Kentucky Machine Works. During the war, he served as a paymaster in the Union army. Later he became collector of internal revenue for the Fifth District of Kentucky, serving until 1868. He completed his career as superintendent of the Western Cement Association, a precursor of Speed Cement Company and then Louisville Cement Company, which was organized by a nephew, James Breckenridge Speed.[157]

Philip Speed died 1 November 1882 and was buried in Cave Hill Cemetery. In 1879 he had arranged for Georgiana Keats Jeffrey to be buried in Cave Hill Cemetery and for George Keats's remains to be moved from Louisville's Western Cemetery to join her.[158]

James Stewart and Willis T. Stewart   Born in Kentucky in 1799, Willis Stewart was a wholesale grocer in Louisville and an active Mason. The Willis T. Stewart Lodge, which continues in existence, is named in his honor. He also invested in the Louisville and Elizabethtown Turnpike, the Kentucky and Louisville Mutual Insurance Company, and the Louisville and Nashville Railroad. Both Willis and his brother James Stewart served on the Harlan Museum board with George Keats. In 1836 the Stewarts invested in northern Texas, buying into the failed Peters Colony. The colony was a tract of 10 million acres from what is today eastern Dallas to Denton.[159] They were joined in the venture by Louisville investor Thomas Coleman. Willis Stewart was buried 19 March 1857 in Cave Hill Cemetery.[160]

Wilkins Tannehill   Born 4 March 1787 in Pittsburgh, Tannehill moved to Louisville, where he served with George Keats as a founder and trustee of the Kentucky Historical Society. Tannehill was an active Clay supporter. In September 1837 he was named Orator of the Day and gave a speech as a cornerstone of the future bridge across the Ohio River was set in place.[161] He also served on the board of managers of the Louisville Medical Institute. In the 1840s he moved to Tennessee to establish a Clay newspaper there, the *Herald*. Tannehill became blind and died in Nashville, Tennessee, on 2 June 1858.

Ariss Throckmorton   The proprietor of the Galt House, neighboring Keats's mill, was Major Ariss Throckmorton. Born 5 February 1789, he had served in the military during the Black Hawk War of 1832. Long the proprietor of the Washington Hall Hotel, he developed the Galt House in 1835 on the northeast corner of Second and Main Streets, where it existed until 1865, when it burned. Throckmorton was also a Bank of Kentucky director with Keats, and they were likely friendly rivals in the hotel business.

Throckmorton's literary claim to fame was related to Frederick Marryat's 1843 stay at the Galt House. The story was later co-opted by Charles Dickens. Given the English author's renown, the semiliterate Throckmorton went to Marryat's room to welcome him and was coolly told that when the guest wanted service, he would call for it. In an anecdote attributed to Dickens, Throckmorton found an excuse—the British gentleman was disturbing a lady in her room—to throw Marryat out on the street.

Throckmorton died 25 December 1868.

Robert J. Ward Sr.   Ward was born 8 January 1800 on a large farm near Georgetown, Kentucky. He practiced law there and ran for the state legislature; at age twenty-eight, Ward was elected speaker of the house. In due course he moved to Louisville, setting up a business as a commission merchant specializing in cotton. Ward served with Keats as a director of the Bank of Kentucky. He also built a large home less than a block from the Keatses at Second and Walnut Streets.[162] He was buried 3 December 1862.

John P. Wenzel   Wenzel, who served as president of the Louisville Hotel Company, was also an insurance executive at the Louisville Fire and Marine Insurance Company and an incorporator of the Merchants Louisville Insurance Company. When Prince Maximilian of Wied (a small house in Rhenish Prussia) visited Louisville in 1832, he carried a letter of introduction to "Mr. Wenzel, a German merchant," who escorted him about town.[163] Although Germans had settled in Brunerstown (Jeffersontown) in 1797 and, by the 1830s, constituted nearly one-third of the white population, they were slow to assimilate. They spoke German in their churches and in their church schools. However, the Germans made many contributions to Louisville, including the introduction of kindergartens to the school system, the establishment of Louisville's first Jewish temple in 1838, and a number of industries that formed the core of the city's manufacturing base.[164] Wenzel was one of only a handful of Germans in George's circle of acquaintances. Few details of his personal life are accessible.

Charles Whittingham Whittingham, a tobacco dealer, traveled to England in 1825 carrying correspondence for George Keats. He was buried 12 March 1872 in Cave Hill Cemetery.

Daniel Wurts Sr. Another incorporator of Merchants Louisville Insurance Company, Wurts was a commission merchant, a form of middleman in entrepôt society. He was an elder in the Presbyterian Church. Of German origin and a leading member of the Kentucky Colonization Society, Wurts hired only free blacks in his household and business, an unusual practice.[165] Over the course of three decades, the Kentucky Colonization Society freed and resettled about 650 Kentucky slaves in Liberia, one of whom became its president. A town north of Monrovia is named Clay-Ashland, for Henry Clay's home near Lexington.

John P. Young Young was a competing lumber merchant who had partnered with George Keats as early as 1829 in land transactions. He then acquired some of the mill equipment after Keats's death. Little else is known about him.

Posthumous

Naomi Joy Kirk Although George Keats did not know Naomi Kirk, who lived a century later, she spent a major portion of her adult life studying him. Born 24 August 1890 in Otisco, Indiana, Kirk taught high school in New Albany, Indiana, until her retirement in 1953. She then served two terms in the Indiana legislature (1954–1957) as a Democrat. Suffering a cerebral hemorrhage in late 1957, she died 20 January 1958 in New Albany.

In 1933 Kirk registered a master's thesis at Columbia University entitled "Shared Porridge: The Life of George Keats." She spoke about the subject on 1 January 1934 before the Filson Club, which published an extract of her talk that year.[166] In 1938 Maurice Buxton Forman published the eight-volume Hampstead edition of *The Poetical Works and Other Writings of John Keats,* an update of his father Harry Buxton Forman's work. Buxton Forman included Naomi Kirk's "Memoir of George Keats," a greatly compressed version of her master's thesis.[167] For the next decade, Kirk attempted to find a publisher for the full text before abandoning the effort. She died without heirs and without a copyright. Her original thesis is on file at Columbia's Butler Offsite Library.

In 1972 Kirk's niece, Helen Scripture Speed of Lexington, donated a copy of Kirk's updated material to the Filson Historical Society (formerly the Filson Club) in Louisville. Mrs. Speed's mother, Bess Kirk Scripture, was Naomi Kirk's older sister. Coincidentally, Mrs. Speed's husband, Percy Hays Speed, was descended from Thomas Speed, an uncle of Philip Speed.[168] Another copy of Kirk's work is in the hands of Mrs. Speed's daughter, Elizabeth "Betsy" Speed Rich of West Glacier, Montana. Betsy Rich recalls her "Aunt Omie" (actually her great-aunt) as a well-known English teacher.[169]

Appendix B

Pertinent Documents

George Keats's Newspaper Contributions

The poem below was presumably contributed to the *Louisville Daily Journal* by George Keats, along with an article about Jacksonian politics.

To the Earth

"The Heavens declare the glory of God: and the firmament shareth his handy work."

—Psalms 19th Chap. 1st v.

Thou'rt lovely when the bright sun's earliest ray
Rests on the smiling mead and sleeping stream,
And gold-tipt hills and mountains far away,
Clothed in the glory of his azure beam,
Shed sweetly over fields with dowerets gay,
Where sparkling rills incessant music keep,
And gliding on, dash o'er their banks their spray
At every fall or moss-clad rock they leap.

But thou'rt lovlier, when the low winds creep,
And thousand lights and shades fantastic play
Through dim twilight of thy valley's deep,
As evening steals her latest beam away—
When in the far-off distance may be heard
The dash of falling waters melt away:
And the wild vespers of the woodland bird,
Mourning the beauty of the dying day.

'Tis then, when every shade is loveliness,
And every passing breath that steals along

243

Is pregnant with the full round tenderness,
And low soft languishment of dying song,
And in the east pale Cynthia lifts her face,
And casts her silvery light in streams abroad,
That in thy smiling lineaments we trace
That perfect loveliness that springs from God.

K.

Democratic-Republican William Taylor Barry and Republican John Pope both served in the U.S. Senate in 1814–1816 and 1807–1813, respectively. As the parties evolved into Andrew Jackson's Democrats and Henry Clay's Whigs, Barry became a Jacksonian and Pope a Whig (also Keats's party). Jackson appointed Barry to be postmaster general (1829–1835) and subsequently ambassador to Spain, although Barry died en route in 1836 and was interred in Liverpool. Pope served as governor of the Arkansas Territory (1829–1835) and later as a U.S. representative (Whig) from Kentucky (1837–1843). In an iteration of Louisville's newspaper wars, Pope was attacked for switching from the Republican Party to the Whigs. Keats wrote a lengthy defense, of which portions of the last two paragraphs follow:

> He [the reader] will discover that Mr. Pope has often been found standing alone, when but yesterday he was surrounded by hundreds: as he really was and is in the two last great controversies in which he so much distinguished himself. And he will come to the same conclusion with myself, that a magnanimous liberality, amidst the bitterness and asperity of party warfare, deserves not to incur charges of fickleness and inconsistency.
>
> Toward Mr. Pope I did not expect to elicit one unkind remark, from any quarter. He has already met his share of unkindness in this life, and I would fain be the last to whom any part of it could be fairly attributed.

REPRESENTATIVE SLAVE CONTRACTS

The first document is a purchase and sale agreement, in which a female slave named Letty and her five children—Frances, Ellen, William, Isaac, and Edward—are being sold by Sarah Taylor Woolfolk, daughter of and heir to the estate of her father, John Sutton III, and by her husband, Richard Allen Woolfolk (in the steamboat supply business), to Dr. Urban Epinitis Ewing. The Woolfolks were represented by her cousin Chapman

Coleman, who appears to have acted as their surety, or guarantor. He was a U.S. marshal and merchant in Louisville and a nephew of John Sutton. Ewing, in turn, sold a slave named Simon to Woolfolk, on behalf of his wife, for $425, all on 6 September 1832. Further, Woolfolk agreed in the document that the subsequent value of the assets, whether in slaves or in other purchased real property, would be for the benefit of his wife Sarah or for any of their children upon their marriages.

The second document is a lease agreement between Chapman Coleman, as owner-lessor, and L. Wilkinson, lessee, for a slave named Saunders, for one year.

These documents were transcribed by myself, Shirley Harmon, and James J. Holmberg. In some cases, the handwritten purchase and sale agreement could not be transcribed due to problematic handwriting or arcane terminology.

Purchase and Sale Agreement

This indenture made on this 6th day of Sptm 1832 by and between Urban E. Ewing of the City of Louisville Kentucky of the first part, and Chapman Coleman of the same place of the other part. Witnesseth that whereas on the 5th day of Sept. 1832 said party of the second part did sell and convey unto the said party of the first part the following negro slaves for life. To wit a negro woman named Letty and her five children To wit Frances a girl, Ellen, William, Isaac and Edward [possibly] Bruce. The consideration of which said slaves was and is nine hundred dollars and said sum being so much of the proceeds of the sale of the interest and share of Mrs. Sarah T. Woolfolk (wife of Richard A. Woolfolk) one of the children and heirs of John Sutton, decd. of in and unto a house and lot on the north side of Main Street in Louisville afd [aforesaid] descended from John Sutton to his children & sold and conveyed by said Woolfolk & wife to said Ewing & whereas also said Richard in part of the sale and purchase for said Sarah's interest in said house and too hath agreed to take and hath taken and received from said Ewing a negro man slave for life named Simon at the sum and price of four hundred and twenty five dollars. But that previous afd sale and conveyance said Richard as an enducement to his said wife Sarah to unite with him in the sale and conveyance afore [aforesaid] did agree with & promise her to invest the proceeds of said sale in negroes or some other productive property to be conveyed to a trustee to be held for her separate use and in pursuance and fulfillment of such his promise and agreement/in faith of which said Sarah alone united as afd this conveyance is made.

This indenture therefore witnesseth that in consideration of the previous and of the sums of money afd, and of the further sum of one dollar now in hand paid said party of the first part hath granted & bargained sold and delivered and by these presents doth grant, bargained, sold and delivered to the party of the second part his heirs & forever the before named negro slaves & the future increase [i.e., children, or issue] of the females and he covenants with the party of the second that said Simon is a slave for life and that he is sound & healthy and that he will warrant the title to said Simon to sd. [said] party of the second part forever. And as to the other named slaves that he will forever warrant the title to them to said second party against the claim or claims of all and every person or persons claiming by this or under him or his heirs, but no one else whatever. In trust & for the purposes following and none other that is to say: that the said second party shall & will permit Mrs. Sarah T. Woolfolk wife of said Richard to have the use, hire and service of said slaves & their increase exclusive of and independent of the said Richard her husband: that the said party of the second part shall and will at any time at and upon the request in writing of the said Sarah sell the whole or any part of sd [said] slaves or their increase and invest the sale money in the purchase of such other slaves or real estate that the said Sarah may request in writing—Second that the said Sarah shall be at liberty by a declaration in writing in the nature of a last will attested by two witnesses, appoint and declare to whom said negros or other property or any part thereof shall go and belong. That on the marriage of any of the children of the said Richard and Sarah she may by writing attested by two witnesses assign to such child so marrying any part of the negroes afd or property acquired by the sale contemplated and provided for as afd; and the better to show his consent hereto that she may deem proper. That any property acquired by sale as afd shall be held & conveyed in the same trusts as herein provided for and created. And said Richard A. Woolfolk unites in this deed to release and convey any supposed right or claim that he may [have] in him to any of the negroes aforesd. And the par-

ties of the first & second part as also the said Richard A. Woolfolk
set hereto their hands & seals this day upon first written.

U. E. Ewing [buyer]

Chapman Coleman [representing the estate as seller, perhaps as
　surety]

R. A. Woolfolk [husband of Sarah Taylor Sutton, representing the
　seller, her father John Sutton III's estate]

Lease Agreement

On or before the first day of January next I promise to pay to
Chapman Coleman Esqr. Seventy dollars for the hire of a negro
man Spencer and a mulatto boy Saunders, until that time and to
give them the customary cloathing and pay all their expenses. Witness my hand and seal this 1st day of January 1832.

L. Wilkinson

GEORGE KEATS'S WILL

Keats's will was drawn up holographically, three days before his death.
Given the difficulty of reading the original handwriting, I have inserted
words in brackets where they appear to be appropriate. The original is
in the Jefferson County, Kentucky, courthouse. (Tables 5 and 6 list the
appraisers' valuation of his property and selected books in his library at
the time of his death.)

I George Keats make the following last will and testament for
which my just debts paid out of my estate and then wish my estate
to be equally divided amongst my children, and wish my wife to
have one third of my real estate for life and one third of my personal estate, but the [divies] of my shares & personal estate to her
to be after the payment of my debts except that I divies to her
two thousand dollars worth of my household property to be taken
by her at the appraisement. I give my executor or two of them
who shall ask [them] to [review] my debts in [banks] and other
debts from time to time and to sell real estate to pay the [sums] of
the cash [due otherwise] paid out of my estate and they may give
mortgages on my real estate for the purposes of securing any of
my debts should they deem an extension of time of payment ben-

eficial to my estate. Lastly I appoint my wife executrix and James Speed and Philip Speed executors of this will. In witness whereof I have hereto set my hand this 21st day of December 1841.
Witness Geo. Keats
James Guthrie
H W Cood
Commonwealth of Kentucky

At a county court held for Jefferson County at the court house in this city of Louisville on the 10th day of January 1842. The foregoing instrument of writing purportedly to be that will and testament of George Keats dec. late of the county and produced in court and proved by the oaths of James Guthrie and H W Cood the subscribing witnesses thereto whereupon the same was established by the court to be the last will and testament of said George Keats dec. and ordered to be recorded and I recorded in my office as clerk of said court.
Attest Curran Pope Clk
By A F [Cartmets] D.C.

Table 5. Appraisers' List of George Keats's Property at His Death

Property	Value
Furnishings (contents of nine rooms, plus garret and kitchen)	
Pianoforte	$150
Six window curtain sets	$200
Various other items	$0.19–$80
Subtotal	$1,966.55
Slaves	
Jesse	$600 (sold for $700)
Hannah	$400 (sold for $300)
Lucy	$250 (sold for $50)
Bank stock	
25 shares Bank of Kentucky	$1,250
2 shares Louisville Savings Institution	$190
10 shares Mechanics Savings Institution	$187.50
Books	
447 books listed (see table 6)	$208.73
Deduction (Georgiana claimed the marital bed)	($50)
Total	$5,002.78 ($2,575.78 realized at sale)

The appraisal was completed by Francis C. Goddard, Felix Smith, and Fortunatus Cosby on 11 February 1842. The sale was completed on 10 March 1842. The Bank of Kentucky stock was pledged at its full value to the Portland Dry Dock Company; the other stocks were not sold at that time. Buyers of the household goods were Messrs. Joyce, Lumly, Mosby, and Spilman and, primarily, H. W. Cood, Keats's mill colleague and successor partner.

Appendix B

Table 6. Selected Contents of George Keats's Library

Author and Title	Author's Comment
Albion, Illinois, newspaper, 3 vols.	From the community that survived after the demise of Wanborough.
John J. Audubon, *Ornithology*	Probably *Ornithological Biography*—extremely valuable.
Francis Beaumont and John Fletcher, 3 vols.	Where John Keats found idea of "writ in water."
Blackwood's Magazine, 4 vols.	Tory journal edited by Sir Walter Scott's son-in-law John Gibson Lockhart; it invented the designation "Cockney school of poetry," which so devastated John Keats.
John Bonnycastle, *Introduction to Astronomy*	
The Bridgewater Treatises	Compendium of natural science texts.
George Washington Burnap, *Lectures to Young Men*	Burnap explored the controversy between Unitarianism and other established Christian theologies.
Thomas Carlyle, *Sartor Resartus*	Although this title was not listed by the appraisers, J. F. Clarke wrote to Emerson that he studied Carlyle with George Keats.
William Ellery Channing, *Discourses*	Channing was a leading Unitarian theologian.
Geoffrey Chaucer, *Works*	
William Cobbett, *Letters*	Possibly one volume of *A Year's Residence in the U.S.A.*
Samuel Taylor Coleridge, *Table Talk*	Commentary on Shakespeare.
Andrew Combe, *Physiology of Digestion*	Acquired after 1838, perhaps due to George Keats's final illness.
Ross Cox, *Adventures on the Columbia River*	History of fur trading for the North West Company.
George Crabb, *The Dictionary of Knowledge*	
Daniel Defoe, *Robinson Crusoe*	
John Dryden, *Plutarch's Lives*, 6 vols.	
Edinburgh Review, 11 vols.	Whig rival of *Blackwood's* that attacked Wordsworth.
George Edwards, *Gleanings in Natural History*	Pre-Audubon book of birds.
Ralph Waldo Emerson, *Essays*	Emerson was a transcendentalist, a friend of Thomas Carlyle, and a biographer of Margaret Fuller, who educated Emma Keats (Speed).
Edward Gibbon, *Decline and Fall of the Roman Empire*, 12 vols.	
Oliver Goldsmith, miscellaneous works	
Capt. Basil Hall, *Travels in North America, 1827–8*	Critique of American society.
Thomas Hamilton, *The Youth and Manhood of Cyril Thornton* and *Annals of the Peninsular Campaign*	Hamilton was a member of the *Blackwood's* coterie.

Pertinent Documents

William Hazlitt, 7 titles — John Keats's sympathizer.

Thomas Hood, *Endless Fun, or the Comic Annual* — Hood married Keats's friend Jane Reynolds; this title was published in 1838.

Samuel Howitt, *Book of Seasons*

David Hume and Tobias Smollett, *History of England* — Covers the time from Julius Caesar to George IV.

James H. Leigh Hunt, *Byron and Contemporaries* — Hunt's essay on John Keats (noting his family's "wretchedness") annoyed George.

Washington Irving, *Salamagundi* — In this satire, Irving coined the term "Gotham" for New York City.

Samuel Johnson, *The Rambler and the Spectator*

Miss Jones, *The False Step and the Sisters*

Ben Jonson's works — Jonson was a contemporary of Shakespeare.

William Kitchiner, *The Cook's Oracle* — A cookbook.

Charles Lamb, *Essays of Elia* — Elia was Lamb's pseudonym.

Valentin M. Llanos, *Sandoval, or the Freemason* — Llanos was Fanny Keats's husband.

Edward Bulwer Lytton, *England and the English*

Sir John Malcolm, *Sketches of Persia*

Masonic Register — Was George Keats a Mason?

Samuel McHenry, *The Practical Distiller*

Thomas Medwin, *Conversations of Lord Byron* — Written at Pisa in 1824.

Thomas Moore, *Irish Melodies* and *Life of Lord Byron* — Moore was Byron's literary executor.

Amelia Opie, 100 vols. of her works — Opie was a radical sympathizer to Godwin.

Thomas Percy, *Reliques of Ancient English Poetry* — Precursor to Romanticism.

George D. Prentice, *Life of Henry Clay* — Prentice was George Keats's friend and the Whig editor of the *Louisville Journal*.

Quarterly Review, 7 vols. — Published Croker's attack on *Endymion*.

William Robertson, *History of America (1777)* — Possibly John Keats's prize from Clarke's School.

Samuel Rogers et al., *Poetry of Rogers Campbell Montgomery et al.* — Contemporary English poets.

Charles Rollin, *Ancient History*, 7 vols. — French compilation of histories.

Walter Scott, 9 titles, including *Poems* — Scott's circle was anathema to John Keats.

Percy B. Shelley, *Essays and Letters* — This may have been Mary Godwin Shelley's 1840 edition.

Johann Spurzheim, *Phrenology* and *Physiognomy* — Spurzheim, the German popularizer of phrenology, died in 1832 in Boston.

Alexis de Tocqueville, *Democracy in America* — Published in 1838.

John Trumbull, *McFingal* — Satirical mock epic poem of the American Revolution.

Appendix B

Adam Waldie, *Select Circulating Library*	A journal of popular literature.
Isaak Walton, *The Compleat Angler*	
Daniel Webster, *Speeches*	Webster was an important Whig, along with Henry Clay.
William Wordsworth, works and poems	Wordsworth was ambivalent toward John Keats.

CHRONOLOGY

Events in the Life of George Keats

1730–1816

13 October 1730	John Jennings is baptized at St. Stephen's Church, Coleman Street, London.
1 November 1736	Alice Whalley (Jennings) is born in Doughty Pasture, Colne, Lancashire.
About 1773	Thomas Keats is born (according to daughter Fanny) in Land's End, Cornwall—a claim never verified.
4 February 1774	John Jennings leases the Swan and Hoop livery stables.
25 February 1774	John Jennings and Alice Whalley are married in St. Stephen's.
29 June 1775	Frances Jennings is baptized at St. Stephen's.
1784	Jennings renews the lease on the Swan and Hoop for twenty-one years.
9 October 1794	Thomas Keats and Frances Jennings are married in St. George's Church, Hanover Square; neither family attends, and there are no witnesses. The couple moves to the Swan and Hoop Inn and Stables at 24 Pavement Row, Moorfields, on London Wall, sometime after the wedding.
31 October 1795	John Keats (JK) is born at an unconfirmed site in London.
18 December 1795	JK is baptized at St. Botolph-without-Bishopsgate.
28 February 1797	George Keats (GK) is born, perhaps above the Swan and Hoop, opposite Moorgate, where Finsbury Circus replaced Moorfields after the demolition of St. Bethlem Hospital.

About 1797–1799	The family moves to Craven Street, north of City Road (presently Cranwood Street in the Borough of Hackney), about a mile north of the Swan and Hoop.
1798	Georgiana Augusta Wylie (Keats) is born; the date is uncertain, but likely sometime before 26 May.
18 November 1799	Tom Keats is born.
28 April 1801	Edward Keats is born.
24 September 1801	GK is baptized at St. Leonard's, Shoreditch, along with Tom and Edward.
1802	Jennings retires from the Swan and Hoop and moves to Ponders End, Edmonton. Thomas Keats takes over the hostelry. The infant Edward Keats dies and is buried in Bunhill Fields, City Road.
3 June 1803	Frances Mary (Fanny) Keats is born.
August 1803	GK and JK enroll in Clarke's School, Enfield.
16 April 1804	Thomas Keats dies in a riding accident and is buried at St. Stephen's. The children stay with grandmother Alice Jennings in Ponders End during school breaks.
27 June 1804	Frances Keats marries William Rawlings at St. George's Church.
8 March 1805	John Jennings dies at age seventy-five in Ponders End.
25 March 1805	The Swan and Hoop lease expires.
1805	Alice Jennings moves to Church Street, Edmonton, with her grandchildren.
Summer 1805	Frances and Rawlings sue her brother, her mother, and the second executor of her father's will.
May 1806	Chancery verdict gives Frances Keats Rawlings a £50 annuity. By this time, she has left Rawlings, who disappears, and is living with Mr. J. Abraham in Enfield.
1808	Midgley Jennings settles John Jennings's estate and pays Frances Keats Rawlings the annuity arrears due to her.
January 1809	Midgley Jennings dies.

Winter 1809	Frances, who is ill with consumption and rheumatism, reconciles with her mother and returns to Alice's home. JK nurses her while on school breaks. Midgley's widow, Margaret Jennings, petitions the Chancery Court to receive all her husband's capital for her children.
13 February 1810	The Chancery Court dismisses Margaret Jennings's suit, awarding her half of Midgley's capital. The other half eventually goes to the surviving Keats siblings (after JK's death). Separately, £1,666 is set aside to guarantee Frances's £50 annuity at 3 percent.
20 March 1810	Frances Keats Rawlings is buried at St. Stephen's, having died at age thirty-five in Edmonton during the second week of March.
July 1810	Alice Jennings relinquishes custody of the Keats children to guardians Richard Abbey and John Sandell.
1811	George III is declared insane; the Regency commences.
September 1811	Abbey withdraws GK and JK from Clarke's School after midsummer term. GK, age fourteen, is apprenticed to Abbey and lives in a dormitory above his tea brokerage at 4 Pancras Lane in the Poultry. JK is apprenticed to surgeon Thomas Hammond in Enfield.
1812	The War of 1812 completes America's separation from England.
1813	Schoolmate Charles Cowden Clarke lends JK Spenser's *The Faerie Queene*, kindling the eighteen-year-old Keats's interest in poetry.
1814	JK writes his first poem. Tom leaves Clarke's School to join George.
19 December 1814	Alice Jennings is buried at St. Stephen's, having died in Edmonton in mid-December at age seventy-eight.
2 February 1815	JK writes sonnet "To Leigh Hunt."
13 February 1815	Wellington defeats Napoleon at Waterloo, followed by recession in England.

July 1815	The Apothecary Act is passed, requiring JK to leave his apprenticeship and train at a hospital.
1 October 1815	JK registers at Guy's Hospital in London. GK introduces JK to Joseph Severn
1816	GK leaves the dormitory to live with Mr. Swan, Abbey's head clerk, at an unknown location. GK meets Georgiana Augusta Wylie (GAW) sometime prior to Valentine's Day.
5 May 1816	JK publishes "O Solitude" in Leigh Hunt's the *Examiner*.
25 July 1816	JK sits for four surgeon's exams, passing them at age twenty in the shortest time and at the earliest age possible.
Summer 1816	JK and Tom, already in poor health, vacation at Margate.
September 1816	GK moves with Tom to 76 Cheapside, around the corner from Abbey.
Autumn 1816	JK begins to associate with Leigh Hunt, James Rice, John Hamilton Reynolds, and the painter Benjamin Robert Haydon, friends he will keep for the rest of his life.
31 October 1816	JK turns twenty-one but has problems obtaining his full inheritance from Abbey.
November 1816	JK moves in with GK and Tom mid-month in Cheapside.
December 1816	JK writes about GAW, describing her as a "nymph of the downward smile."
1 December 1816	Hunt publishes "Three Young Poets" in the *Examiner*, citing Shelley, Keats, and Reynolds as representatives of a "new school of poetry."
Late December 1816	JK informs Abbey of his decision to abandon medicine for poetry.

1817

1817	Habeus corpus is suspended in England.
3 March	JK's first volume, *Poems*, is published by C. and J. Ollier.

March	The three brothers move to lodgings at 1 Well Walk in Hampstead, GK having left Abbey's employ after five years. GK and GAW are engaged.
September	GK and Tom holiday in France. JK visits Oxford.
28 November	JK finishes *Endymion*.
13 December	GK takes Tom to Teignmouth, seeking a better climate for his health.
21 December	JK's letter to GK and Tom defines "negative capability." JK publishes his first theatrical review.
27(?) December	JK writes his "beauty overcomes" letter to his brothers in Teignmouth.

1818

January–February	JK revises *Endymion*. GK enjoys a flirtation with the Jeffrey sisters.
23 January	JK writes his "intellectual powers" letter to his brothers.
16 February	JK describes Hazlitt's influence.
28 February	GK returns to London to claim inheritance.
4 March	JK relieves GK at Teignmouth
14 March	JK finishes *Endymion*.
18 March	GK pays JK's bills; sends £20.
Spring	Morris Birkbeck's *Notes on a Journey in America*, written in 1817, is published by Taylor and Hessey, leading to emigration excitement.
April	JK writes "Isabella, or the Pot of Basil"; *Endymion* is published. John W. Croker lambastes JK in the *Quarterly Review*.
21 April	JK writes his "grateful to brothers" letter, also called the "disinterestedness" letter.
May	*Blackwood's* first critique of JK appears.
28 May	GK and GAW marry at St. Margaret's, Westminster, and take up lodgings at 28 Judd Street, near Brunswick Square, Bloomsbury.
June	The *British Critic* critiques JK.
22 June	GK and GAW leave London for Liverpool,

	accompanied on stagecoach by JK and Charles Brown, on the first leg of their voyage to America.
27 June	JK explains his poetic theories to GK and GAW in the first of several lengthy letters, culminating 28 January 1820.
29 June	JK's journal letter, written during his Scotland trip, begins.
5 July	GK and GAW set sail from Liverpool on the *Telegraph*.
Summer	Fanny leaves Miss Tuckey's School to live with the Abbeys in Walthamstow.
23 July	JK begins his second journal letter from Scotland—this one to Tom Keats.
6 August	JK's letter to Mrs. Wylie praises George and mentions "sorrow and joy."
8 August	JK returns to Hampstead to nurse Tom and meets Fanny Brawne.
26 August	GK and GAW land in Philadelphia.
August–December	JK works on "Hyperion."
29 October	JK's letter to GK notes that he expects to "be among the English poets."
Late October	Disillusioned by Wanborough, GK and GAW arrive in Henderson, Kentucky, where they live with John James Audubon.
Fall	GK invests in a boat, with disastrous consequences.
1 December	Tom Keats dies at 1 Well Walk, Hampstead.
December	JK moves in with Charles Brown in Wentworth Place (now the Keats House) and lives there for seventeen months of prolific composition. Psychological bonds between GK and JK are severed. JK writes in a journal letter to GK, "in singing never mind the music."
3 December	Illinois becomes a state.
25 December	JK becomes committed to Fanny Brawne; they have an "understanding."

Chronology

1819

1819	Panic of 1819 commences, ending the Era of Good Feelings and lasting to 1823.
January (?)	GK and GAW settle in Louisville; he is employed at the Prentice and Bakewell mill.
January	JK writes "The Eve of St. Agnes."
13–17 February	JK writes "The Eve of St. Mark."
14 February–29 March	JK's journal letter to GK and GAW describes his works in progress and reveals his depression.
21 April–May	JK writes "La Belle Dame sans Merci" and the odes.
June (?)	Georgiana Emily Keats (the future Mrs. Alfred Gwathmey) is born in Louisville.
15 June	JK describes himself as "engaged" to Fanny Brawne.
July–August	JK writes "Lamia Part I" and *Otho the Great and the Fall of Hyperion* on the Isle of Wight.
August–October	JK writes "Lamia Part II" in Winchester.
September	JK's journal letter to GK and GAW describes his theories of poetry and includes "To Autumn."
December	GK returns to London to raise money from Tom Keats's estate.

1820

13 January	JK's journal letter to GAW summarizes humanity and critiques the clergy.
28 January	GK departs London for Liverpool, where he will sail for America on the *Courier,* leaving JK with £20 less than the total of his debts.
3 February	JK has his first lung hemorrhage in Wentworth Place, commencing his "posthumous year."
13 February	JK offers to break his engagement with Fanny Brawne.
3 March	The Missouri Compromise admits Missouri as a slave state.
22 June	JK has a second lung hemorrhage and moves to Leigh Hunt's house.

July	*Lamia, Isabella, The Eve of St. Agnes, and Other Poems* is published and well reviewed.
August	*Lamia* receives critical praise. JK leaves Hunt and is nursed by Fanny Brawne at Wentworth Place.
17 September	JK sails for Italy with Joseph Severn.
8 November	GK writes in his last letter to JK that he is unable to provide funds; the letter is diverted by Brown.
15 November	JK and Severn arrive in Rome.
30 November	JK writes his last known letter, to Brown.
18 December	Rosalind Keats is born in Louisville.

1821–1879

23 February 1821	JK, age twenty-five, dies of tuberculosis at 26 Piazza di Spagna, Rome, and is buried there on 26 February at Cimitero Acattolico (Protestant Cemetery).
27 April 1821	GK acquires a one-third interest in Prentice and Bakewell's sawmill, including the underlying property—the first of more than 114 transactions to follow.
21 July 1821	George IV is crowned.
21 March 1823	George accesses the Infant Legatee funds in Chancery.
25 October 1823	Emma Frances Keats (the future Mrs. Philip Speed) is born.
2 December 1823	The Monroe Doctrine is introduced—no European adventurism.
1824	GK is appointed water warden for Preservation Engine Fire Company.
28 February 1825	Isabel Keats is born.
18 March 1825	GK pays off the last of JK's debts.
20 April 1825	A gristmill is added to the sawmill in a partnership with Daniel Smith.
1825	GK joins the philosophical society.
30 March 1826	Fanny Keats marries Valentin Maria Llanos y Gutierrez at the Church of St. Luke, Chelsea.
2 April 1826	Rosalind Keats dies in Louisville.

20 April 1827	Richard Abbey is interviewed by John Taylor, who does not publish it on the advice of Richard Woodhouse. The "Abbey Memoir" is finally published in 1924 by Amy Lowell.
3 November 1827	GK is appointed to the Ohio Bridge Commission.
November 1827	John Henry Keats is born.
May 1828	GAW visits London with Georgiana Emily, age nine, and John Henry, age six months.
1828	Leigh Hunt's encomium to JK annoys GK.
4 March 1829	Andrew Jackson is inaugurated president.
17 December 1829	The gristmill is sold to the Atkinson brothers.
February 1830	Clarence George Keats is born.
May 1830	GK asks Dilke to enjoin Brown from publishing JK's *Life*.
26 June 1830	William IV, formerly Duke of Clarence, becomes King of England.
1830	GK joins the Unitarian Church and is one of the incorporators of Louisville Merchants Insurance Company.
19 June 1830	GK partners with Daniel Smith in the timber business.
1831	GK becomes a curator of the Louisville Lyceum. Keats and Smith begin a property-buying spree.
6 (?) May 1832	In GK's last known letter to Fanny Keats Llanos, the family finances are resolved.
1832	GK participates in forming the Louisville Hotel Company and becomes a trustee and treasurer of the Kentucky Historical Society and a director of the Bank of Kentucky.
2 March 1833	Ella Keats (the future Mrs. George Nicholas Peay) is born.
1834	President Jackson attacks the Bank of the United States.
11 December 1834	John Howard Payne visits the Keatses in Louisville.
1834–1838	GK befriends James Freeman Clarke.
1835	GK completes his home, known as the "Englishman's palace," on Walnut between

	Third and Fourth Streets. The railway boom commences in England.
23 February 1836	The Battle of the Alamo is fought.
1836	Alice Ann Keats (the future Mrs. Edward Morton Drane) is born. GK is considered for a foreign mission to raise capital for the Bank of Kentucky, but flotation is canceled due to market conditions. He becomes an incorporator of the Mechanics Savings Institution and president of the Louisville Charitable Society.
4 March 1837	The Panic of 1837 commences and does not end until 1840.
20 June 1837	Victoria becomes Queen of England.
1837	GK becomes chairman of the Harlan Museum.
1838	Samuel F. B. Morse invents a telegraphic code.
1839	GK becomes director of Lexington and Ohio Railroad Company and a trustee of Louisville College.
1839–1840	Emma Keats studies under transcendentalist Margaret Fuller in Rhode Island and Boston.
1841	GK starts to make good on his endorsement of Thomas Bakewell's loan from the Portland Dry Dock Company.
January 1841	GK joins the Louisville City Council, representing the Fourth Ward.
March 1841	GK waives the right to enjoin a JK biography, and Brown gives materials to Richard Monckton Milnes.
9 June 1841	Emma Keats marries Philip Speed in the Unitarian Church; GK is pleased.
24 December 1841	GK dies at age forty-four of a gastrointestinal disease, possibly tuberculosis.
March 1842	The bank acquires the Keatses' house but allows GAW to remain for about two years.
1842	Charles Dickens tours America, including Louisville.
5 January 1843	GAW marries John Jeffrey, twenty years her junior, in the Unitarian Church.

Chronology

April 1843	James Freeman Clarke publishes "The Character of the Late George Keats" in the *Dial*.
20 October 1843	Isabel Keats dies, a likely suicide, in the Englishman's palace.
21 June 1844	The Englishman's palace is sold by the bank to James Trabue.
8 September 1845	Jeffrey sends transcripts of JK's letters to Milnes.
1848	Richard Monckton Milnes (later Lord Houghton) publishes the *Life, Letters, and Literary Remains of John Keats*, the first (partial) publication of the remaining letters provided by Jeffrey.
10 August 1850	George Keats Gwathmey is born to Georgiana and Alfred Gwathmey; Alfred then leaves home.
24 November 1850	Alfred Gwathmey dies of cholera in the Charity Hospital in New Orleans.
June 1855	Georgiana K. Gwathmey dies at age thirty-six.
19 February 1861	Clarence George Keats dies of tuberculosis at age thirty-one in Evansville, Indiana.
1861–1865	The Civil War is fought.
November 1872	George Nicholas Peay disappears to Montreal with stolen funds.
5 April 1879	Georgiana Keats Jeffrey dies and is buried in Cave Hill Cemetery in Louisville. GK and Isabel Keats are disinterred from Louisville's Western Cemetery and reburied next to Georgiana.

1881–2011

1881	JK's letters to Fanny Brawne are published.
18 February 1881	John Jeffrey dies at age sixty-three and is buried in Cave Hill Cemetery.
15 June 1881	Alice Keats Drane dies in Frankfort, Kentucky, at age forty-five and is buried in Cave Hill Cemetery.
1882	Clarence Keats Drane leaves Kentucky and reappears as Keats Courtenay in a 1902 marriage in Australia.
10 September 1883	Emma Keats Speed dies at age fifty-nine.

Chronology

14 August 1885	Valentin Llanos dies in Madrid at age eighty-nine.
12 March 1888	Ella Keats Peay dies at age fifty-five.
16 December 1889	Fanny Keats Llanos dies at age eighty-six in Madrid and is buried in the Partio de Sante Mario section of the cemetery at San Isidoro with her husband.
1914–1918	World War I is fought.
7 May 1917	John Henry Keats dies at age ninety in Missouri, where he was a farmer.
October 1924	The Englishman's palace is torn down, to be replaced by a store annex.
1933	Naomi Joy Kirk completes her never-published Columbia master's thesis "The Life of George Keats."
2011	Denise Gigante publishes *The Keats Brothers: The Life of John and George.*

NOTES

Abbreviations

BL   Jack C. Stillinger, *The Letters of Charles Armitage Brown* (Harvard University Press, 1966)

EOL   John W. Kleber, ed., *The Encyclopedia of Louisville* (University Press of Kentucky, 2001)

FHS   Filson Historical Society, Louisville

FK   Fanny Keats (later, Llanos)

GAW   Georgiana Augusta Wylie Keats (later, Jeffrey)

GK   George Keats

HOFC   *History of the Ohio Falls and Their Cities* (L. A. Williams, 1882)

HOL   Ben Casseday, *The History of Louisville* (Hull and Brother, 1852)

JK   John Keats

KC   Hyder Edward Rollins, *The Keats Circle*, 2nd ed., 2 vols. (Harvard University Press, 1965)

KF   Lawrence M. Crutcher, *The Keats Family* (Butler Books, 2009)

KI   Robert Gittings, *The Keats Inheritance* (Heinemann, 1964)

KL   Hyder Edward Rollins, *Letters of John Keats*, 2 vols. (Harvard University Press, 1958)

KSMB   *Keats Shelley Memorial Bulletin*

LCD   *Louisville City Directory*

LPP   *Louisville, Past and Present*, comp. M. Joelin (John P. Morton, 1875)

MKC   Hyder Edward Rollins, *More Letters and Poems of the Keats Circle* (Harvard University Press, 1955)

TK   Tom Keats

Preface

1. *MKC*, 10. This work was appended to *KC*, vol. 2, with certain corrections but no change in pagination. All *MKC* citations are from the 1965 edition of *KC*.

2. James Freeman Clarke (1810–1888) befriended George and published a nine-page "Memorial Sketch" of him in the August 1843 edition of the *Dial*, which he edited along with Ralph Waldo Emerson. The article was republished in Clarke's *Memorial and Biographical Sketches* (Houghton Mifflin, 1878), 221–29. Clarke's favorable characterization of George, brief as it is, survives as the primary contemporary description of his character.

3. Naomi Joy Kirk (1890–1958) contributed a twenty-five-page article to *The Poetical Works and Other Writings of John Keats*, ed. Harry Buxton For-

man, rev. by Maurice Buxton Forman, 8 vols. (Charles Scribner's Sons, 1938), 1:lxxiii–xcviii. A précis was also published in the *Filson Club History Quarterly* 8 (April 1938): 88–96.

The Pivotal Year: 1827–1828

1. The entity's name changed frequently, from Prentice and Bakewell to Smith and Keats to Keats and Smith to George Keats and Company, as noted here and as advertised in the 1832 *LCD*. Later it became Keats, Smith and Young; finally, after George's death, the name was changed to F. S. Smith and H. W. Cood.

2. Josiah Stoddard Johnston, *Memorial History of Louisville,* vol. 1 (American Biographical Publishing Co., 1896), 77–78.

3. GK to FK, February 1824, *MKC,* 17.

4. At the time, Louisville's border was about where Eighth Street is today. Shippingport was separated by the canal, which ran westward approximately to Thirtieth Street. It was north of Portland, which is now Louisville's West End. The canal's locks run from about Twenty-seventh to Thirtieth Streets. At the time of their construction, they were the widest and deepest locks in America, exceeding those of the longer Erie Canal.

5. Corn Island was inhabited in the spring of 1778, although its settlers moved to "Fort on Shore," at Twelfth Street, in the fall of that year. Clark may have been perpetrating a ruse on Corn Island, never intending to settle it. He initially used it to train his men for the Illinois campaign, as well as to allay Indian fears that he was seizing their land ashore until the settlers became sufficiently strong to do so. The island, which appears clearly on a map in *HOL,* was opposite Twelfth Street. During various canal reconstructions and other city projects, Corn Island's limestone was quarried. What was left of the island finally disappeared behind a 1920s dam construction.

6. The 1830 census listed 10,341.

7. Depending on the season, the chutes beside the falls could be navigated downstream with care, but not at all during periods of very low water.

8. A steamboat had appeared on the Thames River in London in 1815.

9. Before its incorporation, the town had trustees. It is not clear whether the trustees named the incorporators or whether they emerged from a town meeting consensus.

10. The last cash distribution, however, was not made until 1832.

11. The chapter "Henderson and Audubon" details this saga.

12. The 1830 census recorded 2,638 African Americans among the population of 10,341 (25.5 percent). Of these, 2,406 were enslaved, as reported in an article by J. Blaine Hudson in *EOL,* 14–18. If Shippingport and Portland were included, the total population was 11,345.

13. Dr. Henry McMurtrie wrote in *Sketches of Louisville* (S. Penn, 1819), 49–50: "Indian Summer . . . was succeeded by a week of changes the most sudden and extraordinary I ever witnessed, the ponds in the town, being frozen and thawed alternately during the same day, which was closed by a night equally as variable. The cold now appeared as though it had commenced in

good earnest; . . . quantities of drifting ice were seen on the Ohio, the ponds were incrusted by it three inches deep."

Abandoned: 1804–1814

1. Jean Haynes published "A Coroner's Inquest, Apr. 1804" in *KSMB* 14 (1963): 46.

2. Named for its adjacency to the south gate of Enfield Close.

3. The coroner's inquest suggests the accident happened very late Saturday night, whereas newspaper reports suggest it was very late Sunday night.

4. John Taylor to his solicitor, Richard Woodhouse, Memoranda on the Keats Family, 23 April 1827 (hereafter cited as the Abbey Memoir), *KC*, 1:304. Taylor (1781–1864), John Keats's publisher, was considering a biography of him in 1827, but he abandoned the project. As part of his preparations, Taylor interviewed Richard Abbey and was surprised by a number of dyspeptic remarks he made about the Keatses. Taylor recorded his notes and sent them to his counselor, Richard Woodhouse Jr. (1788–1834), and together they decided not to publish them. Amy Lowell (1874–1925) came upon the memoir and elected to publish portions of it in her book *John Keats* (Houghton Mifflin, 1925). The memoir is reprinted in full in *KC*, 1:302–9. The original copy of the interview is housed at Harvard.

5. Abbey Memoir, *KC*, 1:304.

6. National Archives, MS 11936/438/792703, insurance record dated 13 August 1806.

7. Abbey Memoir, *KC*, 1:303, 305. Census records indicate a J. Abraham living in Enfield.

8. Ibid.

9. The National Archives at Kew maintains an online historical currency converter calculator, which indicates a 38-to-1 multiplier between 1810 and 2012. A conversion of 1810 pounds sterling to 2012 U.S. dollars, on this basis, might be 60 to 1. Economists also look at consumer prices, average wages earned, and other measures, such as health, to produce higher ratios. The Jennings estate would be valued at £516,800 by the Kew method but considerably higher by various other methods. At £1 to $1.57, the estate's value would translate, on a currency basis, to more than $800,000 in 2012 and several times that amount based on a broader economic analysis.

10. John Jennings's will was drawn up on 1 February 1805, seven months after Frances's remarriage, with the assistance not of a solicitor but of a land surveyor named Joseph Pearson.

11. Margaret was the daughter of Huntingdonshire clergyman William Peacock.

12. Edward Holmes to Richard Monckton Milnes, 9 December 1846, quoted in Milnes's *Life, Letters, and Literary Remains of John Keats*, 3 vols. (Edward Moxon, 1848), 1:7. Holmes (1797–1859) was a student, junior to John Keats, at Clarke's School.

13. The original documents filed with the Chancery spell Sandell's middle name as Nowland; however, a few subsequent writers erroneously spelled

it Rowland. Likewise, many other names throughout this story are subject to various spellings. As a result, there may be spelling inconsistencies because I attempted to replicate the spellings used document by document.

14. JK to FK, 2–4 July 1818, *KL*, 1:314.

15. Hereafter, often referred to simply as Mrs. Wylie; during my research for *KF*, I determined that her maiden name was Ann Griffin.

16. JK to Mrs. Wylie, 6 August 1818, *KL*, 1:358. This letter from Inverness was written six weeks after George and Georgiana had departed for America and just prior to John's return to London after aborting his Scottish walking trip due to illness.

Family Origins: 1773–1804

1. *KF*, 1–9.

2. Upon Thomas Keats's death in 1804, his widow said he was thirty years old. When Fanny Keats Llanos registered the birth of her child, Rosa Matilde Llanos, in November 1833 in Valladolid, Spain, she noted that the child's grandfather was "Mr. Thomas Keats of Lands' End, Cornwall," as reported by her descendant, Fernando Juan Paradinas, in "Evidence in Spain," *KSMB* 18 (1967): 23. He is in possession of a page from her Bible, likely a Protestant Bible confiscated at the Spanish border upon her crossing.

3. A Thomas Keast was baptized in St. Sennen's Parish in 1776, which would have made him twenty-eight on the date of Thomas's death, not thirty, as Frances Keats stated.

4. Walter Jackson Bate, *John Keats* (Harvard University Press, 1963), 700.

5. Robert Gittings, *John Keats* (Little, Brown, 1968), 9–11. After Thomas Keats died, a woman named Elizabeth Keats, who described herself as his sister, paid the Swan and Hoop's poor rates for St. Stephen's Church to the tax collector. No other record of her has been found.

6. William Sharp, *Life and Letters of Joseph Severn* (Charles Scribner, 1892), 54. Sharp quotes from Severn's journal of the voyage. Subsequent writers have challenged many points in Sharp's book, likely the result of Severn's faulty memory. That John Keats went ashore, however, is accepted by most Keats scholars and also by Severn biographer Sue Brown in *Joseph Severn: A Life* (Oxford University Press, 2009), 69–70.

7. Amy Lowell, *John Keats*, 2 vols. (Houghton Mifflin, 1925), 1:6.

8. Jean Haynes, in a 12 January 2011 e-mail, wrote, "I have been searching for the birthplace of Keats' father, Thomas, since 1957. The name is legion in various forms from Buckinghamshire through Berks, Hants, Wilts, Devon, Somerset and Cornwall and in Staffordshire and another version in Worcestershire." Richard Keats, descended from the Corfe Castle line, noted in an 11 January 2011 e-mail that a "Thomas Keats, perhaps a cousin, was fined £20 for smuggling stone in 1803, perhaps explaining why things were kept quiet."

9. Dwight E. Robinson, "Notes on the Antecedents of John Keats: The Maritime Hypothesis," *Keats Shelley Journal* 34 (1984): 22–52. Robinson overlooks John's literary interest in Beaumont and Fletcher's *Philaster*, which used

the "writ in water" language. His thesis has been discounted by genealogical researchers.

10. Sheila Keats, *The Keat(e)s Family from the 1600's to the 20th Century* (Ruddocks, 2006), 25–26.

11. William A. W. Jarvis, "The Jennings Family," *KSMB* 20 (1969): 44–46, quotes Robert A. J. Jennings from a 1968 interview. Robert was a great-great-great-grandson of John Jennings. Alternatively, Gittings, *John Keats*, 439–40, states that John Jennings's parents were Martin and Mary Clementson Jennings from London. Phyllis G. Mann, in "Keats' Maternal Relations," *KSMB* 15 (1964): 32–34, challenges Gittings's research but provides no alternative explanation.

12. St. Stephen's was destroyed by German bombs in 1940 and was not rebuilt.

13. According to Gittings, *John Keats*, Midgley was a common name in Colne.

14. Dame schools in England were neighborhood affairs, often run by elderly women in their homes, where they taught the children reading, writing, and basic skills such as sewing. Their quality ranged from little more than day-care centers for the working classes to schools that provided a reasonable elementary-level education. When the government instituted mandatory education beginning in 1880, the dame schools faded away.

15. Charles Cowden Clarke and Mary Cowden Clarke label Thomas Keats a "principal servant" in *Recollections of Writers*, ed. Robert Gittings (Centaur Press, 1969), 121. The article on Keats was originally published in the February 1874 edition of *Gentleman's Magazine*; the book was originally published in 1878.

16. Located at the address today is a pub called Keats at the Globe, a few yards from the Moorgate tube station.

17. Gittings, *John Keats*, 6.

18. According to Lowell, *John Keats*, 1:5, the witnesses were John Brough and Mary Sut, who are otherwise lost to history.

19. GK to Charles W. Dilke, 20 April 1825, *KC*, 1:288.

20. *KC*, 1:303.

21. Clarke and Clarke, *Recollections of Writers*, 121.

22. Richard Monckton Milnes, *Life, Letters, and Literary Remains of John Keats*, 3 vols. (Edward Moxon, 1848), 1:4, drew from James Henry Leigh Hunt's not necessarily accurate *Lord Byron and Some of His Contemporaries* (Henry Colburn, 1828) in writing that John was supposedly a seven-month baby, his birth hastened by Frances's "passionate love of amusement."

23. Fanny was baptized 17 June 1803 at St. Botolph-without-Bishopsgate, according to Marie Adami, *Fanny Keats* (Oxford University Press, 1937), 14–15. Fanny unwaveringly held to the 1803 birth date, although her guardian Richard Abbey maintained in 1824 that she was born in 1804.

24. Craven Street has since been renamed Cranwood Street, in the borough of Hackney, not to be confused with the better-known Craven Street in Westminster. The street consisted of row houses, most of which have been displaced by commercial development. Adami includes a photograph of the street, likely predating 1900, in *Fanny Keats*.

25. Gittings, *John Keats*, 17.

26. A spavin is a swelling of the horse's tibiotarsal joint, causing it to become distended.

27. From the Old Bailey Proceedings Online of 1674–1834, as transcribed 2003–2007. Mathews's sentence was probably commuted, as there is no separate death record, and such sentences were often reduced. Courtesy of Jean Haynes.

28. GK to Dilke, 20 April 1825, *KC*, 1:288. George Keats's spelling, capitalization, and punctuation are left intact, as are those of all the original texts quoted.

Clarke's Schoolboys: 1803–1810

1. GK to Dilke, 20 April 1825, *KC*, 1:284–85.

2. Benjamin Robert Haydon, *The Autobiography and Memoirs of Benjamin Robert Haydon*, ed. Tom Taylor (1853; reprint, Harcourt Brace, 1926). Haydon comments on John Keats at 1:252.

3. Adami quotes a letter from Fanny: "We never lived with them [Frances and Rawlings], but went at once to my grandmother who disapproved of the marriage." Marie Adami, *Fanny Keats* (Oxford University Press, 1937), 18.

4. Norman Kilgour (husband of Dorothy Hewlett) describes Sandell in "Mrs. Jennings' Will," *KSMB* 13 (1962): 25. Otherwise, the financial details are from *KI*.

5. Eleanor Abbey's marriage document was signed with an *X*. John Keats's letters suggest her illiteracy, but she may have learned to read, as she appears to have read some letters to Fanny.

6. Taylor wrote of the Abbeys' ward, "Of late she has drooped and pined. They are afraid she is going into a Decline, but Mr. Abbey suspects that she has become acquainted with the unhappy Story of her real Parents & that secret Grief is consuming her Health & Spirits." *KC*, 1:307.

7. An extensive correspondence developed between John and Fanny and continued throughout her childhood. These letters form the primary basis of the internal Keats family story. Fanny showed her cache to Joseph Severn in Rome in 1861, but his disingenuous review of the letters—saying they had been written to a child—combined with Fanny's reticence, led to their being sequestered until 1878. Finally, at age seventy-five, Fanny released them. It was then that the family stories began to be reconstructed, followed by Amy Lowell's publication of Richard Abbey's brief memoir recorded ninety-seven years earlier.

8. Robert Browning, "Popularity," verse 13.

9. Richard Monckton Milnes, *Life, Letters, and Literary Remains of John Keats*, 3 vols. (Edward Moxon, 1848), 1:5.

10. *KI*, 8. It is also possible that the £2,000 was the capitalized value of the Swan and Hoop's earnings of, for example, £65 at a 3 percent interest rate.

11. Midgley Jennings became a marine after Clarke's School and served with the British Navy in a battle against the Dutch at Camperdown on 11 October 1797. Posted to HMS *Russell*, he reportedly served as a decoy for Admiral

Adam Duncan, both of them being tall. The Dutch repeatedly shot at him, missing both him and Duncan, according to Dutch admiral Jan Willem de Winter.

12. Richard D. Altick, *The Cowden Clarkes* (Oxford University Press, 1948), 13–16.

13. When the train line was extended to Enfield in 1840, Clarke's School became the Enfield station. Part of its façade is preserved today in the Victoria and Albert Museum, whose Acquisition Monograph 324:1–10 (1907) attributes the design to Wren. The pieces are in deep storage at the museum and are unavailable.

14. Charles Cowden Clarke, "Note on the School-House of Keats at Enfield," in *The Poetical Works and Other Writings of John Keats,* ed. Harry Buxton Forman, rev. by Maurice Buxton Forman, 8 vols. (Charles Scribner's Sons, 1938), 4:341–45. Clarke left disparate notes about his father's school, many of them published in his and his wife Mary Cowden Clarke's *Recollections of Writers,* ed. Robert Gittings (Centaur Press, 1969). Clarke also wrote numerous articles that were published in *National Magazine, Atlantic Monthly,* and *Gentleman's Monthly* during the 1860s and 1870s. His wife, born Mary Novello, took to calling herself Mary Cowden Clarke professionally.

15. Nicholas Roe describes the Enfield Academy as a "Cockney Schoolroom" in *John Keats and the Culture of Dissent* (Oxford University Press, 1997), 27–50.

16. Clarke and Clarke, *Recollections of Writers,* 120–57.

17. Altick, *The Cowden Clarkes,* 13–22.

18. Clarke and Clarke, *Recollections of Writers,* 1–29. Clarke refers in numerous places to life at Clarke's School, from which the preceding paragraphs were consolidated.

19. Joseph Severn, "Biographical Notes on Keats," sent to Milnes around October 1845, in *KC,* 2:138.

20. Charles Brown, *The Life of John Keats,* ed. Dorothy Hyde Bodurtha and Willard Bissell Pope (Oxford University Press, 1937), 42.

21. Clarke and Clarke, *Recollections of Writers,* 123.

22. GK to Dilke, 7 May 1830, *KC,* 1:327–28.

23. Edward Holmes to Milnes, 9 December 1846, *KC,* 2:163–64.

24. The Clarke's School alumni are identified from sundry sources; however, no alumni list survives. John Clarke left the school in Enfield in 1810; he died in 1820.

25. Clarke and Clarke, *Recollections of Writers,* 124.

Youths about London: 1811–1818

1. JK to Ann Wylie, 6 August 1818, *KL,* 1:358.

2. GK to Charles W. Dilke, 7 May 1830, *KC,* 1:327.

3. The business was called Abbey Cock and Company. Abbey was partnered with John Cock and William Johnson, although the latter withdrew from the partnership in 1821.

4. Over the years, Pancras Lane, around the corner from St. Mary-le-Bow Church, has shrunk; today, it is essentially a short alley leading up to the load-

ing dock of a modern office tower. Its location is on the cusp of where Cheapside becomes Poultry in the Newgate section of London.

5. Formerly known as Miss Caley's School.

6. Marsh Street became High Street; the site of the Abbeys' house, around the corner on Blackhorse Road, became the location of the St. James Street train station.

7. FK to GK, 31 May 1826, *KC*, 1:297.

8. Hermione deAlmeida, *Romantic Medicine and John Keats* (Oxford University Press, 1991).

9. Edmonton is about eight miles due north of the City of London (it is now located within London). Enfield is about two miles northwest of Edmonton. Ponders End is about a mile north of central Edmonton and about a mile east of Enfield. Walthamstow is six miles north of London and just southeast of Edmonton.

10. George defended his accounts vis-à-vis John, stating that there was a "£200 *premium* to Mr. Hammond." GK to Dilke, 10 April 1824, *KC*, 1:277. See also *KI*, 46–47.

11. Charles Cowden Clarke and Mary Cowden Clarke, *Recollections of Writers*, ed. Robert Gittings (Centaur Press, 1969), 125.

12. GK to Dilke, 20 April 1825, *KC*, 1:284

13. Clarke and Clarke, *Recollections of Writers*, 144.

14. Guy's Hospital, situated south of the Thames in southeast London, was affiliated with St. Thomas's Hospital. It was spun off from St. Thomas's to treat the incurably ill when they were discharged. Guy's still survives in the twenty-first century, and one of its additions is the tallest hospital building in the world. It numbers many groundbreaking medical scientists among its alumni, along with Keats.

15. John Keats's notebook with lecture notes was published as *Anatomical and Physiological Notebook*, ed. Maurice Buxton Forman (1934; reprint, Haskell House Publishers, 1970).

16. GK to Dilke, 10 April 1824, *KC*, 1:277. George's calculation should have summed £170, but he was writing eight years later in approximations.

17. Abbey had dispersed £500 to John by 4 June 1818, according to a retroactive accounting undertaken by Charles W. Dilke's brother William in 1824, in an effort to resolve the dispute between Dilke and Charles Brown. William Dilke did not itemize any of the expenditures up to that date. The sum of John Keats's Clarke's School, Hammond, and Guy's Hospital fees would have approximated £500. William Dilke's accounting is reprinted in *KI*, 78. The Guy's lodging fee is cited in Robert Gittings, *John Keats* (Little, Brown, 1968), 61, quoting alumnus William Knighton in an article in *Guy's Hospital Gazette*, 13 October 1908, 440.

18. There is inconsistent information about John's roommates. Gittings named George Cooper and Frederick Tyrrell. Henry Stephens claimed to be one in a letter to George Felton Mathew, dated March 1847 (thirty years after the fact), sent as a contribution to Milnes's forthcoming biography and reprinted in *KC*, 2:207. He also named George Wilson Mackereth, who

remained close to Stephens throughout his life, and Tyrrell. Stephens became a doctor in Redbourne, Hertfordshire, and ultimately made his fortune by inventing in 1832 a blue-black ink that enabled the fountain pen. An additional possible roommate was named Walter Dendy; another friend at the time was Charles Severn.

19. Henry Stephens to George Felton Mathew, March 1847, *KC*, 2:209–10.

20. Ibid., 209.

21. GK to JK and TK, August 1816, *KL*, 1:104.

22. George Felton Mathew, to whom Keats wrote a verse letter, fell out with the group after 1815, as their liberal tendencies were at odds with his own conservatism. Milnes contacted him in 1846, and Mathew provided the best description of the boys' activities during 1815. Mathew, an aspiring poet himself, sank into oblivion as editor of an obscure law journal and was attempting to support twelve children. He wrote to his cousin Anne, whom he had not seen in thirty years, to ask for her assistance in writing the letter to Milnes. To his probable surprise, Anne had turned into a godly hellfire-and-brimstone critic of Keats and the whole group.

23. Ann Wylie was buried at St. John the Baptist, Hoxton, on 13 March 1835. Her age was recorded as seventy-three, indicating her birth in 1762.

24. Georgiana's true age is debatable. James Freeman Clarke, in his August 1843 "Memorial Sketch" of George in the *Dial*, states that Georgiana was sixteen years old when she married George in 1818. But Georgiana may have been less than truthful about her age on several occasions. In 1852 her age was listed as thirty-six in a U.S. Census document. Actually, she was about fifty-six at the time, so this could have been a transcription error. Phyllis G. Mann (*KSMB* 13 [1962]) examined the marital allegation at the Faculty Office of the Archbishop of Canterbury in Lambeth Palace, which issued marriage licenses, and the St. Margaret's Parish Register and found that Mrs. Wylie (signing her name clearly as Anne, although elsewhere the *e* was omitted) stated Georgiana's age as "twenty upwards" on 26 May 1818, yet she was under twenty-one at the time and required parental assent. Therefore, Georgiana was born between 27 May 1797 and 26 May 1798. Georgiana may have confirmed her 1797–1798 birth date in a 4 November 1828 disembarkation document when she arrived in New York off the *Britannia*; there, she gave her age as thirty, as recorded in Elizabeth Patty Bentley's *Arrivals in New York* (Genealogical Publishing Company, 2000), 662. Keats writers and scholars, beginning with Charles Cowden Clarke and John Taylor, later perpetuated the notion, begun by James Freeman Clarke, of Georgiana's incorrect, younger age.

25. Mrs. Wylie had a sister, (Mary) Amelia Griffin Millar, also a widow, who lived with her daughter Mary. She evidently had a spacious leasehold in Henrietta Street, close by Covent Garden, where John Keats dined with them all. She subleased lodgings to Henry Wylie as well as to Mary Waldegrave and Mary Ann Keasle. Henry Wylie married Mary Ann Keasle, whom John cordially disliked, in a ceremony attended by Mary Waldegrave, John Keasle, and a Mary Amelia (unreadable, but probably Millar). By 18 June 1820 Mrs. Millar was dead.

26. The poem was also copied with "To Emma" written at the top (not to be confused with a separate poem titled "To Emma"). It remains unclear who Emma was, although one possibility is Emma Severn, sister of Dr. Charles Severn. Charles and John were fellow medical students in 1816 at Guy's Hospital, the former having been an apothecary in Harlow. Emma Severn was the author of *Anne Hathaway: or, Shakespeare in Love*, published in three volumes in 1845. Dr. Severn edited in 1839 *The Diary of John Ward*, a Stratford vicar, and was a committed Shakespearean. To date, the biographers of John Keats, also a devoted Shakespearean, have ignored Dr. Severn and Emma. She wrote to Milnes on 25 August 1848 (*KC*, 2:255) that her brother knew Keats "very intimately." They are not known to be related to artist Joseph Severn. Jack Stillinger suggests in *John Keats Complete Poems* (Belknap Press of Harvard University Press, 1978), 421, that Keats wrote the poem for Mary Frogley, a friend of the Mathews. Also, George Felton Mathew may have had a sister named Emma. In any event, the poem was not exclusively written for Georgiana, although she may have thought so at the time.

27. Haslam was also the son of a partner in Framptons, a wholesale grocer, and he assumed the partnership when his father died.

28. JK to GK and GAW, 14–31 October 1818, *KL*, 1:392.

29. Charles Dickens serialized *Bleak House* in twenty installments between March 1852 and September 1853. One of his primary characters was Harold Skimpole, whom Dickens acknowledged and all his friends immediately recognized as an excellent portrayal of the amoral Leigh Hunt. *Bleak House* was Dickens's term for the Chancery Court, where he worked as a law clerk prior to his writing career.

30. It is unknown which school they attended.

31. Composed 18 November 1816.

32. The walk from Cheapside to Romney Street was about three miles.

33. Written in 1816, this sonnet was first published in 1817, a year before George and Georgiana's marriage.

34. John Keats mentioned Hodgkinson several times in his letters to Fanny. Initially, his references were to Hodgkinson's handling of his accounts. He wrote to Fanny on 28 August 1819 (*KL*, 2:148): "Have you heard any further mention of his [Abbey's] retiring from Business? I am anxious to hear wether Hodgkinson, whose name I cannot bear to write, will in any likelihood be thrown upon himself." Then, on 5 July 1820 (*KL*, 2:305), he wrote: "No one can regret Mr. Hodgkinson's ill fortune: I must own illness has not made such a Saint of me as to prevent my rejoicing at his reverse." It is uncertain what Hodgkinson said or did to George or what ultimately happened to him. Hodgkinson remained with Abbey until sometime prior to 23 August 1820, when Abbey wrote to John (*KL*, 2:331): "You know it was very much against my will that you lent your money to George—In my settlement with him Mr. Hodgkinson omitted a 50£ bill which he had drawn from America & not then due, so that he got this 50£ more than I knew at the time—Bad debts for the last two years have cut down the profits of our business to nothing, so that I can scarcely take out enough for my private expence—It is therefore not in my

power to lend you any thing." It is possible that Abbey separated from Hodgkinson at this time. John's reference to Hodgkinson's "ill fortune" involved his supposed suffering from consumption. John wrote to George and Georgiana on 17 March 1819 (*KL*, 2:77): "Mr. A . . . observed how strange it was that Hodgkinson should have been not able to walk two months ago and that now he should be married." In a letter to George dated 31 May 1826 (*KC*, 1:299–300), Fanny mentioned that "Hodgkinson [is] prosperous I believe." According to Joanna Richardson, "New Light on Mr. Abbey," *KSMB* 5 (1953): 30n. Hodgkinson died 25 July 1832 at age seventy-four.

35. Brown to Dilke, 20 January 1830, *BL*, 305.

36. A letter from John to George was addressed to 62 Bread Street, and a Thomas Wilkinson, auctioneer, was listed at 19 Bread Street, according to a 22 April 1817 advertisement in the *Times* and a listing in Johnstone's *1817 London Directory.* John loaned a book of poems to Charles Wilkinson of New North Street, Red Lion Square (*KL*, 1:129n), but the two Wilkinsons were separate individuals. No other aspect of George's short-term relationship to Thomas Wilkinson survives.

37. Nicholas Roe's *Fiery Heart: The First Life of Leigh Hunt* (Random House, 2005), 267–96, provides a full description of the circle.

38. In a 3 March 1819 letter to George and Georgiana, John referred to himself as the "Count de Cockaigne" (*KL*, 2:69).

39. Hoxton, the neighborhood where Georgiana's brother Charles settled and where her mother died, was also considered part of Cockney London. A generally accepted definition of Cockney London is anywhere within earshot of the Bow Church bells; this can encompass up to a five-mile diameter, depending on the winds, which generally blow from the northwest.

40. Clive Sansom, "Keats's Accent," *KSMB* 14 (1963): 43–45.

41. Charles Jeremiah Wells attended Clarke's School, where he befriended Tom Keats. John Keats dropped Wells after he played a practical joke on the dying Tom, penning him a flirtatious correspondence from a make-believe woman, Amena Bellefilia.

42. James Ollier left the publishing business in the 1830s, moving to Boston and then to New York, where he became a journalist. He died in Panama in 1851, presumably on his way to cover the California gold rush.

43. Haydon (1786–1846) incorporated John Keats's face into his monumental work *Christ's Entry into Jerusalem,* painted from 1814 to 1820 and now housed at Mount St. Mary's Seminary in Cincinnati, Ohio. Haydon, who borrowed money from Keats but never repaid him, later went to debtor's prison. He then attempted suicide by shooting himself with a pistol. When the bullet failed, he slit his throat and died at age sixty-one.

44. Charles Brown wrote to John Taylor on 23 August 1819 (*KL*, 2:145) that John Keats had loaned an estimated £230 to various friends, with nothing repaid. Haydon attempted to borrow money from Keats on several occasions. Twice John asked Abbey to release funds for the artist, but Abbey turned him down. Keats gave Haydon £30 of his own living expenses, which Abbey refused to replace.

45. C. and J. Ollier to GK, 29 April 1817, in *The Letters of John Keats,* ed. Maurice Buxton Forman (Oxford University Press, 1947), 101–12n. The letter was first printed in the *Athenaeum,* 7 June 1873.

46. *KC,* 1:308.

47. Abbey Memoir, *KC,* 1:307–8.

48. *KI,* 36–37.

49. Teignmouth (pronounced *tin-muth*) is the modern spelling; it was also spelled Teignemouth. The Teigne River, which flows through it, is pronounced *tayne.*

50. Brown to Dilke, 20 January 1830, *BL,* 304. George wrote to Dilke on 18 October 1826 (*KC,* 1:301): "he [John] advanced some when Tom went to Lyons." No other reference to this trip survives, although Lowell speculates that if it occurred, it was in September 1816, not 1817. Amy Lowell, *John Keats,* 2 vols. (Houghton Mifflin, 1925), 1:172.

51. John Keats wrote to Benjamin Bailey, his host at Oxford, on 8 October 1817 (*KL,* 1:171): "The little Mercury I have taken has corrected the Poison and improved my Health." Later in the century, Abraham Lincoln was prescribed mercury to deal with depression.

52. FK to Harry Buxton Forman, 1 July 1881, in Marie Adami, *Fanny Keats* (Oxford University Press, 1937), 199.

53. By "disinterested"(a William Hazlitt term), John meant that she could submerge her own interests into those of others—namely, George.

54. The basic primer for the history of tuberculosis is René Dubos and Jean Dubos, *The White Plague, Tuberculosis, Man and Society* (Rutgers University Press, 1952). Its second chapter, "Death Warrant for Keats" (11–17), deals explicitly with the poet's health history.

55. The story is modeled after Giovanni Boccaccio's first tale in the fourteenth-century *Decameron,* which was introduced to Keats by Hazlitt and Reynolds.

56. JK to Richard Woodhouse, 21 September 1819, *KL,* 2:174.

57. GK to Marianne [*sic*] and Sarah Jeffrey, 6 March 1818, *KC,* 1:16.

58. GK to JK, 18 March 1818, *KC,* 1:18.

59. JK to Marian and Sarah Jeffrey, 4 June 1818, *KL,* 1:290.

60. Angus Graham-Campbell, "John Keats and Marian Jeffrey," *Keats Shelley Journal* 13 (1984): 40–50.

61. JK to Bailey, 21 and 25 May 1818, *KL,* 286–87.

62. E. M. Forster, *Abinger Harvest* (Harcourt Brace, 1936), 232–41.

63. GK to FK, February 1824, *MKC,* 16. George's faith in Abbey would last two more years.

64. George's 10 April 1824 letter to Dilke (*KC,* 1:278) provides a loose accounting of the funds he took to America on his second trip, totaling £700. He realized £440 from Tom Keats's estate, was repaid £100 by Abbey to cover debts from Tom and John, and was given another £100 by John (the source of endless controversy between Dilke and Brown); "a further sum from himself [Abbey] made up the 700£." The further sum can be imputed as Abbey's £60 investment in George's American venture.

65. These are twenty-first-century street descriptions.

66. *KC*, 1:308.

67. Abbey Memoir, *KC*, 1:308–9.

68. Richardson, "New Light on Mr. Abbey," 26–31.

69. *KC*, 1:304. This was Abbey's opinion despite the fact that Thomas Keats had left an estate of £2,000, which would have equaled £125,000 (retail price adjustment)—or £1.4 million (equivalent earnings) in 2011 terms—according to MeasuringWorth.com.

70. Severn fathered an illegitimate child, Henry, who was born on 31 August 1819, as detailed in Grant F. Scott, *Joseph Severn: Letters and Memoirs* (Ashgate, 2005), 26–27, and in Sue Brown, *Joseph Severn: A Life* (Oxford University Press, 2009), 56. Scott's book is the standard edition of Severn's letters. Brown effectively bought a son by impregnating his maid, Abigail Donahue, and then abandoning her and taking the child to Italy, away from the reach of the law. Shelley left his pregnant wife and child for Mary Godwin. Most of the others had neither married nor formed families.

71. *KI*, 47–48.

72. Abbey Memoir, *KC*, 1:307, referring to a December 1817 interview.

73. JK to GK and GAW, 17 March 1819, *KL*, 2:77.

74. JK to GK, 12 November 1819, *KL*, 2:208.

75. JK to FK, 20 December 1819, *KL*, 2:237.

76. JK to GK and GAW, 3 March 1819, *KL*, 2:70.

77. JK to Miss Jeffrey, 31 May and 9 June 1819, *KL*, 2:112–13, 116.

78. JK to Dilke, June 1819, *KL*, 2:114.

79. JK to Reynolds, 24 August 1819, *KL*, 2:146.

80. Explained in a letter from John Keats to Benjamin Robert Haydon, 17 June 1819, *KL*, 2:119–20.

81. William Hazlitt, *Table-Talk*, published as articles in the *London* and *New Monthly* magazines, and then in book form in 1822.

82. JK to GK and GAW, 31 December 1818, *KL*, 2:19.

83. JK to Benjamin Bailey, 10 June 1818, *KL*, 1:293.

84. GK to FK, 5 June 1825, *MKC*, 30.

85. Alice Lee Keats, "Family Recollections," undated but probably 1935 or 1936, in response to queries by Maurice Buxton Forman, on file in the Buxton-Forman Collection at the University of Delaware.

86. GK to Dilke, 14 March–8 October 1836, *KC*, 2:25.

87. GK to FK, 5 June 1825, *MKC*, 30.

88. Dilke's annotated copy of Milnes is in the Morgan Library, New York. Dilke meant to describe Georgey as an "Indian" when he wrote "indiana."

89. Mrs. Wylie's brother, Robert Griffin, had migrated in the 1790s to Montreal, where he established a soap manufactory centered in the area now called Griffintown. Later he became the first clerk of the Bank of Montreal. He and his wife, Mary, had fifteen children. Two of them, Henry (20 August 1791–8 May 1848) and Frederick (1799–1897), a solicitor, married women named Porteous, a Scottish surname. The Griffins were prospering in North America when Mrs. Wylie approved her daughter's marriage and emigration plan.

90. GK to Dilke, 12 February 1833, *KC*, 2:15. "Mrs. R" was Charlotte Cox Reynolds, wife of George Reynolds and mother of John Keats's friend John Hamilton Reynolds (Keats considered her a bluestocking).

91. Mrs. Wylie was living at Great James Street, Gray's Inn, at the time of her death and was buried in St. John the Baptist Church, Hoxton (Hackney), on 13 March 1835. Her son Charles Gaskell Wylie was also buried there in 1839.

Separation and Emigration: 1818

1. The full title of Birkbeck's pamphlet is *Notes on a Journey from the Coast of Virginia to the Territory of Illinois*. Birkbeck's partner, George Flower, arranged for its initial publication in 1817 by Caleb Richardson of Philadelphia. In London, he assigned the first English edition to James Ridgway and Sons in 1818, with printing by Severn and Company. Later that year, Taylor and Hessey brought out the second English edition. Also in 1818, Thomas Larkin reprinted the pamphlet in Dublin. Asher Miner of Doylestown, Pennsylvania, published the second American edition in 1819. Publication in Paris followed in 1819.

2. George Flower, *History of the English Settlement in Edwards County Illinois* (Fergus Printing Co., 1882), 20. Flower drafted his manuscript in 1860, when he was eighty. In 1882 his manuscript was given to the Illinois Historical Society. Chapters 5 and 6 (pp. 95–142) provide the basis for this synopsis. Flower's circumspect account of his relationship with Birkbeck, saying that neither spoke ill of the other, is at odds with that of William Faux, who wrote *Memorable Days in America, Including Accounts of Mr. Birkbeck's Settlement in the Illinois* (W. Simpkin and R. Marshall, 1823).

3. Different accounts claim that Birkbeck's purchase totaled 26,400 acres. William Faux, writing from Wanborough at the time, stated it was 16,000.

4. Birkbeck, *Notes on a Journey*, 6–7.

5. George wrote to John Taylor around 18 June 1818, referring to Taylor's letter of introduction to Birkbeck (*KC*, 1:29). John referred to Birkbeck several times, including in JK to GK and GAW, 14 October 1818, *KL*, 1:398.

6. William Blake, "Merlin's Prophecy," in *The Complete Poetry and Prose of William Blake,* ed. David V. Erdman (Anchor Books, 1988), 473.

7. George Keats's great-grandson, William H. Crutcher, married Mary Buford Wood, a great-great-great-great-grandniece of Daniel Boone.

8. This refers to Wyoming, Pennsylvania, not the future state.

9. Wanborough soon disappeared, subsumed by the town of Albion, two miles east.

10. William Cobbett, *A Year's Residence in the United States of America*, 3 pts. (Sherwood, Neely and Jones, 1818–1819), ii. He was writing from North Hempstead, Long Island, New York. Cobbett, a political essayist and gadfly, sometimes used Peter Porcupine as a nom de plume. He was on the run several times from libel suits and was jailed for sedition in 1810–1812, after writing about a British army mutiny. In 1832 he was elected to Parliament. At heart, Cobbett was a nostalgic English farmer with a dreamy notion of democracy that had not been achieved to his liking in England, France, or America.

11. JK to GK and GAW, 14 February 1819, *KL*, 2:60.

12. Cobbett, *A Year's Residence*, 560–61, 563–64, 573.

13. Thomas Hulme, *Hulme's Journal*, extracted from Cobbett, *A Year's Residence*, 23–24. Hulme's journey to Illinois followed George Keats's by about one month.

14. Henry Bradshaw Fearon, *Sketches of America: A Narrative of a Journey of Five Thousand Miles through the Eastern and Western States of America with Remarks on Mr. Birkbeck's "Notes" and "Letters"* (Hurst, Rees, Orme and Brown, 1818), 401–2.

15. Faux, *Memorable Days in America*, 298.

16. Ibid., 285.

17. JK to Benjamin Bailey, 10 June 1818, *KL*, 1:293.

18. Dilke claimed ancestry to a Wentworth who was an anti-Crown dissident member of Parliament during the reign of Queen Elizabeth I. This was likely either Peter (1524–1597) or Paul (1533–1593) Wentworth, brothers and Puritan members of Parliament. Peter was briefly jailed when he spoke in Parliament about Elizabeth's encroachments on the powers of Parliament.

19. GK to Dilke, 24 November–14 December 1833, *KC*, 2:15.

20. Naomi Kirk interviewed certain Keats family members during the 1930s. They provided an oral history, none of which Kirk documented, about George and Georgiana's wedding, including such details as the bracelet. Alice Speed McDonald (1876–1964), a granddaughter of George and Georgiana, contributed accounts to both Kirk and Amy Lowell.

21. GK to John Taylor, c. 18 June 1818, *KC*, 1:30.

22. John vanWyhe, *The History of Phrenology*, excerpted in Wikipedia, 27 March 2010.

23. John wrote to Severn on 6 June 1818 (*KL*, 1:291): "The Doctor says I mustn't go out"—not a propitious omen for the arduous trip commencing two weeks later. Carol Kyros Walker retraced the trip in *Walking North with Keats* (Yale University Press, 1992). They hiked from Lancaster to Inverness, covering more than 600 miles in forty-four days. They walked through the Lake District, around Ambleside and Keswick, and along the lochs approaching Inverness. They also traveled by coach during certain stretches north of Carlisle and boated to Belfast and the Island Mull.

24. *KL*, 1:75; JK to GK and GAW, 14–31 October 1818, *KL*, 1:392.

25. Robert Gittings, *John Keats* (Little, Brown, 1968), 218.

26. JK to Bailey, 10 June 1818, *KL*, 1:293; this followed the short note to Severn on 6 June 1818 explaining that his doctor would not let him go out.

27. GK to Dilke, 10 April 1824, *KC*, 1:276–81.

28. Henry Stephens to George Felton Mathew, March 1847, *KC*, 2:212.

29. JK to GK and GAW, 24 October 1818, *KL*, 1:403.

30. JK to GK and GAW, 14 October 1818, *KL*, 1:392.

31. William Amphlett, *The Emigrant's Directory to the Western States of North America* (Longman, Hurst, Rees, Orme, and Browne, 1819), 1.

32. Ibid., 2–3.

33. Walker, *Walking North with Keats*, 8–11.

34. National Archives and Records Administration, Washington, D.C., in Walker, *Walking North with Keats*, 8–11.

35. *Lincoln Courier,* 19 June 1819, reprinted in *KSMB* 28 (1977): 30.

36. Naomi Kirk, "The Life of George Keats" (master's thesis, Columbia University, 1933), 52. Her source was unnamed, but it was likely Alice Speed McDonald.

37. JK to GK and GAW, 14–31 October 1818, *KL,* 1:405. Georgiana Emily Keats was born in Louisville, presumably in May or June 1819. The page that might have recorded her birth in the Keats Bible was removed and lost.

38. In a letter to Drury dated 26 January 1820, Taylor refers to him as "dear Cousin" and asks that Drury extend "kind Love to Mrs. Jas." (*KC,* 1:100–102). Taylor's mother was a sister of Drury's father. Drury was a dry goods seller, as was Tallant, sometimes described as Drury's partner.

39. Cobbett published his book in three parts, his piece on Birkbeck being the last. He dated it 10 December 1818. Fearon's book first went to press after 2 October 1818, when he finished his preface from Essex, England.

40. Amphlett, *Emigrant's Directory,* 69–71.

41. Ibid., 72–74.

42. Ibid., 83.

43. Fearon, *Sketches of America,* 197–98.

44. Timothy Flint, *Recollections of the Last Ten Years* (1826; reprint, Southern Illinois University Press, 1968), 13.

45. James Freeman Clarke, *Memorial and Biographical Sketches* (Houghton Mifflin, 1878), 225–26.

46. Indians called a section of the town Red Banks, after the clay bluffs descending to the river. When Henderson was chartered in 1797, the former name went out of usage.

47. JK to GAW, 13 January 1820, *KL,* 2:242.

48. However, Illinois historian Paul M. Angle notes that Birkbeck was Flower's best man at his marriage to Andrews in his introduction to John Woods, "Two Years Residence on the English Prairie of Illinois," in *Early Western Travels, 1748–1846,* ed. Reuben Gold Thwaites (Arthur H. Clark, 1904; reprint, Lakeside Press, 1968), xxiii.

49. Flower, *History of the English Settlement,* 101.

50. Emma Keats Speed told Oscar Wilde in 1882 that George and Audubon visited the Rappites, the only reference to such a trip. It is not confirmed in Audubon's journals.

51. JK to GAW, 15 January 1820, *KL,* 2:243. The second "duck" was Thomas Campbell's "Gertrude of Wyoming," published in 1809.

52. Charles Dickens, *Martin Chuzzlewit* (Chapman and Hall, 1843; reprint, Penguin Books, 1999). On pages 358–66 of the reprint edition, Dickens recounts Chuzzlewit's arrival at New Thermopylae (Shawneetown) and his reaction to Eden (Wanborough).

53. John is presumed to have burned George's letters, along with others, before departing for Rome, although he loaned one dated May 1819 to William Haslam, which was unaccountably returned in shreds.

54. JK to GK and GAW, 14–30 October 1818, *KL,* 1:398.

55. Ibid., 391.

56. Keats borrowed the "witching time of night" theme from *Hamlet*. After George released the poem, it was published in the August 1837 edition of *Ladies Companion*. This version is accepted by Jack Stillinger, editor of *John Keats Complete Poems* (Belknap Press of Harvard University Press, 1978), 221–22. Stillinger's is regarded as the standard edition of Keats's poetry.

57. Amy Lowell, *John Keats*, 2 vols. (Houghton Mifflin, 1925), 2:118. See also Dorothy Hewlett, *Adonais: A Life of John Keats* (Bobbs Merrill, 1938), 241. Hewlett does not cite a source for Haslam's letter, and no copy remains.

58. Until 1839, an envelope was charged postage as a second sheet. Thus, letters were folded, with the center section of the back page used as the address panel, and the sheet was sealed with wax at the back. These were called stampless covers, as stamps were not yet in use.

59. The two-penny post gave rise to the expression, "you can have my two cents' worth."

Henderson and Audubon: 1818–1819

1. Shirley Streshinsky, *Audubon: Life and Art in the American Wilderness* (University of Georgia Press, 1998), 96. Streshinsky, in turn, credits Stanley Clisby Arthur, *Audubon: An Intimate Life of an American Woodsman* (Harmonson, 1937), 121.

2. Richard Rhodes, *John James Audubon* (Alfred A. Knopf, 2004), 125.

3. JK to GAW, 15 January 1820, *KL*, 2:244.

4. As recounted by James Freeman Clarke, *Memorial and Biographical Sketches* (Houghton Mifflin, 1878), 226. Another version is told by Alice Ford in *John James Audubon* (University of Oklahoma Press, 1964), 99.

5. Spalding Trafger, manuscript dated 8 July 1906, in Henderson (Kentucky) Public Library Manuscript Room.

6. Streshinsky, *Audubon*, 95.

7. John James Audubon, "Myself," in *Writings and Drawings* (Library of America, 1999), 789.

8. Arthur, *Audubon*, 84–86. Robert Speed (b. 1787) was a son of Joseph; Joseph, in turn, was a first cousin of Judge John Speed. The latter's son, Philip Speed, who was a second cousin to Robert, married George Keats's daughter Emma Frances in 1841.

9. Audubon, "Myself," 790.

10. Clarke, *Memorial and Biographical Sketches*, 225–26.

11. *Audubon v. Bowen et al.*, 1819, Henderson Court Docket 1944, State of Kentucky Archives, Frankfort. When the Henderson County clerk transferred the files to Frankfort in 2003, all that remained of the file was a "pull card" indicating that it had been signed out in 1938; the slightly illegible name appears to be "Kork." This may have been Naomi Joy Kirk, who was conducting research at that time. If Kirk returned the file, it was not misfiled because Kentucky archivist Tim Tingle searched every Henderson file and did not find it. Kirk's manuscript, however, refers to the case.

12. First Judicial Court, State of Louisiana, Case 2358.

13. The continuation was handed down 20 November 1819. On 20 May 1820 the case was discontinued, or dropped, by the court.

14. Ford, *John James Audubon*, 104.

15. Mileage references are "river miles" from Captain Rick Rhodes, *The Ohio River in American History* (Heron Island Guides, 2008), 169–89. Land miles might have varied slightly.

16. Audubon, "Myself," 790–91.

17. Arthur, *Audubon*, 88.

18. Ibid., 93.

19. JK to GK and GAW, 17 September 1819, *KL*, 2:185–86.

20. JK to GK and GAW, 21 September 1819, *KL*, 2:211.

21. Judge Haggin, 15 June 1825, in *William and Samuel Bowen v. Burnet Marshall*.

22. John Gilmer Speed, *Letters and Poems of John Keats*, 3 vols. (Dodd Mead, 1883), 1:79n.

23. Thomas W. Bakewell, "Sketch of the Life of Thomas Woodhouse Bakewell Written by Himself," ed. Bruce Sinclair, *Filson Club History Quarterly* 40 (1966): 240–48. The original six-page manuscript is in the Durrett Collection at the University of Chicago.

24. Ibid., 235–39. Sinclair provides no documentation of Keats's investment in the *Pike*.

25. Nicholas's brother's grandson was President Theodore Roosevelt.

26. Maralea Arnett, "Audubon Faces an Identity Crisis," in *A History of Henderson County* (Audubon Printers, 1975), 24.

27. George H. Yater, "George Keats," in *EOL*, 457. He appears to have picked up on the John Gilmer Speed version.

28. Many of these suits were filed with the intent of obtaining a more senior position in the chain of debts, as with present-day liens.

29. Lucy Audubon followed her husband in a carriage loaned to her by Dr. Adam Rankin. Rankin's wife was Elizabeth Speed Rankin, sister of the above-mentioned Judge John Speed.

30. Streshinsky, *Audubon*, 98.

31. Arthur, *Audubon*, 92.

32. Audubon was in Louisville by 12 February 1819, when he advertised his services as a portrait painter in the *Weekly Western Courier*. The Keatses likely preceded him, staying initially with a family named Peay. John Peay (1775–1835) and Mildred Lightfoot Nabb Peay (c. 1772–1835), who were in the Louisville area at the time, became the grandparents of George Nicholas Peay, who married Ella Keats in 1854.

33. This may have been George's own money, indirectly circulating through Audubon, his creditors (including Bakewell), and back to Keats.

34. John James Audubon, *The 1826 Journal of John James Audubon*, ed. Alice Ford (Abbeville Press, 1987), 86. Ford's unvarnished transcription is from the original Audubon manuscript. Maria R. Audubon's sanitized two-volume compilation of Audubon's journals (published by Charles Scribner in 1897) omitted all references to Georgiana Keats.

35. John Francis McDermott, *Audubon in the West* (University of Oklahoma Press, 1965), 26. Georgiana was forty-five. Jeffrey, born in 1817 in Edinburgh, Scotland, was twenty-six.

36. Ford, *John James Audubon*, 339.

37. Streshinsky, *Audubon*, 261.

38. GK to Dilke, 20 April 1825, *KC*, 1:290; confirmed by an indenture filed with the Jefferson County Court, 1821 Deed Book, 87.

39. Rhodes, *John James Audubon*, 99.

Louisville: 1819

1. Their early residence in Louisville is unclear. It may have included a stay at the Indian Queen, with the Bakewells, or with John Peay and his family, or perhaps all three. Gwathmey's grandson Alfred married Keats's daughter Georgiana Emily sometime after 1841.

2. Henry Bradshaw Fearon, *Sketches of America: A Narrative of a Journey of Five Thousand Miles through the Eastern and Western States of America with Remarks on Mr. Birkbeck's "Notes" and "Letters"* (Hurst, Rees, Orme and Brown, 1818), 243, 242, 246.

3. Ibid., 247–49.

4. Prentice and Bakewell initially operated an iron foundry, fabricating parts for steamboat engines, on the site. They added a mill about the time of Keats's arrival.

5. Dr. Henry McMurtrie, *Sketches of Louisville* (S. Penn, 1819), 117–19, 121.

6. Ibid., 122–24.

7. Ibid., 124–25.

8. Ibid., 126–33.

9. Ibid., 134.

10. Ibid., 117.

11. Maria R. Audubon, ed., *Audubon and His Journals,* 2 vols. (Dover Publications, 1960), 2:487–90.

12. James Freeman Clarke, in *Western Messenger,* June 1836, reprinted in *KL*, 1:3.

13. T. S. Eliot, *The Use of Poetry and the Use of Criticism* (Faber and Faber, 1973), 100. See also Grant F. Scott, ed., *Selected Letters of John Keats* (Harvard University Press, 2002), xxii.

14. Speed was missing one, JK to GK and GAW, 12 November 1819, subsequently published in *KL*, 2:228. This came into the hands of Colonel Frank Marx Etting, who willed it to the University of Pennsylvania. Etting's endorsement noted that it had been given to him by Mrs. Philip Speed.

15. Editor Hyder Edward Rollins cites a number of "lost letters" (*KL*, 1:9–13): seven of these were from John to George (one was also to Tom) prior to George's emigration, and perhaps four more were written to him in America.

16. These do not reveal all the dimensions of John Keats, as his important letters to Fanny Brawne and other friends are not included here.

17. JK to GK and TK, 5 January 1818, *KL*, 1:198. I have accepted the dating of letters in *KL*, which is somewhat at odds with Speed's.

18. JK to GK and TK, 21, 27(?) December 1817, *KL*, 1:193.

19. Aileen Ward, *John Keats: The Making of a Poet* (Viking Press, 1963), 161.

20. *KL*, 1:194.

21. JK to GK and TK, 23 January 1818, *KL*, 1:214.

22. JK to GK and TK, 21 April 1818, in John Gilmer Speed, *Letters and Poems of John Keats,* 3 vols. (Dodd Mead, 1883), 1:16. This letter is not included in *KL.*

23. JK to TK, 3–9 July 1818, *KL*, 1:320.

24. JK to Ann G. Wylie, 6 August 1818, *KC*, 1:358.

25. JK to GK and GAW, 14 October 1818, *KL*, 1:392. This is Rollins's transcription; Speed led with "Your welfare."

26. Ibid., 394.

27. Ibid., 395.

28. Ibid., 397.

29. Ibid., 404. "Nighing" translates most closely to "near."

30. JK to GK and GAW, 16 December 1818–4 January 1819, *KL*, 2:16. Dubois wrote *My Pocket Book* (Verner Hood and Sharp, 1808), from which this was extracted.

31. JK to GK and GAW, 14 February–3 May 1819, *KL*, 2:62–63; this passage is from 14 February.

32. Ibid., 3 March, *KL*, 2:68.

33. Ibid., 19 March, *KL*, 2:79.

34. Ibid., 16 April, *KL*, 2:92.

35. Ibid., 3 May, *KL*, 2:108.

36. JK to GK and GAW, 17–27 September 1819, *KL*, 2:185.

37. Ibid., 20 September, *KL*, 2:200–201.

38. Ibid., 21 September, *KL*, 2:208.

39. Ibid., *KL*, 2:210.

40. Ibid., 24 September, *KL*, 2:213.

41. JK to GAW, 13–28 January 1820, *KL*, 2:239–40, 241, 242, 243, 244, 245–46.

A Dismal Return: 1820

1. JK to GK and GAW, 14 October 1818, *KL*, 1:391.

2. Haslam's letter, lost, is inferred from JK to GK and GAW, 16 December 1818–4 January 1819, *KL*, 2:4.

3. John wrote to Abbey "with great anxiety" on 7 July 1819 (*KL*, 2:131–32), requesting that he make George's funds available to him through the offices of Haslam.

4. JK to GK and GAW, 17 September 1819, *KL*, 2:184.

5. JK to GK and GAW, 12 November 1819, *KL*, 2:228–29.

6. JK to GK and GAW, 21 September 1819, *KL*, 2:210.

7. JK to GK and GAW, 12 November 1819, *KL*, 2:231.

8. In the absence of a birth record, the date is estimated from JK to GK and GAW, 14–31 October 1818, *KL*, 1:405. In the section dated 31 October, John acknowledges Georgiana's pregnancy, most likely announced in a lost letter from George written in August or September, following the couple's arrival in Philadelphia on 26 August 1818.

9. GK to FK, 25 May 1820, *KC*, 1:109; GK to JK, 18 June 1820, *KL*, 2:295.

10. Dr. Henry McMurtrie, *Sketches of Louisville* (S. Penn, 1819), 147.

11. GK to JK, 8 November 1820, *KC*, 1:169.

12. GK to FK, 28 April 1824, *MKC*, 20. Fanny Brawne favored her brother Samuel over her sister Margaret.

13. JK to GAW, 13–28 January 1820, *KL*, 1:239–48.

14. *KI*, 51.

15. GK to JK, 18 March 1818, *KC*, 1:17–18.

16. They looked into the matter following George's 10 April 1824 letter to Dilke, defending his actions. This was confirmed by GK to Dilke, 20 April 1825, *KC*, 1:285–86.

17. Brown to Dilke, 6 September 1824, *BL*, 183.

18. GK to Dilke, 10 April 1824, *KC*, 1:278–79.

19. Fanny Brawne to FK, 18 September 1820, in *Letters of Fanny Brawne to Fanny Keats,* ed. Fred Edgcumbe (Oxford University Press, 1937), 3.

20. GK to FK, 30 January 1820, *MKC*, 12–13. Rollins believes the letter was written the day before.

21. JK to FK, 6 February 1820, *KL*, 2:251. His two-penny letter arrived in Walthamstow postage unpaid.

22. GK to FK, 30 January 1820, *MKC*, 12. The passenger manifest, recorded in film M237, reel 1, at the National Archives and Records Administration, confirms that "George Keates, age 28" and a "merchant," was on board.

23. Brown to Milnes, 9 April 1841, *KC*, 2:102.

24. Scholars have dated the hemorrhage to 3 February 1820, despite conflicting accounts by Brown and Taylor.

25. Most Keats scholars believe that John was actually thinking about disengaging from his relationship with Fanny Brawne, but he never said it directly to her. Perhaps he did not want to expose her to his downward spiral into death.

26. Fanny Brawne to FK, 23 May 1821, *Letters of Fanny Brawne*, 33–35.

27. *KC*, 1:217.

28. Eric Hall McCormick, *The Friend of Keats: A Life of Charles Armitage Brown* (Victoria University Press, 1989), 60. On 19 March 1841 Brown handed over to Milnes the manuscript on John Keats's life on which he had based his 21 December 1836 Plymouth lecture.

29. Brown and Haslam wrote to George on John's behalf. If he wrote directly, the letters have been lost.

Getting Established: 1820–1826

1. Carl F. Kramer, *Visionaries, Adventurers and Builders* (Sunnyside Press, 1999), 100–108.

2. The Black Ball line advertised monthly service between New York and Liverpool, the passage taking fifteen to sixteen days eastbound and thirty-six days westbound, with ships leaving Liverpool the first day of each month.

3. GK to Dilke, 20 April 1825, *KC*, 1:290.

4. John Keats wrote to Fanny Keats on 1 April 1820 (*KL*, 2:284): "I have not heard from George yet since he left liverpool. Mr. Brown wrote to him as from me the other day." A letter posted in March would have arrived in Louisville in May.

5. GK to JK, 18 June 1820, *KL*, 2:295. Natchez is actually 130 miles from New Orleans.

6. GK to JK, 8 November 1820, *KC*, 1:168. The letter was opened by Brown in London and was not forwarded to John in Rome.

7. George wrote to his sister Fanny in February 1824 (*MKC*, 16): "The last time I heard from you was thro' our dear John." Since the last known letter from John to George was dated 12 November 1819, this implies that another (since lost) was sent after 28 January 1820, when George left London.

8. GK to JK, 8 November 1820, *KC*, 1:168.

9. Ibid., 169.

10. JK to GAW, 17 January 1820, *KL*, 2:244.

11. Jefferson County Deed Book, 1821, 87.

12. Rosalind's birth date is the only one remaining in George's Bible, the family data page having been removed.

13. Alternatively, she may have been named for Emma Severn, a sister of the poet's friend Dr. Charles Severn at Guy's Hospital. One copy of Keats's valentine poem ("Hadst thou liv'd in days of old") was inscribed "To Emma," and she may have known George as well. The poem titled "To Emma" was written in 1815, when Keats was socializing with the Mathew family. George Felton Mathew had several sisters, one of whom may have been named Emma. E. De Sélincourt, *The Poems of John Keats* (Methuen, 1905), 562–63, notes that Keats's "To Emma," found in Richard Woodhouse's transcript of *The Fall of Hyperion and Other Poems,* was first published by Harry Buxton Forman in 1883, substituting "Georgiana" on line 1 for "my dear Emma" and "And there Georgiana" for "There beauteous Emma" on line 11. De Sélincourt also notes that "Emma or Emmeline, according to the exigencies of metre, was the name by which Wordsworth referred to his sister Dorothy, and there can be little doubt that Keats is influenced by this fact when he veils the identity of his future sister-in-law under the same *nom de plume.*"

14. Jane Austen's *Emma* also has a character named Isabella Woodhouse.

15. A descendant, Keats Noyes Carlton, presented the Bible to me.

16. GK to FK, 7 January 1822, *MKC*, 14–15.

17. Dr. John P. Harrison, writing in the *Philadelphia Medical Journal,* quoted in *HOL*, 163.

18. GK to JK, 8 November 1820, *KC*, 1:169.

19. GK to FK, February 1824, *MKC*, 17.

20. Ibid.

21. GK to FK, 15 April 1826, *MKC*, 35.

22. George Keats was buried in Western Cemetery in December 1841 and was subsequently moved to Cave Hill Cemetery, along with daughters Isabel and Georgiana Emily Gwathmey, by his son-in-law Philip Speed. Rosalind was not moved to Cave Hill, suggesting that she had never been moved from the original cemetery to the Western. The old graveyard's site is now called Baxter Park, housing a youth center.

23. GK to Dilke, 20 April 1825, *KC*, 1:289–90.

24. GK to Dilke, 12 July 1828, *KC*, 1:316.

25. *Louisville Public Advertiser,* 17 December 1829. The first notice was repeated on 11 January 1830.

26. The flour millers were Alsop and Swing, Richard and John Atkinson, John Slaughter, and David Steward, all located at the opposite end of town.

27. The site was taken over by the Belknap Hardware Company, which grew from the time of the Civil War into a giant hardware manufacturer and wholesaler. In its day, Belknap was the region's equivalent of a Home Depot distribution center.

28. GK to Dilke, 20 April 1825, *KC,* 1:289, 291–92.

29. *The [Louisville] Focus of Politics, Commerce and Literature,* 22 December 1829 (hereafter cited as *[Louisville] Focus*).

30. A sample slave lease contract is included in the appendix.

31. GK to Valentin Llanos, 10, 11 July 1828, *MKC,* 45.

32. GK to Dilke, 1 March 1838, *KC,* 2:30.

33. *HOL,* 156.

34. GK to Dilke, 20 April 1825, *KC,* 1:289. An extract of one such article, concerning a political contretemps between William T. Barry (1784–1835) and John Pope (1770–1845), is included in the appendix.

35. GK to Dilke, 11 May 1832, *KC,* 2:148–49.

36. 1829 Jefferson County Deed Book, EE:502, records the transaction from the Bank of the United States for $2,600.

37. *[Louisville] Focus,* 19 January 1830.

38. *HOFC,* 1:251. Craik served from 1844 to 1882.

39. JK to Brown, 30 November 1820, *KL,* 2:360.

Who Failed the Poet? 1820–1821

1. Benjamin Robert Haydon, *The Autobiography and Memoirs of Benjamin Robert Haydon,* ed. Tom Taylor (1853; reprint, Harcourt Brace, 1926), 1:253.

2. JK to Brown, 30 November 1820, *KL,* 2:360.

3. Keats's "posthumous" existence dates from September 1819, when he completed "Lamia." Keats wrote to Brown on 30 November 1820 (*KL,* 2:359): "I am leading a posthumous existence."

4. Copied from englishhistory.net/keats.

5. A gallipot was a small earthenware jar used by apothecaries to mix drugs.

6. Lowell attributes this character to Alain-René Lesage's farcical opera *Gil Blas.* Amy Lowell, *John Keats,* 2 vols. (Houghton Mifflin, 1925), 2:85.

7. Copied from englishhistory.net/keats.

8. Lockhart's particulars are summarized from Andrew Lang's *The Life and Letters of John Gibson Lockhart,* 2 vols. (John C. Nimmo, 1897). Lang maintains that Lockhart did not write the early "Z" reviews but may have penned the August 1818 review. Wilson's biographical data are drawn from *Encyclopedia Britannica,* 11th ed.

9. Bailey to Taylor, 28 April 1821, *KC,* 1:237, refers to a duel between John Scott (the same person George and Tom visited in Paris, but unrelated to Sir Walter), editor of *London Magazine,* and Jonathon Henry Christie, Lockhart's agent in London. They quarreled over Lockhart's treatment of Scott's Cock-

ney contributors and met to settle the dispute at 9:00 PM on 16 February 1821 (one week before Keats's death in Rome) on a farm between Hampstead and Camden Town. Christie's second shot killed Scott. The collection taken up for Scott's family became a noted radical cause. Other letters, all in *KC*, include Bailey to Taylor, 8 May 1821, 1:244; Bailey's notes on his conversation with Lockhart, 8 May 1821, 1:245–47; Bailey to Taylor, 10 May 1824, 1:281–82; Bailey to Milnes, 7 May 1849, 2:286, 288; and Bailey to Milnes, 11 May 1849, 2:299–300.

10. Haydon, *Autobiography*, 1:265.

11. JK to Hessey, 8 October 1818, *KL*, 1:374.

12. JK to GK and GAW, 14 October 1818, *KL*, 1:393–94.

13. JK to GK and GAW, 19 February 1819, *KL*, 2:65.

14. Percy Bysshe Shelley, preface to *Adonais* (Pisa, 1821), 4. Shelley had *Adonais* printed in Pisa, where he was living, and sent to London. An abridged version appeared in the *Literary Chronicle*, 1 December 1821.

15. George Gordon (Lord) Byron, *Don Juan*, last two lines of stanza 60, canto XI, as reprinted in Joanna Ferguson, *Lord Byron* (Folio Society, 1988), 144.

16. Shelley, preface to *Adonais*, 5.

17. GK to Dilke, 10 April 1824, *KC*, 1:280.

18. William Hazlitt, written in January 1821 and reprinted in Herschell Baker, *William Hazlitt* (Belknap Press of Harvard University Press, 1962), 250.

19. JK to FK, 21 April 1820, *KL*, 2:287.

20. JK to Fanny Brawne, 5 July 1820, *KL*, 2:303.

21. GK to JK, 18 June 1820, *KC*, 1:114.

22. Severn to Haslam, 1, 2 November 1820, *KL*, 2:353.

23. Clark to unknown, 27 November 1820, *KL*, 2:358.

24. Clark to unknown, 3 January 1820, *KL*, 2:366–67.

25. Recounted in Severn to Taylor, 26 January 1821, *KL*, 2:372–73.

26. Brown to JK, 21 December 1820, *KL*, 2:364.

27. Brown to Haslam, 10(?) December 1820, *KC*, 1:175.

28. Haslam to Severn, 4 December 1820, in Grant F. Scott, *Joseph Severn: Letters and Memoirs* (Ashgate, 2005), 111.

29. William Sharp, *Life and Letters of Joseph Severn* (Charles Scribner, 1892), 72–73; also confirmed in Scott, *Joseph Severn*, 111.

30. Brown to Haslam, 5 January 1821, *KC*, 1:187.

31. Brown to Severn, 15 January 1821, *KC*, 1:201. A subsequent compilation, *New Letters from Charles Brown to Joseph Severn*, ed. Grant F. Scott and Sue Brown (Romantic Circles Electronic Edition, University of Maryland, 2010), includes many letters not in *KC*. The editors' introduction casts Brown in a generally positive light—a minority view—based on his continued involvement with Severn through the 1830s.

32. GK to Brown, 3 March 1821, *KC*, 1:222.

33. Clark to unknown, 27 November 1820, *KL*, 2:358. The recipient may have been a man named Gray, an agent or employee of Taylor. Lowell thought he was Samuel Edward Gray, a pharmacologist who may have introduced Clark to Keats's London physician, Dr. Darling.

34. Taylor and Hessey to GK, 17 February 1821, *KC*, 1:214–15.

35. Taylor to Drury, 19 February 1821, *KC*, 1:219.

36. Dilke to GK, September 1838, *KC*, 2:33.

37. Dilke to GK, 12 February 1833, *KC*, 2:10.

38. Brown to Milnes, 19 March 1841, *KC*, 2:51–52.

39. Eric Hall McCormick, *The Friend of Keats: A Life of Charles Armitage Brown* (Victoria University Press, 1989), 185.

40. The most detailed accounts of Charles Brown's feud with Charles Dilke can be found in *BL*, 21–27, and Jack Stillinger, "The Brown-Dilke Controversy," *Keats Shelley Journal* 11 (Winter 1962): 39–45. Stillinger was guided by the information contained in Brown's letters, which in turn was dependent on Brown's memory of what the poet had told him. Robert Gittings studied the issue in *KI*, working with information from multiple sources, commencing with Chancery documents. Stillinger and Gittings arrive at generally opposite conclusions about George's culpability. Most scholars, beginning with Milnes and including Brown's own biographer Eric Hall McCormick, absolve George.

41. GK to Dilke, 20 April 1825, *KC*, 1:285.

42. GK to FK, February 1825, *MKC*, 25.

43. JK to GAW, 15 January 1820, *KL*, 2:243.

44. GK to Dilke, 20 April 1825, *KC*, 1:290.

45. A detailed chronology of John Keats's life is in *KL*, 1:29–61.

46. Recounted in Severn to Brown, 27 February 1821, draft in City of London Records Office, as cited by Robert Gittings, *John Keats* (Little, Brown, 1968), 428–29; an abridgment is contained in *KC*, 2:94.

Settling Affairs: 1821–1828

1. *KI*, 1–82, is the principal source for this chapter. Gittings credits solicitor Ralph Thomas, who in 1885 painstakingly examined the original Chancery documents while on retainer to Sidney Colvin (Thomas also represented Fanny Keats Llanos). Gittings accepted Thomas's original conclusions (curiously, Colvin did not understand them) after examining the Chancery documents himself.

2. Robert Gittings, *John Keats* (Little, Brown, 1968), 18–20.

3. The National Archives at Kew online currency converter indicates a 38-to-1 historical ratio, the pounds-to dollar conversion being $1.57. Alternative indices, factoring in health, leisure, and other lifestyle components, suggest higher ratios, even up to the 100s-to-1.

4. John Jennings's will is copied in full in *KI*, 8–9.

5. *KI*, 59–65.

6. Ibid., 66–70.

7. Ibid., 30.

8. Public Records Office, Chancery Lane C.33.576, in *KI*, 31.

9. Based on the notes of Ralph Thomas in *KI*, 79–81.

10. The Sweetingburgh entry in table 1 is sourced to Public Records Office, C33.616ff and C33.809, as cited in *KI*, 36. Ralph Thomas noted separate items within the same date as "do," for "ditto"; I assumed the final recipients. The capital disbursement data are transcribed from *KI*, 79, 81. The Frances Keats

Rawlings Life Account closure is from *KI*, 80, and the Infant Legatees Account closure is from *KI*, 82.

11. JK to Benjamin Bailey, 10 June 1818, *KL*, 1:293. The sentence structure implies that the "earlier misfortunes" preceded his birth, giving rise to various speculations, one being that Thomas Keats was illegitimate.

12. Midgley Jr.'s story is told in William Dalrymple, *The Last Mughal* (Alfred A. Knopf, 2007), 57–60, 71–72, 88, 98, 112, 132, 135, 141–43, 150n.

13. JK to GK and GAW, 17 September 1819, *KL*, 2:185.

14. JK to GK and GAW, 12 November 1819, *KL*, 2:231.

15. JK to Haydon, 8 March 1819, *KL*, 2:42.

16. *KL*, 2:331.

17. Fanny's baptismal record is in the London Metropolitan Archives. Based on this, Abbey may have been right about her 1804 birth date, although she always maintained she was born in 1803.

18. GK to Abbey, 18 March 1825, *MKC*, 28.

19. FK to GK, 31 May 1826, *KC*, 1:298.

20. GK to Dilke, 18 October 1826, *KC*, 1:301.

21. Charles G. Wylie to Taylor, 17 August 1828, *KC*, 1:317.

22. GK to Dilke, 14 November 1829, *KC*, 1:321, 324.

23. Dilke to GK, 12 February 1833, *KC*, 2:9.

24. GK to Dilke, 7 May 1830, *KC*, 1:330.

25. Dilke to GK, September 1838, *KC*, 2:34.

26. GK to Dilke, 18 October 1826, *KC*, 1:301.

27. According to the Ralph Thomas manuscript, c. 1885–1886, uncataloged, in the Keats House Collection. Fanny Keats Llanos asked Thomas to retrieve the balance of the funds in Chancery prior to 1887, and Sidney Colvin asked him to summarize the Chancery accounts, from which this analysis is drawn. Thomas's notes are reproduced in *KI*. Fanny's accounts are described in *KI*, 52–53.

28. An English pound is worth about $1.57 in 2012, a rate that has fluctuated over the decades.

29. *KC*, 1:330.

30. GK to Reynolds, 6 May 1832, *MKC*, 65–66.

31. Fanny Brawne to FK, 23 May 1824, in *Letters of Fanny Brawne to Fanny Keats*, ed. Fred Edgcumbe (Oxford University Press, 1937), 33.

32. *MKC*, 72–74. The poems were included in the sale of letters by Dr. Paradinas to Arthur Houghton.

33. At least one other poem, entitled "Julia to the Wood Robin," has been discovered above the initials G. K. However, the same poem was found in Richard Woodhouse's papers with other John Keats transcripts. If "Julia" were George's, which is improbable, it likely dated from about 1817. Reginald Spofforth published his piano canzonet *Julia to the Wood Robin* in 1816.

The Legacy Deferred: 1821–1848

1. *KC*, 1:cxlii. Edmund Blunden, *Keats's Publisher: A Memoir of John Taylor* (Jonathan Cape, 1936), 92–93, also cites a similar notice published 4 June 1821 in the *Morning Chronicle*.

2. Brown to Severn, 14 August 1821, *BL*, 86–87.

3. *KC*, 1:cxliii.

4. GK to Dilke, 20 April 1825, *KC*, 1:288.

5. Edmund Blunden, *Shelley and Keats as They Struck Their Contemporaries* (C. W. Beaumont, 1925), 82.

6. Herschell Baker, *William Hazlitt* (Belknap Press of Harvard University Press, 1962), 250.

7. James Henry Leigh Hunt, *Lord Byron and Some of His Contemporaries* (Henry Colburn, 1828), 408–9.

8. GK to Dilke, 12 May 1828, *KC*, 1:313–14.

9. GK to Dilke, 7 May 1830, *KC*, 1:326–27.

10. Brown to Dilke, 20 January 1830, *BL*, 306.

11. GK to Dilke, 7 May 1830, *KC*, 1:325.

12. Ibid., 329–30.

13. William Sharp, *Life and Letters of Joseph Severn* (Charles Scribner, 1892), 177.

14. *BL*, 332–33.

15. *KC*, 2:52–101.

16. Brown's manuscript is reproduced in Charles (Armitage) Brown, *The Life of John Keats,* ed. Dorothy Hyde Bodurtha and Willard Bissell Pope (Oxford University Press, 1937), 39–91; the clarifying notes and corrections of the editors follow at 93–122.

17. Eric Hall McCormick, *The Friend of Keats: A Life of Charles Armitage Brown* (Victoria University Press, 1989), 149.

18. GK to Dilke, 14 March 1836, *KC*, 2:24.

19. GK to Dilke, 1 March 1838, *KC*, 2:30.

20. Brown to Severn, 23 August 1838, *BL*, 348.

21. McCormick, *Friend of Keats,* 173–75.

22. Taylor to Edward Moxon, 30 September 1845, *KC*, 2:128.

23. GK to Dilke, 20 April 1825, *KC*, 1:287–88.

24. GK to Dilke, 14 March, 8 October 1836, *KC*, 2:23.

25. Dilke to GK, September 1838, *KC*, 2:33.

26. Brown to Milnes, 14 March 1841, *KC*, 2:50.

27. Sharp, *Life and Letters of Joseph Severn,* 191.

28. The Taylor-Moxon agreement of 30 September 1845 is in *KC*, 2:128.

29. Richard Monckton Milnes, *Life, Letters, and Literary Remains of John Keats,* 3 vols. (Edward Moxon, 1848), 1:xxxvi; see also 2:39–45.

30. At the time, Dilke was recommending John Hamilton Reynolds, rather than Charles Brown, as the best biographer, an opinion that George accepted.

31. Jeffrey to Milnes, 13 May 1845, *KC*, 2:117–18.

32. Jeffrey to Milnes, 8 September 1845, *KC*, 2:123.

33. The transcripts are now housed at Harvard's Houghton Library.

34. John Gilmer Speed, *Letters and Poems of John Keats,* 3 vols. (Dodd Mead, 1883), 1:ix.

35. GK to Dilke, 1 March 1838, *KC*, 2:30.

Prosperity: 1828–1841

1. GK to FK Llanos, 5 March 1829, *MKC*, 51.
2. GK to Dilke 7 May 1830, *KC*, 1:331.
3. *HOFC*, 255.
4. Karl Bernhard, Duke of Saxe-Weimar-Eisenach, *Travels through North America*, 1828, reprinted in *HOFC*, 257.
5. *HOFC*, 264, 287.
6. *HOL*, 185, 193.
7. 1822 Jefferson County Deed Book, 87.
8. *[Louisville] Focus*, 13 December 1826, reel 4515, FHS.
9. Ibid., 24 March 1824.
10. *HOL*, 181–82.
11. *HOFC*, 280.
12. George H. Yater, "Fourteenth Street Bridge," in *EOL*, 315–16.
13. *[Louisville] Focus*, 9, 16, 23, 30 December 1828.
14. Also referred to as Bardstown Turnpike and presently known as Bardstown Road.
15. *HOFC*, 266.
16. GK to Dilke, 12 July 1828, *KC*, 1:315.
17. GK to FK, 6 May 1832, *MKC*, 67–68.
18. Unitarianism traces to the 1540s in Poland and Transylvania.
19. Osgood to Milnes, 26 November 1875, *KC*, 2:348.
20. *LCD*, 1832, 141.
21. Emma Keats Speed Sampson to Kirk, 13 December 1933, Naomi Kirk Collection, FHS.
22. Fuller, a transcendentalist who helped edit the *Dial*, became a journalist for Horace Greeley, a feminist, and a sympathizer to the Italian revolution. She had a child with Giovanni Ossoli; all three were killed in a shipwreck off Fire Island in 1850.
23. Robert D. Richardson Jr., *Emerson: The Mind on Fire* (University of California Press, 1995), 175.
24. Winander is an alternative spelling of Windermere.
25. The original letter has been lost.
26. Hyder Edward Rollins, *Keats' Reputation in America to 1848* (Harvard University Press, 1946), 46.
27. Paul Wolf Holleman, in *EOL*, 415.
28. *LCD*, 1832, 138.
29. *HOFC*, 1:266.
30. Ibid.
31. Thomas D. Clark, "Building Libraries in the Early Ohio Valley," *Journal of Library History* 6, no. 2 (1971): 111.
32. Louisville Hotel Company records, including Minute Book, 5 May 1832–10 January 1835, containing stockholder, director, and officer lists, FHS.
33. *LCD*, 1832, 154.
34. Ibid., 154–55.

35. Caleb Atwater, *Remarks Made on a Tour to Prairie du Chien* (1831), reprinted in *Louisville: A Guide to the Falls City* (M. Barrows and Company, 1940), 24.

36. James Silk Buckingham, *English Traveler's Observations* (London, 1841), reprinted in *HOFC*, 289.

37. 1834 Jefferson County Deed Book, QQ: 328, 329, 353. Ann E. F. Smith was the widow of the Reverend Daniel Smith; he was apparently not related to Keats's partner Daniel Smith, also married (first) to an Ann.

38. The Doric portico was added by James Trabue, who purchased the dwelling after George's death.

39. When the assets of George's estate were inventoried in 1842, three household slaves were also in residence. Jefferson County Kentucky Inventory and Settlement Book, 11:387.

40. GK to Dilke, 20 April 1825, *KC*, 1:289.

41. GK to FK, 5 June 1825, *MKC*, 30.

42. GK to Dilke, 24 November–14 December 1833, *KC*, 2:15.

43. William IV, previously the Duke of Clarence (1765–1837), ascended the English throne in 1830.

44. GK to Dilke, 24 November–14 December 1833, *KC*, 2:13.

45. Bertha-Monica Stearns, "John Howard Payne as an Editor," *American Literature* 5, no. 3 (November 1933): 215–28.

46. Basil W. Duke, *History of the Bank of Kentucky, 1792–1895* (John P. Morton, 1895), 25. Duke (1838–1916), a general officer for the Confederacy, participated with his brother-in-law John Hunt Morgan in the notorious Morgan's raid into Ohio and Indiana. His son, Calvin Duke, married Jenny Ewing Speed, a great-granddaughter of George Keats.

47. Ibid., 39–41, 133. Their child, George Keats Gwathmey, was born 10 August 1850.

48. *LCD*, 1832, 155.

49. GK to Dilke, 8 October 1836, *KC*, 2:25.

50. GK to Dilke, 1 March 1838, *KC*, 2:31.

51. John Keats referred to Briggs on two occasions: JK to FK, 12 May 1819, *KL*, 2:110, and JK to GAW, 13 January 1820, *KL*, 2:242. Briggs carried letters back and forth between George in Kentucky and his correspondents in England. George refers to him several times: GK to Dilke, 10 April 1824, *KC*, 1:281; GK to Dilke, 20 April 1825, *KC*, 1:283; GK to Mrs. Dilke, 19 March 1829, *KC*, 1:319; GK to Dilke, 14 November 1829, *KC*, 1:320.

52. Jerry W. Markham, *A Financial History of the United States* (M. E. Sharp, 2001), 1:149.

53. Harrison died after thirty-two days in office.

54. Isabel McLennan McMeekin, *Louisville, the Gateway City* (Julian Messner, 1946), 94.

55. Thomas D. Clark, in *Register of the Kentucky Historical Society* 31 (January 1933): 9–28.

56. *HOFC*, 277.

57. Lewis Collins and Richard H. Collins, *Historical Sketches of Kentucky* (L. A. and U. P. James, 1848), 1:40.

58. Henry C. Pope himself was killed in a duel in 1848.

59. *HOL*, 183.

60. *LPP*, 229.

61. *HOFC*, 283.

62. Ron D. Bryant, in *EOL*, 474; *HOFC*, 284.

63. Laws of Kentucky, chap. 704 (1835), 128.

64. Media archive, Smithsonian American Art Museum.

65. James R. Robertson to J. R. and A. H. Carson, 9 May 1836, Harlan Museum Minute Book, 1837–1838, FHS.

66. Harlan Museum Minute Book, 1837–1838, FHS.

67. Alice Ford, *John James Audubon* (University of Oklahoma Press, 1964), 268.

68. Francis Hobart Herrick, *Audubon the Naturalist*, 2 vols. (D. Appleton, 1917), 1:427.

69. Ford, *John James Audubon*, 286.

70. Ibid., 297.

71. M. W. Caldwell and G. L. Bell Jr., "Of German Princes and North American Rivers: Harlan's Lost Mosasaur Snout Rediscovered," *Netherlands Journal of Geosciences* 84–3 (2005): 207–11. Harlan obtained the snout from Major Nathaniel A. Ware, who had bought it from a trader.

72. Abstract from Richard Harlan's *Journals* (American Philosophical Society, 2003), 1–9.

73. Ford, *John James Audubon*, 268. No surviving records tie Harlan through Audubon to Bakewell or to the Harlan Museum in Louisville. A letter from Nathaniel A. Ware to Samuel Brown, dated 30 December 1821 (FHS), refers to Ware acting as Brown's agent in the purchase of Harlan's Museum, a previous entity. Connection to the 1837 museum is imputed.

74. Louisvillians revived the museum idea in 1871 with the Louisville Polytechnic Institute. After several moves, it was absorbed by the Louisville Free Public Library in 1908. In 1975 the Louisville Museum of History and Science (the present Louisville Science Center) opened on Main Street, a short walk from the Louisville Museum's original location. A number of the Science Center's artifacts are from the library and possibly date back to the Polytechnic Institute. There is a remote chance that some items, including rocks and an eagle allegedly stuffed by Audubon, date to the Harlan Museum or the Louisville Museum.

75. *HOFC*, 288.

76. Josiah Stoddard Johnston, *Memorial History of Louisville*, vol. 1 (American Biographical Publishing Co., 1896), 235–36.

77. "A Brief History of the University of Louisville," University of Louisville website.

78. GK to Dilke, 1 March 1838, *KC*, 2:29.

79. Louisville Medical Institute, *Catalogue of the Officers and Students* (Prentice and Weissinger, 1839), 10.

80. George H. Yater, in *EOL*, 665.

81. Charles Dickens, *American Notes for General Circulation* (Chapman and Hall, 1842), 214.

82. *Louisville Journal,* 5 June 1839.

83. Dickens describes fellow passengers on a steamboat trip from Louisville to St. Louis in *American Notes,* 215.

84. James Freeman Clarke to Emerson, 30 April 1838, in James Freeman Clarke, *Autobiography, Diary and Correspondence,* ed. Edward Everett Hale (Houghton Mifflin, 1891), 121.

85. A copy of the letter is on display at Farmington, now a house museum.

86. Dickens, *American Notes,* 212. Dickens belonged to a line of British travel writers who arrived in America with a point of view. The writers were often Tories who had difficulty with the American democracy and scoffed at the efforts of Henry W. Longfellow (1807–1882) and others to create a distinctly American culture. Not incidentally, Dickens was among those writers who were angry at the lack of a copyright treaty, which enabled American publishers to pirate their works without compensation.

87. *HOFC,* 287.

88. The Belknap site at First and Main Streets was taken over by Humana Inc., which maintains in its lobby a display of photographs and historical memorabilia from the Belknap Company.

89. Maximilian, Prince of Wied, "Travels in the Interior of North America, 1832–1834," in *Early Western Travels, 1748–1846* (Arthur H. Clark, 1906), 22:157. Maximilian's primary interests were the flora and fauna.

90. One of Louisville's darkest moments was 6 August 1855, "Bloody Monday," when nativists burned large swaths of Catholic German and Irish neighborhoods, killing twenty-two.

Ruin and Death: 1841

1. Ralph Waldo Emerson, "The Conservative," delivered 9 December 1841 at Boston Masonic Temple.

2. GK to Dilke, 12 July 1828, *KC,* 1:315.

3. Alice Ford, *John James Audubon* (University of Oklahoma Press, 1964), 400.

4. 1842 Jefferson County Deed Book, 58:412.

5. Billy Bakewell was the Louisville agent for the Red River Steamship Company.

6. Letter from Mildred Fry Bullitt (Mrs. William Christian Bullitt), written from Ox Moor (later called Oxmoor), the Bullitt estate, to her son John, a student at Centre College, 20 December 1841, Bullitt Family Letters, FHS. William Neville Bullitt (1802–1867), who succeeded George in the City Council from the Fourth Ward, was her cousin-in-law.

7. Alice Speed McDonald, a granddaughter, told Kirk it was a stomach ailment. George's son John Henry, who was fourteen when his father died, said it was tuberculosis. If so, it had an unusually rapid onset.

8. The will is included in the appendix.

9. *KC,* 1:cviii

10. Martha Bullitt to John Bullitt, 21 January 1842, Bullitt Family Papers, FHS.

11. Cood signed his name either Holiday or Holliday; the *LCD* spelled it Holaday.

12. Georgiana predeceased Jeffrey on 3 April 1879. In a further irony, when Jeffrey died on 18 February 1881, his estate redounded to his nieces and nephews, some of whom lived in Scotland.

13. John Jeffrey to Milnes, 26 July 1845, *KC*, 2:122: "his estate . . . paid about twenty cents in the Dollar of his debts."

14. Daniel and Ann Smith had two sons, Richard and Felix, whose lives are unrecorded except by references in the city directory. Both worked in the mill, which became Smith and Cood after George's death.

15. Jesse, a male, was valued at $600, Hannah at $400, and Lucy at $250.

16. The Economic History Association website (measuringworth.com) calculates that the $44,000 in 1842 securities and household effects would be worth $1.13 million in 2012, based on a fairly conservative Consumer Price Index measure. The value of the sawmill, outside the estate, was not calculated.

17. *Maysville (MO) Herald,* September 1911.

18. Upon John Jeffrey's death, his brother Alexander Jeffrey contributed an obituary to the *Lexington Daily Press,* claiming, "He set free and settled in Canada all the slaves he acquired by his marriage" (*KC*, 1:civ). This was an embellishment of the truth, as the slaves were sold.

19. 1842 Jefferson County Court Minutes Inventory Book, 2:399.

20. 1842 Jefferson County Court Records, Book 59:263.

21. Ibid., Book 65:551.

22. 1844 Jefferson County Court Records, Book 65:549.

23. Ibid., Book 64:147–48.

24. The filings, or indentures, do not specify the individual amounts owed.

25. Jefferson County Deed 64:148 notes Jeffrey's land purchase on Green Street, between Third and Fourth Streets, for $1,312.50, recorded 9 July 1844.

26. Trabue added a portico and columns to the house.

27. Jefferson County Deed 63:362, recorded 17 September 1844.

28. 1844 Jefferson County Court Records, Book 64:147. An anomaly in the recorded documents is that Isabel (Isabella) was dead and may have been listed as a deceased beneficiary, while Ella was inconsistently listed or omitted. Love and Craig appear to have been acting as guardians ad litem for the minor Keats children, or perhaps as Georgiana and John Jeffrey's counsel. James Guthrie and James Speed, on whom George relied, were uninvolved.

29. James Freeman Clarke to Margaret Fuller, November 1834, in James Freeman Clarke, *Autobiography, Diary and Correspondence,* ed. Edward Everett Hale (Houghton Mifflin, 1891), 107.

30. James Freeman Clarke, *Memorial and Biographical Sketches* (Houghton Mifflin, 1878), 221–22, 223, 228–29.

31. Hyder Edward Rollins, *Keats' Reputation in America to 1848* (Harvard University Press, 1946), 94–95. Milnes drew extensively from Clarke's sketch, word for word, without attribution.

32. James Freeman Clarke to Houghton, 20 October 1875, *KC*, 2:344.

33. Richard Monckton Milnes (Lord Houghton), *The Aldine Edition of the British Poets* (Bell and Daldy, 1876), xxvi, reprinted in *KC*, 2:346fn.

34. Reverend Samuel Osgood, *Eighteen Years: A Reminiscence of Kentucky* (Knickerbocker Gallery, 1855), reprinted in *The Atlantic Souvenir for 1859* (Derby and Jackson, 1859), 48.

35. Samuel Osgood to Lord Houghton, 26 November 1875, *KC*, 2:347–48.

36. John Jeffrey to Alexander Jeffrey, 31 January 1854, Alexander Jeffrey Papers, FHS.

37. GK to FK Llanos, 25 May 1820–6 January 1821, *KC*, 1:110.

38. When Chatsworth, the estate of George Keats Speed, was subdivided in the 1890s, Thomas B. Crutcher was head of the Public Works Commission. A great-grandson of George, he arranged for the naming of the street.

Aftermath: 1842–

1. GAW to Alexander Jeffrey, undated, Alexander Jeffrey Papers, FHS; see also *KC*, 2:124–27.

2. The poem was published in the *Louisville Journal,* October 1843.

3. Jeffrey to Milnes, 26 July 1845, *KC*, 2:122.

4. Jeffrey to Milnes, 8 September 1845, *KC*, 2:123.

5. Georgiana and Alice rejoined the Unitarian Church that year.

6. Ella Keats to Jeffrey, 20 May 1852, Alexander Jeffrey Papers, FHS.

7. Georgiana was also prone to fibbing about her age, telling Clarke that she was four years younger than she actually was. On a passport application taken out when she was fifty-six, her age was listed as thirty-six, so far wrong that it might have been a clerical error.

8. A detailed account of the Jeffreys and all the Keats children can be found in *KF.*

9. Marie Adami, *Fanny Keats* (Oxford University Press, 1937), 151.

10. John Henry Keats told the *Maysville (MO) Herald* in September 1911 that he was born "in melancholy" (perhaps because he was named for his deceased uncle) in November 1827; no other record of his birth survives.

11. Jeffrey to Alexander Jeffrey, 4 August 1850, Alexander Jeffrey Collection, FHS.

12. Susan Bullitt (1829–1907, daughter of Mildred) to John Bullitt, 14 March 1849, Bullitt Family Papers, FHS.

13. Jeffrey to Alexander Jeffrey, 17 June 1855, Alexander Jeffrey Collection, FHS.

14. Emma Frances Keats Speed to FK Llanos, 7 April 1878, *MKC,* 103, refers to a chain of previous correspondence.

15. Emma Keats Speed to FK, *MKC,* 43.

16. Lord Houghton noted Peay's notoriety in a 6 November 1875 letter to James Freeman Clarke, *KL,* 2:346.

17. *KF,* 187–254.

18. A grandson, Geoffrey T. Wood of Dubbo, New South Wales, suggested to me that Drane had intermingled too closely with African Americans and was "told to leave."

19. *KF,* 318–33. See also, Lawrence M. Crutcher, "Finding the Keats Family," *Keats Shelley Review* 25, no. 1 (April 2011): 3–9.

Appendix A:
The George Keats Circle of Friends and Acquaintances

1. Faculty Office, Calendar of Marriage Allegations, Lambeth Palace Library, in Robert Gittings, *John Keats* (Little, Brown, 1968), 4. His father, Jonathan Abbey, a farmer in Healaugh, moved farther east to Skipwith, where Abbey was christened on 13 August 1765. Gittings, *John Keats,* 33.

2. As early as 23 August 1820, Abbey wrote to John Keats, "Bad debts for the last two years have cut down the profits of our business to nothing" (*KL,* 2:331).

3. On 8 March 1827 Abbey was pickpocketed by Sarah Forrester, age sixty-three; she took a handkerchief worth three shillings. At the Old Bailey trial in April 1827, he still described himself as a tea dealer. Forrester was found guilty and confined for one year.

4. *KL,* 1:62.

5. Jean Haynes, "Richard Abbey's Resting Place," *Keats Shelley Review* 24 (October 2010): 12. His age was listed as seventy-five, which implies a 1761–1762 birth; this is at odds with the Marital Allegation in Lambeth, indicating a 1765 birth. It is possible that Haynes meant Mare Street, in South Hackney.

6. Joanna Richardson, "New Light on Mr. Abbey," *KSMB* 5 (1953): 26–31.

7. JK to GK and GAW, 16 December 1818, *KL,* 2:8.

8. Joanna Richardson, *Fanny Brawne: A Biography* (Vanguard Press, 1952), 26. This sketch was compiled from a synopsis of Richardson's book, whose factual underpinnings have been challenged by subsequent scholars.

9. Gittings is the proponent of Fanny as the subject of "Bright Star"; not all scholars are certain.

10. A cornelian is a semiprecious stone, normally of a reddish hue.

11. Richardson, *Fanny Brawne,* 140.

12. Jane Campion's 2009 movie *Bright Star,* for which Andrew Motion was script adviser, portrays her in this sympathetic light.

13. A 12 July 1890 memorandum from Charles (Carlino) Brown Jr., son of Charles Brown, to Fred Holland Day (1864–1933) provided the bulk of Brown's biographical data. *KC,* 1:liv–lxii.

14. Carlino was describing his mother here.

15. Eric Hall McCormick, *The Friend of Keats: A Life of Charles Armitage Brown* (Victoria University Press, 1989), 213.

16. The term *apoplexy* may have been used interchangeably with *epilepsy;* he had suffered a seizure in 1834 in Florence. It also may have been a stroke.

17. Gillian Iles, "New Information on Keats' Friend Charles 'Armitage' Brown and the Brown Family," *Keats Shelley Journal* 40 (1991): 146–66, provides extensive background on Brown.

18. "History of the House," Keats House website.

19. GK to Dilke, 12 May 1828, *KC,* 1:315.

20. *KC,* 1:lxxx–lxxxvi.

21. Ibid., lxxxvi–xc.

22. Frederick Locker-Lampson, *My Confidences* (Smith, Elder, 1896).

23. A copy, inscribed as having been donated by John Gilmer Speed, resides at the Keats Shelley House, Rome. It is possible that Emma Keats Speed commissioned the copy. Her correspondence indicates a curiosity as to Fanny Keats Llanos's appearance. Keats House, Hampstead, holds two other copies.

24. Marie Adami, *Fanny Keats* (Oxford University Press, 1937), 1–293.

25. *KC*, 1:cxvii–cxxxvi.

26. The painting was donated to the Keats Shelley House, Rome, by John Gilmer Speed. It appears that Henry Wylie retrieved it from John's estate and sent it to George in Louisville.

27. GK to Dilke, 11 May 1832, *KC*, 2:4.

28. Sue Brown, *Joseph Severn: A Life* (Oxford University Press, 2009).

29. *KC*, 1:cxxxvii–cxliv; see also Edmund Blunden, *Keats's Publisher: A Memoir of John Taylor* (Jonathan Cape, 1936).

30. St. Martin Outwich Marriage Register, Guildhall Library.

31. St. Thomas Apostle Baptism Registry, Guildhall Library.

32. James Wylie's parents were James Wylie and Anne Porteous, innkeepers. Two of Ann Griffin Wylie's nephews, Henry and Frederick Griffin, sons of Robert Griffin, married Mary Porteous and Jane Porteous, respectively, in Canada, although the Porteous family was of Scottish descent. The Porteous-Griffin and Wylie-Porteous connections are fully documented, whereas the link between James Wylie and Ann Griffin is inferential.

33. National Archives, Public Records Office, 12/4424, 4487.

34. St. John the Baptist Burial Register, London Metropolitan Archives.

35. Georgiana's scrapbook includes a French visa application for Charles dated August–November 1819 in which his age is stated as *19 ans*. His Shoreditch death certificate, dated 5 June 1839, states his age as thirty-nine.

36. West Hackney Baptism Register, London Metropolitan Archives; Parliamentary Papers, vol. 133.

37. GK to Dilke, 12 July 1828, *KC*, 1:316.

38. His date of birth is inferred from his burial record. He was buried in Nunhead on 30 October 1846 at age sixty-three.

39. Sometimes also spelled Keysell.

40. Marriage Register, St. George Bloomsbury, London Metropolitan Archives.

41. JK to GAW and GK, 14 February–3 May 1819, *KL*, 2:68–69. Rollins dates the passage 3 March, whereas Maurice Buxton Forman, in *The Poetical Works and Other Writings of John Keats* (Charles Scribner's Sons, 1938), 7:241–42, dates it 18 February.

42. JK to GAW, 13–28 January 1820, *KL*, 2:247.

43. FK to GK, 31 May 1826, *KC*, 1:299.

44. GK to FK, 24 March 1831, *MKC*, 64.

45. Several excellent Audubon biographies, especially that of Alice Ford, were used as sources for this extremely brief sketch, which focuses only on his early years in Kentucky and the overlap with George Keats.

46. Earlier, the Mechanics and Traders Bank had been headed by David James. Letters from James to William G. Bakewell, dating from 24 June 1841 to 1 November 1843 (FHS), relate to boat charters and commercial shipping matters. James's niece, Mary Ann James, married Clarence George Keats on 12 January 1853, coincident with Bakewell's presidency of the partially James-owned bank.

47. Thomas W. Bakewell, "Sketch of the Life of Thomas Woodhouse Bakewell Written by Himself," ed. Bruce Sinclair, *Filson Club History Quarterly* 40 (1966): 235–48. See also *The Family Book of Bakewell * Page * Campbell*, comp. B. G. Bakewell (Wm. G. Johnston, 1896), 33–40.

48. Historical Sketches, Montgomery County (Pennsylvania) Historical Society.

49. The *[Louisville] Focus,* eight days later, recorded it as a Monday evening, 17 November 1828.

50. *Family Book of Bakewell,* 43–44.

51. Bakewell, "Sketch of the Life," 245.

52. Ella Keats Peay obituary, following her death on 12 March 1888. The unidentified clipping is likely from the *Louisville Courier-Journal.*

53. *HOFC,* 271–72.

54. *LCD,* 1832–1838.

55. *HOFC,* 442–45.

56. *LPP,* 305–18.

57. Ibid., 89–90.

58. Formerly Switzerland, but annexed by France.

59. Alice Ford, *John James Audubon* (University of Oklahoma Press, 1964), 104–5.

60. John Goff, "The Last Leaf," *Register of the Kentucky Historical Society* 59 (1961): 331–42.

61. U.S. Genealogy Net, 2001.

62. *KC,* 1:283n. Rollins cites Paxton's *Supplement to the New Orleans Directory* (1824), in which Briggs is colisted with Gordon and Forstall, merchants. He appears in the 1827 and 1830 directories with them, but not in the 1835 directory.

63. Jerry W. Markham, *A Financial History of the United States* (M. E. Sharp, 2001), 1:149.

64. *New Orleans Daily Picayune,* 4 April 1864, 2.

65. Garden District National Register 71000358 (1971).

66. *New Orleans Bee,* 3 April 1874 (in French).

67. *New York Times,* 20 April 1903.

68. *LPP,* 252.

69. George Yater, *Two Hundred Years at the Falls of the Ohio* (Filson Club, 1987), 107.

70. Laws of Kentucky, 1834, chap. 448, sec. 32d, Acts of the General Assembly.

71. Buchanan family records.

72. *HOL,* 184–85.

73. 1847 Journal of Proceedings, Annual Convention of Protestant Episcopal Church of Kentucky.

74. *New International Encyclopedia*; Marcus Buford, *A Genealogy of the Buford Family in America* (San Francisco, 1903), 213–14.

75. GK to FK Llanos, 12 July 1828, *MKC*, 49–50.

76. Bullitt was disbarred in 1817 after challenging Ben Hardin to a duel. Although the disbarment was lifted, he left the law in 1820.

77. E. Polk Johnson, *A History of Kentucky and Kentuckians* (Lewis Publishing Co., 1912), 2:607.

78. Most Kentuckians would compress this sentence, saying the Bullitts and Gwathmeys were "kinfolks."

79. *LPP*, 120–25.

80. George Baber, in *HOFC*, 483–85; see also Josiah Stoddard Johnston, *Memorial History of Louisville* (American Biographical Publishing Co., 1896).

81. Robert M. Ireland, in *EOL*, 150.

82. Diana Stradling and J. Garrison, *American Queensware—The Louisville Experience, 1829–37* (Chipstone, 2001), 1–7. John Bull is variously referred to as John Bell, but it is most likely the same person.

83. Kentucky General Assembly Statutes Book.

84. *HOFC*, 252–53.

85. John C. Pillow, in *Louisville Courier-Journal*, 1989 (date missing).

86. Robert D. Richardson Jr., *Emerson: The Mind on Fire* (University of California Press, 1995), 175.

87. The passage was included in John's 25–27 September 1818 letter to his brother Tom, written during his Scottish tour with Charles Brown.

88. Carl W. Stover and Jerry L. Coffman, "Seismicity of the United States, 1568–1989" (U.S. Geological Survey paper, 1993).

89. Audrea McDowell in *EOL*, 322. She cites Robert A. Burnett, "Louisville's French Past," *Filson Club History Quarterly* 50 (April 1976): 5–27, and *LPP*, 216–19.

90. Henry Wylie to Dilke, 15 February 1837, *KC*, 2:25n.

91. *LCD*, 1838 and 1843.

92. John Wilson Townsend, *Kentucky in American Letters, 1784–1912* (Torch Press, 1913), 119–20. Townsend obtained certain materials relating to Georgiana Keats Jeffrey, apparently found in Lexington, that he subsequently sold to the Houghton Library at Harvard. These include a photograph of Georgiana's granddaughter Alice Lee Keats. See also Johnston, *Memorial History of Louisville*, 2:64, 78.

93. Johnson, *History of Kentucky and Kentuckians*, 2:997.

94. *LCD*, 1843–1844.

95. Dr. U. E. Ewing, slave leasing document dated 6 September 1832, FHS.

96. GK to Dilke, 1 March 1838, *KL*, 2:29.

97. Dr. Emmet Field Horine, *Daniel Drake, Pioneer Physician of the Midwest* (University of Pennsylvania Press, 1961), 327–28, 334–35.

98. *Boston Medical and Surgical Journal* 70 (1864): 205–9.

99. Timothy Flint, *Recollections of the Last Ten Years in the Valley of the Mississippi* (1826; reprint, Southern Illinois University Press, 1968).

100. Kentucky General Assembly Book, 1834, 503.

101. Louisville Board of Trade, "A Tribute to the Memory of William Garvin," 1869.

102. John Findling and Jennifer Lavery, *A History of the First Unitarian Church of Louisville, Kentucky* (n.p., 2005), 1–12.

103. James Guthrie to George Meriwether, 7 December 1831, FHS.

104. Drawn from an article by George H. Yater in *EOL*, 362–63.

105. Anna Russell Des Cognets, *Gov. Garrard of Kentucky* (James M. Byrne, 1898).

106. Various postings in Ancestry.com.

107. Laws of Kentucky, 1836.

108. *Nathaniel Hardy, 1795–1848*, published in 1995 for the 200th anniversary of his birth by S. I. George, Lucy Brice Daust, and B. E. Clement, copy in FHS.

109. Nathaniel Hardy to Caroline Hardy (Miles), 3 October 1836, letter 2 in *Nathaniel Hardy, 1795–1848*.

110. M. W. Caldwell and G. L. Bell Jr., "Of German Princes and North American Rivers: Harlan's Lost Mosasaur Snout Rediscovered," *Netherlands Journal of Geosciences* 84–3 (2005): 207–11.

111. Miami University alumni listing.

112. *HOL*, 203.

113. James Guthrie resided on Walnut Street, one block east.

114. This version was published as an article by Lucian V. Rule in *Historic Towns of the Southern States,* ed. Lyman P. Powell (G. P. Putnam's Sons, 1900), 528–30.

115. Basil W. Duke, *History of the Bank of Kentucky, 1792–1895* (John P. Morton, 1895), 39–42.

116. *EOL*, 429; *LPP*, 26.

117. U.S. National Library of Medicine, National Institutes of Health website.

118. Helen McIver, *Genealogy of the Jaffrey-Jeffrey Family* (published privately, 1925), 3. His parents were John Armstrong Jeffrey and Elizabeth McConnell Jeffrey. The date is consistent with Jeffrey's tombstone in Louisville's Cave Hill Cemetery. Scotland had no government mandate to record births until 1855. ScotlandsPeople.gov has assembled the available parish baptismal records; however, none documents Jeffrey's date or place of birth.

119. Obituary in the *Lexington Daily Press,* 20 February 1881, *KC*, 1:ciii–civ.

120. Alexander Jeffrey and John Jeffrey Letters, FHS.

121. John Jeffrey to Alexander Jeffrey, 24 December 1855, Alexander Jeffrey Letters, FHS.

122. John Jeffrey Papers, FHS.

123. *HOFC*, 273

124. Smithsonian American Art Biographies, 2010; *New York Times* obituary, 1 February 1889.

125. Carl F. Kramer, *Visionaries, Adventurers and Builders* (Sunnyside Press, 1999), 83–84.

126. Biographical Dictionary of the U.S. Congress.

127. Louisa H. A. Minor, *The Meriwethers and Their Connections* (Joel Munsell's Sons, 1892).

128. Peter Richard Guetig and Conrad Selle, *Louisville Breweries* (Louisville, 1995), extracted in *EOL*, 117.

129. Margaret L. Merrick, in *EOL*, 657.

130. *Knickerbocker Magazine,* 1855, 27–36.

131. Obituary, *New York Times,* 15 April 1880.

132. *HOFC,* 277.

133. *Twentieth Century Biographical Dictionary of Notable Americans,* ed. Rossiter Johnson and John Howard Brown (Biographical Society, 1904).

134. *EOL,* 697. The unsigned piece cites Donald B. Towles, *The Press of Kentucky, 1787–1994* (Lexington, 1994).

135. Johnston, *Memorial History of Louisville,* 1:491–94.

136. Duke, *History of the Bank of Kentucky,* 52.

137. Multiwords.de—a Prather family website.

138. John Prentice, *The Laird of Stone,* prenticenet.com.

139. Letter from Thomas Bakewell, 26 March 1834, in Susan Lewis Shaffer, *Letters,* as cited by Ford, *John James Audubon,* 440.

140. *HOL,* 183–84.

141. Prentice was a Mason (*HOFC,* 285), and George may have been one as well.

142. Thomas D. Clark, in *EOL,* 722–23.

143. Kincaid A. Herr, *The Louisville & Nashville Railroad, 1850–1963* (University Press of Kentucky, 2000), 6.

144. Horine, *Daniel Drake,* 123, 126, 153–63.

145. *HOFC,* 254; *LPP,* 327–32.

146. Dr. Henry M. Bullitt, *An Address of the Life and Character of the Late Dr. Coleman Rogers, M.D.* (Bull and Brother, 1855).

147. J. Winston Coleman, *The Rowan-Chambers Duel* (Winburn Press, 1976), 1–15.

148. Steven Tackler, "John Rowan and the Demise of Jeffersonian Republicanism in Kentucky, 1819–31," *Register of the Kentucky Historical Society* 78 (Winter 1980): 1–26.

149. *LPP,* 237–45.

150. Melville O. Briney, "History of James Rudd," *Louisville Times,* 5 March 1959.

151. Kentucky Heritage Council Newsletter, 1995.

152. *EOL,* 820.

153. *HOFC,* 240.

154. Ibid., 482–83; Thomas Speed, *Records and Memorials of the Speed Family* (Courier-Journal, 1892), 104–15; James J. Holmberg article in *EOL,* 842.

155. James Freeman Clarke, *Memorial and Biographical Sketches* (Houghton Mifflin, 1878), 217–18.

156. Speed, *Records and Memorials,* 93–108.

157. Ibid., 128–29. James Breckenridge Speed was the son of William Pope Speed, another child of Judge John Speed.

158. The body of Isabel Keats (1825–1843) was also moved.

159. Catherine Connor and Seymour V. Connor, "Kentucky Colonization in Texas," *Register of the Kentucky Historical Society* (January 1953–October 1954): 29.

160. The cemetery has multiple entries for James Stewart, the likeliest being a 19 April 1867 interment.

161. Lewis Collins and Richard H. Collins, *Historical Sketches of Kentucky* (L. A. and U. P. James, 1848), 41. Lewis Collins's original 1848 book was updated through 1874 by his son Richard.

162. *HOFC*, 563–65.

163. Maximilian, Prince of Wied, "Travels in the Interior of North America, 1832–1834," in *Early Western Travels, 1748–1846* (Arthur H. Clark, 1906), 22:157–58.

164. C. Robert Ullrich et al., "Germans," in *EOL*, 338–39.

165. Karolyn Smardtz Frost, *I've Got a Home in Glory Land* (Farrar Straus Giroux, 2007), 77–79.

166. Naomi J. Kirk, "George Keats," *Filson Club History Quarterly* 8 (1934): 88–96.

167. John Keats, *The Poetical Works and Other Writing of John Keats*, ed. Harry Buxton Forman, rev. by Maurice Buxton Forman, 8 vols. (Charles Scribner's Sons, 1938), 1:lxxiii–xcvii.

168. Thomas Speed, who authored *Records and Memorials of the Speed Family*, was a grandson of Thomas Speed of Cottage Grove, Bardstown.

169. Letter from Betsy Speed Rich to the author, 1 February 2007.

BIBLIOGRAPHY

Books, Articles, and Dissertations

Adami, Marie. *Fanny Keats*. Oxford: Oxford University Press, 1937.

Adams, Alexander B. *John James Audubon*. New York: G. P. Putnam's Sons, 1966.

Allison, Young Ewing. *The City of Louisville and a Glimpse of Kentucky*. Louisville: Louisville Board of Trade, 1887.

Altick, Richard D. *The Cowden Clarkes*. London: Oxford University Press, 1948.

Amphlett, William. *The Emigrant's Directory to the Western States of North America*. London: Longman, Hurst, Rees, Orme and Browne, 1819.

Arnett, Maralea. "Audubon Faces an Identity Crisis." In *A History of Henderson County*. Henderson, KY: Audubon Printers, 1975.

Arthur, Stanley Clisby. *Audubon: An Intimate Life of an American Woodsman*. New Orleans: Harmonson, 1937.

Atwater, Caleb. *Remarks Made on a Tour to Prairie du Chien*. 1831. Reprinted in *Louisville: A Guide to the Falls City*. New York: M. Barrows and Company, 1940.

Audubon, John James. *Audubon, by Himself,* edited by Alice Ford. Garden City, NY: Natural History Press, 1969.

———. *The 1826 Journal of John James Audubon,* edited by Alice Ford. New York: Abbeville Press, 1987.

———. "Myself." In *Writings and Drawings*. New York: Library of America, 1999.

Audubon, Maria R., ed. *Audubon and His Journals*. 2 vols. New York: Dover Publications, 1960.

Baker, Herschell. *William Hazlitt*. Cambridge, MA: Belknap Press of the Harvard University Press, 1962.

Bakewell, B. G., comp. *The Family Book of Bakewell * Page * Campbell*. Pittsburgh: Wm. G. Johnston, 1896.

Bakewell, Thomas W. "Sketch of the Life of Thomas Woodhouse Bakewell Written by Himself," edited by Bruce Sinclair. *Filson Club History Quarterly* 40 (1966).

Bate, Walter Jackson. *John Keats.* Cambridge, MA: Harvard University Press, 1963.

Bernhard, Karl, Duke of Saxe-Weimar-Eisenach. *Travels through North America.* Philadelphia: Carey, Lea and Carey, 1828.

Birkbeck, Morris. *Notes on a Journey from the Coast of Virginia to the Territory of Illinois.* Multiple publishers from 1817, including London: James Ridgway, 1818.

Blake, William. "Merlin's Prophecy." In *The Complete Poetry and Prose of William Blake,* edited by David V. Erdman. New York: Anchor Books, 1988.

Blunden, Edmund. *Keats's Publisher: A Memoir of John Taylor.* London: Jonathan Cape, 1936.

———. *Shelley and Keats as They Struck Their Contemporaries.* London: C. W. Beaumont, 1925.

Brawne, Fanny. *Letters of Fanny Brawne to Fanny Keats,* edited by Fred Edgcumbe. New York: Oxford University Press, 1937.

Briney, Melville O. "History of James Rudd." *Louisville Times,* 5 March 1959.

Brown, Charles (Armitage). *The Life of John Keats,* edited by Dorothy Hyde Bodurtha and Willard Bissell Pope. New York: Oxford University Press, 1937.

———. *Some Letters and Miscellanea,* edited by Maurice Buxton Forman. London: Oxford University Press, 1937.

Brown, Sue. *Joseph Severn: A Life.* N.p.: Oxford University Press, 2009.

Buckingham, James Silk. *English Traveler's Observations.* London, 1841. Reprinted in *History of the Ohio Falls and Their Cities.* Cleveland, OH: L. A. Williams, 1882.

Buford, Marcus. *A Genealogy of the Buford Family in America.* San Francisco: n.p., 1903.

Buley, R. Carlyle. *The Old Northwest Pioneer Period, 1815–1840.* Bloomington: Indiana University Press, 1951.

Bullitt, Dr. Henry M. *An Address of the Life and Character of the Late Dr. Coleman Rogers, M.D.* N.p.: Bull and Brother, 1855.

Burnett, Robert A. "Louisville's French Past." *Filson Club History Quarterly* 50 (April 1976).

Butler, Edward Mann. *A History of the Commonwealth of Kentucky.* Louisville: Wilcox, Dickerman and Company, 1834.

Byron, (Lord) George Gordon. *Don Juan.* Reprinted in Joanna Ferguson, *Lord Byron.* London: Folio Society, 1988.

Caldwell, M. W., and G. L. Bell Jr. "Of German Princes and North Ameri-

Bibliography

Bibliography

can Rivers: Harlan's Lost Mosasaur Snout Rediscovered." *Netherlands Journal of Geosciences* 84–3 (2005).

Caldwell, Stephen A. *A Banking History of Louisiana*. Baton Rouge: Louisiana State University Press, 1935.

Carlyle, Thomas. *Sartor Resartus*. Fraser's, 1833–1834. Reprint, Oxford World Classics, 1987.

Casseday, Ben. *The History of Louisville*. Louisville: Hull and Brother, 1852.

Clark, Thomas D. "Building Libraries in the Early Ohio Valley." *Journal of Library History* 6, no. 2 (1971).

———. *A History of Kentucky*. Lexington, KY: John Bradford Press, 1960.

Clarke, Charles Cowden, and Mary Cowden Clarke. *Recollections of Writers*. 1878. Reprint, edited by Robert Gittings. Fontwell, UK: Centaur Press, 1969.

Clarke, James Freeman. *Autobiography, Diary and Correspondence*, edited by Edward Everett Hale. Boston: Houghton Mifflin, 1891.

———. *Memorial and Biographical Sketches*. Boston: Houghton Mifflin, 1878.

———. "Memorial Sketch of George Keats." *Dial*, August 1843. Reprinted in James Freeman Clarke, *Memorial and Biographical Sketches*. Boston: Houghton Mifflin, 1878.

Cobbett, William. *A Year's Residence in the United States of America*. London: Sherwood, Neely and Jones, 1818–1819.

Coleman, J. Winston. *The Rowan-Chambers Duel*. Lexington, KY: Winburn Press, 1976.

Collins, Lewis, and Richard H. Collins. *Historical Sketches of Kentucky*. Covington, KY: L. A. and U. P. James, 1848.

Colvin, Sidney. *John Keats—His Life and Poetry, Friends, Critics, and After-Fame*. London: Macmillan, 1917.

———. *Keats*. London: Macmillan, 1887.

Connor, Catherine, and Seymour V. Connor. "Kentucky Colonization in Texas." *Register of the Kentucky Historical Society* (January 1953–October 1954).

Croker, John Wilson. Review of *Endymion*. *Quarterly Review*, April 1818.

Crutcher, Lawrence M. "Finding the Keats Family." *Keats Shelley Review* 25, no. 1 (April 2011).

———. *The Keats Family*. Louisville: Butler Books, 2009.

Dalrymple, William. *The Last Mughal*. New York: Alfred A. Knopf, 2007.

De Almeida, Hermione. *Romantic Medicine and John Keats*. New York: Oxford University Press, 1991.

Bibliography

Des Cognets, Anna Russell. *Gov. Garrard of Kentucky.* Lexington, KY: James M. Byrne, 1898.

De Sélincourt, Ernest. *The Poems of John Keats.* London: Methuen, 1905.

Dickens, Charles. *American Notes for General Circulation.* London: Chapman and Hall, 1842. Reprint, Penguin Classics, 1985.

———. *Bleak House.* London: Bradbury and Evans, 1852–1853 [originally published in twenty installments]. Reprint, Penguin Books, 1996.

———. *Martin Chuzzlewit.* London: Chapman and Hall, 1843. Reprint, Penguin Books, 1999.

Dubois, Edward. *My Pocket Book.* London: Verner Hood and Sharp, 1808.

Dubos, René, and Jean Dubos. *The White Plague, Tuberculosis, Man and Society.* New Brunswick, NJ: Rutgers University Press, 1952.

Duke, Basil W. *History of the Bank of Kentucky, 1792–1895.* Louisville: John P. Morton, 1895.

Durrett, Reuben Thomas. *The Centenary of Louisville.* Louisville: John P. Morton, 1893.

Eliot, T. S. *The Use of Poetry and the Use of Criticism.* London: Faber and Faber, 1973.

Emerson, Ralph Waldo. "The Conservative." Speech delivered 9 December 1841 at Boston Masonic Temple. In *Nature: Addresses/Lectures,* 1849. Reprint, Cambridge, MA: Harvard University Press, 1971.

Faux, William. *Memorable Days in America, Including Accounts of Mr. Birkbeck's Settlement in the Illinois.* London: W. Simpkin and R. Marshall, 1823.

Fearon, Henry Bradshaw. *Sketches of America: A Narrative of a Journey of Five Thousand Miles through the Eastern and Western States of America with Remarks on Mr. Birkbeck's "Notes" and "Letters."* London: Hurst, Rees, Orme and Brown, 1818.

Findling, John, and Jennifer Lavery. *A History of the First Unitarian Church of Louisville, Kentucky.* Louisville: n.p., 2005.

Flint, Timothy. *Recollections of the Last Ten Years.* 1826. Reprint, Carbondale: Southern Illinois University Press, 1968.

Flower, George. *History of the English Settlement in Edwards County, Illinois.* Chicago: Fergus Printing Company, 1882.

Ford, Alice. *John James Audubon.* Norman: University of Oklahoma Press, 1964.

———. *John James Audubon: A Biography.* New York: Abbeville Press, 1988.

Forster, E. M. *Abinger Harvest.* New York: Harcourt Brace, 1936.

Frost, Karolyn Smardtz. *I've Got a Home in Glory Land.* New York: Farrar Straus Giroux, 2007.

Garrod, H. W. *Keats.* Oxford: Clarendon Press, 1926.

Gittings, Robert. *John Keats.* Boston: Little, Brown, 1968.

————. *John Keats: The Living Year.* Melbourne: Heinemann, 1954.

————. *The Keats Inheritance.* London: Heinemann, 1964.

————. *The Mask of Keats—A Study of Problems.* Melbourne: William Heinemann, 1956.

Gittings, Robert, and Jo Manton. *The Story of John Keats.* New York: E. P. Dutton, 1963.

Goff, John. "The Last Leaf." *Register of the Kentucky Historical Society* 59 (1961).

Graham-Campbell, Angus. "John Keats and Marian Jeffrey." *Keats Shelley Journal* 13 (1984).

Hall, Capt. Basil, R. N. *Travels in North America in the Years 1827 and 1828.* Vol. 3 of 3. Edinburgh: Robert Cadell, 1830.

Harlan, Richard. Abstract from his *Journals.* Philadelphia: American Philosophical Society, 2003.

Haydon, Benjamin Robert. *The Autobiography and Memoirs of Benjamin Robert Haydon,* edited by Tom Taylor. New York: Harcourt Brace, 1926.

Haynes, Jean. "A Coroner's Inquest, Apr. 1804." *Keats Shelley Memorial Bulletin* 14 (1963).

————. "Richard Abbey's Resting Place." *Keats Shelley Review* 24 (October 2010).

Hebron, Stephen. *John Keats: A Poet and His Manuscripts.* London: British Library, 2009.

Herr, Kincaid A. *The Louisville & Nashville Railroad, 1850–1963.* Lexington: University Press of Kentucky, 2000.

Herrick, Francis Hobart. *Audubon the Naturalist.* 2 vols. New York: D. Appleton, 1917.

Hewlett, Dorothy. *Adonais: A Life of John Keats.* Indianapolis: Bobbs Merrill, 1938.

Hilton, Timothy. *Keats and His World.* London: Thames and Hudson, 1971.

History of the Ohio Falls and Their Cities. Cleveland, OH: L. A. Williams, 1882.

Horine, Dr. Emmet Field. *Daniel Drake, Pioneer Physician of the Midwest.* Philadelphia: University of Pennsylvania Press, 1961.

Hunt, James Henry Leigh. *Lord Byron and Some of His Contemporaries.* London: Henry Colburn, 1828.

Iles, Gillian. "New Information on Keats' Friend Charles 'Armitage' Brown and the Brown Family." *Keats Shelley Journal* 40 (1991).

Bibliography

Jarvis, William A. W. "The Jennings Family." *Keats Shelley Memorial Bulletin* 20 (1969).

Joelin, M., comp. *Louisville, Past and Present.* Louisville: John P. Morton, 1875.

Johnson, Dr. Leland, and Charles E. Parrish. *Triumph at the Falls: The Louisville and Portland Canal.* Louisville: U.S. Army Corps of Engineers, 2007.

Johnson, E. Polk. *A History of Kentucky and Kentuckians.* Chicago: Lewis Publishing, 1912.

Johnston, Josiah Stoddard. *Memorial History of Louisville.* Chicago: American Biographical Publishing Company, 1896.

Keats, John. *Anatomical and Physiological Note Book,* edited by Maurice Buxton Forman. 1934. Reprint, New York: Haskell House Publishers, 1970.

———. *John Keats Complete Poems,* edited by Jack C. Stillinger. Cambridge, MA: Belknap Press of the Harvard University Press, 1978.

———. *The Letters of John Keats,* edited by Maurice Buxton Forman. London: Oxford University Press, 1947.

———. *Letters of John Keats to Fanny Brawne Written in the Years MDCCCXIX and MDCCCXX,* edited by Harry Buxton Forman. New York: Scribner, Armstrong and Company, 1878.

———. *The Poetical Works and Other Writings of John Keats,* edited by Harry Buxton Forman. 4 vols. London: Reeves and Turner, 1883.

———. *The Poetical Works and Other Writings of John Keats* [Hampstead ed.], edited by Harry Buxton Forman, revised and augmented by Maurice Buxton Forman. 8 vols. New York: Charles Scribner's Sons, 1938.

———. *Selected Letters of John Keats,* edited by Grant F. Scott. Cambridge, MA: Harvard University Press, 2002.

Keats, Sheila. *The Keat(e)s Family from the 1600's to the 20th Century.* Lincoln, UK: Ruddocks, 2006.

Kirk, Naomi J. "The Life of George Keats." Master's thesis, Columbia University, 1933.

———. "Memoir of George Keats." In vol. 1 of *The Poetical Works and Other Writings of John Keats* [Hampstead ed.], edited by Harry Buxton Forman, revised and augmented by Maurice Buxton Forman. 8 vols. New York: Charles Scribner's Sons, 1938.

Kleber, John W., ed. *The Encyclopedia of Louisville.* Lexington: University Press of Kentucky, 2001.

Kramer, Carl F. *Visionaries, Adventurers and Builders.* Jeffersonville, IN: Sunnyside Press, 1999.

Lang, Andrew. *The Life and Letters of John Gibson Lockhart*. 2 vols. London: John C. Nimmo, 1897.

Livesley, Brian. *The Dying Keats—A Case for Euthanasia?* Kibworth-Beauchamp, UK: Matador, 2009.

Locker-Lampson, Frederick. *My Confidences*. London: Smith, Elder, 1896.

Louisville Board of Trade. "A Tribute to the Memory of William Garvin." 1869.

Louisville Medical Institute. *Catalogue of the Officers and Students*. Louisville: Prentice and Weissinger, 1839.

Lowell, Amy. *John Keats*. 2 vols. Boston: Houghton Mifflin, 1925.

Mann, Phyllis G. "Keats' Maternal Relations." *Keats Shelley Memorial Bulletin* 15 (1964).

Markham, Jerry W. *A Financial History of the United States*. Armonk, NY: M. E. Sharp, 2001.

Maximilian, Prince of Wied. "Travels in the Interior of North America, 1832–1834." In *Early Western Travels, 1748–1846*. Cleveland, OH: Arthur H. Clark, 1906.

McCormick, Eric Hall. *The Friend of Keats: A Life of Charles Armitage Brown*. Wellington: Victoria University Press, 1989.

McDermott, John Francis. *Audubon in the West*. Norman: University of Oklahoma Press, 1965.

McIver, Helen. *Genealogy of the Jaffrey-Jeffrey Family*. Published privately, 1925.

McMeekin, Isabel McLennan. *Louisville, the Gateway City*. New York: Julian Messner, 1946.

McMurtrie, Dr. Henry. *Sketches of Louisville*. Louisville: S. Penn, 1819.

Milnes, Richard Monckton (Lord Houghton). *The Aldine Edition of the British Poets*. London: Bell and Daldy, 1876.

———. *Life, Letters, and Literary Remains of John Keats*. 3 vols. London: Edward Moxon, 1848.

Minor, Louisa H. A. *The Meriwethers and Their Connections*. Albany, NY: Joel Munsell's Sons, 1892.

Motion, Andrew. *Keats*. Chicago: University of Chicago Press, 1997.

Muschamp, Edward A. *Audacious Audubon*. New York: Brentano's, 1929.

Paradinas, Fernando Juan. "Evidence in Spain." *Keats Shelly Memorial Bulletin* 18 (1967).

Parson, Donald. *Portraits of Keats*. Cleveland, OH: World Publishing, 1954.

Payling, Catherine, curator. *Keats and Italy: A History of the Keats Shelley House in Rome*. Rome: Edizioni Il Labirinto, 2005.

Plumly, Stanley. *Posthumous Keats*. New York: W. W. Norton, 2008.

Bibliography

Prentice, John. *The Laird of Stone.* prenticenet.com.

Prichard, Alvyn L., transcriber. *Early Kentucky Settlers: The Records of Jefferson County, Kentucky.* Baltimore: Genealogical Publishing Company, 1988.

Rhodes, Capt. Rick. *The Ohio River in American History.* St. Petersburg, FL: Heron Island Guides, 2008.

Rhodes, Richard. *John James Audubon.* New York: Alfred A. Knopf, 2004.

Richardson, Joanna. *Fanny Brawne: A Biography.* Great Britain: Vanguard Press, 1952.

———. *Lord Byron and Some of His Contemporaries.* London: Folio Society, 1988.

———. "New Light on Mr. Abbey." *Keats Shelley Memorial Bulletin* 5 (1953).

Richardson, Robert D., Jr. *Emerson: The Mind on Fire.* Berkeley: University of California Press, 1995.

Riebel, R. C. *Louisville Panorama.* Louisville: Liberty Bank, 1954.

Robinson, Dwight E. "Notes on the Antecedents of John Keats: The Maritime Hypothesis." *Keats Shelley Journal* 34 (1984).

Roe, Nicholas. *Fiery Heart: The First Life of Leigh Hunt.* London: Random House, 2005.

———. *John Keats and the Culture of Dissent.* Oxford: Oxford University Press, 1997.

Rollins, Hyder Edward. *The Keats Circle.* 2nd ed. 2 vols. Cambridge, MA: Harvard University Press, 1965.

———. *Keats' Reputation in America to 1848.* Cambridge, MA: Harvard University Press, 1946.

———. *Letters of John Keats.* 2 vols. Cambridge, MA: Harvard University Press, 1958.

———. *More Letters and Poems of the Keats Circle.* Cambridge, MA: Harvard University Press, 1955.

Rollins, Hyder Edward, and Stephen Maxfield Parrish. *Keats and the Bostonians.* Cambridge, MA: Harvard University Press, 1951.

Rossetti, William Michael. *Life of John Keats.* London: Walter Scott, 1887.

Rule, Lucien V. "Louisville, the Gateway City to the South." In *Historic Towns of the Southern States,* edited by Lyman P. Powell. New York: G. P. Putnam's Sons, 1900.

Scott, Grant F. *Joseph Severn, Letters and Memoirs.* Aldershot, UK: Ashgate, 2005.

Scott, Grant F., and Sue Brown, eds. *New Letters from Charles Brown to Joseph Severn.* College Park: University of Maryland, Romantic Circles Electronic edition, revised 2010.

Sharp, William. *Life and Letters of Joseph Severn*. New York: Charles Scribner, 1892.

Shelley, Percy Bysshe. *Adonais*. Pisa: n.p., 1821.

Smith, Z. F. *School History of Kentucky*. Louisville: Courier Journal Job Printing Company, 1891.

Speed, John Gilmer. *The Letters and Poems of John Keats*. 3 vols. New York: Dodd, Mead, 1883.

Speed, Thomas. *Records and Memorials of the Speed Family*. Louisville: Courier-Journal, 1892.

Stearns, Bertha-Monica. "John Howard Payne as an Editor." *American Literature* 5, no. 3 (November 1933).

Stillinger, Jack C. *The Letters of Charles Armitage Brown*. Cambridge, MA: Harvard University Press, 1966.

————. *The Texts of Keats's Poems*. Cambridge, MA: Harvard University Press, 1974.

Stover, Carl W., and Jerry L. Coffman. "Seismicity of the United States, 1568–1989." U.S. Geological Survey paper, 1993.

Stradling, Diana, and J. Garrison. *American Queensware—The Louisville Experience, 1829–37*. N.p.: Chipstone, 2001.

Streshinsky, Shirley. *Audubon: Life and Art in the American Wilderness*. Athens: University of Georgia Press, 1998.

Tackler, Steven. "John Rowan and the Demise of Jeffersonian Republicanism in Kentucky, 1819–31." *Register of the Kentucky Historical Society* 78 (Winter 1980).

Thomas, Samuel W. *Views of Louisville since 1776*. Louisville: Courier Journal, 1971.

Townsend, John Wilson. *Kentuckians in History and Literature*. New York: Neale Publishing, 1907.

————. *Kentucky in American Letters, 1784–1912*. Cedar Rapids, IA: Torch Press, 1913.

Twentieth Century Biographical Dictionary of Notable Americans, edited by Rossiter Johnson and John Howard Brown. Boston: Biographical Society, 1904.

Wade, Richard C. *The Urban Frontier*. Chicago: University of Chicago Press, 1959.

Walker, Carol Kyros. *Walking North with Keats*. New Haven, CT: Yale University Press, 1992.

Ward, Aileen. *John Keats: The Making of a Poet*. New York: Viking Press, 1963.

Welby, Adlard. *Welby's Visit to North America*. London: J. Drury, 1821.

Woods, John. "Two Years Residence on the English Prairie of Illinois." In *Early Western Travels, 1748–1846*, ed. Reuben Gold Thwaites. Cleveland, OH: Arthur H. Clark, 1904.

Yater, George. *Two Hundred Years at the Falls of the Ohio*. Louisville: Filson Club, 1987.

Archival and Documentary Resources

Annual Convention of Protestant Episcopal Church of Kentucky, 1847 Journal of Proceedings

Biographical Dictionary of the U.S. Congress

British Library
    George Keats Notebook, 1820.

British Museum

City of London Records Office

Eckstrom Library, University of Louisville

Filson Historical Society (formerly the Filson Club)
    Martha Bullitt (Mrs. William Christian Bullitt) letters, 1841–1842.
    Dr. Urban E. Ewing, slave purchase document dated 6 September 1832.
    S. I. George, Lucy Brice Daust, and B. E. Clement. *Nathaniel Hardy, 1795–1848*. Published for the 200th anniversary of his birth, 1995.
    Harlan Museum Co. Minute Book, 1837–1838.
    Alexander Jeffrey Collection.
    Naomi J. Kirk Collection.
    Louisville Hotel. Corporate Records Book, 1832–1852.

Garden District National Register (1971)

Henderson County (Kentucky) Courthouse

Houghton Library, Harvard University
    Georgiana Augusta Keats (née Wylie). Scrapbook, c. 1815–1825.

Jefferson County Archives, Louisville

Keats House, Hampstead, London

Kentucky General Assembly Statutes Book

Kentucky Heritage Council Newsletter (1995)

Kentucky State Archives, Frankfort

London Metropolitan Archives

Louisville City Directory. A facsimile edition, reprinted in 1970, exists for 1832; other years are on microfilm.

[Louisville] Focus of Politics, Commerce and Literature, 1829–1830, on microfilm

Montgomery County (Pennsylvania) Historical Society

Bibliography

Morgan Library, New York
National Archives Public Records Office at Kew
National Portrait Gallery, London
Smithsonian American Art Biographies (2010)
Speed Art Museum, Louisville
University of Chicago, Durrett Collection
    Thomas W. Bakewell. "Sketch of the Life of Thomas Woodhouse Bakewell Written by Himself." 6 pp., original manuscript.
University of Delaware Library
    Buxton Forman Papers

ILLUSTRATION CREDITS

ABBREVIATIONS

BM   British Museum
FHS   Filson Historical Society
HOFC   *History of the Ohio Falls Cities and Their Counties* (L. A. Williams, 1882)
KH   Keats House, Hampstead
KSH   Keats-Shelley House, Rome
MHL   J. Stoddard Johnston, *Memorial History of Louisville* (American Biographical Publishing Co., 1896)
NPG   National Portrait Gallery, London
SAM   Speed Art Museum, Louisville

CREDITS

COVER
Front   George Keats, KSH
Back   Keats memorial, Cave Hill Cemetery, Louisville

ENDLEAVES
Front   Cities of London and Westminster, by William Faden, 1801, British Library Board, amended by Emily Coon
Back   City of Louisville and its enlargements, by city surveyor Edward D. Hobbs, in 1832 *Louisville City Directory*, amended by Emily Coon

GALLERY FOLLOWING PAGE 176
Illustration credits are listed in order of appearance.
George Keats, KSH
Livery and tavern in Little Moorfields, BM
Swan and Hoop layout, City of London Records Office
Row houses in Craven Street, reproduced from Marie Adami, *Fanny Keats* (Oxford University Press, 1937), amended by Emily Coon
St. Leonard's at Shoreditch, Wikipedia Open Content License
Tom Keats, KSH
Gate to Bunhill Fields, 2007 photograph by author
Edmonton house, BM
Edmonton Center, Southwark High Street, originally in Dr. David Hughson (pseudonym for Edward Pugh), *London, Being an Accurate*

317

Illustration Credits

History and Description of the British Metropolis and Its Neighborhood (J. Stratford, 1806), courtesy of KH

Enfield marketplace, in Dr. David Hughson (pseudonym for Edward Pugh), *London, Being an Accurate History and Description of the British Metropolis and Its Neighborhood* (J. Stratford, 1806)

Clarke's School at Enfield, KSH

Charles Cowden Clarke, NPG

Rev. Midgley John Jennings, courtesy of Society for the Propagation of the Gospel, Bodleian Library, Oxford University

John Keats, copy at NPG; the original is housed at the Fitzwilliam Museum Library, University of Cambridge

Joseph Severn, NPG

Maria Dover Walker Dilke, KH

Fanny Brawne, KH, courtesy of Robert Goodsell

Charles Brown, courtesy of Dennis J. King

Charles Wentworth Dilke, KH

St. Mary-le-Bow Church, BM

John Hamilton Reynolds, NPG

Hampstead Heath, 1840, engraving by William Westall (1765–1836), published by Charles Tilt

James Henry Leigh Hunt, NPG

Percy Bysshe Shelley, KSH

Benjamin Robert Haydon, NPG

Lord George Gordon Byron, KSH

John Taylor, reproduced from Edmund Blunden, *Keats's Publisher* (Jonathan Cape, 1936), in which the author attributed its ownership to Mrs. Cartwright-Taylor

Richard Monckton Milnes, NPG

St. Margaret's Church, BM

Great Ormes Head, photograph by author

Packet *Antarctic*, Royal Museum of Greenwich

Keelboats and flatboats, in *The Planting of Civilization in Western Pennsylvania* (University of Pittsburgh Press, 1939), Carnegie Library of Pittsburgh

John James Audubon, Photo Researchers, Inc.

Thomas Woodhouse Bakewell, in *The Cardinal* (Audubon Society of Sewickley Valley, July 1934), Carnegie Library of Pittsburgh

James Berthoud, SAM

Nicholas Berthoud, SAM

Ohio rapids from Clarksville, FHS

Indian Queen Hotel, FHS

Bank of Louisville, undated photograph, FHS

Illustration Credits

Map of Louisville, 1819, in Henry McMurtrie, *Sketches of Louisville* (S. Penn, 1819)

City of Louisville from the Indiana shore, FHS

Beargrass Creek joins the Ohio River, originally printed by Charles Chardon aîné, Paris, FHS

Fourteenth Street Bridge, FHS

Louisville and Portland locks, FHS.

Steamboat for sale, FHS

Advertisement for return of runaway slave, *Louisville Public Advertiser*, 28 June 1827

George and Georgiana Keats silhouettes, courtesy of Elizabeth M. Dunn

Emma Frances, Isabel, and Georgiana Emily Keats silhouettes, courtesy of John S. Speed

George Keats's home, courtesy of Mark Willis

Green and Sixth Streets, Photographic Archives, Eckstrom Library, University of Louisville

Louisville Hotel, SAM

View of Main Street, Louisville, SAM

Oakland House and Race Course, SAM

Lexington and Ohio Railroad letterhead, FHS

University of Louisville, Photographic Archives, Eckstrom Library, University of Louisville

Farmington, Library of Congress Performing Arts Collection

Lucy Gilmer Fry Speed, Historic Homes Foundation

Judge John Speed, Historic Homes Foundation

Philip Speed, in Thomas Speed, *Records and Memorials of the Speed Family* (*Courier Journal*, 1892)

Emma Keats Speed, courtesy of Mark Willis

James Speed, in James Speed (his grandson), *James Speed, a Personality* (John P. Morton, 1914)

Ella Keats Peay, courtesy of Mark Van Alstyne

Isabel Keats's grave marker, photograph by author

Georgiana Augusta Wylie Keats Jeffrey, FHS

Valentin Maria Llanos y Gutierrez, courtesy of Dr. Fernando Juan Paradinas

Fanny Keats Llanos, courtesy of Dr. Fernando Juan Paradinas

Fanny Keats Llanos, reproduced from Marie Adami, *Fanny Keats* (Oxford University Press, 1937), amended by Emily Coon

Dr. Theodore Samuel Bell, reproduced from *HOFC*

Sen. George Mortimer Bibb, FHS

John H. Brand, FHS

William Christian Bullitt, *HOFC*

Illustration Credits

Judge William Fontaine Bullock, *HOFC*

Edward Mann Butler, photograph of painting at Capitol Art Gallery, Frankfort, Kentucky, FHS

Samuel Casseday, *HOFC*

James Freeman Clarke, courtesy of Trustees of the Boston Public Library

Dr. Joshua Barker Flint, FHS

William Garvin, in *MHL*

James Guthrie, FHS

Richard Harlan, Wikipedia Open Content License

Jacob Keller, FHS

Sen. Humphrey Marshall, FHS

George W. Meriwether, FHS

Samuel Osgood, Print Collection, Miriam and Ira D. Wallach Division of Art, Prints and Photographs, New York Public Library

Judge Henry Pirtle, *HOFC*

George Dennison Prentice, FHS

Dr. Coleman Rogers, FHS

Judge John Rowan, FHS

James Rudd, FHS

Leven Lawrence Shreve, *MHL*

Willis Stewart, FHS

Robert J. Ward Sr., *HOFC*

INDEX

Abbey, Eleanor Jones, 19, 85, 192, 270n5

Abbey, Jonathan, 298n1

Abbey, Richard: account, 54, 96, 137, 139; adopted daughter, 19, 270n6; biographical sketch, 191–92; career suggestions for JK, 10; clarifying accounts, 90; confusion about estate details, 3, 90, 93, 120, 130–37; custody of children, viii, 7, 18, 255; death of, 298n5; defense of, 41–44, 98; discourages poetry, 35; employs GK, 27; exonerates GK, 97, 121; firm of, 271n3, 274–75n34; gift to GK, 139; indentures JK to Hammond, 28; on Jennings and Keats families, 5–6, 12; and Fanny Keats, 13, 25, 98, 132–33; GK's faith in, 276n64; GK's power of attorney, 2; memoir of, 144, 261, 267n4, 270n7; origins, 298n1; pickpocketed, 298n3; refuses loan to JK, 274–75n34; releases GK's inheritance, 52–53; in Walthamstow, 272n9; withdraws Keatses from school, 7, 24, 255

Abraham, J., 6, 254, 267n7

accent, Cockney, 34

Adami, Marie, xiii, 153, 186, 269n23, 269n24

Adams, John Quincy, 167, 213, 227

Ainslie, Hew, 228

Albion, Illinois, 64–65, 250, 278n9

Amphlett, William, 56–57, 59–62

Anderson, James, 236

Anderson, Thomas, 203

Anderson, William, 204

Aristotle, on physiognomy, 53

Arthur, Stanley Clisby, 76, 281n1

Atkinson, John, 108, 261, 287n26

Atkinson, Richard, 107–8, 261, 287n26

Atwater, Caleb, 162

Audubon, John James: attack on, 73, 211; biographical sketch, 207–8; business model, 3; compliments GK's persistence, 181; episode with finances, 71, 76; on Georgiana, 76–77; gristmill fails, 70; Harlan Museum, 168; hosts Keatses, ix, 63, 69–76; on Jeffrey, 77; JK calls dishonest, 90; lawsuits with Bowen, 71–73; leaves Henderson, 76; on Louisville's residents, 83; monument, 78; as a naturalist, 63, 77; publications, 77, 169; steamboat investment, 3

Audubon, John Woodhouse, 168

Audubon, Lucy Bakewell, ix, 69, 75, 76, 91, 208, 209, 282n29

Audubon, Maria R., 282n34

Audubon, Victor Gifford, 168, 209

Austen, Jane, 106

Bachman, Jane, 169

Bailey, Benjamin, 35, 37, 40, 45, 52, 54, 86, 116, 144, 198

Bakewell, Alicia Matthews (Mrs. William G.), 173–74, 209

Bakewell, Benjamin, 208

Bakewell, Elizabeth Rankin Page (Mrs. Thomas W.), 69, 70, 208

321

Index

Index

Hoxton, London, 201, 273n23, 275n39, 278n91
Hughes, James, 160, 203
Hulme, Thomas, 51, 279n13
Hunt, James Henry Leigh, 3, 35, 36, 38, 48, 112, 114–16, 138, 144–48, 152, 194, 198, 255, 256, 259, 260, 269n22, 274n29; circle of, 31, 34, 48, 144, 198; as a journalist, 21, 51, 195; posthumous JK sketch by, 143, 251, 261, 269n22, 274n29
Hunt, John, 31

Illinois, viii, x, 2, 46, 48–52, 58, 59, 61, 63, 72, 108, 185, 188, 208, 214, 226, 231, 258, 266n5, 279n13
immortal dinner, 35
Indian Queen Hotel, 79–81, 222, 283n1
Indians, 1, 49, 50, 59, 214, 266n5, 280n46
"Influence of Tea upon the *Ladies*, The" (GK), 140
inheritance, Keatses', viii, x, xiv, 2, 6, 24, 25, 33, 36, 39, 40, 46, 47, 52, 76, 93, 123–24, 130, 132, 134, 137–39, 176, 196, 256, 257
Irving, Washington, viii, ix, 251
"Isabella, or the Pot of Basil" (JK), 39, 106, 257
Isle of Wight, 37, 43, 93, 193, 198, 259

Jackson, Andrew, 47, 110, 164, 165, 212, 228, 234, 244, 261
Jacob, John Jeremiah, 157, 158, 162, 170, 172, 203, 204, 206, 229, 234, 235; biographical sketch, 224–25
Jacob, Richard, 224
Jacob, Thomas Prather, 224–25
James, David, 300n46
James, John H., 188
Jarvis, Dr. Edward, 167, 206; biographical sketch, 225

Jefferson Seminary, 111, 161, 169, 216, 221
Jeffrey, Alexander, 183, 226, 296n18
Jeffrey, Elizabeth McConnell, 302n118
Jeffrey, John, 177, 178, 180, 185, 187, 238, 263, 296n12, 296n25, 296n28, 302n118; biographical sketch, 225–26; Cave Hill memorial to GK, 78, 175, 186; and Clarence, 185, 188; genealogy, 302n118; marries Georgiana, 77, 151, 175, 183, 262; and Milnes, 151–52, 186, 263
Jeffrey, John Armstrong, 302n118
Jeffrey, Mrs. Margaret, 39, 52
Jeffrey, Marian, 39, 40, 43, 257
Jeffrey, Sarah, 39, 40, 257
Jenks, Edward, 189
Jennings, Alice Haworth Whalley (GK's grandmother), 11, 27, 163, 191, 192, 197, 253–55; "discreet parent," 18, 19; estate issues, 7, 36, 93, 124–27, 130, 131, 134–36, 139; as "Granny-good," 7; names trustees, 24, 42
Jennings, Edward (GK's uncle), 11
Jennings, John (GK's grandfather), 6, 11–12, 18, 28, 71, 253, 254, 267n10; death of, 124, 197; estate of, 93, 123–25, 130–31, 133–35, 139, 175, 267nn9–10, 269n11
Jennings, John (GK's great-grandfather), 11, 269n11
Jennings, Margaret Alice (GK's cousin), 127
Jennings, Margaret Peacock (Mrs. Midgley), 7, 44, 93, 95, 125, 127, 130, 131, 255, 267n11
Jennings, Martin (GK's speculative great-grandfather), 269n11
Jennings, Mary (GK's great-grandmother), 11, 269n11
Jennings, Mary Ann (GK's cousin), 127

Index

Jennings, Midgley John (GK's uncle), 6–7, 11, 20; estate issues, 124, 125, 126–27, 130, 254, 270–71n11

Jennings, Rev. Midgley John, Jr. (GK's cousin), 127, 130

Jennings, Robert A. J., 269n11

Jesse (GK's slave), 163, 176, 249, 296n15

Johnson, Andrew, 229, 236

Johnson, William, 132, 192, 271n3

Johnston, Dr. James Chew, 169, 205; biographical sketch, 226–27

Jones, Isabella, 39, 55, 106

Jonson, Ben, 178, 251

journal letters: JK to GAW, 95, 101, 259; JK to GK, 56, 67, 258, 259; JK to TK, 86, 258

Judd Street, London, 53, 257

"Julia to the Wood Robin" (GK?), 290n33

Kean, Edmund, 34

Keasle, John (also Keysell), 201, 273n25

Keast, Thomas, 9, 10, 268n3

Keat (alternative spelling of Keats), 9

Keat, John, 9

Keate, Dr. Robert, 9

Keate, Shilson, 9

Keate, Dr. Thomas, 9

Keate(s), Dr. William, 9

Keat or Keats of Corfe Castle, Devon, 10

Keats, Alice Lee (GK's granddaughter), 45, 301n92

Keats, Clarence George (GK's son), 2, 163, 178, 183, 186, 188, 261, 263, 300n46; works for Jeffrey, 185

Keats, Edward, (GK's brother), 13

Keats, Elizabeth (GK's speculative aunt; of Stratfield Mortimer), 9

Keats, Elizabeth (GK's speculative aunt; of Swan and Hoop), 6, 268n5

Keats, Frances Jennings (GK's mother), vii, 5–7, 11, 12–13, 16, 17, 18, 34, 105, 122, 253, 254, 255, 267n10, 268n3, 270n3; aspires to Harrow for sons, 3, 16, 19; Chancery issues, 124, 125–31, 133, 135; death of, 24, 255; marries William Rawlings, 5, 254; "passionate love of amusement" of, 269n22

Keats, Frances Mary (GK's sister; Fanny; Mrs. Valentin Llanos), vii, xiii, xiv, 1, 2–3, 7, 9, 13, 17, 18, 25, 86, 95, 104, 106, 117, 121, 138, 140, 155, 158, 163, 171, 179, 181, 187, 188, 196, 198, 202, 214, 251, 253, 254, 260, 261, 264, 268n2, 269n23, 270n3, 270n7, 274–75n34, 290n17; and Abbey, 13, 19, 25, 27–28, 41–45, 53, 85, 98, 99, 136, 137, 191, 192, 258; biographical sketch, 197–98; and Fanny Brawne, 98, 99, 138, 193; Chancery saga, 36–38, 90, 96, 128–37, 139–40, 147, 289n1, 290n27; children not living with mother, 270n3; unaware of GK's death, 186

Keats, Frederick, 10

Keats, George (GK): and Abbey, 7, 24, 27–28, 33, 41, 44, 52–54, 76, 93, 96, 98, 131; accepted in Louisville society, ix, 1, 106; advertises to buy slaves, 109; on American politics, 110; anger at *Blackwood's*, 117; applies for inheritance, 128, 132, 136; assimilates into Kentucky life, 152; and Audubon, 69–78; Bakewell loan guarantee, x, 173, 176, 208; bank loans, 158–59; bankruptcy, 174, 176, 181, 208; bank trip to London proposed, 165; bedridden, 106;

Index

Keats, Georgiana Augusta Wylie
(GAW; Mrs. George, also Mrs.
John Jeffrey), 297n5, 299n35,
301n92; age and description, 2–3,
30, 38, 44–46, 49, 52–55, 74, 93,
163, 200–201, 273n24, 297n7; and
Audubon, 74, 76–77, 208, 282n34;
crossing to Illinois, 49, 56–59,
61–65, 69, 71, 199; and Jeffrey,
151, 175, 177, 180, 183, 185, 225–
26, 296n12, 296n28; letters from
JK, viii, 43, 55–56, 59, 66, 84–91,
95, 101, 105, 116, 121, 185, 193,
268n16, 275n34, 275n38, 284n8,
286n13; in London, 27, 31–32,
38–40, 94, 128, 134, 155, 184–88;
in Louisville, ix, 76, 79, 81, 82, 84,
106, 163, 174–78, 181, 207, 218,
238, 249, 254, 256, 263; marries
GK, 46, 53, 279n20; "Nymph of
the Downward Smile," 33
Keats, Isabel (GK's daughter), 2,
39–40, 106, 163, 178, 224, 260,
296n; death of, 183–84, 186, 187,
263, 286n22, 304n158; poem by
Prentice to, 184, 232
Keats, John (JK), and Abbey,
36, 41–42, 98; agrees to GK's
American venture, 35; "amen to
nonsense," 91; apprentices to
Hammond, 27–29; on Audubon,
ix, 76, 90; biographers of, xi, xiii,
3, 123, 153, 188; on Birkbeck,
65; black moods of, 23; and
Fanny Brawne, xi, 55, 67, 85, 87,
94–95, 117, 140, 192–94, 197,
198, 258, 259, 260, 263, 285n25;
and Brown, xi, 2, 31, 54–55, 97,
99–101, 112, 114, 117–18, 121–
23, 136, 143–44, 146, 193–95,
199, 258, 260; Brown as putative
biographer, 23, 148; "burden of
society," 52; burns letters, 280n53;
on Byron, 90; career options, 43;

on church, 88; at Clarke's School,
5, 7, 17, 20–25; Cockney accent,
speculative, 34; copyrights, 143,
149–50, 196; critics of, 77, 113–
17; death, causes of, 111, 117–18,
122; death of, 1, 3, 120; debts of,
cleared by GK, xi, 2, 90, 96, 99,
121, 133, 139–40, 180, 259–60,
276n64; difficult personality,
17–18; on "disinterestedness," 38,
44, 86, 88, 257, 276n53; "earlier
misfortunes," 130, 181, 290n11;
Endymion, 34, 37, 39–40, 114,
117, 132, 139, 144, 149, 180,
196, 199, 251, 257; estate issues,
family, 4, 7, 9–11, 13, 17, 19, 45,
123–24, 163, 253, 260, 284n3;
final farewell to GK, 93–101;
finances, xiv, 43, 54, 95, 100, 102,
104, 118, 123, 136–40, 276n64;
gravestone inscription of, xii, 10,
114; at Guy's Hospital, 29, 32,
42–43, 122, 128, 272n14, 272n17,
274n26; in Haydon's painting,
275n43; health of, 39, 54, 101,
117–18, 121–22; hemorrhages of,
99, 101, 111–12, 117, 122, 139,
259, 285n24; on Hodgkinson,
274–75n34; and Hunt's circle,
31, 34–35, 36, 38, 42; and Isabella
Jones, 39–40, 55, 106; and Mary
Ann Keasle, 95, 201, 273n25; and
Fanny Keats, 18, 38, 42–43, 139,
197–98, 202, 270n7, 285n4; and
GK, xiii–xiv, 4, 8, 27, 30, 33, 46,
94–95, 105, 123, 174, 180–81,
285n4; TK's illness and death, 17,
38–39, 88, 93; legacy of, defined
by others, xi, 4, 120–21, 143–
53, 164, 185, 187; letters to GK
and GAW, xi, xiii–xiv, 43, 56, 58,
63–67, 69, 73, 84–88, 90–91, 93,
105, 283n15; letters written by, 10,
33, 43, 56, 63, 67, 84–91, 98, 101,

Index

Index

Penn, Shadrack, 167, 205, 232;
biographical sketch, 230
Pennsylvania, 3, 50, 59, 61, 64, 65,
103, 219, 234, 278n8
Peter, Arthur Robert, 177
Philadelphia, viii, 31, 51, 56, 57,
58–59, 60, 64, 69, 71, 80–81, 94,
104, 106, 119, 155, 168–69, 199,
207, 209, 220, 223, 227, 231, 258,
284n8
philosophical society. See Keats,
George (GK): philosophical
society
phrenology, 53, 108, 157, 171, 179, 251
phthisis. See consumption;
tuberculosis
physiognomy, 53
Pierce, Franklin, 109, 157–58, 222
Pierpont, Rev. John, 159
Pirtle, Judge Henry, 159, 170, 206,
221, 233; biographical sketch,
230–31
Pirtle, Jane Ann Rogers, 233
Pitot, Judge James, 72
Pitt, William, 110
Pittsburgh, 1–2, 59–60, 61–62, 70, 71,
81, 83, 103, 109, 167, 172, 208,
209, 227, 233, 239
Plymouth, Devonshire, 10, 147–48,
195, 285n28
Poe, Edgar Allan, 53
Ponders End, Edmonton, 12, 18, 34,
254, 272n9
Pope, Godfrey, 167, 212
Pope, Henry C., 167, 212, 294n58
Pope, John, 244, 287n34
Pope, William Fontaine, 212
Pope, William Hamilton, 203, 204,
205, 212; biographical sketch, 231
Pope, Worden, 105, 231, 236
Porcupine, Peter. See Cobbett,
William
Porteous, Jane and Mary, 277n89,
299n32

Porter, Jim, 170
Portland (section of Louisville), 1,
166, 266n4
Portland Dry Dock Co., x, 173, 174,
176, 206, 208, 228, 249n, 262
"posthumous" existence. See Keats,
John (JK): "posthumous"
existence
Poultry (section of London), 7, 10,
27, 43, 54, 191, 255, 272n4
Prather, Thomas, 160
Prather, William, 160, 203;
biographical sketch, 231
Prentice, David, 70–72, 74, 76, 78,
81–83, 93, 209; biographical
sketch, 231–32; GK as executor
of estate of, 74; as mill partner of
GK, 104–5, 156, 162, 208
Prentice, George Dennison, 167,
180, 181, 184, 206, 207, 210, 212,
219, 228, 230, 251, 303n141;
biographical sketch, 232–33;
writes GK's obituary, 174, 232
Prescott, Gen. Robert, 200
Preservation Engine Co., 157, 260
Princeton, Indiana, 63, 64, 84
Procter, Bryan Waller, 34

"Quaker's Horse," 35
Quaritch, Bernard, 189

Rankin, Dr. Adam, 282n29
Rankin, Elizabeth Speed, 282n29
Rapp, George, 65
Rappites, 65, 280n50
Rawlings, William, vii, 5–6, 18, 124,
126, 254, 270n3
Reading, Berkshire, 9
Red Banks (former section of
Henderson), 63, 280n46
Redbourne, Hertfordshire, 54,
273n18
Regency era, 42, 47, 255
Reynolds, Charlotte Cox, 95, 278n90

Index

Index

Index

Stewart, Isaac, 163
Stewart, James, 204, 205, 304n160; biographical sketch, 238
Stewart, Willis T., 177, 205; biographical sketch, 238
St. George's Church, Hanover Square, 5, 12, 201, 253, 254
Stillinger, Jack C., 153, 274n26, 281n56, 289n40
St. Leonard's Church, Shoreditch, 13, 254
St. Margaret's Church, Westminster, 53, 257, 273n24
St. Mary-le-Bow Church, Cheapside, 34, 36, 192, 271n4, 275n39
St. Stephen's Church, Coleman Street, 7, 11, 13, 253, 254, 255, 268n5, 269n12
Sully, Thomas, 227
Susquehanna River, 50
Sut, Mary, 269n18
Swan (Abbey's head clerk), 30, 256
Swan and Hoop, 5, 6, 11–14, 17, 30, 124, 126, 253, 254, 268n5, 270n10
Sweetingburgh, Mary (GK's great-aunt), 125, 126, 128–31, 289n10

Tallant, James, 59, 63, 134, 144, 200, 280n38
Tannehill, Wilkins, 158, 204, 206, 210; biographical sketch, 239
Tarascon, John, 211, 218
Tarascon, Louis Anastasius, 210–11, 218
Taylor, John, 34, 53, 59, 96, 115, 116, 118, 122, 151, 196, 198, 199, 270n6, 273n24, 280n38, 285n24; and Abbey, 12–13, 19, 35, 41–42, 144, 192, 261; attempts JK biography, 120, 143–45, 267n4; biographical sketch, 199–200; copyright issues, 143, 149–51; and JK's advance, 100, 119–20, 133–34, 139, 199

Taylor and Hessey, publishers, 35, 39, 40, 48, 132, 134, 139, 143, 144, 149, 199, 257, 278n1
Teignmouth, Devonshire, 37–40, 43, 48, 52, 84–86, 97, 257, 276n49
Telegraph (packet), 56, 58
Tennyson, Alfred, Lord, 151
Terry, Daniel, 116
Thomas, Ralph, 135, 198, 289n1, 289n10, 290n27
Thomson, James, 50
Thoreau, Henry David, 167
Throckmorton, Ariss, 165, 170, 204; biographical sketch, 239
Tolstoy, Lev Nikolayevich, vii
Town, Ithiel, 158
Trabue, James, 177, 263, 293n38, 296n26
transcendentalism, 156, 160, 167, 171, 173
Trimble, Justice Robert, 220
tuberculosis, 13, 122, 135, 160, 174, 260, 262, 263, 276n54, 295n7
Tunstall (sawmill operator), 82
Turner (GK's courier), 67
two-penny post. *See* mail
Tyler, John, 166, 211
Tyler, John H., 203, 234
Tyler, Levi, 176
Tyler, Mary Jacob (Mrs. John William), 224
Tyrrell, Frederick (roommate of JK), 272–73n18

Unitarianism, 89, 159, 221, 250, 292n18; church, 89, 157, 159–60, 221, 250; church in Louisville, 157, 159, 170, 171, 207, 217, 221, 226, 228, 229, 235, 238, 262; GK as, 78, 111, 160, 261
University of Louisville, 157, 161, 169, 216, 221–22, 224, 229–30, 237
Utopia, viii, 50, 65

Index

Topics in Kentucky History
James C. Klotter, Series Editor

Books in the Series

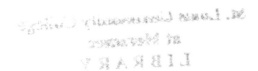

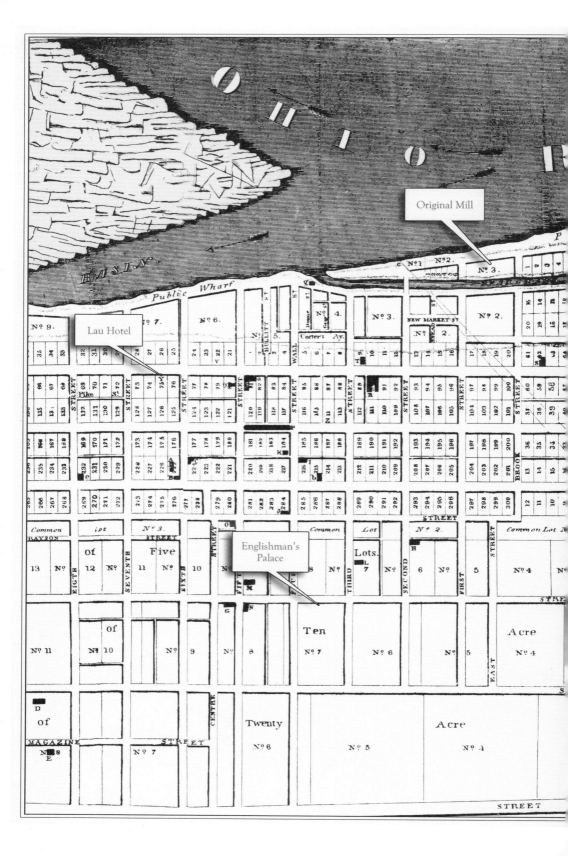